T0385055

THE STORY OF ARCHITECTURE

THE STORY OF ARCHITECTURE

WITOLD RYBCZYNSKI

Yale University Press | New Haven and London

Published with assistance from the Nancy Batson Nisbet Rash Publication Fund.

yalebooks.com/art

Designed by Yve Ludwig.
Set in Mercury Text, designed by Jonathan Hoefler and Tobias Frere-Jones, and Whitney, designed by Tobias Frere-Jones.
Printed in Singapore

Library of Congress Control Number: 2021951352
ISBN 978-0-300-24606-3
A catalogue record for this book is available from the British Library.

This paper meets the requirements of ANSI/NISO Z 39.48-1992 (Permanence of Paper).
10 9 8 7 6 5 4 3 2 1

Jacket illustrations: (front) Giovanni Paolo Panini, *Interior of the Pantheon, Rome*, c. 1734 (detail of fig. 19); (back) National Assembly, Dhaka, Bangladesh. Louis Kahn, 1962–83. Interior (detail of fig. 143)
Sketches by Witold Rybczynski:
P. ii: Propylaea seen from Parthenon
P. xii: Tholos, Delphi
P. 46: Notre-Dame, Paris
P. 102: Laurentian Library (Michelangelo), Florence
P. 158: Schemerlbrücke (Otto Wagner), Vienna
P. 216: Notre-Dame du Haut (Le Corbusier), Ronchamp
P. 276: Richards Medical Research Building (Louis Kahn), Philadelphia

To Shirley Hallam (1944–2021),
once more and forever

Also by Witold Rybczynski

Paper Heroes
Taming the Tiger
Home
The Most Beautiful House in the World
Waiting for the Weekend
Looking Around
A Place for Art
City Life
A Clearing in the Distance
One Good Turn
The Look of Architecture
The Perfect House
Vizcaya (with Laurie Olin)
Last Harvest
My Two Polish Grandfathers
Makeshift Metropolis
The Biography of a Building
How Architecture Works
Mysteries of the Mall
Now I Sit Me Down
Charleston Fancy

Any historian who has lived long enough to experience what happens as the present becomes the past has a story to tell about the way the outlines change with increasing distance.

— *E. H. Gombrich*

Architecture is a visual art, and the buildings speak for themselves.

— *Julia Morgan*

Contents

A Note to the Reader

Architecture is concerned not only with beauty but also with function, construction, and building materials, thus the art of architecture is inseparable from its practice. This has several implications. Buildings are expensive, so economics is always lurking in the background. Architects do not work alone but with assistants, builders, craftsmen and, above all, clients; hence the practice of architecture has always involved both collaboration and compromise. Like all human endeavors, architecture has a history. "History is not the past," the novelist Hilary Mantel observes. "It is the method we have evolved of organizing our ignorance of the past." My method of organizing the past is to select a few buildings from each period, and to describe the circumstances surrounding their commission, construction, and use. "The most famous works are really often the greatest by many standards," wrote the great art historian E. H. Gombrich, and many of my examples are well known, because these are the buildings that have influenced successive generations. Most are not museum pieces; people still worship in the Great Mosque of Damascus, look at paintings in the Louvre, and study in the New York Public Library. Because buildings last such a long time, those that remain in everyday use and are admired and cherished become living reminders of time-tested rules. It is for this reason that old architectural styles, or fragments of old styles, endure—or are revived.

On the whole, I have not included unbuilt works in this account. With a few exceptions the buildings discussed are still in existence and may be visited, which the reader is encouraged to do because, as the architect Julia Morgan wisely observed, buildings speak for themselves. But whom do they address? Architecture, especially public architecture, speaks to us all, and when there is a divergence between critical and popular taste, which is often the case in recent times, I have tended to favor the latter. Small, obscure buildings in out-of-the-way places have sometimes exercised an unduly large influence on practitioners, but I have tended to focus on the prominent works. I have also often favored individual architects, because innovation is frequently a key element of my story. Inevitably, in chronicling the main course of events, I have had to leave out many excellent works. Nor have I included what Bernard Rudofsky called "architecture without architects," the everyday structures that constitute the bulk of the built environment; theirs is a separate history. I have not given equal attention to all parts of the world; this is primarily although not exclusively the story of the Western canon. That is not to slight regions that often have their own unique architectural accomplishments—Norwegian stave churches, Polish wooden synagogues, the Hausa mosques of Niger—but I have chosen examples that best convey the principal thrust of the strain of architectural thought that has most influenced me. At the same time, like a meandering river shifting its course, the story of architecture has taken many unexpected twists and turns, and these I have followed.

I
THE ANCIENTS

1

Buildings Last a Long Time

Brittany, fifth millennium BC

Isn't architecture just a fancy name for building? Or, to put it another way, isn't architecture just a name for fancy building? If fancy means out of the ordinary, architecture is always that. Although the human need for shelter is primordial, what distinguishes a work of architecture from a cave in the hills, a lean-to in the forest, or a tent in the desert is its ambition: not only to accommodate a practical function but also to celebrate, honor, pay homage, and, yes, to impress.

Architecture stands apart from the everyday world. Fashions change from season to season; the useful lives of smartphones and computers are measured in years; cars last a decade—an automobile that is more than twenty-five years old is considered an antique. The thirty-year-old Cunard ocean liner that brought my parents and me to Canada from England was scrapped only three years later, thanks to the growing popularity of air travel; and the supersonic Concorde was in service for only twenty-seven years. Buildings are different—they last a long time. Unlike technological devices, which are designed to do one job until something better comes along, buildings can have many lives. The Roman Pantheon was built as a temple, and five hundred years later it was turned into a church; the great Byzantine basilica of Hagia Sophia in Constantinople was a church for almost a thousand years before being converted into a mosque; the Church of Sainte-Geneviève in Paris, begun in 1758 by Louis XV, became a secular mausoleum thanks to the French Revolution. Many of the world's famous art museums started life as something else: the Uffizi Gallery in Florence originally housed the offices of Renaissance magistrates; the Louvre in Paris and Vienna's Belvedere were palaces; the Prado, in Madrid, was designed as a museum of natural history; and the National Portrait Gallery in Washington, D.C., was originally the federal patent office. Cities are full of buildings that change uses: banks that become restaurants, mansions that are converted into office buildings, offices that turn into apartments. The loft building in which I am writing was built more than a hundred years ago as an industrial workplace; today, people live in it.

Of course, buildings represent a major investment of time, money, and materials, so it makes sense to use them for a long time. But it is not just a question of economics. Highclere Castle in England, known to television viewers as the fictional Downton Abbey, has been the home of the same family since the seventeenth century and, just as in the television series, the identity of its owners is intertwined with the architecture of the house. Some buildings survive because they are irreplaceable; music halls such as Vienna's Musikverein, Amsterdam's Concertgebouw, and Boston's Symphony Hall, which all date from the nineteenth century, have endured because they are exemplary places in which to listen to music. Some buildings are national icons. Who could imagine tearing down the British Houses of Parliament, the Kremlin, or the U.S. Capitol? And some buildings are simply too beautiful to live without: Sainte-Chapelle in Paris, the Ca' d'Oro in Venice, the Taj Mahal in Agra.

Architecture is a reminder of previous ages, but old buildings are also a functioning part of the present. We admire them and we use them. We maintain them and adapt them, and we rebuild them when they are damaged or destroyed. After the two-hundred-year-old Doge's Palace in Venice was ravaged by fire in the sixteenth century, its delicate Gothic facade was restored to its original state. After the President's House in Washington, D.C., was burned by the British during the War of 1812, it was repaired and its charred stone exterior painted white, hence its later name. More recently, following German reunification, the Frauenkirche in Dresden, which was badly damaged by bombs in the Second World War, was rebuilt in all its Baroque splendor. The war-damaged seventeenth-century Royal Palace in Berlin, demolished by the East German authorities in 1950, was likewise rebuilt after reunification.

"We shape our buildings, thereafter our buildings shape us," observed Winston Churchill. He was speaking during a parliamentary debate about the fate of the House of Commons, which had been destroyed during the Second World War. The choice was to rebuild the old chamber or to build a brand new one. Churchill supported the former course and argued that the cramped, intimate room had become an essential part of British political life. Old buildings, whether they are houses of parliament or concert halls, not only shape our behavior; they are like valued friends. They accompany us throughout our lives and, even if their functions change, remain comforting constants in a changing world. Buildings also remind us of the people who built them, people who were like us yet unlike us. And we are grateful for what they have left us. Will people in the future be grateful for what we have built?

▪ ▪ ▪ ▪ ▪

One of the oldest surviving buildings in the world stands on a windswept Brittany headland overlooking the English Channel. Construction began around 4800 BC during the Neolithic period, the end of the Stone Age. Known as the Cairn of Barnenez, it is a cumulus—that is, a burial mound. This manmade stone pile, two hundred and forty feet long, eighty feet wide, and thirty feet high, contains eleven tombs. Each tomb is located deep inside the cairn and reached by a stone passage. The tombs, which resemble caves, are built of stone, and in most a single slab forms the ceiling. The tombs and passages were constructed first, then the exterior wall was built with larger stones carefully fitted together, and the leftover space was filled with rubble. Archaeologists have determined that the individual tombs were built over a period of six hundred years and that the cairn was enlarged at least once and represents the work of several generations (fig. 1). Each tomb has its own passage, and all the entrances face south, away from the sea. The cairn has an irregular form, but this is not simply a pile of stones; its stepped pyramidal ends are carefully shaped.

The construction of the burial mound did not require complex engineering. The passages were roofed with slab-like stones, called megaliths. Like all the stones, these were not dressed and were laid without mortar. But Barnenez does incorporate a refinement. The largest tombs, roughly circular in plan and ten feet in diameter, were too large to be roofed with single slabs. Instead, flat pieces of slate or granite were laid with progressively projecting courses that eventually met in the center, creating a domed interior. This technique is called corbeling, and until the Romans popularized arched construction many thousands of years

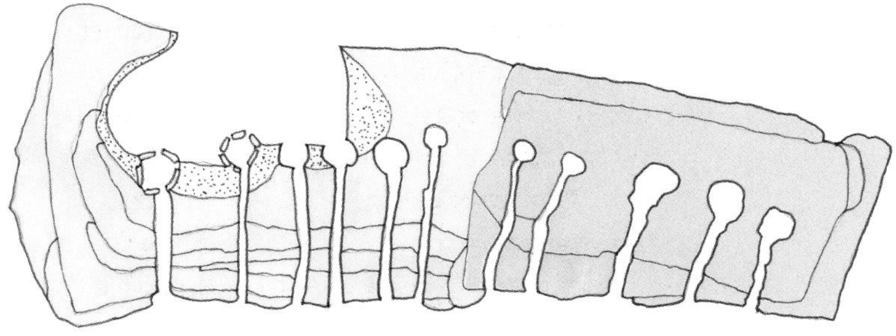

1 Cairn of Barnenez, Brittany, c. 4800 BC. Plan. The shaded right half was built first; the missing portion on the upper left is the result of quarrying in the 1950s.

later, corbeling was how openings, vaults, and domes were spanned. Although some of the Barnenez tombs were rebuilt when the cairn was restored in the twentieth century, others are intact after more than six thousand years, attesting to their builders' skill.

It has been estimated that the Brittany cairn is composed of more than ten thousand tons of granite and dolerite, some of it local but many pieces transported from at least a mile away. How were the megaliths, which weigh several tons each, moved? Perhaps on rollers, or perhaps on sleds dragged over greased timber tracks by scores of workers—we can only speculate. The megaliths were manhandled into place, and it has been estimated that up to a hundred workers would have been needed to move and erect the heaviest stones. That required people to take time off from hunting, fishing, and farming, meaning there had to have been agreement in these small communities about cooperating on such a monumental endeavor. That is why architecture is often referred to as a social art; it brings us together.

We know very little about how the cairn was used. Was it visited regularly by the descendants of those interred, like a modern cemetery? Was it a sacred precinct, standing apart from everyday life, or was it cheek by jowl with the houses of its builders? Those rude shelters were made of impermanent materials, probably wattle and daub—wood and earth—and none have survived. Thus we have more evidence of how Neolithic people buried their dead than of how they actually lived. This is a reminder that the story of architecture, especially ancient architecture, is always the story of the survivors, those buildings that were durable enough to last, or were considered important enough—or valuable enough—to preserve.

There is archaeological evidence of active burials at Barnenez over a period of at least two thousand years, well into the Bronze Age, which is a remarkably long period for the useful life of a building. We can only gaze in admiration at the achievement that the cairn represents. Like many monumental works of architecture, it is first the size that impresses. The cairn makes us feel small, but at the same time proud—humans like us built this. The cairn shares another quality with many works of architecture: it takes its place in the landscape, both standing out and fitting in. The headland location is visible from a distance—from the sea as well as from land. The deliberately arranged stone walls are obviously manmade, yet they suit their rocky surroundings. The land slopes down at the north end, and photographs of the stepped architecture suggest to me the prow of a great vessel carrying the souls of the departed out to sea (fig. 2).

What does the Cairn of Barnenez tell us about its Neolithic builders? They likely believed in an afterlife. They had a feeling for the landscape and were drawn to the sea—many of the burial mounds are in coastal locations. But who

2 Cairn of Barnenez. The stepped architecture suggests the prow of a great vessel carrying the souls of the departed out to sea. The tomb entrances are plainly visible on the south side.

was entombed in this impressive structure? Were they chieftains and clan leaders, or are these family graves? We simply don't know. The acidic soil of Brittany has ensured that the human remains have disappeared long ago. The builders did leave some evidence, in addition to pottery shards, arrowheads, and stone axes. The interior walls of the passages and tombs are adorned with engravings and paintings. Some of the motifs are geometrical—vertical and horizontal zigzag lines—and others represent images: a head with flowing hair, bull's horns, and a bow shape that may be associated with hunting. Similar motifs have been found elsewhere in Brittany and as far away as Spain, which suggests some sort of communication between these distant Stone Age communities. Although the black and red markings of the Barnenez cairn are not as accomplished as the evocative deer and bison paintings of the much older Lascaux caves in southwestern France, this evidence of creativity is nevertheless touching and immediately establishes a human presence. The ancient paintings are also a reminder of the universal human need to decorate; frescoes, carvings, and mosaics are an important part of the architecture story throughout the ages.

The Cairn of Barnenez was originally one of a pair—Kerdi Bras and Kerdi Bihan in the Breton language—which survived untouched for thousands of years after they ceased to be actively used. The two cairns, which were three hundred feet apart, were formally identified as prehistoric burial mounds only in 1807. In the twentieth century they were acquired by a local building contractor, and in the 1950s he mercilessly leveled Kerdi Bihan, the smaller of the two, using the stone as building material. The municipality stepped in, and Kerdi Bras, which the contractor had started to dismantle, was saved from destruction and restored. André Malraux, who was the French minister of culture at the time, called the burial mound a "megalithic Parthenon." With some exaggeration, he meant that forty-three hundred years before the Greeks built what is considered one of the greatest works of ancient architecture, prehistoric man had already felt the need to create commemorative structures that would last—and tell a story to future generations. In other words, to make something that we call architecture.

2

Houses of Eternity

Upper and Lower Egypt, third millennium BC

About five hundred years after the Brittany cairn was completed, a different sort of prehistoric tomb appeared thousands of miles away in the Nile Valley. The ten-by-twenty-foot rectangular walled structure of sun-dried brick, partly buried in the desert sand, was outside the city of Hierakonpolis, the capital of Upper Egypt. What became known as Tomb 100 was excavated by British archaeologists in 1898. The wooden superstructure was long gone, and because the tomb had been recently plundered there was no direct evidence as to who might have been interred here, although the stone and clay shards suggested that it might have been someone of importance. Tomb 100, which no longer exists, is famous because it contained the oldest known Egyptian tomb painting, which now resides in the Egyptian Museum in Cairo. The eight-foot-long fragment of a battle scene shows a flotilla of high-prowed reed boats, as well as warriors fighting, capturing cattle, and leading prisoners. This prehistoric Bayeux Tapestry is much more refined than the rough scratchings of Barnenez.

The ancient Egyptians attached great importance to the afterlife and filled their tombs with precious objects and personal effects that the soul of the deceased would need in the next world. This attracted grave robbers, and during the First Dynasty, beginning around 3200 BC, tombs began to be housed in massive vault-like structures with flat roofs and sloping walls. These so-called mastabas were likewise built of sun-dried bricks—Nile silt mixed with chopped straw, molded and left out in the sun to dry. The mute walls gave no hint of the interior, which usually included one or more richly decorated rooms where offerings could be deposited. A small, inaccessible room called the serdab contained a seated statue of the deceased, visible through a small aperture that allowed the soul of the deceased to move about. A sealed trapdoor in the roof provided access to a shaft that led to the underground burial chamber containing a stone sarcophagus with mummified remains (fig. 3). The bulky mastabas must have been an imposing presence in the flat, featureless desert. Rising as high as twenty or thirty feet, the structures were geometrically precise compared to the roughly shaped Brittany cairn—forms *in* the landscape rather than *of* the landscape.

The ancient Egyptians called these bunkers "houses of eternity." The largest belonged to the king, who, according to religious belief, was a divine intermediary between the gods and his people (the title "pharaoh" dates from a later period). High-ranking dignitaries rated smaller versions. The tomb of Akhethotep, a royal adviser who came from a long line of high officials—his mother had been the overseer of female physicians—was built around 2400 BC in Saqqara, a sprawling necropolis outside Memphis, the capital of the Old Kingdom. This mastaba, a hundred feet long, fifty feet wide, and more than twenty feet high, also contained the remains of Akhethotep's son Ptahhotep. Although wives were sometimes buried alongside their husbands, there is no evidence of other family members. The entryway, surmounted by a lintel bearing Akhethotep's name, opened into a wide passage leading to a central hall whose ceiling was supported by four pillars. The hall accommodated the large groups that attended the funeral ceremonies and regularly visited the tomb, leaving food offerings for the departed. Two adjoining chapels were dedicated to the father and son; the actual sarcophagi were in deep underground tombs. The interior of Akhethotep's chapel, today in the Louvre, is covered in beautiful polychromed carvings in shallow relief. These depict the occupant's funerary banquet, as well as scenes from his everyday life—officiating, hunting, and farming—and are accompanied by hieroglyphic descriptions. The west wall contains a narrow false door representing a portal to the underworld.

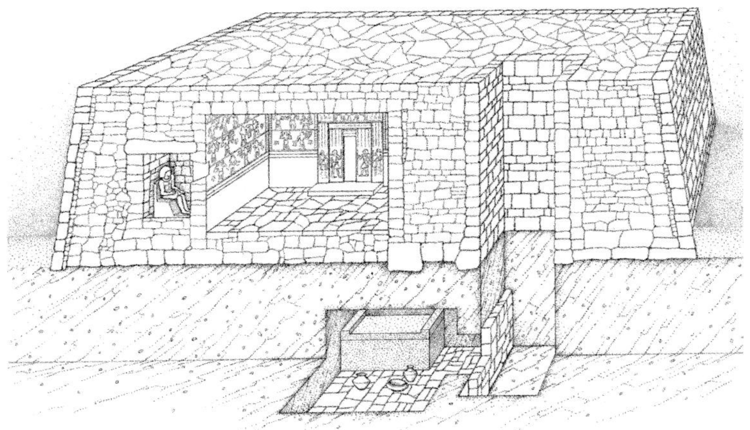

3 Cross-section through a stone mastaba showing an interior chamber for offerings and the serdab, a small room containing a statue of the deceased. A vertical shaft leads to the underground tomb.

The elaborate carvings in Akhethotep's mastaba were possible because the construction material was not sun-dried brick but limestone. The switch to stone occurred two hundred and fifty years earlier when King Djoser, the founder of the Third Dynasty and the unifier of Upper and Lower Egypt, built a large mastaba at Saqqara. To give it greater durability—and presumably additional distinction—he ordered that the mastaba be constructed of limestone rather than sun-dried brick. This change reflected the growing wealth of the Old Kingdom, for while mud bricks could be inexpensively fabricated on the building site, limestone had to be quarried, dressed, and transported long distances.

Djoser's funerary complex, which included the mastaba, ancillary structures, and a surrounding wall, required more than six hundred thousand tons of limestone in all. The person in charge of this massive construction project was the king's vizier, Imhotep. A contemporary inscription refers to Imhotep as "administrator of the great palace, hereditary lord, Greatest of Seers . . . the builder, the sculptor, the maker of stone vases." Does that make him the first architect? Although this polymath was not identified as an architect—no such formal position existed in ancient Egypt—that was in effect his role. Djoser must have been a demanding master, for Imhotep enlarged the mastaba several times during its decades-long construction. He made the structure wider and longer, and then extended it in an unexpected direction: vertically. He added three progressively smaller mastaba-like platforms, one on top of the other. The king must have been pleased with the result, and in a final burst of building Imhotep further enlarged the base until it was about four hundred by three hundred and fifty feet, adjusted the platforms to suit, and added two more steps. He lined the exterior with blocks of smooth white limestone—long since disappeared. The resulting six-step pyramid, which was completed around 2648 BC, rose two hundred feet above the desert floor (fig. 4). This impressive height was possible only because limestone is more than twenty times stronger in compression than is sun-dried brick—a brick pyramid this tall would have collapsed of its own weight. Djoser's Step Pyramid is generally considered the world's earliest large-scale structure of cut stone.

It requires a considerable leap of the imagination to go from a squat mastaba to a stepped pyramid. There must have been a palpable sense of excitement during the construction of the tomb as Imhotep evolved the new potent shape. Such singular moments are rare in the story of architecture, but every so often an individual such as an architect, a craftsman, or an ambitious client invents something entirely unexpected. Such pioneering works are not always the most beautiful—the stepped pyramid form is less evocative than later smooth pyramids—but they can alter the course of future building.

4 King Djoser's Step Pyramid, Saqqara. Imhotep, 2667–2648 BC. The innovative form was arrived at through trial and error. The white limestone cladding of the pyramid has long since disappeared.

The powerful symbolism of a giant staircase ascending to the sky was not lost on Djoser's successors. Later kings not only built step-pyramid tombs for themselves but also constructed small step pyramids throughout the kingdom, not as tombs but as monumental markers. The pyramid had become a regal icon. Yet Djoser's Step Pyramid was not the ultimate prototype. It was one of his successors, Sneferu, the first king of the Fourth Dynasty, who was responsible for the classic pyramid as we know it. During his thirty-year reign Sneferu built no fewer than three pyramids. The first was at Meidum, about thirty-five miles south of Saqqara. There is some evidence that the project may have been started by his predecessor Huni, the last king of the Third Dynasty. The traditional seven-step design was larger and steeper than Djoser's, and seventy feet taller, and Sneferu's modifications included a dramatic change: he filled in the steps to create smooth sloping sides. The classic pyramid shape was born.

It is not known whether the inspiration for this momentous change came from Sneferu or from his unknown vizier. It required extraordinary skill in finishing and setting stone to create perfectly flat angled planes at this giant scale, but the new project was unsuccessful. For reasons that are not entirely clear, the pyramid suffered a catastrophic collapse during construction—all that remains is a ruined portion of the original stepped core. Sneferu immediately began a second pyramid, this time at Dahshur, closer to Saqqara. It was a similar design but larger—it would be three hundred and fifty feet tall. The height was the result of an extremely steep slope angle—sixty degrees. However, when the massive

5 King Sneferu's pyramids at Dahshur, c. 2600 BC. The Red Pyramid (right), completed in 2580 BC, became the model for future builders. The upper portion of the distant Bent Pyramid was completed with a lower slope.

structure was half finished, it started showing signs of uneven settlement resulting from excessive weight, inadequate foundations, or subsoil conditions.

When the Dahshur pyramid started to list, the indomitable Sneferu ordered his builders to stop work and to start a third pyramid, a mile away. This time the slope of the sides was decreased to a conservative forty-three degrees, which reduced the structure's weight. The unprecedentedly large base (722 feet per side) produced a pyramid that was 344 feet tall—taller than anything previously built. It would have been doubly impressive because the exterior was faced with gleaming white limestone. Medieval scavengers would strip away the surface, revealing the reddish limestone core that gives the pyramid its modern name, the Red Pyramid (fig. 5).

There is a postscript to Sneferu's pyramid-building saga. After the Red Pyramid was finished, Sneferu ordered his builders to return to Dahshur to complete the abandoned pyramid. They somehow solved the settlement problem. A thick stone girdle was added around the unfinished portion, the slope was decreased to fifty-four degrees, and, to further reduce the weight, the slope of the new upper portion was decreased to forty-three degrees, the same as the Red Pyramid. The result is an ungainly gambrel shape that nevertheless has stood the test of time; the so-called Bent Pyramid is the only Egyptian pyramid whose smooth limestone facing has survived intact (see fig. 5).

Sneferu's son, Khufu (better known by his Hellenic name Cheops), established his own necropolis at nearby Giza, and, determining to outdo his father, he built an even taller pyramid. His builders adopted a steeper slope (fifty-one degrees) than the Red Pyramid, and, with a base of 750 feet, the pyramid rose 481 feet, the tallest manmade structure in the world—and so it would remain for the next thirty-eight-hundred years. Cheops's pyramid was celebrated as one of the Seven Wonders of the Ancient World, known simply as the Great Pyramid.

The core of the Great Pyramid is constructed of rough-hewn limestone blocks quarried next to the building site. The blocks of Djoser's Step Pyramid had been relatively small, but as the size of pyramids increased, so did the size of the blocks. A contemporary photograph gives a sense of the engineering accomplishment that the Great Pyramid represents (fig. 6). The blocks are laid in courses—more than two hundred of them. The lower courses are roughly four-foot cubes and double cubes weighing five to ten tons; higher up, the blocks are three-foot cubes weighing two to three tons. The pyramid was topped with a pyramidion, a capstone of granite or diorite, inscribed with the king's name and religious symbols, and covered in gold leaf. The Great Pyramid was originally faced in milky white limestone quarried in Tura, eight miles upstream—not a thin veneer but large facing blocks that were cut and shaped with copper saws and chisels at the quarry, then transported down the Nile by barge to the building site. Limestone was soft and easily worked, but it was incapable of supporting the long spans required for the tombs within the pyramid, which were constructed of polished granite from distant Aswan, at the southern end of the kingdom. Granite was also used for the massive blocks that sealed the entrance to the gallery that led to the king and queen's tombs deep within the pyramid. These blocks were the largest in the pyramid—some weighed as much as fifty tons. The hard granite

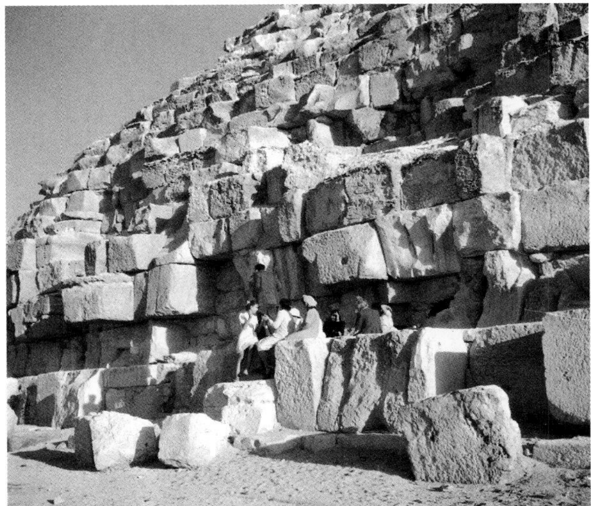

6 Great Pyramid of Cheops, Giza, 2580–2560 BC. The rough-hewn blocks, each weighing about five tons, are laid in regular courses, diminishing in size with height. The exterior was originally clad in smooth blocks of Tura limestone.

was laboriously quarried and worked with pounding stones made of gneiss, diorite, and granite, as well as with polishing abrasives. The paving stones around the base of the pyramid are basalt, a hard volcanic rock from the Western Desert.

Once transported to the building site, the limestone blocks had to be dragged to their final location. This was done by gangs of men using temporary earthen ramps. At least, that is our best guess, for there is no direct evidence of the precise method. After the blocks were positioned, the cracks between them were filled with mortar made from gypsum. It is unclear how the builders managed to create the perfectly flat sloping sides using only measuring rods, squares, stretched lines, and plumb bobs. The achievement is all the more impressive considering the size of the workforce; it has been estimated that the Great Pyramid employed as many as fifteen hundred masons to set the stones in place, in addition to fifteen thousand quarrymen and stone-haulers. Although prisoners were used as slave labor, most of the workers were not slaves but skilled craftsmen, many of whom had worked on Sneferu's pyramids. Cheops's massive pyramid was completed in a remarkable fourteen years.

The ancient Egyptians were not the world's only pyramid builders. Step pyramids serve as platforms, either for temples, in the case of the Khmer pyramids in what is present-day Cambodia, or for ceremonies, in the case of Mayan and Aztec pyramids in pre-Columbian Mexico. The step pyramids built by the ancient Koguryo civilization, which existed on the Korean peninsula and parts of Manchuria, most closely resemble the Egyptian pyramids, being royal tombs whose interiors are likewise covered in evocative paintings. But the smooth Egyptian pyramids remain unique in design, size, and execution. They are architecture as the expression of a particularly stable and long-lived civilization, not merely distinctive forms but models of the society that built them: hierarchically ordered, self-confident, and perfectionist.

3

Enter the Column

Saqqara, third millennium BC
Luxor, second millennium BC

The Great Pyramid was part of a complex that included two mortuary temples, mastabas for court officials, and three smaller pyramids for Cheops's wives. The precedent for this arrangement was King Djoser's Step Pyramid at Saqqara, and it is worth examining the latter in more detail. Djoser's forty-acre funerary compound was consciously modeled on his royal palace in nearby Memphis in order to provide a familiar setting where the king's soul might reenact everyday rituals in the afterlife. The surrounding thirty-five-foot-high limestone wall was divided into vertical panels and contained fifteen gateways. Only one of the gates was functional—the rest were false doors intended exclusively for the spirit of the deceased. Although built in stone, the single entrance, the false doors, and the paneled wall were characteristic of an old-fashioned sun-dried brick mastaba. This combination of innovation and tradition continued throughout.

The entrance, which still exists, is casually located near one corner and is not a grand portal but a tall, unadorned slot about four feet wide. This narrow passage opens into a colonnaded gallery that leads to a ceremonial court in front of the pyramid. Facing a smaller court is a row of what archaeologists call "dummy buildings," solid limestone replicas of the brick pavilions that stood on the grounds of the actual palace. In addition to a small mortuary temple and two storehouses for offerings, there is a limestone mastaba whose burial chamber is a smaller version of the one beneath the pyramid. The interior of this slightly mysterious structure—why a second tomb?—is decorated with beautiful turquoise tiles, and the exterior has a spectacular bas-relief frieze consisting of cobra heads.

The cobra heads are the direct result of the recent shift to building with stone: unlike sun-dried brick, limestone could be carved, and the Egyptians were skilled carvers, experienced in making vases and pots out of hard granite, porphory, and basalt. The carvers emulated many of the features of traditional

7 King Djoser's burial compound, Saqqara, 2650 BC. The carved ends of the piers outside the entrance gallery are three-quarter columns, whose vertical striations resemble bundled papyrus reeds. The piers originally carried a limestone slab ceiling.

mud-brick construction: palm-log roof beams, papyrus matting, and created faux wooden doors complete with carved hinges. Even the dimensions of the limestone blocks mimicked sun-dried bricks. Such imitation happens frequently in the story of architecture when builders are confronted with a brand-new material, whether it is limestone, cast iron, or reinforced concrete. The first impulse is to reproduce a familiar form; it is only later that new shapes emerge.

Let us return to the colonnaded gallery at Saqqara. The long-gone ceiling of limestone slabs was supported by two rows of twenty-two-foot-tall columns. At least they look like columns. Because Egyptian masons had no experience building freestanding masonry columns, they conservatively braced the columns with short side walls. At the end of the gallery, four piers consisting of paired sets of similarly braced three-quarter columns formed a gateway to the ceremonial court (fig. 7). And what elegant columns! The shaft, which is gently tapered, has a pronounced base, and the capital, which has not been preserved, is surmounted by a simple rectangular cap called an abacus. The columns are delicately striped with convex striations. What was the inspiration for this unusual architectural detail? In traditional construction, mud brick was unsuitable for structural columns, and because timber was rare (cedar had to be imported from Lebanon), columns were often made by bundling papyrus reeds and tying them with cords. These bundled reeds were the model for the vertical striations of the shafts in the Saqqara entrance gallery. (Elsewhere in the compound, the striations are concave, anticipating the rounded grooves, or flutes, that are features of later Greek architecture.) The profiles of some of the shafts mimic the swelling shape of bound papyrus. In addition, there are walls with rows of slender half-round columns attached—or "engaged"—to the wall's surface. These columns are surmounted by capitals carved in plant forms such as open leaves and deadheaded flowers. There are no freestanding columns in Djoser's compound.

If this were a movie, it would be time for a fanfare, for the appearance of the column in Saqqara represents a great moment in the story of architecture. Almost miraculously, all the elements of the classic column emerged at once: a clearly defined base, a tapered and swelling shaft, fluting, a capital, and an abacus. I am tempted to credit Djoser's vizier Imhotep with this remarkable invention, although it could have been the work of a particularly gifted mason. Another curious fact: it is often assumed that engaged columns were an adaptation of freestanding columns, but Djoser's burial compound suggests that it was the engaged column that appeared first.

▪ ▪ ▪ ▪ ▪

The ancient Egyptians were skilled builders, and it did not take them long to learn how to construct freestanding columns. Columns proliferated—in colonnades, in galleries surrounding arcaded courts, and especially in hypostyle halls, that is, halls whose flat stone roofs were supported by grids of closely spaced columns, which were required because the granite beams used to support the roof slabs could span only about twenty feet. The mortuary temple of Rameses III, the last of the great pharaohs, has several such halls. Built in the twelfth century BC, this temple is in Medinet Habu on the west bank of the city of Luxor, and it is representative of the increasingly sophisticated architecture of the New Kingdom. The mortuary temple—Rameses's actual burial place is outside the city in the Valley of the Kings—measures about two hundred feet by five hundred feet and stands in a sixteen-acre compound that included a palace where the king and his retinue resided during their periodic visits to the holy city, which was about five hundred miles up the Nile from Memphis. The palace was built of sun-dried brick (stone construction was limited to tombs and funerary buildings) and has all but disappeared, but the stone temple is one of the best preserved in ancient Luxor.

The entrance to the temple is through a monumental portal flanked by sandstone walls called pylons (fig. 8). Eighty feet high, the tapered forms were a conscious reference to the slope-sided walls of mastabas, albeit hugely magnified. The pylons, which remind me of giant billboards, are covered in carved

8 Rameses III's mortuary temple, Medinet Habu, Luxor, 1186–1153 BC. The slots in the tapered pylon walls originally accommodated flagstaffs.

hieroglyphics and pictorial scenes; four slots originally held tall flagstaffs flying colored pennants dedicated to individual gods. The central portal leads to a courtyard that served as a forecourt for the temple and the adjoining royal palace; the two sides are lined by shaded porticos. A second set of pylons, with a portal of red granite that held a cedar door covered in gold and hammered copper, marks the entrance to the temple proper. The doorway opens to another courtyard with a surrounding peristyle, or columned arcade. That is as far as most people went. Beyond an imposing set of double doors was the sacred precinct, which included a large peristyle hall, two smaller halls, a square chamber containing a model of the royal barge, assorted secondary chapels, treasuries, and ceremonial rooms. At the termination of the processional axis was the sanctuary itself, the holy of holies, a small, narrow chamber with the cult image of the god Amon.

Compared to such earlier funerary buildings as Djoser's complex at Saqqara, which has an improvised quality, the studied plan of Rameses III's temple incorporated biaxial symmetry and a rigorous geometry (fig. 9). Like the old mastabas, the exterior consisted of blank walls. The sequence of courtyards and major rooms was carefully orchestrated: as one penetrated the temple, the ceilings became lower, the spaces smaller, the architecture more intense. The atmosphere changed, too, from a sunny forecourt to a shaded peristyle, to a dimly lit hall with overhead clerestories, to two increasingly murky halls, terminating in a pitch-black sanctuary. All these spaces were laid out along a processional axis. There is considerable sophistication in the labyrinthine arrangement of the sacred precinct, whose secondary rooms are shoehorned into the leftover space in order to preserve the symmetry of the main halls. This part of the temple, unlike the two forecourts, is largely ruined today, although the outlines of the halls and rooms are plainly visible.

Columns, contrasting with the horizontal lines of floors, walls, and ceilings, are the vertical exclamation points of this architecture. The forecourts contain square piers with attached carved human figures representing the pharaoh, as well as bulging papyrus columns, some with capitals shaped like open saucerlike flowers, and others in the shape of closed buds (fig. 10). The peristyle halls had similar columns supporting the ceiling and a clerestory over the taller central aisle. The limestone was given a thin coat of plaster, whitewashed, and the sunk relief carvings were picked out in bright colors. The surfaces of columns, walls, beams, and ceilings were all finished this way. The aim of the inscriptions and images was not to enhance or ornament the architecture but rather to document and commemorate the life and achievements of the pharaoh.

There were more than eighty columns in Rameses III's mortuary temple; half were used to support the roofs of the two hypostyle halls. We have become used to large spaces such as sports arenas, convention halls, and airport terminals roofed over by single spans, and the architectural impact of a hypostyle hall, with its forest of columns, is very different. As in a forest, where one is mainly aware of the trees, the main experience is of the columns, and one catches only fragmentary glimpses of the space itself.

Rameses's temple took about a dozen years to build and was completed in 1196 BC. Although it had been more than fifteen hundred years since Imhotep had introduced the engaged column in Djoser's funerary compound, the conservative

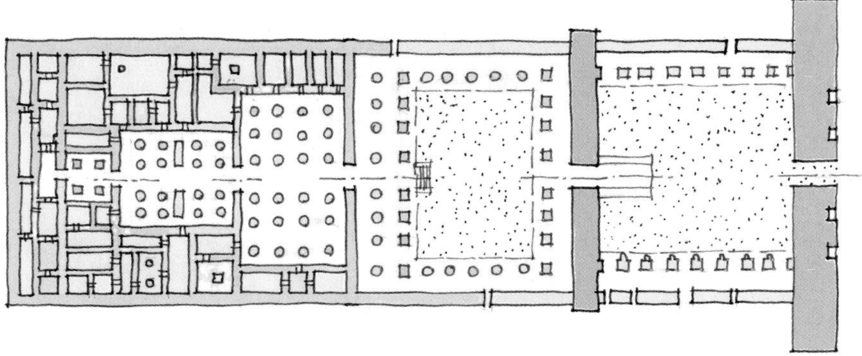

9 Rameses III's mortuary temple. Plan. The symmetrical design is arranged around a processional way that passes through progressively smaller spaces, culminating in the sanctuary.

10 Rameses III's mortuary temple. The massive bulging columns of the peristyle court have stylized capitals shaped like closed papyrus buds. The columns, beams, ceilings, and walls are carved in shallow sunk relief and painted.

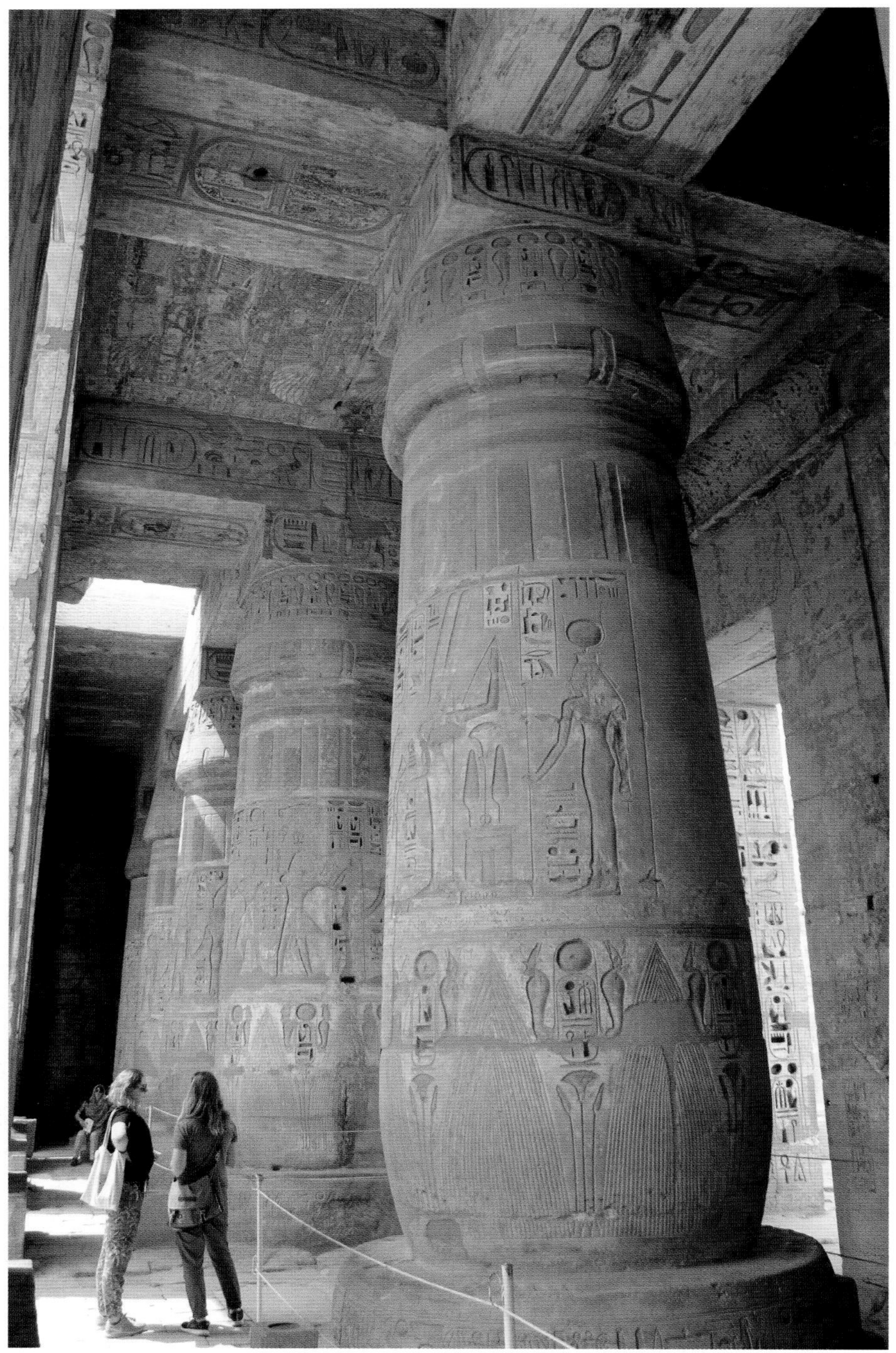

Egyptian builders continued to model column capitals on plants: the papyrus, which was the emblem of Lower Egypt; the lotus, the emblem of Upper Egypt; and the ubiquitous palm. Over time, these capitals were stylized and simplified, like the smooth closed-bud capitals in Rameses's temple. The shafts were smooth, fluted, or covered in hieroglyphics. The largest surviving columns in Rameses III's mortuary temple are twenty-three feet tall and five and a half feet in diameter, and the columns of the largest hypostyle hall in ancient Egypt, the great hall of Karnak, are seventy feet tall and ten feet in diameter. The human figure shrinks to antlike proportions next to such Brobdingnagian architecture.

4

The Birthplace

Athens, fifth century BC

At this point in the story, one might have expected that Egyptian architecture, which was so skillfully constructed and conceived—and so long-lived—would have become the model for succeeding generations of builders. Instead, the birthplace of the architecture that would inspire architects for more than two thousand years was not the Nile Valley but a remote corner of the eastern Mediterranean. Greek civilization took root on and around the mountainous Peloponnese peninsula among fifteen hundred or so self-governing city-states, the largest of which were Athens, Sparta, Corinth, and Thebes. Sharing a common language and culture, sometimes rivals and sometimes confederates, these seafaring peoples established far-flung colonies on the shores of the Mediterranean—in Macedonia, along the coastal region of Asia Minor, in Sicily, and as far away as North Africa and Spain. Settlements in Asia Minor brought the Greeks into conflict with the mighty Persian Empire, which—against all odds—they ultimately defeated. The leading city-state was Athens, with a population of about one hundred thousand. Its social organization was unique: a form of democracy that, among other things, encouraged creative individuals in many fields, including literature, drama, the plastic arts, and, not least, architecture.

The temple architecture commonly associated with ancient Greece appeared in the sixth century BC. Greek religious rituals occurred out of doors, and the temple was not a place of communal worship but a combination of sanctuary and treasury, a repository for cult statues, sacrificial offerings, and war trophies. The temple stood in a sacred precinct, generally in a natural setting outside the city. The earliest temples consisted of a windowless mud-brick chamber (cella) covered by a tiled gable roof and fronted by a timber-columned portico. Sometimes the portico was enlarged into a colonnade that encircled the cella. When the Greeks switched to more permanent materials they reproduced the old buildings in stone, just as the Egyptians had done two thousand years earlier, although the timber rafters that supported the heavy tiled roof remained unchanged. Greek builders spaced the columns close together to account for the limited span of the stone lintels. The ruins of the oldest such temple, the Temple of Artemis in Corfu, date from about 580 BC and are of limestone; later temples were built of white Parian or Pentellic marble, which has a beautiful appearance, was easy to carve, and was abundant in the region. The dressed blocks were laid without mortar and reinforced against earthquakes with bronze clamps and pins. The temples were not large by Egyptian standards—the Corfu temple was seventy-seven feet wide and one hundred and sixty feet long—for the Greeks had neither the manpower nor the resources to undertake mammoth projects. While transporting the marble elements was laborious and depended on large gangs of laborers, the straightforward architecture did not place excessive technical demands on the builders.

Temple design did not change much over the next hundred and fifty years. The size of the cella and the exact number of columns varied, but whether the temple was dedicated to Artemis, Apollo, or Poseidon, the basic plan remained the same: a windowless sanctuary surrounded by a colonnade. The design of the columns, which were constructed of stacked marble drums, was influenced by earlier Egyptian examples: a tapered shaft, concave flutes, a simple upside-down saucer as a capital, and a square abacus. Such columns were referred to as Doric, after the Dorian region of western Greece where they originated. The abacus supported a marble beam (the architrave), above which ran a frieze consisting of grooved rectangles (triglyphs) and panels (metopes) that were sometimes decorated with relief carvings. Above the frieze was a projecting cornice. These component parts, called an entablature, were derived from the pegged details of the original wooden temples.

The culmination of Greek temple architecture is the Parthenon, which stands on the Acropolis, a rocky promontory in the center of Athens (fig. 11). Greek temples varied from three bays to nine bays wide and had different lengths. The Parthenon, which falls in the middle of this range, is seven bays by sixteen, one hundred and one feet wide and two hundred and twenty-eight feet long. Like all temples, it stands on a stepped platform (stylobate). The cella is asymmetrically divided into two windowless chambers (fig. 12), each with its own doorway; internal columns supported the bulky timber rafters that carried the heavy marble roof tiles. The smaller square chamber served as the city treasury, and the larger housed the sculptor Phidias's colossal statue of Athena, the goddess of the city. The statue—long gone—is described as made of gold and ivory, realistically painted and decked out with precious gems, altogether garish by modern

11 Parthenon, Athens. Ictinus and Callicrates, 447–432 BC. This temple was the pinnacle of Greek temple architecture, which had been refined over more than a hundred years.

standards. (A bronze statue of the goddess stood outside.) The glowing Pentellic marble temple looks chaste today, but it, too, was adorned: the frieze and sculptural features were picked out in colors, and key elements were gilded, such as the capitals and the floral ornaments (acroteria) at the four corners of the roof. Bas-relief sculpture was an integral part of Greek temples, although the Greeks, unlike the Egyptians, used the art to complement the architecture. There were three chief locations: the pediments, or triangular gable ends, which were filled with figural sculpture; the metopes, which were carved with individual motifs in deep relief; and the upper part of the cella wall, which carried a continuous sculptural frieze in low relief. Most temples incorporated sculpture in only one or two of these locations; the Parthenon had elaborate sculpture in all three. This lavishness was probably because the temple was not a conventional cult shrine but a sort of war memorial, built shortly after Greek victories over the Persians and erected on the site of a temple that had been destroyed by the invaders. In a Phoenix-like gesture, the new building incorporated some of the material of the old temple in its fabric.

What is remarkable about the Parthenon is that while it is monumental—the thirty-four-foot-high columns are six feet in diameter—it is not overpowering.

There is no front or back; instead, the surrounding colonnade invites entry at any point. The result is a sense of openness and freedom. Nor is there a hierarchy to the component parts, which appear to be in perfect harmony. It is a cliché that a work of art is complete when nothing can be added or taken away, but, despite its ruined state and the notable absence of its sculptural elements, that is the feeling we have looking at the Parthenon—it is perfect.

The building of the Parthenon was spearheaded by Pericles, the leading Athenian statesman, assisted by his friend Phidias, the sculptor. Construction of a Greek temple was the responsibility of the *architekton,* the "chief builder," and the architects of the Parthenon were Ictinus and Callicrates. Architects directed the quarrying of the marble, supervised the construction, and oversaw numerous refinements. For example, although Greek temple columns appear to be tapered cylinders, they were regularly given a gently swelling profile (entasis); corner columns were sometime made slightly thicker and were spaced closer to give added visual weight to the corners of the building; for the same reason, columns were not plumb but were made to lean slightly toward the center of the building; and instead of being perfectly flat, the stylobate could be made slightly convex, a curve that might be echoed in the entablature. The precise purpose of these subtle adjustments, which immeasurably complicated the masons' job, is unclear. The refinements may have been derived from Egyptian precedents, they may have been optical correctives, or they may have reflected an artistic wish to avoid a mechanical appearance and to make the building more organic—that is, more human. Most Greek temples include one or two of these features—there are temples with flat stylobates, with columns that do not lean, and there is at least one temple whose columns have no entasis. The magisterial Parthenon incorporates *all* of the subtle refinements.

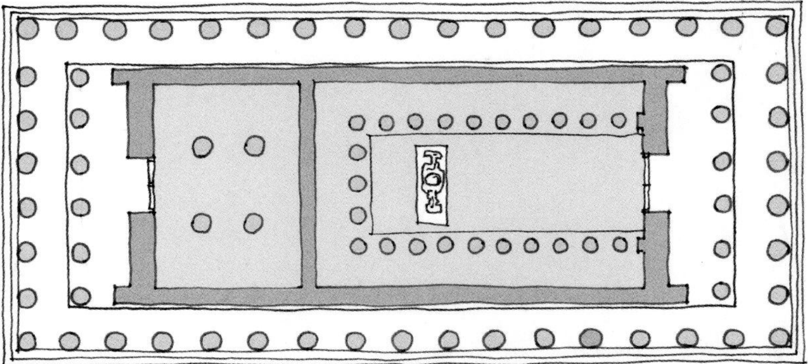

12 Parthenon. Plan. The larger chamber housed a statue of Athena. The interior columns were required to support the timber roof. Note the row of smaller columns at each end.

No sooner had the Parthenon been completed than Pericles commissioned the architect Mnesikles to design a second building. We don't know why Ictinus and Callicrates were passed over. Perhaps their many architectural refinements had been too costly, or perhaps there was a falling out between Phidias and the architects. The new project was a propylaea, or gateway, located on a slope at the edge of the outcrop. Mnesikles used the traditional architectural vocabulary of columns, entablature, and pediments, but he had to accommodate a more complex plan—a ceremonial entryway flanked by two wings, one of which housed a ritual dining hall (fig. 13). A steep exterior stair led up the hill to the entry facade, which resembled a pedimented temple front but with a subtle refinement: the space between the two central columns was slightly enlarged to accommodate the pathway. These columns are Doric, but the interior colonnade is different: Ionic. Ionic columns originated in Ionia, a colonized region on the Aegean coast of Asia Minor (Anatolia in present-day Turkey), and they were distinguished by more slender shafts and spiral-shaped capitals, which reflected a different sensibility, perhaps influenced by Persian architecture. Unlike Egyptian capitals, which were based on plant forms, the symbolism of the Ionic spirals, or volutes, remains obscure; they could stand for rams' horns, seashells, or paper scrolls. Because of their slender form and delicate capitals, Ionic columns were sometimes characterized as "feminine" compared to the sturdy "masculine" Doric. The ancient Greeks called their varieties of columns *genê,* from *genos,* meaning

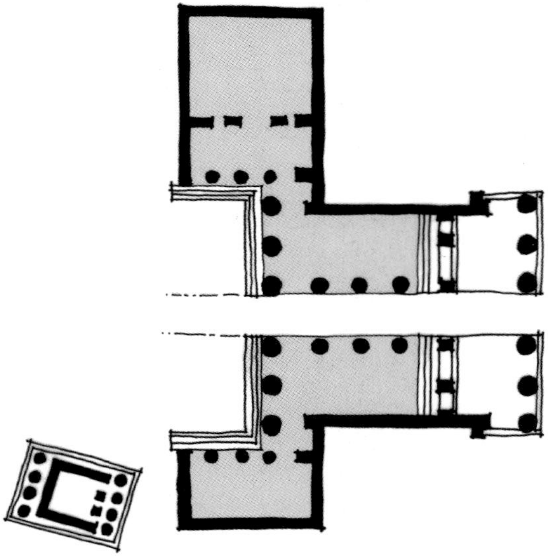

13 Propylaea, Athens. Mnesikles, 437–432 BC. Plan. The gateway to the Acropolis was approached by a pathway from the left. The northern wing contained a banqueting hall. The small building at lower left is the Temple of Athena Nike.

14 Temple of Athena Nike, Athens. Callicrates, c. 420 BC. The simple arrangement of cella and porticos was based on a traditional model. The columns are Ionic.

families or clans. It was not until the sixteenth century and the Italian Renaissance that architects began to refer to the combination of column and entablature as an "order," which connotes a sense of systematic organization that did not exist for the ancient builders.

Construction of the Propylaea was interrupted by the outbreak of the second Peloponnesian War with Sparta, and the south wing of the building was never completed, nor were the two even larger wings framing the east side of the building. Ten years later, two more buildings were added to the Acropolis. The first was a small temple next to the Propylaea (fig. 14). Only seventeen and a half feet wide, it was dedicated to Athena Nike, the goddess of victory, a hoped-for outcome in the ongoing struggle with Sparta. The architect was Callicrates, back on the job following the death of Phidias and Pericles. The traditional plan consists of a cella with only front and rear porticos instead of a full colonnade. The four slender fluted Ionic columns at each end are made of single pieces of marble, and instead of triglyphs and metopes, a continuous frieze depicts battlefield scenes of Athenian victories.

The top of the Acropolis is a flattish rocky plateau extending over about seven acres. The fourth major building is some distance from the Parthenon. The so-called Erechtheion was a key religious shrine for the ancient Athenians because it housed their most precious relic, the wooden cult statue of Athena that, according to legend, came directly from the gods. The building stood next to a sacred olive tree, said to have been planted by Athena herself. The architect of the Erechtheion is unknown—it may have been Mnesikles. Whoever he was, he faced a challenging commission: not only the need to incorporate several shrines—some preexisting—to various gods and goddesses, but also to accommodate a steeply sloping site. To complicate matters further, the budget was

15 Erechtheion, Athens, 421–406 BC. Topography, religious considerations, and budgetary constraints conspired to produce an unusual building. The caryatid porch is on the right; the infill walls and windows of the rear portico are a later addition.

reduced partway through construction due to wartime demands, and the design had to be modified. The result is an asymmetrical building with no two facades the same. The cella has an Ionic portico at each end, and attached to the side walls are two dissimilar projecting porches (fig. 15). The building was originally decorated with a dark blue limestone frieze, covered with white marble reliefs; the facades were embellished with decorative moldings and rosettes; the columns were painted and gilded; and the details of the entablature were picked out with gilt bronze and colored beads.

An unusual feature of the Erechtheion is found in the smaller of the two porches whose flat roof is supported not by columns but by six draped female figures standing on a low parapet wall. Columns in the form of human figures, called caryatids, were not uncommon in ancient Egypt, but they are rare in Greek architecture. It is a measure of the architect's boldness that he introduced this unusual feature into such a prominent building. The caryatids, like the building's asymmetry, are odd, yet oddly affecting. The Erechtheion tempers the Parthenon's austere perfection with a delicate grace.

Architecture depends on many variables: craftspeople and artists who can realize the work, and patrons who have the wherewithal—and the inclination—to pay for it. In the case of a large building such as the Parthenon, which took fifteen years to build, it also depends on unswerving community support. We have seen how the Propylaea was never completed and how the design of the Erechtheion was cut back; the temptation to compromise, alter, and trim is ever present during a long building process. That the Parthenon and many other Greek temples were fully and consistently realized required that all the variables fall into place.

■ ■ ■ ■ ■

Like the colossal structures of pharaonic Egypt, the buildings on the Acropolis had a symbolic role. They did not celebrate a divine ruler, however, but the city itself, the *polis*. Perhaps for the first time, architecture was used to honor civic rather than regal virtues. According to Plato, the "just city" represented wisdom, courage, moderation, and justice; the Acropolis, built on the site of an ancient citadel in the heart of Athens, was the polis's visible civic soul. Only citizens were permitted in the sacred precinct. They marched there en masse during the Panathenaia, the religious festival that included athletic, musical, and poetical contests, and their everyday lives were carried on in the shadow of the limestone promontory. The buildings on the Acropolis were emblematic of the prosperity and power of their city, of their imperfect democracy (which did not extend to women, the foreign-born, and chattel slaves), as well as of the divine protection afforded by their patroness, the goddess Athena.

The first time I climbed up to the Acropolis was as a student on a European summer road trip. I had studied Greek temples in class, but I was confused. What was going on? The buildings seemed randomly scattered on the rocky hilltop. There was no grand processional axis, and the casual layout did not follow any geometrical scheme that I could see. Plato described democracy as a "charming form of government, full of variety and disorder, and dispensing a sort of equality to equals and unequals alike," and variety and a certain amount of disorder certainly characterize the four buildings on the Acropolis. Although two of them incorporate bilateral symmetry, the Propylaea and the Erechtheion do not—both take into account complicated functional demands, both are adjusted to fit the topography, and both combine columns of different kinds and scales. And there is definitely a sort of equality to the architecture; the same elements are used in the large Parthenon and in the tiny Temple of Athena Nike. In other words, although Greek architecture was a template, it was one that was flexible and even had room for radical innovations such as the caryatid porch. There were conventions, but these could be judiciously interpreted—or even ignored. The same elements could be used for a temple like the Parthenon and a civic building like the Propylaea.

Greek architecture, with its three kinds of columns (the third, the Corinthian, which appeared later and was used infrequently, had an elaborate capital that combined Ionic volutes with acanthus leaves) and its carefully defined and proportioned entablatures, has sometimes been described as a language. It is a very loose metaphor. Greek architecture depended on established conventions rather than hard and fast rules. The Greeks were a logical people who pioneered arithmetic and geometry and devised a written alphabet that was the ancestor of Latin and Cyrillic, but they left no architectural treatises or handbooks, and there is no evidence that they designed their buildings according to strict prescriptions. These seagoing traders and merchants were pragmatic realists who saw the world as it was, which is what they portrayed in their art. At the same time as they pursued a humanist ideal, they also believed in conquering heroes and vengeful gods. This split personality caused them to produce buildings that are both disciplined and imaginative, constrained by tradition yet open to invention, resolutely conservative and at the same time radically new.

Classical Greece provided the foundation of Western culture in many fields: mathematics, history, drama. Alfred North Whitehead wrote, "The safest general characterization of the European philosophical tradition is that it consists of a series of footnotes to Plato." It would not be a large exaggeration to say that the European architectural tradition consists of a series of footnotes to Periclean Athens. Greek temples demonstrate an enduring lesson: how to transform simple construction into Beauty. Generations of architects would be inspired, even sometimes overawed, by these extraordinary buildings, for the ancient temples underline another key feature of the story of architecture: this account is not, at its root, about progress. Unlike science and technology, architecture does not evolve or improve. Instead, it consists largely of new interpretations and reinterpretations of old—sometimes very old—insights. And it began in Greece on a very high note; there is nothing crude or primitive about a building like the Parthenon. It is both fully formed and perfectly achieved—and pregnant with possibilities.

5

Mighty Arches

Orange, first century BC
Rome, first and second centuries AD

The Roman Republic was founded shortly before the construction of the Parthenon, and in the succeeding centuries, Rome conquered the Mediterranean world and established an empire that eventually stretched from Ægyptus in the south to Britannia in the north. Although Achaea, which included the Peloponnese and Attica, became a Roman province, Athens remained an important cultural center, and the prestige of Greek art was paramount; wealthy Romans collected Greek sculpture and admired Greek architecture. Roman architects often followed Greek models but adapted and modified them to the needs of their own society in amphitheaters, public baths, and basilicas.

Whereas the Greeks relied chiefly on trabeated construction (columns and beams) and used arched construction only in tombs, Roman builders used arches, vaults, and domes in a variety of buildings, including spectacular bridges and aqueducts. These engineering structures were unadorned, but important civic buildings required something more, which, in architectural terms, meant something Greek. With characteristic ingenuity, the Romans combined Greek columns and architraves with semicircular arches—in effect, building with arches and decorating with columns. Put like that, it sounds simple, but this represented a major discovery and an important addition to the architect's toolbox.

The triumphal arch was one of the Romans' most durable architectural inventions—two thousand years later versions were still being built, in Paris, London, Munich, Saint Petersburg, New York, Mexico City, and New Delhi. Roman arches, which commemorated major military victories and other notable public events, were built in the provinces as well as in Rome, and there are surviving examples all over Europe, the Middle East, and North Africa. The arch typically straddled an important thoroughfare. An impressive example stands in the town of Orange in Provence, France, which was then the Roman province of

Gallia Narbonensis (fig. 16). This arch was erected in the first century BC on the via Agrippa to commemorate the victories of the Second Legion, whose veterans founded the town. The details of the arch are much eroded today, but originally all the surfaces were covered in low-relief sculpture depicting battle scenes, war booty, and victorious centurions lording it over submissive prisoners. The imposing structure has square proportions: sixty-five feet wide and sixty-five feet high. There are three openings, a large arch over the roadway and two smaller side arches for pedestrians. The Greek architectural elements include four giant engaged columns beneath an entablature and a central pediment. Although the arches carry the actual weight of the structure, it is the giant columns that catch the eye. The columns are three-quarter round and fluted. The showy Corinthian columns—a Roman favorite—have a characteristically plain architrave and frieze and an elaborate cornice framing the arched opening. Unlike Greek columns, which stood on the ground, Roman columns were typically elevated on tall bases, or plinths. The pyramidal composition of the arch draws the eye upward toward the center of the attic story, which was originally topped with martial statuary. The custom of placing statues on rooftops was an Etruscan legacy. The curious effect, still visible in many neoclassical buildings today, makes the architecture literally subservient to the human figure.

The Orange arch is a jingoistic celebration of military conquest, but there is nothing primitive about the architecture. This is not just an appliqué patchwork of ancient motifs; there is a clear hierarchy. The central arch, with its taller opening and pediment, dominates the composition. The spacing of the columns accommodates the various openings, and the difference in height is masked by flattened engaged columns, called pilasters, that echo the columns and appear to support the arches. (The pilasters are Tuscan, a simplified Roman version of the Greek Doric.) Engaged columns and pilasters were occasionally used in Greek temple interiors, but the Romans gave them a dominant symbolic role. Pilasters serve no structural function—in a sense, they are optical illusions—but they are a clever way of suggesting columns in buildings where structural columns are not actually required.

The Romans used two different techniques for masonry construction. The Orange triumphal arch was built the old-fashioned way, with dressed limestone blocks, a technique called *opus quadratum.* The other technique was *opus caementicium,* or concrete work. Roman concrete was made by mixing pozzolana (volcanic ash) and lime, adding water, and combining this paste with stone aggregate. The region around Rome was rich in pozzolana, as well as in timber for fueling lime kilns, and because concrete was less expensive than quarried

16 Triumphal Arch, Orange, first century BC. Greek columns meet Roman arches.

stone, opus caementicium became the preferred building technique. Concrete was ideally suited to arched construction because all the material in an arch is in compression, and unreinforced Roman concrete was strong *only* in compression.

Roman builders became adept at using concrete for arches, barrel vaults, cross vaults, and domes. Among the largest concrete structures were amphitheaters. These were based on outdoor Greek theaters whose semicircular seating was carved out of hillsides. The Romans built similar theaters—one still exists in Orange—but they also translated the form into freestanding circular or oval structures with seating surrounding the performance area. The tiered seating was supported by barrel and groin vaults, which also spanned the circling ambulatories and stairs. The concrete surfaces were generally lined with brick or stone, or stuccoed and covered with decorative painting.

The largest amphitheater was the Colosseum in Rome, which could accommodate as many as eighty thousand spectators (the name was derived from the colossal hundred-foot statue of the emperor Nero that stood nearby). The

Colosseum was begun by the emperor Vespasian and completed in AD 80 by his son and successor, Titus. Vespasian had come to the throne following a brutal civil war, and the Colosseum was part of a campaign to establish his legitimacy with the Roman public. The massive oval structure was quickly and cheaply built of concrete and brick, and the builders had little time—or money—for refinements; they were concerned chiefly with creating reasonable sightlines, channeling the movement of crowds of people, and accommodating the backstage requirements beneath the arena—the gladiator barracks, prisoner cages, animal pens, access tunnels, ramps, and elevators that served the brutal spectacles that the Colosseum contained. Present-day views of the partially ruined building give a misleadingly picturesque impression; the monumental structure, with its row upon row of superimposed arched openings, must have been overwhelming.

There is a notable exception to the Colosseum's utilitarian architecture: the curved facade. Equivalent in height to a modern ten-story building, it consists of three open ambulatories. The builders could have left the brick-lined concrete exposed, but Vespasian wanted something impressive, and the brick is covered by travertine slabs attached with bronze clamps and dowels. The design uses the familiar arch-and-column motif. Which kind of column did the unknown architect use? All three. The first level is sturdy Doric, the second delicate Ionic, and the third ornate Corinthian, a vertical hierarchy that would become the model for superimposed columns in multistory buildings for centuries to come (fig. 17). All the half-columns are the same diameter (because Doric columns have more vertical proportions, the lowest ambulatory is taller) and the simplified entablatures are identical on all three levels; the third level includes a cornice, which became redundant when Titus added a fourth story to the building. Designed to look like an attic, the topmost wall has flattened Composite pilasters (Composite is an elaborate Roman fusion of Ionic and Corinthian) and is punctuated by square openings. The spaces between the openings originally held decorative bronze shields; a row of protruding brackets supported wooden masts that carried a retractable canvas canopy over the seating.

■ ■ ■ ■ ■

The apotheosis of vaulted construction was the dome, and the biggest Roman dome was that of the Pantheon, a circular temple in the Campus Martius. Begun by the emperor Trajan on the site of an earlier temple, the building was completed around AD 125 by Hadrian. The precise function of the Pantheon is not altogether clear. Although it contained statues of the gods, it was not a cult temple. Hadrian

17 Colosseum, Rome, AD 70–80. The upper portion of the travertine facade combines Ionic and Corinthian columns with arched construction; the attic story contains Composite pilasters. The protruding brackets at the top originally supported wooden masts that carried a retractable canvas sunshade.

is known to have held court here, and there is evidence that it was occasionally used as a place of public assembly.

It is possible that the designer of the Pantheon was Trajan's favorite architect, Apollodorus, who was also responsible for the Forum and the Baths of Trajan. Apollodorus, an experienced military engineer and a native of Damascus, is sometimes credited with introducing Middle Eastern dome construction to Rome. The hemispherical dome of the Pantheon sits on a tall drum whose brick exterior is almost entirely unadorned—the relieving arches in the curved wall are plainly visible. The domed drum is pragmatically mated to a massive entry portico with the form of a pedimented Greek temple. The deep portico, with sixteen Corinthian columns made out of single pieces of smooth Egyptian granite, is the dominant architectural feature of the exterior (fig. 18). The dome itself is barely visible, its lower portion obscured by a series of so-called step-rings whose extra weight was needed to counter the dome's horizontal thrust. The upper portion of the flattish dome was originally covered in gilded bronze tiles.

The dark, forbidding portico does not prepare one for the interior. The windowless space is brightly lit by daylight coming from a thirty-foot-diameter opening (oculus) at the top of the dome (fig. 19). Drains in the marble floor carry off the rainwater. The overall height of the dome is equal to its diameter—142 feet. The dome sits on eight piers that are separated by deep alcoves spanned by entablatures supported on giant fluted Corinthian columns made of colored marble. The dome seems to float above the vast space. The builders went to great lengths to reduce the actual weight of the dome, decreasing its thickness from twenty-one feet at the base to four feet at the oculus and using progressively lighter aggregates (terra-cotta, volcanic pumice, and porous limestone) in the upper portions. The deep coffers were likewise intended to reduce weight, the divisions acting as structural ribs, while the oculus ingeniously solved the problem of spanning the flat portion of the dome. The square coffers originally held gilded bronze rosettes or stars—the effect must have been like a giant sky. The atmosphere in this vast space is ethereal, a blend of spectacular engineering and wonderfully lyrical architecture; Michelangelo described it as an "angelic and non-human design." Like the Parthenon, the Pantheon represents a seminal architectural achievement of the first order, and the concept of a circular domed room would make regular reappearances—in a church in seventeenth-century Italy, in an eighteenth-century country house in England's Lake District, in a museum in nineteenth-century Berlin, as a reading room in Victorian London, as a university library in Jeffersonian Virginia, and, a hundred years after that, as the entrance rotunda of the National Gallery of Art in Washington, D.C.

18 Pantheon, Rome, AD 113–25. Plan. The circular domed temple is entered through a deep Corinthian portico.

Opposite:
19 Pantheon. Interior. By the eighteenth century, when it was painted by Giovanni Paolo Panini, the temple had been long since been converted into a Christian church.

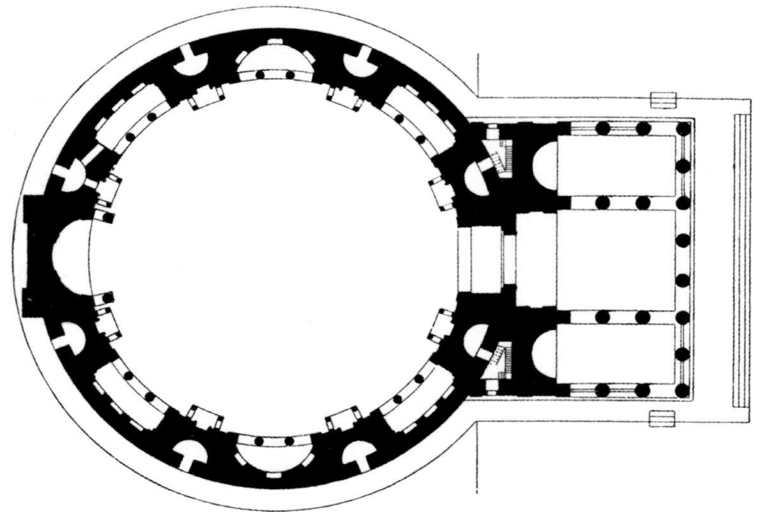

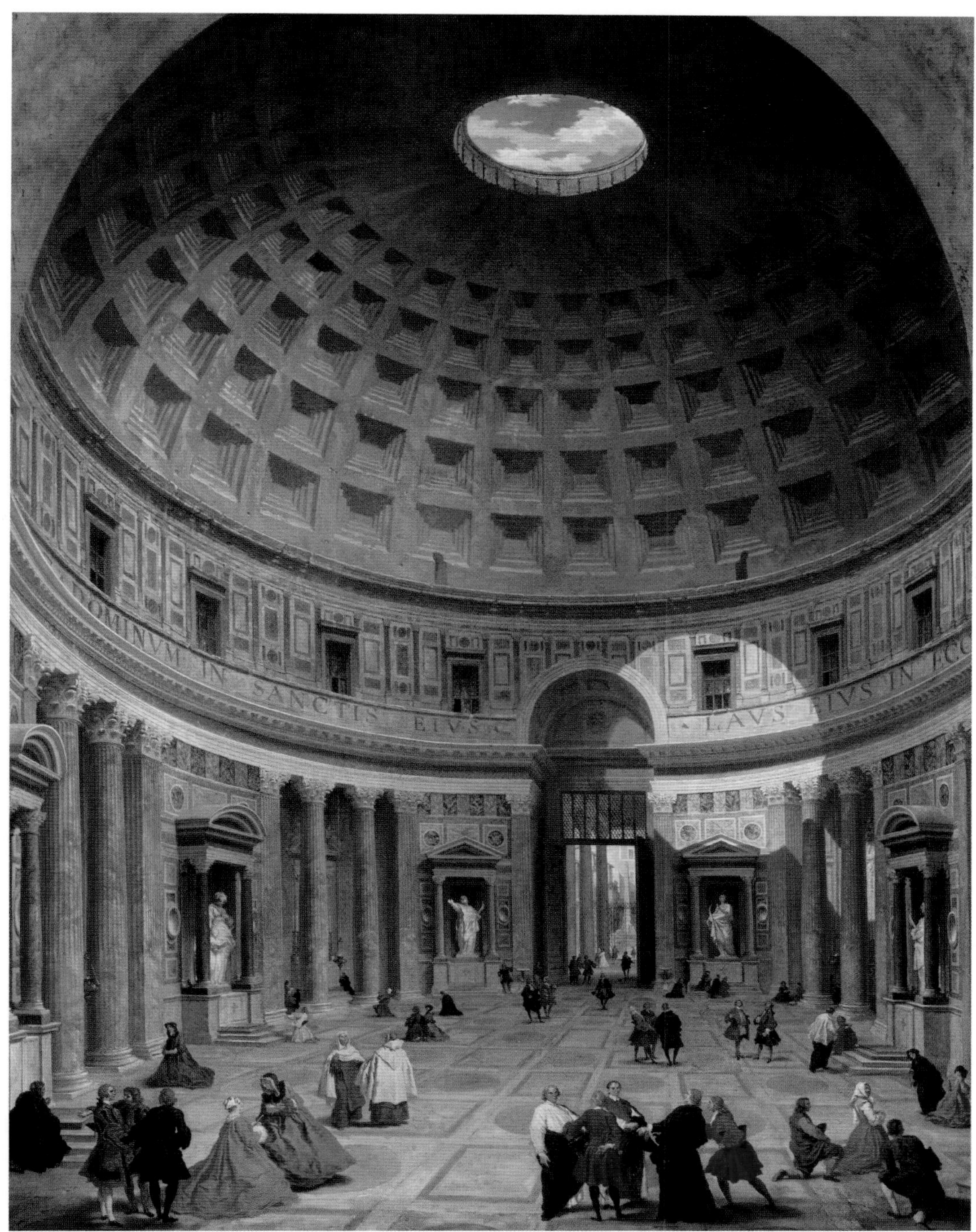
DOMINVM IN SANCTIS EIVS
LAVS EIVS IN

6

Sailing to Byzantium

Constantinople, sixth century

The largest buildings in Rome were the imperial baths. A combination of spa and community center, these public complexes—open to all Roman citizens, women and men—included hot and cold baths, athletic facilities, libraries, and lecture halls. The Baths of Caracalla in the southern part of the city were surrounded by extensive gardens and covered more than sixty acres; only fragments of the immense concrete vaults of the bathing halls survive today. The basilica was another large civic building, a combination town hall and courthouse used for public meetings and legal proceedings. The spacious interior, lit by tall clerestory windows, often had one or two flanking aisles separated by colonnades, and an apse with a dais at one end where the magistrates sat. The largest basilica, of which only a ruined portion remains, was located in the Roman Forum (fig. 20). This monumental building, begun by the emperor Maxentius and completed by Constantine in AD 312, was modeled on the great hall of the Baths of Caracalla. The main space was roofed by three giant concrete cross vaults spanning more than eighty feet; the aisles on each side were covered by barrel vaults. The apse at the end held a colossal seated statue of the emperor Constantine, remnants of which are displayed today on the Capitoline Hill.

Constantine officially recognized Christianity in AD 313, and the religion became dominant throughout the Roman Empire. Unlike the polytheistic Romans, who had private household shrines, and whose public ceremonies took place outdoors, Christians required spaces for group worship. New types of buildings are rarely pure inventions—they are usually adaptations of an existing type, and the first Christian churches were no exception. But what to adapt? The typical Roman temple could not serve as a model—its small sanctuary was inappropriate for large gatherings, and in any case it represented pagan beliefs. The basilica, a prestigious civic building with no religious connotations, provided a well-lit nave and aisles that could easily accommodate large groups; the apsidal end could hold the altar and the assembled clergy. A double-aisled basilica was the model for the large church that Constantine ordered to be built on the site of Saint Peter's grave in Rome. The aisles were divided by columns reused from earlier Roman buildings; the gabled roof was timber. What is now referred to as Old Saint Peter's accommodated up to four thousand congregants and became the chief pilgrimage church of Christendom.

The largest Christian church was not in Rome, however. In AD 324, Constantine moved his capital to Byzantium, which he renamed Constantinople (today Istanbul). In time, the Roman Empire split into western and eastern portions, and although the former fragmented and declined in importance, the latter flourished, and Constantinople grew into the largest and richest city in Europe. The Church of the Holy Apostles, which was started by Constantine and completed by his son Constantius II, was not a basilican plan but a cruciform with a central dome. That church and its successor were destroyed by fire. In 532, the emperor Justinian, whose reign lasted almost forty years, ordered a new cathedral as part of an ambitious building program for the city. He entrusted the work to Anthemios, a Greek born on the coast of Asia Minor (present-day Anatolia), and Isidorus, from nearby Miletus. Both men were scholars; Anthemios was a scientist and inventor, and Isidorus was a geometer and teacher of stereometry and physics. It was an unconventional choice because this remarkable emperor intended to erect an unconventional building.

The architectural concept for the Church of the Holy Wisdom, or Hagia Sophia in Greek, could be crudely described as a combination of the Basilica

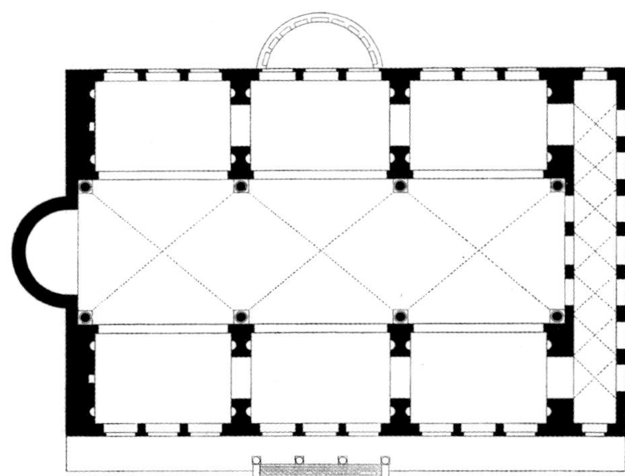

20 Basilica of Maxentius, Rome, AD 308–12. Plan. Used for public meetings and legal proceedings, the central space measured 83 by 265 feet. The arrangement of nave and side aisles would influence early Christian churches.

of Maxentius and the Pantheon. The nave and the flanking aisles resemble the former, but the hundred-foot-wide nave is not spanned by vaults but by a single dome (fig. 21). Whereas the dome of the Pantheon sits atop a cylindrical drum, the base of the dome of Hagia Sophia is square. Byzantine builders, who were fascinated by dome construction, arrived at a solution for combining these two shapes: a spheroid section of wall that enabled the transition from a circle to a square. This crucial architectural device, called a pendentive, made it possible to combine domes—which were more evocative than simple vaults—with rectilineal plans, which were more practical than circular rooms. The pendentive was still novel when Hagia Sophia was being planned, and it had never been used at such a large scale, which may be why Justinian chose a pair of scientists to be his architects.

The dome of Hagia Sophia is supported on four immense arches. The north and south arches flanking the aisles are filled with arcades and windows, while the east and west arches open into large half-domes to create an elongated nave. The

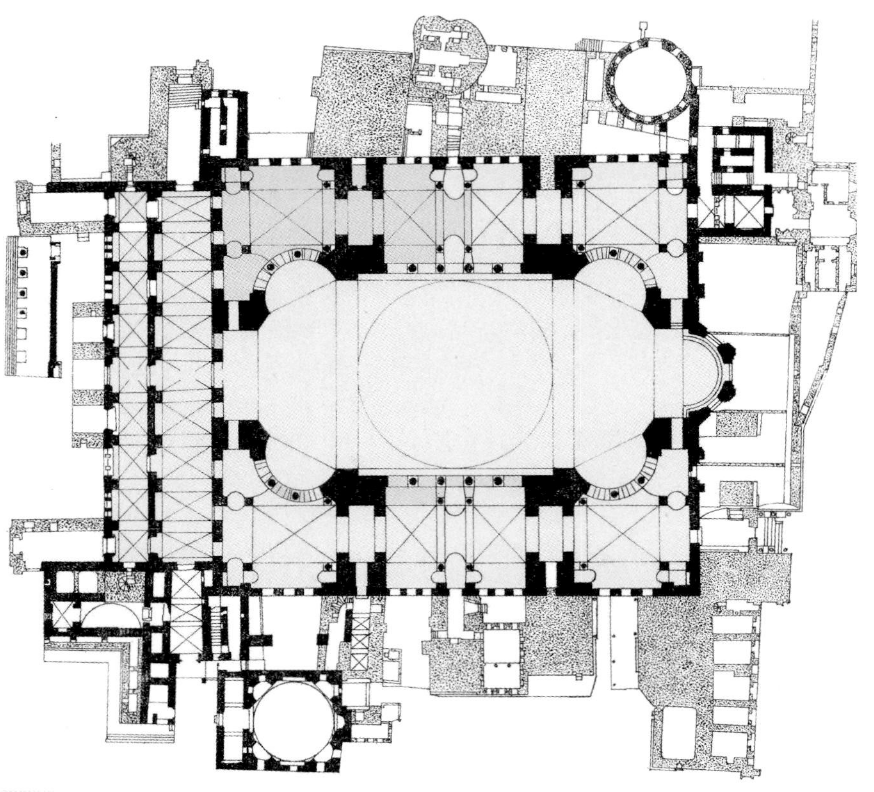

21 Hagia Sophia, Istanbul. Anthemios and Isidorus, AD 532–37. Plan. The church was entered through a narthex on the left. Although the nave and aisles are clearly visible, the basilican concept is modified by the addition of a vast Pantheon-like dome. The shaded structures surrounding the church were added over the centuries.

chancel occupies the east end and houses the altar and an apse with tiered seating for the assembled clergy. The congregants assembled in the nave and spilled into the side aisles; the upper galleries were reserved for women. There were no pews. On ceremonial occasions, the imperial retinue occupied the nave and the faithful were relegated to the side aisles and galleries. The half-dome of the less elaborate west end marked the entrance, which was reached through a vaulted narthex.

Hagia Sophia is neither purely centralized nor purely axial—it is a combination of the two. Centralized because of the great dome, and axial because the half-domes forcefully extend the nave in an east-west direction. The axial geometry is complicated by two large apses that intersect the half-domes on the diagonal. There is no simple hierarchy to this composition, and the views are broken up in a manner that defies easy description. Rhythms of threes, fives, and sevens resonate throughout: the arcades of the two-story galleries consist of seven arches above and five below, the large apses have seven above and three below. This combination of dome, interlocked half-domes, apses, arches, and pendentives had never before been attempted. It is breathtaking.

Hagia Sophia was begun in 532 and completed in less than six years. The workforce is said to have numbered ten thousand. The speed of construction was partly the result of imperial impatience and partly due to the construction method. The eight major piers that support the dome and the two half-domes are stone, but the rest of the building—the vaults as well as the walls—is brick. Byzantine builders built brick vaults and domes that were thinner and lighter than those of their Roman counterparts: several layers of long, thin bricks were set in beds of a very thick mortar paste mixed with brick dust. Long iron tie-bars below the springing of the arches and vaults countered the horizontal thrust. At Hagia Sophia, Anthemios and Isidorus, probably egged on by Justinian, pushed building technology to the limit. For example, they made the large dome lower and flatter than a true hemisphere, and even before construction was finished this produced excessive horizontal thrust in the side wall that required heavy buttress walls on the exterior. Thirty years later the dome collapsed in an earthquake; it was rebuilt by Isodorus's nephew, who reduced the horizontal thrust by making the dome taller and adding structural ribs. This ribbed dome, repaired twice over the centuries, is what survives today.

The site of Hagia Sophia is a commanding promontory overlooking the Bosphorus, the strait that joins the Sea of Marmara and the Aegean to the Black Sea. Then as now the great dome was a prominent feature of the city's skyline, yet the builders showed little interest in the exterior. The complex forms are a straightforward expression of the various structural elements: large double

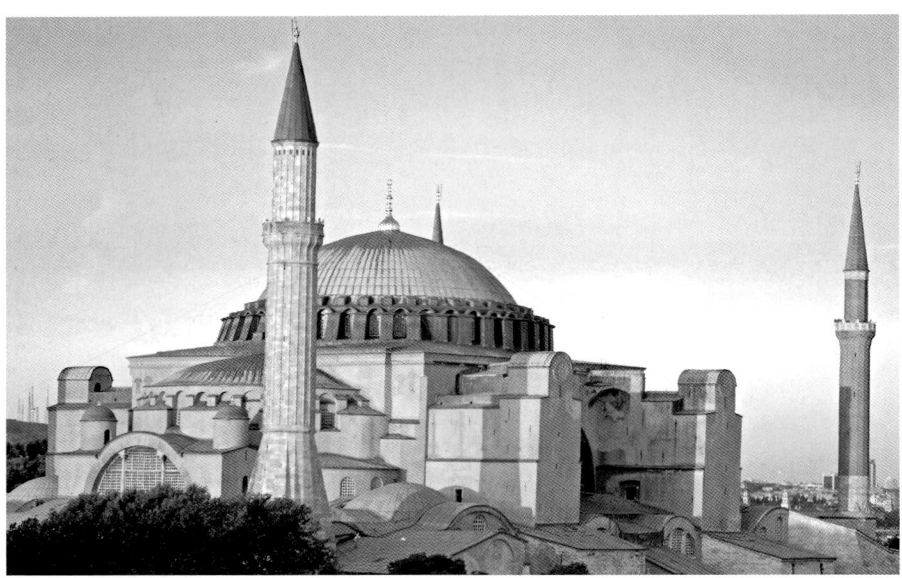

22 Hagia Sophia. The great double buttresses counter the thrust of the dome. The minarets are an Ottoman addition, constructed when the basilica was turned into a mosque.

buttresses brace the dome on the north and south, and a cascade of half-domes does the same on the east and west (fig. 22). Unlike most Greek and Roman monuments, the plain stuccoed exterior includes neither columns, pediments, nor pilasters—in fact no ornamental features of any kind. In that sense, Hagia Sophia is more like an Egyptian temple, saving its architectural drama for the interior.

Light is at the heart of the experience of Hagia Sophia. The base of the dome contains forty arched openings—one in each ribbed segment. In addition, there are scores of small windows filled with panes of colored glass: blue, green, purple, yellow, and ivory. Early Christian custom proscribed statues, which were considered pagan, but allowed two-dimensional images in the form of frescoes and mosaic murals. The brick piers are covered in sheets of multicolored marble. The monolithic column shafts are polished white marble, porphyry (a purple igneous stone), and green serpentine. Some of the columns, which were brought to Constantinople from the far reaches of the Roman Empire, are spolia, that is, repurposed fragments of ancient Greek and Roman buildings. The magical effect of sunlight shimmering on the multicolored stone and the gold and glass mosaics that cover the interior surfaces of the vaults and domes was captured by the painter John Singer Sargent during a nineteenth-century visit (fig. 23).

The religious schism between Eastern Orthodoxy and the Roman Church is mirrored in Byzantine architecture, which moved away from its Roman roots. Builders abandoned the pedimented temple front, replaced entablatures with

23 Hagia Sophia. The painter John Singer Sargent visited the basilica in 1891 and captured the breathtaking interior in this sketch.

arches and vaults, relegated columns to a subordinate role, and dispensed with engaged columns and pilasters altogether. When extra structural support was required they pragmatically paired columns, something that was not done by Roman builders. The columns sometimes had stylized capitals with vestigial Ionic volutes and Corinthian foliage, but not fluting or entasis. To make the transition between the relatively narrow capital and the wide springing of the arch,

24 Hagia Sophia. The wedge-shaped carved marble imposts of Byzantine columns were designed to carry arches rather than an entablature. Note the vestigial Ionic volutes. The book-matched marble of a pier is visible in the background.

Byzantine builders replaced the abacus with a wedge-shaped block called an impost. The impost was elaborately decorated and sometimes replaced the capital altogether. At Hagia Sophia, the imposts and capitals are made of gleaming white Proconnesian marble from the nearby island of Marmara. The Marmara carvers became skillful at working the soft stone, and they developed a technique of undercutting with drills that produced a delicate, lacy overlay of stylized plant leaves, animals, and geometrical patterns (fig. 24). Individual craftsmen introduced their own variations, so that a Byzantine colonnade might contain a variety of dissimilar capitals and imposts—very different from a uniform Greek and Roman colonnade. The most dramatic departure from classical practice was the way that the interior hid—rather than dramatized—the structure. In Hagia Sophia, the marble paneling blends the massive piers supporting the dome with neighboring walls, making the former disappear. This creates the illusion that the flattened dome—the vault of heaven—is unsupported, serenely floating overhead.

▪ ▪ ▪ ▪ ▪

The extraordinary architecture of Hagia Sophia was the result of several factors: Justinian's desire to build something startlingly new; the architects' interest in geometry; the long-standing Byzantine fascination with domes and centralized plans; the builders' prowess in constructing brick vaults and domes; and the stone-carvers' decorative skills. But there was something else at play, something more elusive: taste. Taste sounds frivolous in the context of something as solid and permanent as a building. Yet taste plays an important role in the story of architecture. Some of the decisions made when designing and constructing a building are dictated by functional needs or by the structural limitations of the materials, and others are influenced by precedent-setting traditions. But the choice of a particular color, pattern, or shape is not necessarily governed by the same constraints. It is a matter of taste.

Chacun à son gout, the French say. Each to his own taste. But in an undertaking as large and complex as a building, where decisions are made by scores of participants—clients, architects, artists, craftsmen, and builders—leaving the myriad choices to personal whim would result in confusion. Successful architecture requires a *shared* taste. This shared taste must not be so narrow as to preclude individual creativity nor so broad as to produce chaos. The taste that guided the builders of Hagia Sophia was a complex blend. Justinian's empire included the entire eastern Mediterranean, a cultural mishmash of Greeks, Slavs, Armenians, Georgians, Syrians, and Turks, as well as a scattering of Christian Arabs and Jews. The inhabitants of Constantinople called themselves "Romans" (the term "Byzantine" was coined in the sixteenth century), but their heritage was really Hellenistic: they spoke Greek, their literature was influenced by ancient Greece as well as Rome, and their cuisine was Greco-Roman with Balkan and Anatolian dishes. Byzantine dress was likewise a mixture: men abandoned the Roman toga in favor of the dalmatica, a sort of tunic, while women, who dressed more modestly than their Roman counterparts, continued to wear the Roman stola, a long pleated dress. In Rome, sumptuary laws governed who could wear what, but Constantine's subjects were under no such constraints. They dressed in rich materials imported from Persia and as far away as China, with which there was a flourishing trade. Mosaic murals depict bejeweled women in elaborately patterned robes and men with layered and richly trimmed outfits. The same lavish taste influenced their architecture.

In English, the term "byzantine" implies complexity and devious intrigue, but the French *byzantin* is more apposite—it means luxurious. That captures the fondness for opulence and magnificent display that is clearly visible in Hagia Sophia. This does not mean that religious belief was not central to the architecture. All the details, from the impost carvings to the sparkling mosaics and the golden lamps, were intended to create the sense of a place set apart from the mundane—an otherworldly retreat. In the tenth century, the pagan ruler of Kievan Rus'—the forerunner of Russia—sent emissaries to his neighbors to learn about Judaism, Islam, and Roman and Orthodox Christianity. After visiting Hagia Sophia his emissaries reported back: "We were led into a place where they serve their God, and we did not know where we were, in heaven or on earth."

II
MIDDLE AGES

7

Mihrabs and Minarets

Damascus, eighth century
Kairouan, eighth and ninth centuries

For thousands of years the story of architecture has been mainly concerned with religious structures—tombs and pyramids in pharaonic Egypt, cult temples in polytheistic Greece and Rome, the basilicas of Christianity. There were significant secular exceptions, such as Assyrian palaces and Roman baths, amphitheaters, and triumphal arches, but it was religious belief that tended to produce the most impressive buildings. This pattern continued under Islam. Originating among the pastoral and nomadic peoples of the Arabian Peninsula, Islam emerged in the seventh century as the Mediterranean world's third great religion after Judaism and Christianity. In the following hundred years, this militant faith spread throughout the entire Middle East including Persia, and from present-day Pakistan in the east to North Africa and eventually as far as the Iberian Peninsula in the west. At first, the followers of this austere desert religion had little interest in elaborate buildings—the early mosques or *masjids* (places of prostration) were simply walled outdoor compounds. But as Islam increased in geographic extent—and became more urban—it was inevitable that its adherents would seek an architectural expression that befit their ascendancy.

In 706, the Umayyad clan's Caliph al-Walid announced that he planned to build a grand mosque in Damascus, the capital of the Arab caliphate. He had already restored the Prophet's Mosque in Medina and the beautiful Dome of the Rock shrine in Jerusalem, and he was determined to endow Damascus with a similarly impressive monument. He chose a prominent location in the heart of the city, a walled sanctuary that had been the site of a Roman temple and was presently occupied by the Cathedral of Saint John. Al-Walid bought the site from the Christians and demolished the fourth-century church. Whether the caliph was the designer of the new mosque is unclear, but he seems to have been personally engaged in the project.

The old sanctuary was encircled by an ancient Roman wall and covered an area about three hundred feet by five hundred feet, roughly the same footprint as Hagia Sophia. The prayer hall of the new mosque would occupy slightly less than half of this area, and the rest would be a courtyard surrounded on three sides by arcaded porticos (fig. 25). The paved outdoor area, used for prayers and intended to recall the courtyard of the house of the Prophet Muhammad in Medina, led to the prayer hall, a vast space divided into three by tall colonnades that carried timber trusses supporting a flat roof. All great architecture is a synthesis of the old and the new, and al-Walid's Great Mosque of Damascus was no exception. The nomadic Arabs had no architectural tradition, but because the region was rich in ancient monuments there was no shortage of models—Roman, Byzantine, and Persian. The Arab builders did not copy these antecedents indiscriminately but adapted them to the demands of their faith. They used the Christian basilica as a model, but because the nave and chancel arrangement was ill-suited to communal Islamic prayer, they dispensed with the latter and turned the symbolic axis of the building ninety degrees (fig. 26). Now the faithful faced the long south wall, the so-called qibla wall, which was oriented to Mecca and whose emblematic center was the mihrab, an intricately decorated niche or apse. Next to the mihrab stood the minbar, a tall pulpit from which the imam addressed the worshippers. Light poured into the space from windows in the back north wall. In Islam, ritual prayers are performed five times daily, but the weekly focal event is the midday Friday prayer, and the prayer hall and courtyard of the Damascus mosque were large enough to accommodate the entire male population of the city.

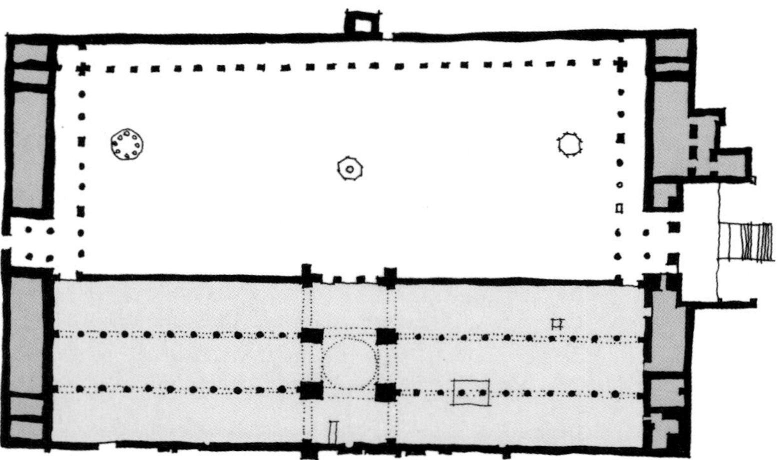

25 Great Mosque of Damascus, 706–15. Plan. The tripartite arrangement of the prayer hall resembles a basilica; the paved courtyard was used for prayers.

26 Great Mosque of Damascus. The architecture was a synthesis of influences: the plan is Christian, the columns and capitals are Roman, the imposts are Byzantine, and the horseshoe arches are Persian. The small domed structure is a shrine to Saint John the Baptist.

A key feature of the mosque is the extensive use of columns, both in the prayer hall and in the porticos of the courtyard. The columns are spolia from the demolished cathedral and also from Byzantine and Roman buildings as far away as Antioch, a distance of almost two hundred miles. The twenty-foot columns in the prayer hall are Corinthian, surmounted by wedge-shaped Byzantine imposts. The arches are horseshoe-shaped, a form that originated in Persia and creates an impression of lightness and grace compared to the more stolid semicircular Roman arch. Horseshoe arches have no structural advantage and they complicate construction, but their delicacy appealed to Arab taste and became a distinguishing mark of Islamic architecture.

The Damascus prayer hall is intersected in the center by a wide aisle facing the mihrab, a slightly awkward arrangement that divides the prayer hall in two. The symbolism of the small dome sitting on a tall octagonal drum in the center of the aisle is unclear, although it may have marked the spot where the caliph knelt during Friday prayer. The dome, like the triangular trusses that supported the roof, was made of wood. Islamic builders borrowed the dome motif—though not the brick dome-building technique—from Byzantium and used it for the same symbolic reason: to represent the vault of heaven. In addition, al-Walid may have wanted the mosque to have a presence in the Damascus skyline. The dome shares that role with three tall minarets, from which the muezzin issued a call to prayer. The minaret directly opposite and across the court from the dome may have been a part of the original plan; the other two minarets were added in the thirteenth and fifteenth centuries.

The interior of the prayer hall, as well as the walls of the porticos encircling the courtyard, is covered in mosaics—another Byzantine borrowing. Because Islam proscribed the depiction of animate beings, the murals depict pastoral scenes with oases and rivers, as well as buildings and imaginary cities. The mosaics are believed to be the work of Byzantine artists and craftsmen, although the motifs are Islamic and may refer to the far-flung caliphate, or they may represent an image of Islamic paradise. In addition, the interior of the prayer hall contains decorative geometric motifs and inscriptions from the Koran. A gilded marble vine scroll, modeled on a similar motif in Hagia Sophia, surrounds the prayer hall, whose walls are clad in gold mosaics and multicolored slabs of marble. All the surfaces are covered in decorative patterns and inlaid decorations. Although the mosque displays architectural elements similar to those found in a Byzantine church—mosaics, arches, and columns—it uses them to different ends. Instead of a hierarchical and complex play of ceremonial spaces, such as Hagia Sophia, the Great Mosque of Damascus is a static composition, a calm place in which everything contributes to a contemplative atmosphere of serenity and communal prayer.

▪ ▪ ▪ ▪ ▪

Ten years after the Damascus mosque was completed, work began on a mosque fifteen hundred miles west, in Kairouan. This Tunisian city is of small consequence today, but in the ninth century it was a leading Islamic intellectual and religious center, the site of an important university, and, like Mecca, Medina, and Jerusalem, an important place of pilgrimage. Kairouan was founded in 670 by Uqba ibn Nafi, the Umayyad general who led the Arab army that conquered the Byzantine province that included present-day Tunisia, western Libya, and eastern Algeria. Uqba chose the site for the city's first mosque, but twenty years later that building had to be rebuilt after being destroyed during a Berber uprising. In 724, to accommodate the growing Islamic population of what was now the capital of Umayyad Ifriqiya, the caliph in Damascus ordered the Kairouan mosque to be enlarged. The old structure was demolished, all except the mihrab, and work began anew. This building was enlarged four times over the next hundred and fifty years, the successive generations of builders maintaining a remarkable consistency and producing a fine example of early Islamic architecture.

The overall layout of the mosque was influenced by the Great Mosque of Damascus: a large walled compound of approximately the same size divided into a prayer hall and a paved courtyard (fig. 27). Because the rectangular compound was laid out so that the narrow end faced Mecca, the prayer hall has more pleasing proportions: a double square in plan, roughly 230 feet by 115 feet. The aisles in the prayer hall are oriented toward the qibla wall. As in Damascus, the flat wooden roof is supported on arched colonnades, but because the arches are smaller and the colonnades closer together, the result is a grid of columns only fifteen feet apart, more like an Egyptian hypostyle hall than a Roman basilica.

As in the Damascus mosque, a central aisle lines up with the mihrab, and, together with a widened space in front of the qibla wall, forms a T-shape in plan. There are two domes. The first, built about a hundred years after construction began, marks the mihrab. The second, built some three decades later when the prayer hall was enlarged, is located over a deep entrance portico facing the courtyard and indicates the direction of Mecca to worshippers in the outdoor space. The mihrab is decorated with carved marble panels, but the mosque contains no mosaics and, on the whole, ornamentation is sparse. The exception is the intricate carving—of the wooden doors, of the wood minbar, and of the wood ceiling, which is painted with floral and geometric patterns that echo the woven carpets that cover the floor. The harsh desert sun was unwelcome, and the small apertures in the hexagonal drum supporting the mihrab dome are the only windows

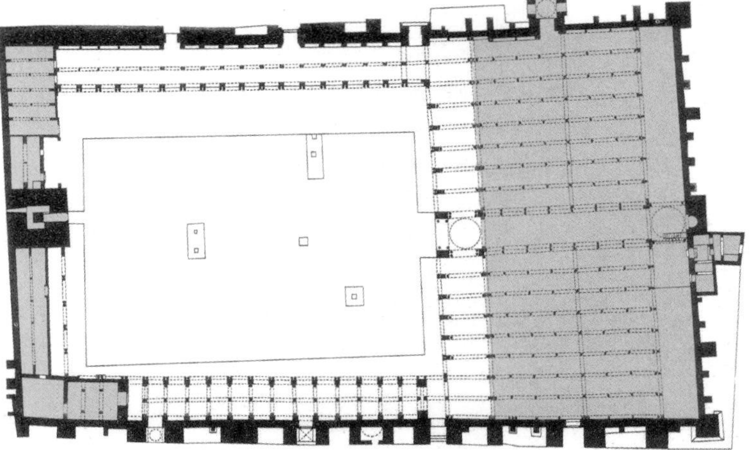

27 Great Mosque of Kairouan, Tunisia, 724–875. Plan. A deep portico forms a transition between the courtyard and the hypostyle prayer hall.

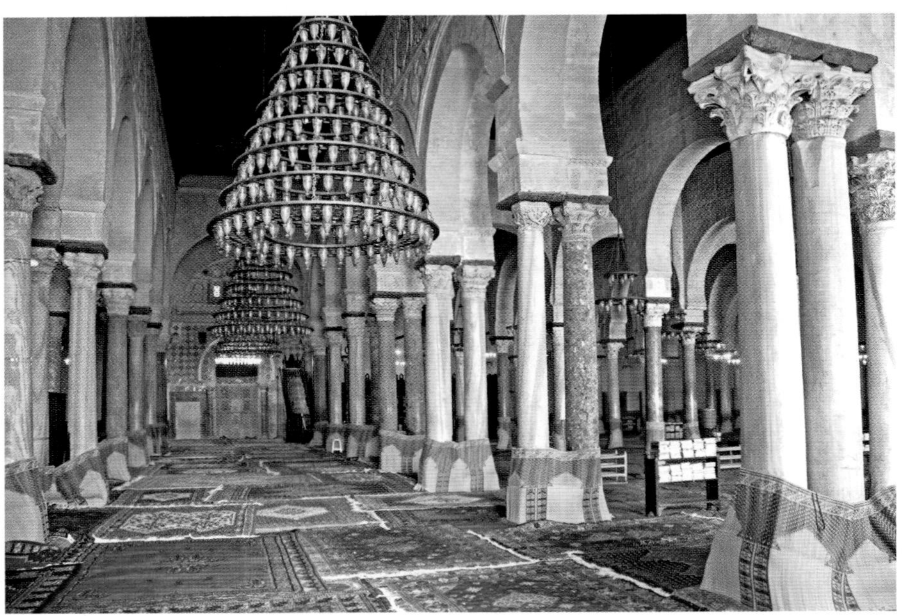

28 Great Mosque of Kairouan. The prayer hall is a forest of columns, chiefly Roman and Byzantine spolia. Paired columns support the arches of the central aisle, which is focused on the mihrab.

in the prayer hall. Daylight enters through a series of doors opening into the portico; in addition, chandeliers illuminate the murky interior. The hemispherical brick domes are only about twenty feet in diameter but beautifully built, with twenty-four lobed segments, concave on the inside and convex on the outside, resembling a pumpkin or gourd.

The engineering knowhow of the builders of the Kairouan mosque was limited; the domes were small and the flat roof was supported on simple beams rather than trusses. The short spans make for an architecture of columns—there are more than four hundred. The shafts are a mixture of white, green, or pinkish marble, gray granite, and red porphyry, with capitals of all types (fig. 28). The vast majority of the columns and capitals are spolia, either retrieved from the ruins of Roman Carthage (only a hundred miles away) or removed from old Byzantine buildings in the region. The builders developed an unusual detail: between the capital and the springing of the arch, where a Byzantine builder would have placed a wedge-shaped impost, they added a tall, straight-sided, undecorated block. This raised the ceiling as well as changed the proportion of the arch. The mosque contains paired and even tripled columns, both in the porticos and within the prayer hall itself, producing an even greater sense of weight, like repeated exclamation points. The arches supported by these columns are of the horseshoe type, but more pronounced than in the Damascus mosque. In

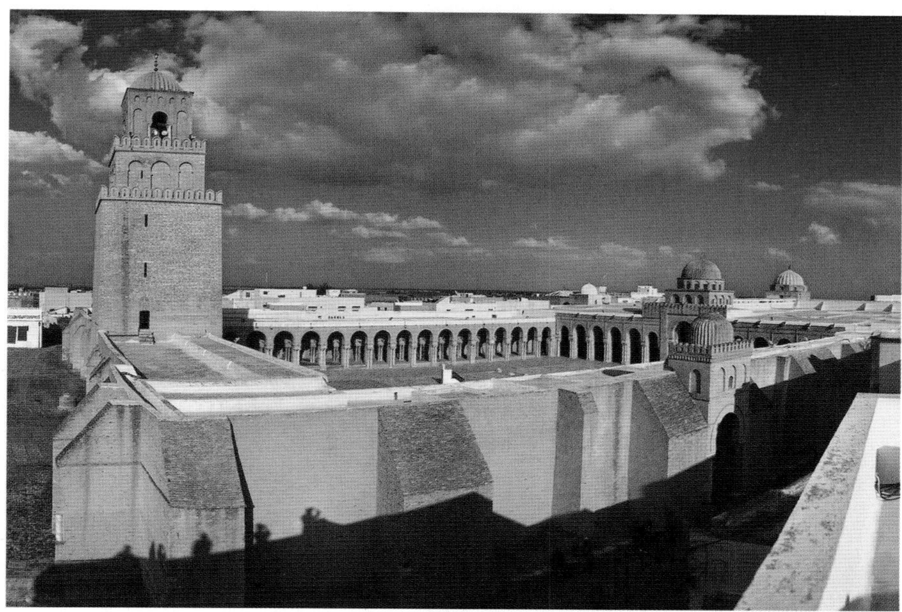

29 Great Mosque of Kairouan. From left: the minaret, the courtyard and its surrounding porticos, and the prayer hall with its two domes. This faultless design was the result of building campaigns that stretched over more than a century and a half.

some locations, such as the main entrance, the arches are pointed. The complex pointed horseshoe shape, which required laying out arcs with four centers, became a favorite of Islamic builders.

The Kairouan mosque, with its variety of arches, is of a more sophisticated design than the earlier Damascus mosque. The prayer hall is better suited to the Islamic liturgy—the arcades are at right angles to the qibla wall and accentuate the direction of Mecca. The T-plan is a further refinement, and the domes are in symbolically meaningful places. The prayer hall and the courtyard achieve a kind of balance; the courtyard is not a simple forecourt but a space of equal significance, with the deep narthex-like portico acting as a link—and a transition—between the two. The minaret is on an axis with the central aisle and the two domes (fig. 29). The Kairouan minaret, one of the oldest in the Islamic world, consists of a tower atop a solid square base. The Arabic root of the word "minaret" means lighthouse or beacon, and the design may have been based on the ancient Pharos of Alexandria, which was then still standing. The entire complex—minaret, domes, courtyard, prayer hall, and surrounding wall—forms a unified composition of great beauty.

8

Cultural Fusion

Ravenna, sixth century
Aachen, ninth century

Architectural ideas circulated around the Mediterranean—from Greece to Rome, from Rome to Byzantium, and from Byzantium to the Middle East. They also traveled north to Frankish Europe. To understand that journey it is necessary to retrace our steps to the sixth century and visit the western half of the old Roman Empire. Losing control of the provinces, Rome grappled with successive waves of invasions by Germanic peoples, and the last emperor was deposed in 476. Two decades later the Germanic king was himself ousted by Theodoric the Great, king of the Ostrogoths, a Christian people from the Balkans. Theodoric's kingdom of Italy included Sicily and Dalmatia, and he established his court in Ravenna, which, following the decline of Rome, remained the capital of the western Roman Empire for almost a century.

In 526, thanks to the generosity of a private benefactor, the bishop of Ravenna began building a church dedicated to Saint Vitalis, a local Christian martyr. Construction proceeded slowly and a decade later was interrupted by an unexpected event. Justinian, firmly enthroned in Constantinople, invaded Sicily in a bid to assert control over the western portion of the old Roman Empire. In a successful campaign his army fought its way up the Italian peninsula, and Ravenna fell in 540. The city became the seat of the Byzantine governor of Italy, and the bulk of the new church was completed under Byzantine rule. It shows. Construction is in the Byzantine manner, using long, thin bricks laid in thick mortar. The capitals and imposts are Byzantine, too, made of Proconnesian marble carved on the island of Marmara. The dome, the floor, and the arches are covered in patterned mosaics, and the cross-ribbed vault over the chancel is decorated with festoons of leaves and flowers. Two panels, which are considered leading examples of Byzantine mosaic work, portray the emperor Justinian and his retinue on one side and the empress Theodora and her attendants on the other.

The splendid church of San Vitale has a centralized plan (fig. 30). The octagonal nave is surrounded by an ambulatory and a second-floor gallery, and is crowned by a fifty-foot-diameter dome sitting on a tall octagonal drum. Seven of the spaces between the piers that support the drum are filled by semicircular columnar niches; the eighth space, on the east side, is open to a vaulted chancel terminated by an apse. The chancel is flanked by two circular chapels. The church is entered on the west side through a narthex whose odd angle may have been the result of a preexisting site condition. The mosaic interior glitters and sparkles thanks to a profusion of arched windows, both in the walls and in the tall octagonal drum.

The capitals, the wedge-shaped imposts, and the mosaics are Byzantine, and the plan and the beautiful semicircular niches resemble the octagonal church of Saints Sergius and Bacchus, which was then under construction in Constantinople (fig. 31). On the other hand, while most Byzantine domed churches had simple rectangular footprints, the octagonal exterior of San Vitale echoes the shape of the nave. Nor is the construction purely Byzantine. The local masons were apparently unfamiliar with thin brick vaulting, and they built the ambulatory roof of wood (the present-day brick vaults date from the twelfth century). For the dome they revived the ancient Roman technique of concentric rings of hollow clay tiles, and they supported the drum on squinches, a Persian device that anticipated the Byzantine

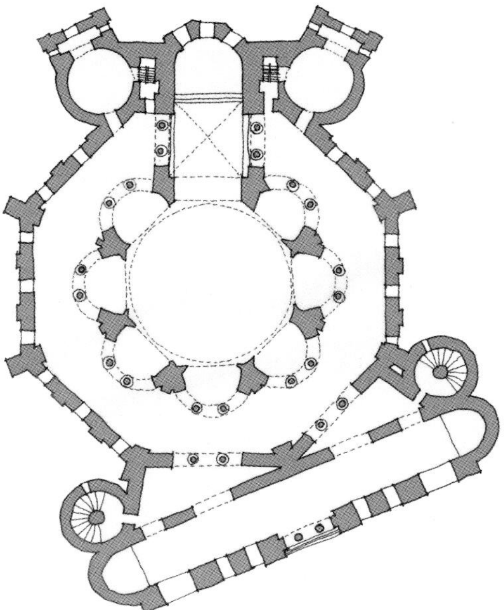

30 San Vitale, Ravenna, 526–47. Plan. The domed hexagon is surrounded by semicircular niches and encircled by a hexagonal ambulatory. The symmetry is interrupted by the chancel and the oddly angled narthex.

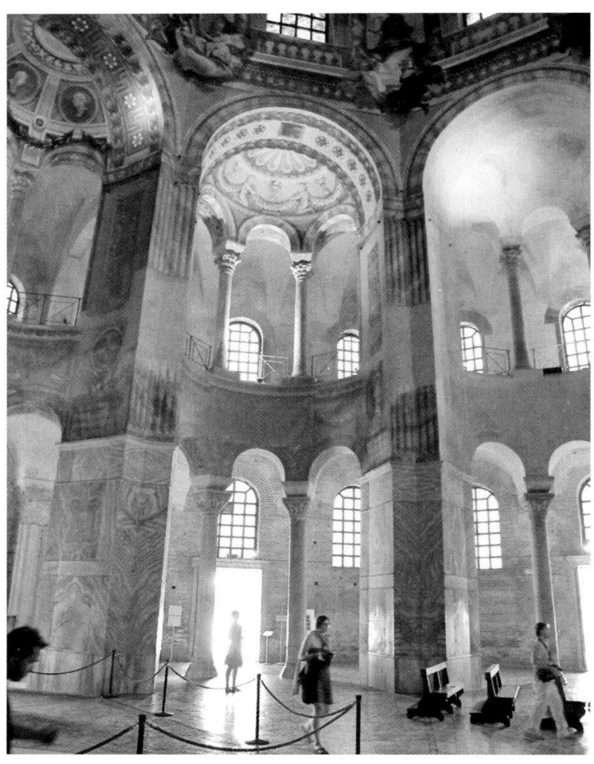

31 San Vitale. Interior. The architecture is a fusion of East and West, of Roman arched construction and Byzantine sensibility. The mosaic work glitters and sparkles thanks to a profusion of arched windows.

pendentive. The architect of San Vitale is unknown to us—he may have been a local builder or, likely, an itinerant Hellene from Constantinople. In any case, he was unusually gifted, for this building represents a remarkable fusion of East and West.

▪ ▪ ▪ ▪ ▪

Two hundred and fifty years after San Vitale was completed, Ravenna came under the rule of the Frankish emperor Charlemagne, whose vast Holy Roman Empire included most of present-day France, Belgium, the Netherlands, Germany, and Switzerland, as well as northern Italy. Like previous Carolingian monarchs, Charlemagne moved his court between royal residences scattered across his sprawling realm. In 792, the emperor decided to establish a permanent home. He could have picked Rome or Ravenna but he decided on Aachen, the old capital of the Franks and his birthplace. Charlemagne regarded himself as a direct successor to the Roman emperors, and the design of his new imperial palace was intended to reinforce that claim. The ensemble of buildings, linked by arcaded galleries and atria, was modeled on the Lateran Palace, an ancient Roman residence that had served as the papal home since the time of Constantine. Charlemagne's palace included the royal residence, administrative offices, an audience hall patterned on an ancient basilica, a Roman-style public bath (one of the attractions of Aachen was its hot springs), and a large chapel. Of these buildings, only the chapel survives today. Its exterior has been much altered by the addition of a Gothic choir, a steeple, and an oddly shaped Baroque roof, but most of the remarkable interior is largely intact.

What came to be known as the Palatine Chapel was modeled on the old church of San Vitale in Ravenna. Charlemagne had visited Italy and been impressed by the splendid building, and he wanted one just like it. This was not simply an aesthetic decision. Ravenna had been the capital of the western Roman Empire, and building a facsimile of its famous church would signal the shift of power to Aachen. And because Ravenna had once been the seat of Byzantine rule in Italy, a replica of the church would also be a thumb in the eye of Justinian's descendant in Constantinople. Charlemagne's chapel is an early example of an occurrence that is common in the story of architecture: the revival. Buildings last a long time—San Vitale was two hundred and fifty years old—and revivals occur when the merits of an earlier epoch are rediscovered and appreciated anew. This appreciation may be driven by the desire to demonstrate a link to an earlier historical era, which was the case with the Palatine Chapel, but it can also be motivated by religious faith, nationalism, and, of course, nostalgia. And sometimes a revival is simply an expression of affection and admiration for the architecture of a particular historical period.

A revival differs from the original in one important respect—the benefit of hindsight. When Ictinus and Callicrates built the Parthenon, they were working within established conventions, but Charlemagne made a conscious decision to revisit San Vitale's Byzantine-influenced style. A revivalist not only decides what to emulate but also how to emulate it—whether to be accurate or sketchy, authentic or impressionistic, total or partial. Inevitably the historic model will need to be modified, sometimes drastically. Although the dimensions of the Palatine Chapel are approximately the same as San Vitale's, there are significant differences: the dome is not a true hemisphere but an eight-sided domical vault; the ambulatory is sixteen sided, making it almost round; and the semicircular niches are replaced by sturdy Roman-looking arches. As a result of the last change, the chapel appears less delicate than San Vitale. This is also due to a change in the construction material—from brick to stone. The gallery is supported by heavy vaults, and the dome is ingeniously braced by the sloping barrel vaults of the gallery.

The imperial Palatine Chapel functioned differently from San Vitale. The second-floor gallery was reserved for the emperor and his retinue and was effectively the principal floor, while the first floor was for churchgoers of lower ranks (fig. 32). The difference was expressed in the architecture: the dark ambulatory of the first floor resembled an undercroft, while the tall upper gallery was brightly lit by arched windows. Further adornment took the form of fluted pilasters with Corinthian capitals, and elaborate bronze balustrades decorated with classicized details and vine scrolls. The balustrades and the bronze doors of the chapel were the work of Frankish artists, and it is likely that Lombard stone carvers also worked on the project. The domical vault was originally covered with a fresco showing a Christ figure in the sky and a frieze of church elders. The architecture is a fusion of Frankish workmanship, Byzantine design, and the now dim memory of Roman architecture. And not just a memory—many of the marble, granite, and porphyry columns were ancient spolia transported from Rome and Ravenna. The beautiful marble slabs that covered the piers and arches of the nave were likewise recycled Roman antiquities.

Charlemagne's chapel was the work of Odo of Metz, a Frankish master builder about whom little is known. Odo used Corinthian columns and Roman wall cladding, but his understanding of ancient architecture was limited. For example, mimicking the triple arched apses of San Vitale he inserted two columns beneath the arches of the triforia, an awkward and structurally redundant solution (fig. 33). The alternating bands of dark and light stone on the arches,

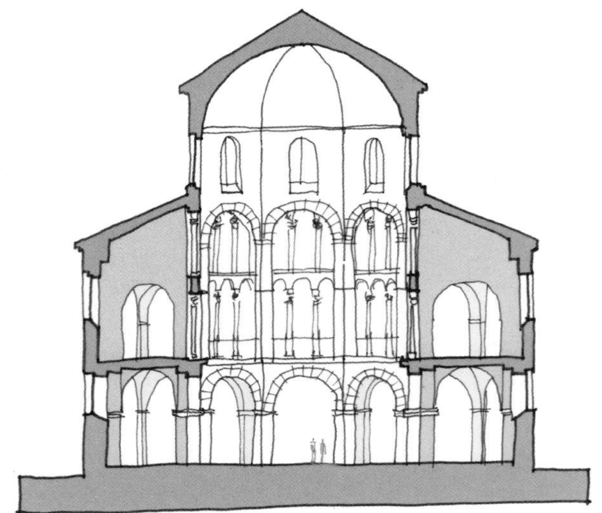

32 Palatine Chapel, Aachen. Odo of Metz, 792–805. Section. The sixteen-sided ambulatory and gallery surround a domed octagonal nave that is more than one hundred feet high.

Opposite:
33 Palatine Chapel. The interior is a fusion of Frankish, Byzantine, and Roman influences. The chandelier is a twelfth-century addition.

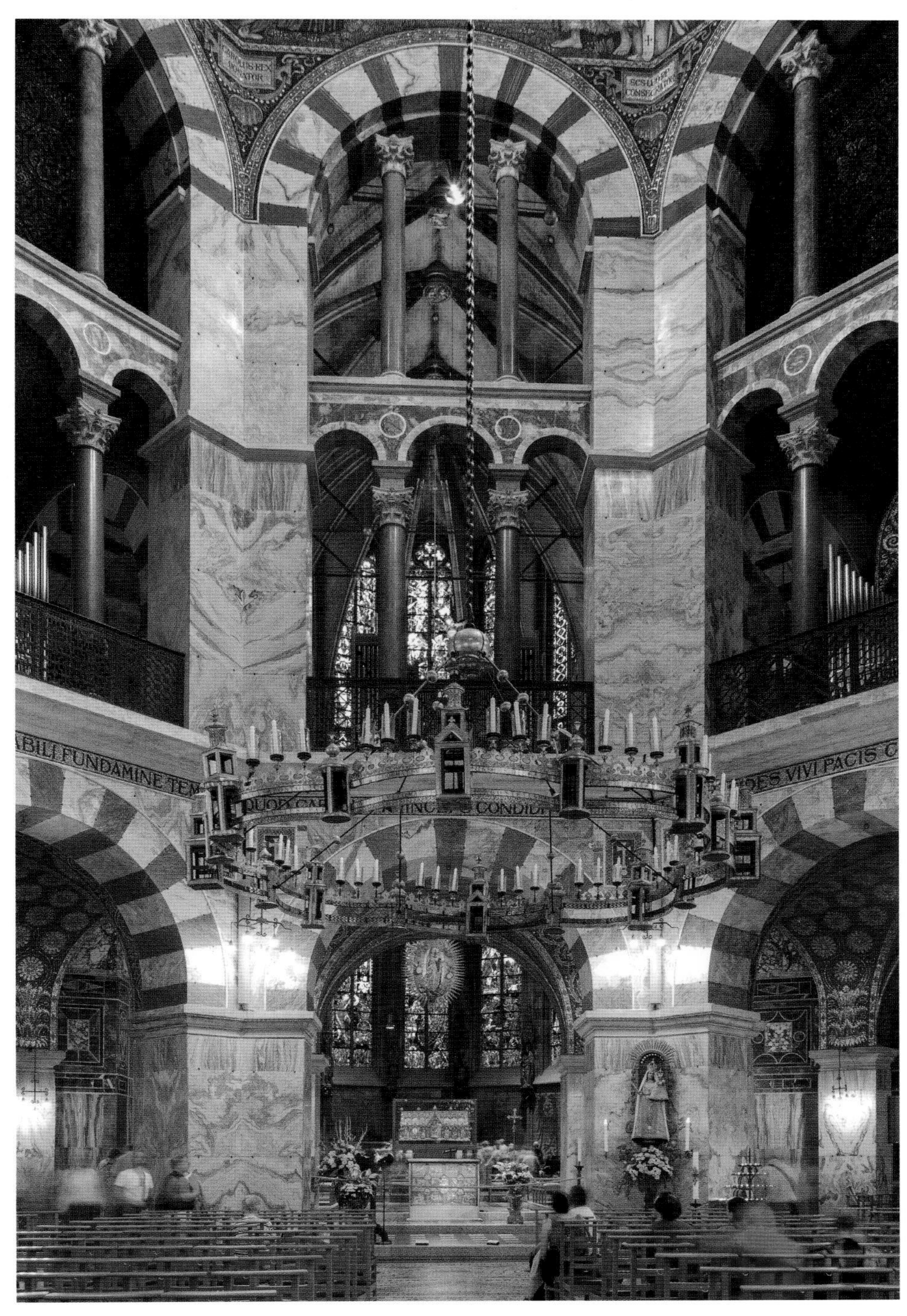
BILI FUNDAMINE TEM
DES VIVI PACIS C

which suited Frankish taste, did not have Roman precedents. The impost blocks, called dosserets, that sit on top of the capitals and support the springing of the arches seem like distant cousins of the wedge-shaped Byzantine impost.

I should not be too hard on Odo. In the days before formal schooling, architectural knowledge was acquired on the job, passed on from master to apprentice. It had been more than three hundred years since the ousting of the last Roman emperor, and when construction ceased altogether, as it did during the Germanic invasions, knowledge of classical building techniques was lost. Few intact Roman buildings were available to serve as models—especially in northern Europe. In any case, it was one thing to admire the Pantheon and quite another to build it; that required a skilled team of artists and artisans—sculptors, mosaicists, and stone carvers, as well as masons, bricklayers, and carpenters. By the eighth century, craftsmen had to innovate in the absence of classical prototypes. Charlemagne may have wanted to re-create the glories of ancient Rome, but Odo had precious little to work with. He did the best he could.

The architecture of the Palatine Chapel has awkward moments, but it represented an earnest attempt to recover the lost heritage of ancient Rome and it deserves our respect. It also contained the germ of something new. At slightly more than one hundred feet tall, the Palatine Chapel was taller than San Vitale, and for many years it remained the tallest domed space north of the Alps. More important, the space *looked* tall. Whereas the semicircular niches of San Vitale create a billowing effect that leads the eye outward, in the Aachen chapel everything leads the eye upward. Even the eight-sided domical vault has a pronounced vertical character. This character is crudely expressed, and occasionally the blending of Roman and Byzantine motifs gets in the way, but it is present nevertheless. This emphasis on verticality opened the door to a new architectural interest that would become a preoccupation of European architects—and would remain so for the next three hundred years.

9

Sacred Citadels

Durham, twelfth century

Although the Palatine Chapel spawned several centralized-plan churches, most Carolingian churches continued to follow the basilican model, with three important modifications. The chancel was extended, which brought more light into the center of the church and produced a symbolically appealing cross-shape plan; a lantern or tall spire was added over the crossing of the transept and the nave; and the western entrance facade was enlarged. The last innovation, called the westwork, was introduced by Odo in the Palatine Chapel and consisted of a monumental doorway flanked by two bell towers, a composition that would influence church builders for centuries to come. Westwork towers, like the crossing spire and the tall nave, further emphasized the verticality that would become the hallmark of medieval cathedrals.

The Normans of northern France were among the most accomplished builders of that period. Descendants of marauding Norse Vikings, they turned the Duchy of Normandy into a formidable maritime power. Their martial culture was combined with an unexpected Christian piety, and in addition to formidable castles and fortifications—beautifully constructed of Caen limestone—they built monasteries, abbeys, and churches. These followed the prevailing round-arch style but with heavier proportions and a more massive appearance. The sturdy Norman churches and cathedrals had a distinctly military character—sacred citadels.

Shortly after the Normans invaded England, William the Conqueror chose Durham, a small Northumbrian town near the Scottish border, as the northern outpost of his new realm. A promontory surrounded on three sides by an oxbow of the River Wear was an ideal site for a castle, within whose walls the Normans built a Benedictine priory and a cathedral. Construction of the latter began in 1093 and was overseen by William de Saint-Calais, a Norman Benedictine monk whom William appointed bishop of Durham. The town was the most important pilgrimage destination in England, as it was the site of the tomb of Saint Cuthbert, a Celtic hermit and the patron saint of Northumbria.

The cathedral was located between the priory and the castle keep. The large cross-shaped plan, squeezed into a constricted site, followed the conventions of the great abbey churches of Normandy: an arcaded nave with aisles interrupted by a transept and leading to a long chancel and a choir (fig. 34). The roof was supported on tall walls that consisted of an arcade, a triforium, and clerestory windows. The nave included a feature introduced in the great abbey church of Jumièges in Normandy, completed in 1066: an arcade of double bays separated by piers and subdivided by columns. The piers were clusters of engaged half-columns—a common design—but the construction of the intermediate columns was unusual. They were hollow tubes of ashlar masonry, sixty feet tall and seven feet in diameter, filled with rubble. These behemoths rivaled the piers in visual impact because their shafts were decorated with boldly incised patterns: fluting, zigzags, lozenges, and, in the transept and chancel, spirals (fig. 35). The spirals are assumed to have been modeled on the columns that surrounded the tomb of the apostle in Old St. Peter's in Rome, but the other patterns are purely decorative. Classical Greek and Roman colonnades consisting of identical columns and Byzantine arcades were an eclectic mix, but the idea of ordered variety was new. Another startling departure: beginning in the second bay of

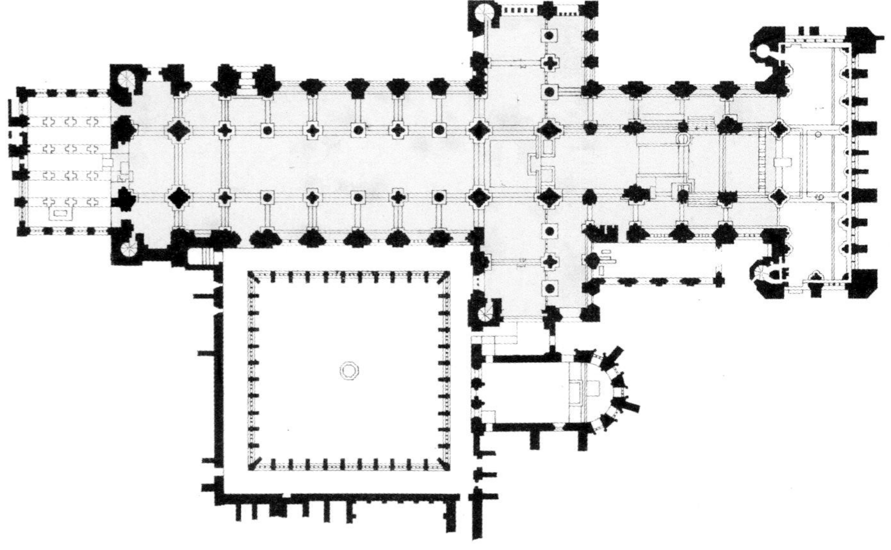

34 Durham Cathedral, 1093–1133. Plan. The shaded portion indicates the original building. The adjoining cloister was part of a Benedictine priory. The Galilee Chapel (left) at the west end was added around 1170, and the hammerhead Nine Altars Chapel (right) was built in 1228.

Opposite:
35 Durham Cathedral. Nave, showing the double bays with piers of clustered half-columns, giant intermediate columns decorated with boldly incised patterns, and arches with carved chevrons. The rose window dates from the thirteenth century; the marble choir screen is a Victorian addition.

the nave, the arches of the arcade and the triforia were decorated with incised chevrons, creating a toothlike effect. Painted chevron patterns had been used in Norman churches, but this was one of the first examples of chevrons carved into the stone.

The Norman architecture of Durham is referred to as Romanesque—a nineteenth-century art historian's term—but there is precious little that is Roman about this building, other than the round arches and the basilican plan. Certainly not the arcade, with its toothlike chevrons and simplified capitals. The massive decorated columns without entasis are more Egyptian than Roman, and the pattern of interlaced arches on the lower walls of the aisles is a reminder that the cosmopolitan Normans, who had outposts in Sicily and Malta, were familiar with Arab architecture. While the wedge-shaped capitals in the triforia recall Byzantine imposts, there are no mosaics or frescoes, no marble revetments or ancient spolia. The Norman builders had moved away from their Carolingian origins, and even further from the latter's roots in antiquity. Despite the incised column decorations and chevrons, which were originally highlighted in painted colors, the overall effect is distinctly unfussy and rather severe—a warrior's architecture.

While the plan of Durham resembled earlier Norman cathedrals, the patterned columns were novel, as were the incised chevrons. Perhaps it was the remote location, so far out of the mainstream, that gave the builders the liberty to experiment. The most radical innovation at Durham was the ceiling. Norman churches typically had timber roofs whose trusses were exposed to the nave below. This common solution was perfectly serviceable, but it created two problems, one practical and one aesthetic: timber roofs were susceptible to fire, and their barnlike appearance undermined the sense of dignity associated with stone architecture. The obvious solution was to build a masonry ceiling. Because lightweight brick vaulting was unknown in northern Europe, Norman builders were obliged to use heavy stone barrel vaults and groin vaults, which not only consumed large amounts of stone and required expensive temporary wooden formwork but also necessitated thickening the walls to support the extra weight. The builders of Durham tried something different: they spanned the forty-foot-wide nave with structural ribs and filled the spaces between with thin stone vaults. The crisscrossing ribs required only minimal formwork, and the light vaults could be built without temporary supports. The inspiration for this cost-cutting technique is unclear. Ribbed vaults were known to the ancient Romans, and they reappeared in medieval Lombard churches. They were also a feature of architecture in Arab countries, which is where the Normans may have seen them. In Durham, as in all later cathedrals, the ribbed vaults carry the ceiling but do not support the roof, which is carried on timber trusses.

The use of a ribbed-vault ceiling has a significant effect. Because the ribs are a continuation of the piers, the eye is led up and across the vaults in one uninterrupted sweep. That makes the architecture even less Roman. In a classical building, the entablature establishes a strong horizontal; in Durham, the strong lines are all vertical. It is also a matter of proportions. The nave of Durham is not particularly high at seventy-three feet, but because it is only forty feet wide it gives the impression of a narrow canyon, a very *long* narrow canyon; the high-ribbed arches march along, one after the other, for almost five hundred feet. With the light filtering in from above, it is a moody, evocative space.

Durham Cathedral was not realized all at once; it underwent additions and modifications over three and a half centuries. Less than forty years after the cathedral was completed, a chapel was planned for the east end to provide a suitably stately setting for Saint Cuthbert's remains. For some reason that project was shelved, and the building materials, which included imported marble columns, instead were used to build an addition at the west end. The result, called the Galilee Chapel, is a kind of narthex (see fig. 34). The wooden roof is supported on four diaphragm walls carried by arches resting on groups of four individual columns—two of marble and two of sandstone. The undersides of the arches are not flat but have roll moldings sandwiched between chevron bands—a detail that was sometimes used in Islamic architecture. The overall effect is remarkable, reminding me of a series of huge toothed cogwheels.

Medieval cathedrals loomed over their surroundings—no other buildings approached them in height or mass, and their landmark towers were visible for miles. Durham Cathedral originally had five towers. The crossing tower was the tallest; two slightly lower towers marked the westwork; and two spires terminated the east end of the choir. Towers were the final phase of construction, and if funds ran low they might remain unbuilt; it took a hundred years before Durham's two westwork towers were completed. These towers—square, largely windowless, with turrets at each corner—resemble the keep of the Tower of London, an earlier Norman building. The 218-foot-tall crossing tower is Durham's most prominent external feature (fig. 36). The original crossing tower was built shortly after the westwork towers, but it was rebuilt and enlarged in the fifteenth century after being twice struck by lightning. Like the westwork towers, it has a battlemented parapet and a martial appearance. The two spires at the east end of the choir were demolished in the mid-thirteenth century in the course of adding a chapel to honor Saint Cuthbert. Because of the steep topography, it was

36 Durham Cathedral. The blocky towers give the building a martial appearance.

impossible to extend the choir, so the chapel took the form of a second transept, creating a hammerhead termination to the church (see fig. 34). The so-called Nine Altars Chapel, which also served as a private chapel for the monks, is the same height as the chancel and the nave. Yet its appearance represents a significant departure from the earlier church, for by the time that construction began in the thirteenth century, religious architecture had undergone a momentous change. That change is the subject of the next chapter.

10

The Allure of the New

Saint-Denis, twelfth century
Paris, thirteenth century

The Nine Altars Chapel of Durham Cathedral is distinguished by having pointed rather than round arches, both in the ribs of the ceiling and in the tracery of the windows. This architectural form had arrived more than a hundred years earlier, in the twelfth century. Architectural innovations generally occur in one of two ways: they either emerge in various guises, here and there, and percolate up into the general consciousness, or, more rarely, they appear fully formed in groundbreaking buildings. The twelfth-century Royal Abbey Church, in the village of Saint-Denis on the outskirts of Paris, is an example of the latter. This venerable basilica, which dated from the eighth century, was an important pilgrimage site that contained the remains of the martyred Saint Denis, the patron saint of France, and was also the traditional burial place of French kings. In 1122, the abbey elected a new head. Abbot Suger (1081–1151), a Benedictine monk, was a learned scholar and a well-traveled diplomat, a confidant of Louis VI as well as of the future king, Louis VII.

In 1135, Suger, who had determined that the old church needed enlarging, embarked on what would be an epochal construction project. He started by demolishing the old Carolingian westwork in order to extend the nave. On the new west front, to ease congestion, the abbot and his unnamed master builder added smaller doors on each side of the traditional central portal. Massive buttresses separate the three doorways, which are decorated with concentric arcs of figural sculpture. The tripartite organization of the facade is further emphasized by twin towers and, between them and above the central portal, a large circular window (fig. 37). Although the twin towers and the round arches of the portals were traditional, this early example of what came to be called a rose window was entirely new.

Once the work on the west end of the church was under way Suger turned his attention to the east end. For some reason he changed builders, perhaps

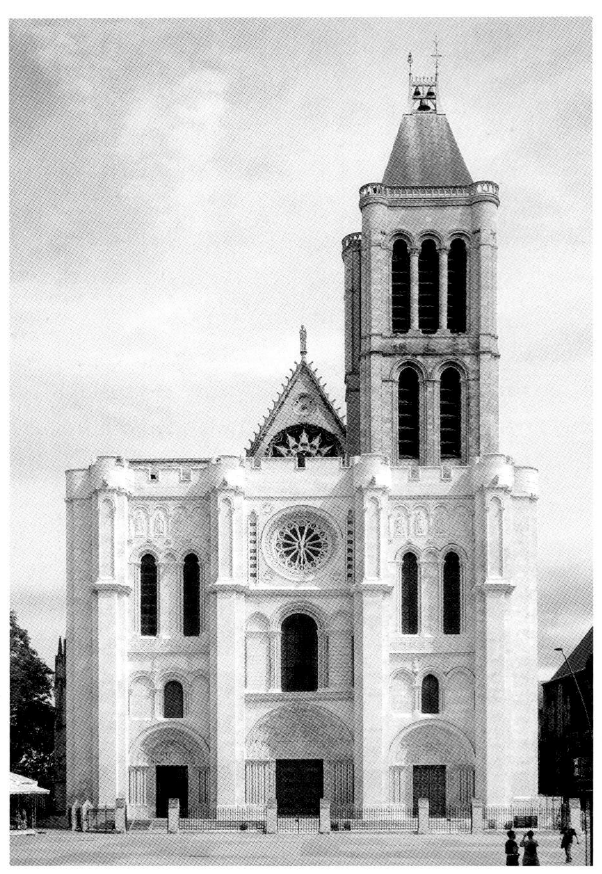

37 Royal Abbey Church of Saint-Denis, 1140–44. West facade. The tripartite organization of the westwork, with three portals and a rose window, was an innovation. The left tower, weakened by a storm, developed structural problems and was dismantled in 1846.

because he had something even more unconventional in mind. He replaced the old chancel with a spacious choir supported by twelve columns, representing the Twelve Apostles, and ringed by an ambulatory and seven chapels. As in Durham, the vaults of the choir and the ambulatory were ribbed. While conventional vaults are supported on thick external walls, ribbed vaults need only individual piers. This enabled Suger and his master builder to do something unusual: they filled the spaces between the piers with windows, both in the chapels and in the upper walls of the choir (fig. 38). This simple change had the far-reaching consequence of flooding the church interior with light. And not just any light, *colored* light. Stained glass was relatively new in northern Europe—the windows of Durham were grisaille, or gray-painted glass. Suger imported craftsmen from Italy and Bohemia who created stained-glass windows illustrating Old and New Testament themes and in the process developed a new cobalt glass that became known as “Saint-Denis blue.” To those used to murky church interiors the effect must have seemed magical. It is unclear if the abbot’s preoccupation with light was liturgical or simply aesthetic. Perhaps both—an inscription in the church reads, “And bright is the noble edifice which is pervaded by the new light.”

In a traditional stone church, the sideways thrust of the heavy ceiling vaults was resisted by the extremely thick exterior walls. In Saint-Denis, the ceiling vaults of the chapel roofs had ribs whose concentrated sideways thrust was resisted by external piers, leaving the rest of the wall as delicate window tracery. What about the thrust of the ribs of the nave ceiling? It was impossible to use piers, which would have intruded into the ambulatory, so Suger or his builder came up with an ingenious solution. He braced the tall nave walls with arches that spanned the ambulatory and landed on the external piers (fig. 39). *Et voilà,* the flying buttress.

Suger’s third innovation at Saint-Denis was equally momentous. Look closely at the arches on the west facade (see fig. 37). Some, like the portals, are round, but others are pointed. Suger used pointed arches throughout the church, in the ribs of the roof vaults as well as in the tracery of the windows. The shape may

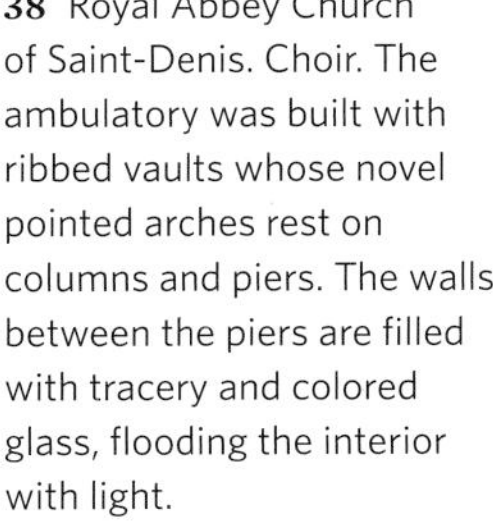

38 Royal Abbey Church of Saint-Denis. Choir. The ambulatory was built with ribbed vaults whose novel pointed arches rest on columns and piers. The walls between the piers are filled with tracery and colored glass, flooding the interior with light.

39 Royal Abbey Church of Saint-Denis. A nineteenth-century lithograph shows the extensive window tracery as well as the flying buttresses that span the ambulatory of the choir and land on external piers.

have been influenced by the Islamic buildings of North Africa, as Christopher Wren surmised, although the evidence for that is inconclusive. The chief advantage of pointed arches is not structural but architectural; unlike a semicircular arch, whose height is governed by its width, the height of a pointed arch can be varied irrespective of the width—it can be flatter or steeper. Moreover, while a semicircular arch has squat proportions, a pointed arch can be given an attenuated shape. Just as the attention of worshippers in a mosque was directed toward Mecca, the prayers of the faithful in a church were directed to heaven, and the arrow-like pointed arch led the eye in that direction—upward.

The ceremonial consecration of the new choir of Saint-Denis in 1144 was attended by Louis VII and by the archbishops of Reims, Rouen, Sens, Bordeaux, and Canterbury. The clerics were impressed by the new architecture of the church, and over the course of the next fifty years, whenever a cathedral was modified or rebuilt—Sens, Noyon, and Laon in northern France, and Canterbury, Wells, and Lincoln in England—the builders used ribbed vaults, stained-glass windows, and pointed arches. That is how, a hundred and forty years later, the pointed arch showed up at the Nine Altars Chapel in Durham. Suger's bold experiment had become the new convention.

We call Suger's new architecture Gothic, a term coined in the sixteenth century; in his day it was referred to simply as "French" or "Frankish." The pointed-arch motif showed up everywhere, not only in the arches of triforia and window tracery but also in the paneling of choir stalls. The architectural change reflected a change in taste; simply put, people liked the arrowhead shape. Perhaps its Arab roots made it appear exotic, or perhaps it was just the pointed arch's novelty that made the old round arch look stodgy and old-fashioned by comparison.

▪ ▪ ▪ ▪ ▪

The sides and backs of medieval cathedrals were hemmed in by streets and houses, but the west front generally faced a public square, which allowed the entire facade to be appreciated from a distance. One of the most beautiful examples of a west front is Notre-Dame in Paris. The cathedral replaced the church of Saint-Étienne, an old basilica that was considered too small and was unceremoniously demolished. Work on the new building started only two decades after the completion of the choir of Saint-Denis, but because construction commenced at the east end and proceeded westward, the front was not finished until a century later. The plan of Notre-Dame is not radically different from that of earlier cathedrals such as Durham, featuring a long nave (this time with double aisles), transepts forming a cross, and an apsidal choir. The cathedral incorporates all of Suger's innovations: pointed arches, stained-glass windows, and flying buttresses. The west front is similar to that at Saint-Denis but more fully resolved. The two tall towers, three entrance portals, and central rose window are arranged in a beautifully balanced composition of three vertical and three horizontal divisions (fig. 40). The vertical divisions, which correspond to the nave and the aisles, are emphasized by thick buttress piers that extend upward to become the corners of the towers. The horizontal divisions—the entrance portals, a windowed story, and an open gallery—intersect with the verticals, like a tic-tac-toe diagram. The center square is filled by a large rose window in the form of a wheel with spokes; at more than thirty feet in diameter, it was the largest rose window yet built. From a distance, the silhouette is dominated by the two blunt towers. Most cathedral towers had steep wooden roofs, and there is evidence that these were originally intended for Notre-Dame, although they were never built.

Details become more apparent as you approach the church. What appear at a distance to be simply deep portals turn out to be an exceedingly rich array of figural sculpture. Medieval churches had always included sculpture, but the idea of a coherent sculptural display in the west front was another of Suger's innovations. At Notre-Dame the main portal represents the Last Judgment, the right portal denotes the coronation of the Virgin Mary, and the left is dedicated to Mary's mother, Saint Anne. The buttresses between the portals contain niches with statues of the first Christian martyr, Saint Étienne, Saint Denis, and draped allegorical figures. Above the portals is a frieze of twenty-eight niches containing statues of the kings of Judah—the so-called Royal Gallery. (The gargoyles, monsters, and other grotesque figures that adorn the roof are nineteenth-century additions.) The faithful entering the cathedral passed beneath an array of images of the Old and New Testaments, of prophets and teachers, saints and sinners, heaven and hell. In an age before literacy and printing these figures provided a key educational function. Not since the friezes and metopes of the Greek temple had figural sculpture played such an important role in a religious building.

Notre-Dame was my first experience of a medieval cathedral. That was 1964, and the newly cleaned facade almost sparkled, but it was the interior that made the biggest impression. The cold surrounding stone was bone-chilling, the vast dark space absorbed all sounds, and the columned piers disappeared into the murk that shrouded the tall ceiling. The nave was more than a hundred feet tall. The stained-glass windows allowed a filtered colored light into the interior, though it was hardly illumination, more like a reflected glow. The ancient stones were so old that they no longer looked cut by humans but like stalagmites in some sort of mammoth cavern. Altogether a mysterious atmosphere, both intimidating and inspiring, uplifting and a little scary.

■ ■ ■ ■ ■

40 Notre-Dame, Paris, 1163–1260. The sober west front carefully balances horizontals and verticals.

Notre-Dame was begun in 1163, only three decades after the completion of the nave of Durham Cathedral, yet in that short interval an architectural sea change had taken place. Traditional societies in which the patterns of everyday life remain unaltered are slow to change, but late medieval European society was not

traditional at all. Population was growing rapidly thanks to agricultural innovations, towns and cities were expanding, and international trade was flourishing because of advances in business and banking. It was a period of far-reaching inventions—windmills, coal mining machinery, mechanical clocks, navigation instruments, and optical devices such as telescopes, eyeglasses, and magnifying glasses. Change was in the air.

The inventive climate of the late Middle Ages introduced a new quality to the art of building—the allure of the new. Architecture had occasionally incorporated radical changes—as when King Sneferu converted the step pyramid to a smooth-faced pyramid, for example. But Sneferu's immediate successors did not depart from his pyramidal model, rather they copied it. Similarly, Roman builders were content to follow their predecessors' lead unless something special was required, as happened in the Colosseum. Medieval cathedral builders were different. After Suger, a spirit of lively competition developed among cities—and among the itinerant master builders whom they employed. Modern art historians have divided cathedral building into successive periods—Early Gothic, High Gothic, Rayonnant, and Flamboyant—which gives the impression of an ordered evolution. But medieval builders did not see it that way. They were pushing the envelope, to use a modern phrase, making naves that were taller and lighter, ribbed vaults that were ever more complex, larger rose windows, more elaborate flying buttresses, taller steeples.

One of the most evocative medieval churches is neither the largest nor the tallest, and it does not even have flying buttresses. The royal chapel of Sainte-Chapelle was built by Louis IX (canonized Saint Louis) as an addition to the royal palace on the Île de la Cité in Paris. Consecrated in 1248, the chapel was built to house precious relics of the Crucifixion, including Christ's crown of thorns, which the king had acquired from Baldwin II, the impoverished emperor in Constantinople. The nave is not large—108 feet long and 67 feet high. Because there are no aisles, flying buttresses were not required, and the exterior walls are braced by piers. The structure supporting the vaults is reduced to what is absolutely necessary; the slender piers are a continuation of the vault ribs, and the rest of the wall, almost its full height, consists entirely of stone tracery filled with stained glass (fig. 41). The builders spared no effort to create a suitable setting for the holy objects and the entire interior was conceived as a precious reliquary. The tracery, ribs, and vaults were gilded and painted in bright colors and patterns, as bright as the brilliant stained glass.

Almost exactly a hundred years had passed since Suger had built the choir of Saint-Denis, and the nave of Sainte-Chapelle perfectly encapsulates his

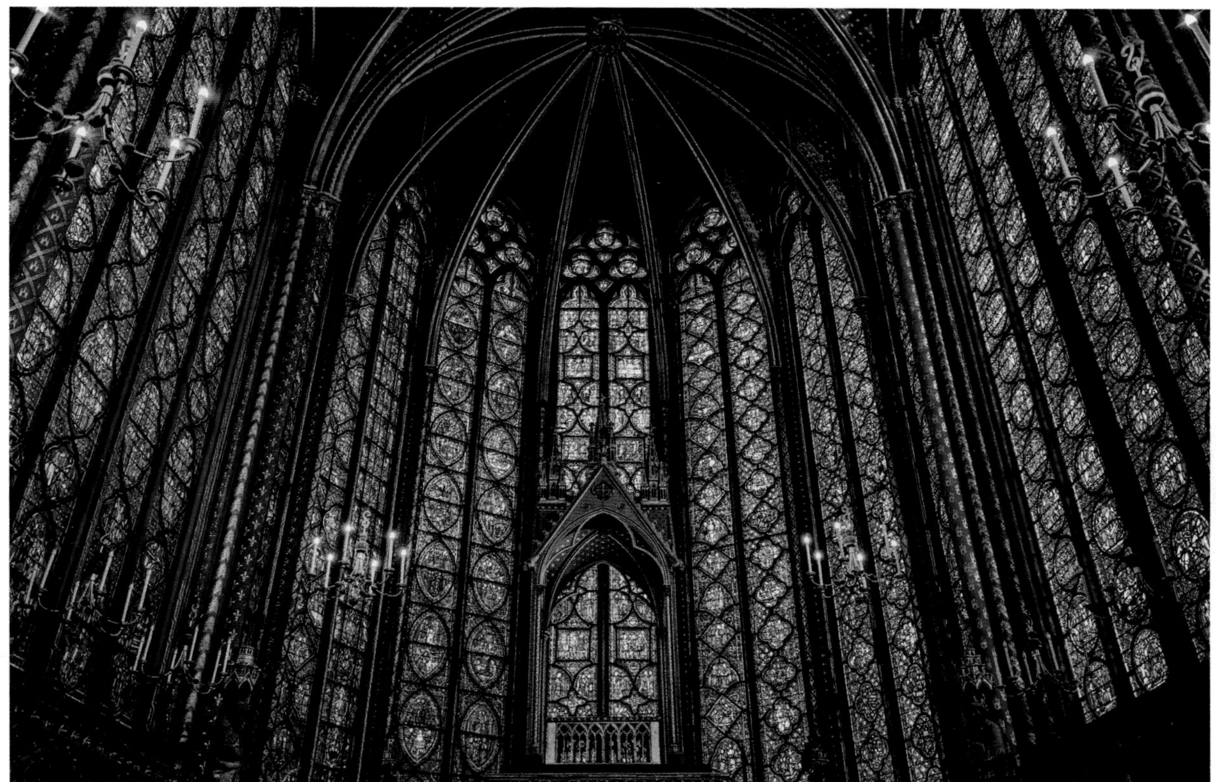

41 Sainte-Chapelle, Paris, 1242–48. The numinous glass architecture represents the apogee of thirteenth-century church building.

transcendent vision of a numinous space defined not by stone but by light. The chapel represents the apogee of Gothic building in northern France. Thirty-six years later, the vaulted choir of Beauvais Cathedral, which was to be twenty feet taller than the tallest cathedral at that time, collapsed while under construction. The choir was completed, but the rest of the cathedral was never finished. There were pressing external reasons for the abandonment—the calamitous fourteenth century witnessed the Black Death and the beginning of the Hundred Years War. Gothic cathedrals continued to be built until the sixteenth century, but it is hard not to see Beauvais as signaling the end of an era. No taller cathedral was ever attempted. Architecture is always a sign of optimism about the future, and it was as if the prodigious effort required to make buildings that were taller, lighter, and glassier had simply run out of steam.

11

The Diffusion of a Style

Ypres and Bruges, fourteenth century
Venice, fourteenth and fifteenth centuries

Abbot Suger did not conceive of the new elements he introduced at Saint-Denis as a style. The profusion of stained glass was intended to create a particular atmosphere, and the stylistic elements such as the pointed arches, ribbed vaults, and flying buttresses were more like accessories. This architecture was originally intended for places of worship, but over time—perhaps inevitably—the new way of building found wider application. Westminster Abbey and Canterbury Cathedral were both attached to Benedictine monasteries, so it was natural that when cloisters, refectories, and chapter houses were rebuilt or expanded they would incorporate pointed arches, ribbed vaulting, and tracery. The newly founded universities in Italy, England, France, and Spain were an outgrowth of monastic and cathedral schools, and when they built quadrangles and college halls, they used similar architecture. Eventually, the pointed arch lost its religious connotation. As happened in ancient Greece, where elements of temple architecture spread to secular buildings, and in Rome, where they appeared in triumphal arches and amphitheaters, the pointed arch became part of an architectural toolkit that could be used in different types of buildings.

Because architecture is expensive, it always depends on economic wherewithal. During the early Middle Ages, only the Crown, the Church, and the monastic orders had the resources to undertake ambitious building projects. But by the fourteenth century, new concentrations of wealth appeared among the independent towns of northern Europe that had broken away from the old feudal order. Banding together in confederations such as the Hanseatic League, merchants organized thriving urban economies, pioneered international trade and banking, and in the process became rich. As so often happens, great wealth found expression in great architecture.

42 Lakenhalle, Ypres, completed 1304, rebuilt 1933–67. This mid-nineteenth-century view shows the massive building with its commanding belfry. The tower of Saint Martin's Church is visible at right.

The Gothic cathedrals that towered over their urban surroundings were a source of civic pride, so it is hardly surprising that their architecture should influence secular buildings. The largest civic buildings at this time were market halls. The town of Ypres in Flanders (present-day Belgium) was renowned throughout Europe for its linen and wool, and its Lakenhalle, or Cloth Hall, dominated the main town square (fig. 42). This immense building, completed in 1304, was more than four hundred feet long with an inner courtyard, and it backed onto a canal from which barges could be unloaded. A belfry served as the town watchtower. The first floor contained merchants' stalls behind a series of forty-eight identical doors. The second floor housed a banqueting hall, meeting rooms for guild members and aldermen, and warehouse space. Brick vaults supported the second floor, and timber trusses carried the roof. The beautiful stone facade included pointed-arch windows, trefoil tracery, and pinnacles decorated with crockets, hook-shaped elements resembling curled leaves, buds, or flowers; every second "window" was a niche that contained paired statues of Flemish nobles. (The building that stands today is a faithful reconstruction, built after the original was all but destroyed following a devastating bombardment of the city during the First World War.) The belfry, with its four pinnacles and crowning lantern, was obviously inspired by a cathedral crossing tower. None of this was intended to detract from Saint Martin's Church next door, but the wealthy members of Ypres's cloth guild were clearly not shy about celebrating the wellspring of their town's prosperity.

Another type of civic building that was accorded special architectural treatment was the town hall. Medieval town halls were not large—there was no municipal bureaucracy—and their chief function was to provide a dignified meeting place for the town council. One of the most beautiful Flemish examples is in Bruges, which was an important market and banking center at the crossroads of northern European and Mediterranean trade routes. In 1376, construction began of a town hall facing Burg Square, the administrative center of the town. The doubled composition of the facade, with its two entrances, reflected the town's two governing councils, each with its own chamber. The steep roof was decorated with crenellations and octagonal turrets, giving the facade a martial air. The pointed arches and trefoil tracery conveyed the small building's symbolic importance, as did the more than forty statues of local nobility and biblical figures standing under the crocketed canopies that were arranged in tiers across the sandstone facade (fig. 43). This flamboyant building used the elements of religious architecture, yet it could not be mistaken for a church. Cathedrals and important churches were freestanding, whereas the town hall, despite its architectural finery, was part of a continuous row of civic buildings and grand residences, presenting only its facade to the square.

▪ ▪ ▪ ▪ ▪

In the thirteenth century, the pointed-arch style spread southward into Italy, and over the next hundred years Gothic cathedrals were built in Orvieto, Siena, Florence, and Milan. The exception was Venice—Venetians saw no need to build a new cathedral because they had Saint Mark's Basilica, a splendid twelfth-century Byzantine church replete with gilded domes and mosaics. Their architectural conservatism was not the result of a lack of funds—the Venetian Republic was probably the wealthiest of all the mercantile city-states. Venice dominated the eastern Mediterranean militarily, and its trade connections reached to northern Europe and as far away as China. International commerce brought Venetians in contact with diverse foreign societies, Islamic North Africa as well as Byzantine Constantinople, and these contacts had cultural as well as commercial effects.

The grandest fourteenth-century civic building in Venice was the Palazzo Ducale, the Doge's Palace, which housed the apartments of the doge (the elected chief of state), the meeting halls of the ruling bodies of the city, and the law courts.

43 Town Hall, Bruges, 1376–1420. The facade incorporates more than forty statues of Flemish nobility. The turrets and crenellations lend this building a martial air.

Located on the most prominent site in the city, facing the harbor and the entrance to the Grand Canal, the Palazzo was the first building encountered by travelers arriving by water. The historic origin of the Palazzo, a large rectangular block with a central courtyard, was a group of buildings that dated from the twelfth century and began to be consolidated in the 1300s, which was when the grand facade facing the lagoon was built. The architecture incorporated numerous Gothic elements: pointed arches in the open colonnade of the first floor, ribbed vaults, tracery in the second-story loggia, and large windows that echoed the arches of the lower arcade in the tall upper story. Figural sculpture is prominent: the capitals of the columns supporting the arcade are carved with various allegorical scenes, and the corner columns of the arcade and the loggia are decorated with biblical sculptural groups. Gothic pinnacles frame the central balcony, which includes a bas-relief of the doge kneeling before the winged lion of Saint Mark.

Venice being Venice, however, the Gothic features are combined with a sensibility that was influenced by contacts with diverse Eastern cultures. The first-floor colonnade is conventionally Gothic, although the columns are short

44 Palazzo Ducale, Venice, 1340–1442. The facade facing the lagoon is an amalgam of Gothic, Byzantine, and Islamic influences.

and stubby and the proportions of the pointed arches are squarish rather than elongated. The variety of capitals is a Byzantine influence. The second-story loggia consists of slender columns supporting cusped ogee (inflected S-shaped) arches that seamlessly turn into rondels filled with quatrefoils, a lacy curtain of Gothic tracery. This tracery is not glazed and acts as a support for the story above—a typical Venetian arrangement. The wall of the upper story, which housed the monumental assembly hall of the Grand Council, is clad in white and pink marble, and the flat textilelike pattern recalls the decorated wall of an Arab mosque. The parapet is decorated with spiky finials alternating with heraldic devices that resemble highly stylized crenellations.

The facade facing the lagoon is well known to all visitors to Venice, who barely give it a second glance, yet it is a most curious composition and bears closer examination (fig. 44). Although the two colonnades and loggia tracery are regular, the placing of the openings in the patterned wall is haphazard: the two large windows on the right, which are the only ones with tracery, have lower sills; the central window, with an ornate frame and balcony, is not centered and is squashed between its neighbors; the rondels above are unevenly spaced. These irregularities are somewhat masked by the pink and white patterned marble, which acts like a kind of wallpaper. What was the reason for this odd arrangement? Were the anomalies the result of the involvement of different builders over the long construction period, or were they caused by the functional demands of the interior? Or was the irregularity simply a matter of taste, a kind of aesthetic insouciance, a refusal to be hidebound, the very opposite of the attitude of ancient Roman builders who preferred an almost military precision. I favor the last reason, for when the Palazzo Ducale was enlarged and the adjacent wing facing the Piazzetta San Marco was completed—almost a century later—the builders repeated the irregularities of the waterfront facade exactly. Throughout the fifteenth and sixteenth centuries the Palazzo Ducale was plagued by fires—the floors and roof are wood—but despite occasional calls to update the exterior, the conservative Venetians consistently rebuilt their quirky version of Gothic. The history of architecture is sometimes described as if it were an ordered succession of discrete styles, but as Palazzo Ducale shows, styles can linger for a long time, and building styles are rarely all of a piece.

During the fifteenth century, the Palazzo Ducale was the most prominent building in the city—after Saint Mark's Basilica—and its architecture influenced other secular buildings, notably the imposing private residences that lined the Grand Canal. The model for the Venetian palazzo was established early in the Middle Ages: a three- or four-story building with an arcaded loggia serving as a boat dock on the canal side, warehouse space on the first floor, and, above, the main living spaces surrounding an internal courtyard. Canal frontage was at a premium, so buildings tended to be narrow and deep, and because the facade in such an arrangement was not load-bearing, it could easily be altered as fashions changed. That is what happened to a palazzo on the Grand Canal not far from the Rialto Bridge. In 1420, Marino Contarini, the head of an influential Venetian clan, one of the twelve founding families of the city, began a renovation of his ancestral home that included a brand-new front. The marble facade was in the Gothic style made fashionable by the Palazzo Ducale, and the result is generally considered the most beautiful palazzo in Venice. The design is attributed to the premier stonecutters of the city, Giovanni Bon (1355–1433) and his son Bartolomeo (1421–1464), who both worked on the Palazzo Ducale.

The Palazzo Contarini facade incorporates three superimposed loggias (fig. 45). The lowest, containing the boat dock, is behind an arcade whose pointed arches are pragmatically combined with a central round arch that allows access to gondolas. The arcade of the second floor—the piano nobile, or main floor—is a more elaborate version of the tracery of the Palazzo Ducale, with ogee arches and quatrefoil-filled rondels, while the third-floor arcade consists of delicate

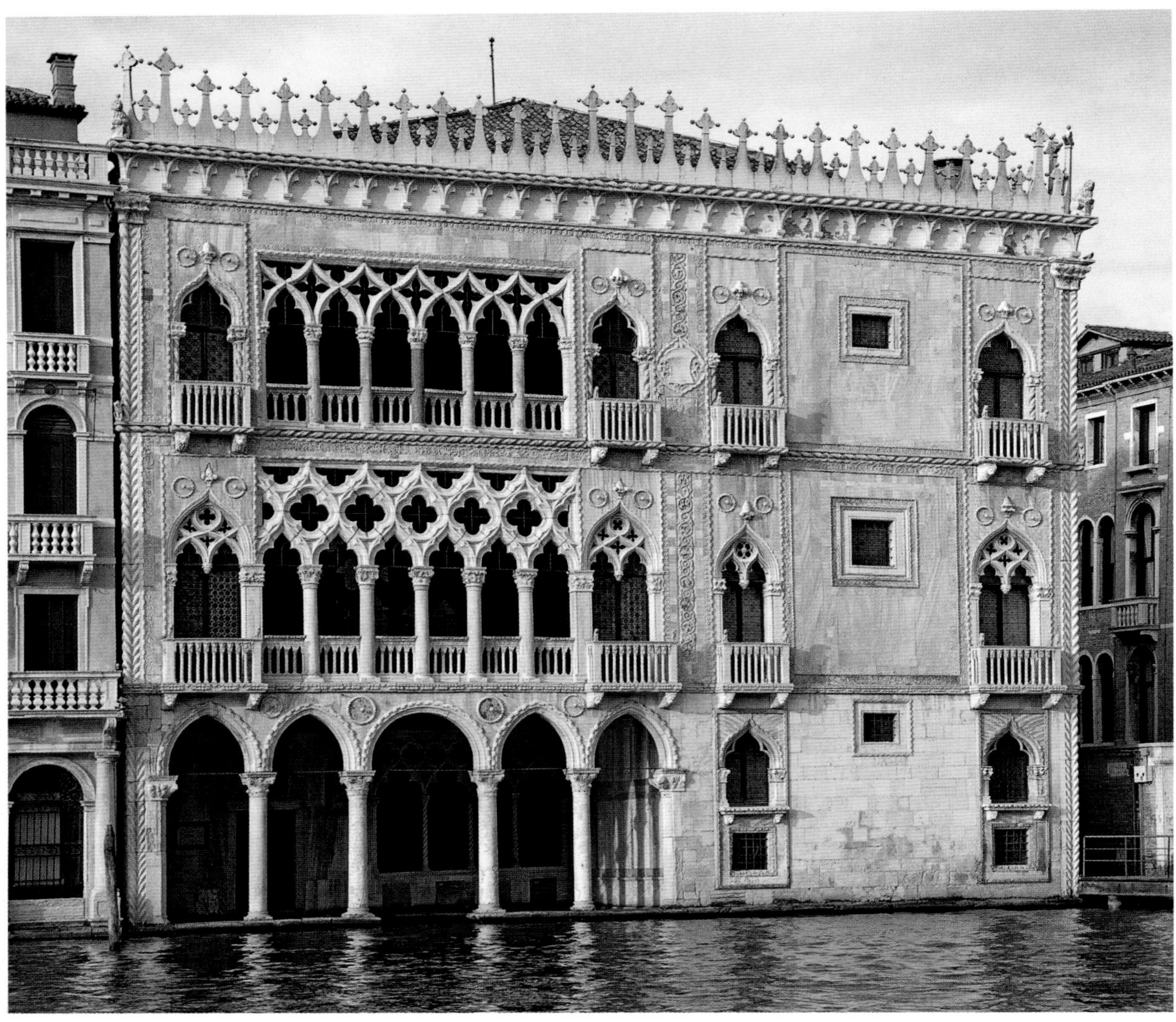

45 Palazzo Contarini, Ca' d'Oro, Venice. Giovanni and Bartolomeo Bon, 1420–40. Gothic motifs are applied to a residential building in a characteristically whimsical fashion.

overlapping ogee arches. The tracery, which recalls Islamic screens, was originally painted in red and ultramarine—the latter was a particularly prestigious color, as its expensive pigment used lapis lazuli brought from China. Details were picked out in gold leaf. The balls of the ornamental crenellations, another Islamic motif, were likewise gilded, which gave the palazzo its nickname, the Ca' d'Oro. There is more: the unusual composition is unexpectedly asymmetrical. The left side contains the three superimposed loggias, and the right side features a blank wall with square windows. The two sides of the pink and white marble facade, which is adorned with braid-like carved stone ornament and serpentine pilasters, are framed by superimposed, not-quite-identical balconies. The complex composition is an architectural tour de force.

In the three hundred years since Abbot Suger built Saint-Denis, the Gothic style had spread over all of Europe. Part of its popularity was that its craftsmanship and virtuosity captured the buoyant mood of the newly prosperous age. The style proved flexible enough to adapt to various types and sizes of buildings; it could serve equally well for a royal chapel or a town hall, a large civic building such as the Palazzo Ducale, or a residence such as the Ca' d'Oro. Moreover, the inherent quirkiness of the secular Gothic style enabled builders to modify their designs to accommodate functional demands. In addition, Gothic proved adaptable to local tastes. It could be cheerfully sybaritic in Venice or severely somber in Flanders, and it could be modified to exhibit differences of national character: more temperate in England and Germany and more flamboyant in Spain and Portugal. This adaptability accounts for the rapid spread of the pointed-arch style in the Middle Ages, and likewise explains its later popularity and its periodic revival.

12

Andalusian Fantasy

Córdoba, eighth to tenth centuries
Granada, fourteenth century

Venetian Gothic architecture is sometimes described as having Islamic influences. This refers to the distinctive architecture of the Muslim rulers of the Iberian Peninsula. In 712, a combined Arab and Berber army crossed from North Africa into Spain, ousting the Germanic Visigoths (Western Goths) who had occupied the old Roman colony of Hispania for three hundred years. It is important to understand that what the Arabs called al-Andalus, which comprised most of present-day Spain and Portugal, was not a colony but a part of the Umayyad caliphate. Islamic civilization—advanced, liberal, and tolerant—had a broad influence on the local culture. Under Islamic rule, the Visigoth feudal system was broken up and smallholdings replaced large fiefdoms. New crops such as sugarcane, citrus fruits, and rice were introduced, as were industries producing textiles, pottery, leather, and paper. The Iberian economy expanded and prospered. The new Arab settlers lived side by side with local Islamic converts as well as Christians and Jews, many of them Arabic-speaking. Thanks in part to this mixing, Islamic Spain developed into an unusually dynamic society that produced significant advances in architecture and the sciences.

The capital of al-Andalus in the eighth century was Córdoba, which became one of the largest cities in Europe and an important center of Islamic learning. The ruler was Emir Abd al-Rahman, a descendant of the Umayyad dynasty of Damascus. Like his forebears, al-Rahman was a builder, and in 784 he began construction of a mosque. (Previously, Islamic worshippers had shared a church with a Christian congregation.) The new mosque followed the model set by the Great Mosque of Kairouan: a walled courtyard and a rectangular prayer hall covered by a flat wooden roof supported on colonnaded arcades that defined aisles oriented toward the mihrab. The emir intended his building to rival the Great Mosque of Damascus, and he specified a similar thirty-foot ceiling. The problem was that the

46 Great Mosque, Córdoba, 784–987. The overlapping double-tiered and banded arches create a hypnotic effect; the Corinthian columns are ancient Roman spolia.

columns available, which were ancient Roman spolia recovered from the church that had stood on the site when al-Rahman purchased it, were less than fourteen feet tall. The builders devised an ingenious solution: instead of using a traditional arcade-plus-triforium, they invented a double-decker arcade. The short Corinthian columns support freestanding horseshoe arches and rectangular piers that extend up to support a *second* set of identical arches carrying the roof beams (fig. 46). The effect of two sets of arches is mesmerizing, especially so because the white stone arches are banded with red brick. Black bands had been used first by al-Walid in the Dome of the Rock in Jerusalem, but using red brick heightened the effect. It is possible that this feature of the Córdoba mosque influenced the banding in Charlemagne's contemporaneous Palatine Chapel in Aachen.

The prayer hall and courtyard of the Córdoba mosque were enlarged three times over the next two hundred years to accommodate the growing Muslim population of the city. A minaret was added, and the courtyard was surrounded by porticos. The unpaved courtyard was planted with citrus trees and palms, making a shady arboreal analog to the forest of columns within. In 961, Caliph Hakam II extended the prayer hall and, perhaps inspired by Kairouan, added a lantern over the mihrab. The scalloped and trefoil arches further the air of fantasy in the interior, as do three small top-lit domes over the maqsura, which was a screened enclosure reserved for the caliph. These domes are supported on interlaced arches that form an eight-pointed star, a structural system that anticipated—on a smaller scale—the ribbed vaulting of Durham and later medieval cathedrals. Together with the courtyard the mosque measures 610 feet long and 445 feet wide, larger than its counterparts in Kairouan and Damascus. The exterior resembles a fortification: tall, buttressed walls with only a few small openings. Where there is ornament, such as around the entrance portals, it has the character of a schematic drawing, with no suggestion of the fantastic world within. In enlarging the mosque, al-Rahman's successors followed his lead and duplicated the double-tiered arcades, producing a remarkably unified building. This highlights another difference between architecture and the other arts: a great painting is the work of a single creative imagination and a single moment, but a great building may be constructed by successive generations of builders over an extended period of time.

The Great Mosque of Córdoba is an impressive building, but it is impressive in a different way from a Gothic cathedral. The structure is not ambitious. The aisles are only twenty feet wide, the arches span a mere ten feet, and the flat wooden ceiling lacks the drama of a soaring vault. The plan is likewise simple; instead of a hierarchic arrangement of aisles and nave, and of transept and crossing, there is only the uniform repetition of aisles, one after the other. The emphasis is on the horizontal rather than the vertical. Despite the domed mihrab, the interior does not have an architectural focus; it is like an enveloping forest or, rather, an enchanted forest. The ancient columns are jasper, onyx, marble, granite, and porphyry, and the interior is also enriched by glittering glass mosaics created by Byzantine craftsmen al-Rahman brought from Constantinople. Gilded mosaics adorn the ribbed vaults of the domes. Much of the ornament takes the form of calligraphy, quotations from the Prophet but highly stylized and almost illegible—unlike in a cathedral, the mosque decorations were not intended to be instructive. The complex interior that surrounded the worshipper invited private contemplation. The present-day visitor will be surprised to find the hypostyle hall interrupted by a Renaissance cathedral nave and transept. These were crudely inserted into the middle of the building in the sixteenth century after the mosque had been converted into a Christian church.

▪ ▪ ▪ ▪ ▪

The lands of the Islamic empire were chronically riven by factional disputes, and al-Andalus was no exception. The Umayyad caliphate was usurped by a Berber insurrection, which itself was overthrown by another rival until, following a destructive civil war, al-Andalus disintegrated into two dozen rival sheikdoms. This allowed the Christian kingdoms of northern Spain—León, Castile, and Navarre—to make territorial inroads. A series of Christian victories led to the capture of Toledo, Córdoba, and Seville, shrinking the area under Muslim rule, and by the thirteenth century the sole surviving Islamic presence on the Iberian Peninsula was the Emirate of Granada, a coastal enclave secure behind the Sierra Nevada mountains.

The emirate was politically aligned with Castile, and thanks to its coastal location it became a prosperous entrepôt for trade between Christian Spain and Islamic North Africa. The city of Granada was a safe haven for Muslims (Arabs and non-Arabs alike) who had been expelled from the recaptured territories, and the city replaced Córdoba as a focus of Islamic culture. On a raised plateau at the northern edge of the city stood the royal palace, the Alhambra (Al-Hamra means "the red one" in Arabic, a reference to the windblown red clay dust that coated the surrounding fortifications). The walled citadel occupied more than five acres and included several palaces as well as barracks, workshops, and even a zoo.

The main palace within the Alhambra was built during the fourteenth century by a succession of sultans of the ruling Nasrid dynasty, notably Ismail I, Yusuf I, and Muhammad V. Arab dwellings were traditionally organized around inner courts, a house type whose origins dated to ancient Egypt, and the Nasrid palace followed this pattern. There was a variety of courts: large and small, grand and intimate, planted and hard-surfaced. The oldest court is on the extreme left of the floor plan (see fig. 47); the adjacent room with six columns was a public

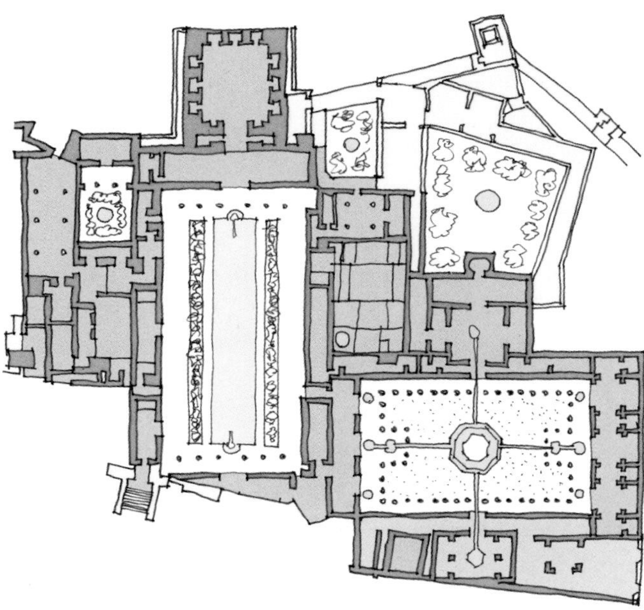

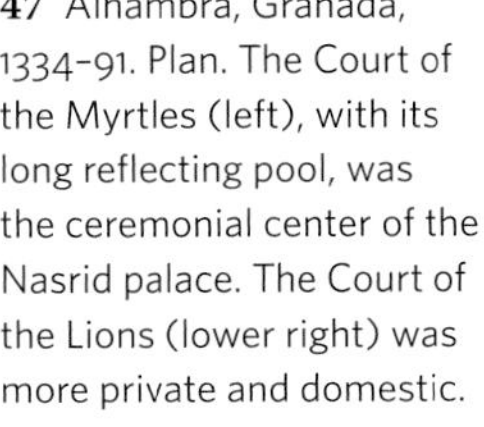

47 Alhambra, Granada, 1334–91. Plan. The Court of the Myrtles (left), with its long reflecting pool, was the ceremonial center of the Nasrid palace. The Court of the Lions (lower right) was more private and domestic.

reception room. To the right of this entrance court is the ceremonial center of the palace, Yusuf I's Court of the Myrtles, whose chief feature was a long reflecting pool flanked by myrtle bushes. The court served as an outdoor anteroom to the towering throne room, which was entered through a cusped arch under an arcaded portico on the north side of the court. The idyllic appearance is deceptive—the Nasrid palace was rife with bloody intrigue. Two of the sultans who built the Alhambra were assassinated, and the third was overthrown by his half-brother but returned to power three years later, after murdering both his usurper and his usurper's usurper.

The portico at the end of the Court of the Myrtles is strikingly graceful (fig. 48). Roman, Byzantine, and Romanesque columns are sturdy and robust, to emphasize their load-carrying function, but the Alhambra columns are extremely slim, effortlessly supporting the stone arcade whose fretwork surface looks like a weightless trellis rather than solid masonry. The round arches of the arcade are stilted—that is, they are extended vertically, which visually lightens them further. Stilted arches, like the imposts over the capitals, were a Byzantine influence; the fretwork and the honeycombed ornamental vault, or mocárabe, of the large central arch were distinctively Arab.

Water is the leitmotiv of the Alhambra; it enlivened the courts, cooled the interior, irrigated the gardens, and supplied the large bathhouse, which had hot and cold pools and a steam room. A system of aqueducts and lifting devices transported water to the palace and created the pressure required to power the many fountains. The most dramatic fountain, an alabaster basin supported by twelve marble lions—a rare case of Islamic figural sculpture—stands in the center of the palace's second major court, built by Muhammad V. The Court of the Lions is divided by four shallow stone channels that meet at the fountain and symbolize the four rivers of paradise as described in the Koran (fig. 49). Today the marble court is paved, but originally flowers and trees surrounded the two open-air pavilions. The paradise garden theme extends to the design of the surrounding arcade, which is even more delicate than in the Court of the Myrtles: the extremely narrow stilted arches are separated by wide bands of solid wall whose lacy fretwork creates the illusion of an immaterial architecture. The sense of airy weightlessness is emphasized by the slenderness of the single, paired, and tripled columns.

48 Court of the Myrtles, Alhambra. A battlemented tower containing the throne room looms over the court. The delicate stilted arches of the portico are decorated with carved fretwork.

When I visited the Alhambra, I was at first disoriented. The palace presents no single architectural image—rather, it is a collage of discrete set pieces, each intended to be experienced separately. The Court of the Lions, for example, is different from the Court of the Myrtles, more private and intimate—and more playful. The same variety is evident in the interiors. The throne room is modestly

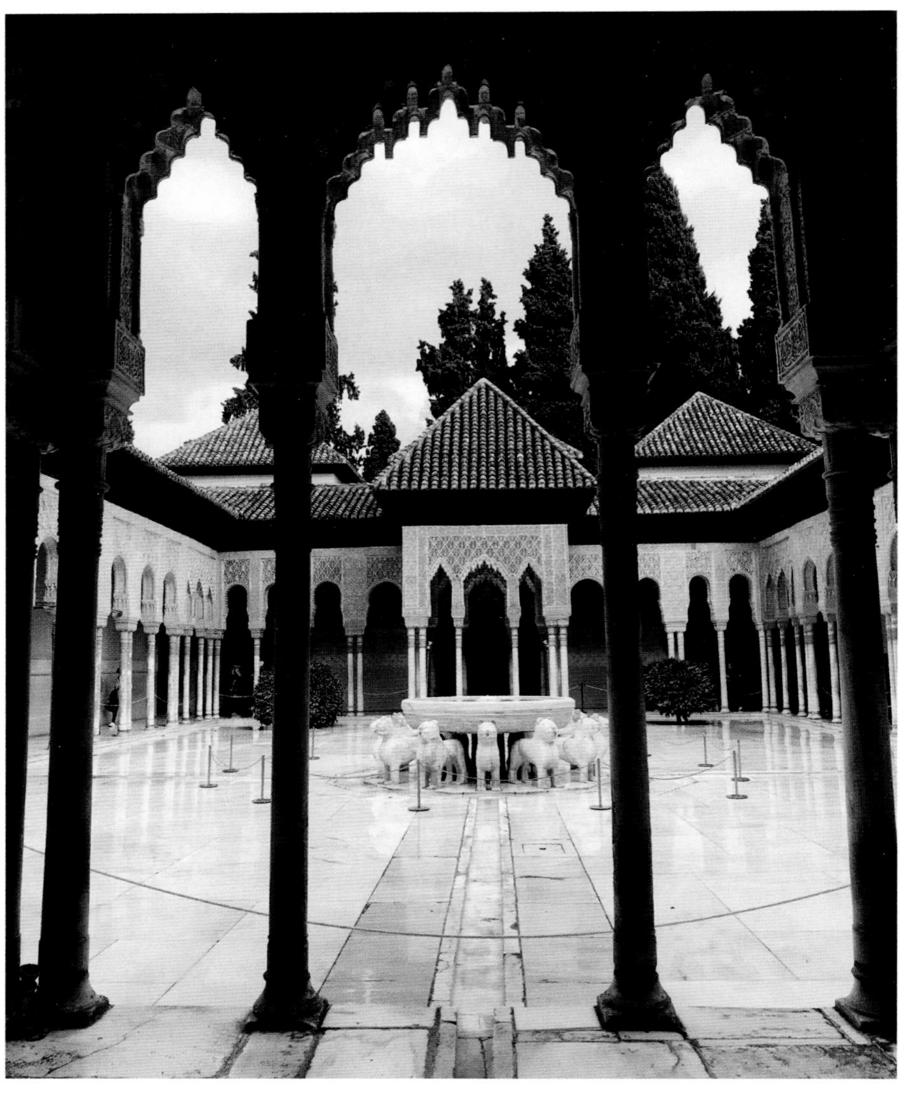

49 Court of the Lions, Alhambra. The scalloped-arch arcades are supported by single, paired, and tripled columns. The water channels extend into the building's interior.

sized, about forty feet square, but it rises to a sixty-foot-high domed wooden ceiling. This is decorated with mocárabe vaulting and white, blue, and gold inlays in the shape of circles, crowns, and stars. The walls are covered in yeseria work, delicately carved plaster arabesques as fine as embroidery. Three sides of the room contain deep niches. The windows, which were originally filled with stained glass, create a murky atmosphere that sharply contrasts with the sunlit court outside.

The royal apartments that surround the Court of the Lions consist of four groups of rooms with extremely tall, dramatic domed ceilings. The room on the north side, referred to as the Hall of the Two Sisters, has three festooned arches leading to sleeping chambers, one of which opens into a small latticed pavilion that overlooks a landscaped mirador, or belvedere. The central room contains a small pool with a water jet that is scaled to floor-sitting; the water is carried outside to the court by a narrow floor channel. The lower part of the walls is covered with geometrically patterned tilework. The room would have been furnished with wall hangings and carpets. Its most extraordinary feature is the ceiling: a carved plaster dome with mocárabe work that resembles gilded stalactites, supported by mocárabe pendentives resting on an eight-sided drum with grilled windows. This dazzling and diaphanous composition seems to float over the room; in reality, the plaster ceiling is suspended from a concealed wooden structure.

Much of the luxurious architecture of the Alhambra was created with distinctly un-luxurious materials—wood and plaster—which reflected the reduced resources of the small emirate. As a vassal state of neighboring Castile, Granada was somewhat isolated from the rest of the Arab world. This isolation produced a unique, highly refined architecture, one little concerned with practicality or structural expression, consumed with craftsmanship, and intent on creating an atmosphere of dematerialized fantasy. It may be far-fetched to see this as the expressive final gasp of a great civilization, as it would be another hundred years before Islamic rule in Granada—and thus Spain—ended. But there is something elegiac about this ephemeral fairyland palace, which seems to celebrate the conclusion of something rather than its beginning.

13

Far East

Beijing, ninth and fifteenth centuries

China is one of the great ancient civilizations, emerging in the Bronze Age and forming a continental empire as early as the second century BC. The formative age of Chinese culture was the stable and prosperous Tang dynasty, which lasted from the seventh to the tenth century AD, roughly contemporaneous with the early European Middle Ages. Literature, painting, calligraphy, and ceramics flourished, as did architecture, whose distinctive features were established at this time. These are evident in one of the oldest surviving wooden temples of this period, the Great East Hall of Foguang, built in 857 and part of a Buddhist monastery. The timber-framed building, seven bays wide and three deep, stands on a raised stone platform (fig. 50). The hipped roof is covered in clay tiles, and the wide, gently curving eaves are supported by richly modeled corbeled wooden brackets, repeated on the interior, where the crisscrossing roof beams and brackets rest on round timber columns. A lattice ceiling conceals most of the roof framing. The Great East Hall was built about the same time as Charlemagne's Palatine Chapel, but it is a very different sort of building: horizontal rather than vertical, built of wood rather than stone, austere rather than ornate, restrained rather than monumental, simple in form but complex in detail.

Following successive periods of fragmentation and consolidation that included a hundred years of Mongol rule, the Ming dynasty reasserted Han sovereignty over a vast empire that included more than a hundred million inhabitants. The third Ming ruler, the Yongle Emperor, came to the throne in 1403 after overthrowing his nephew, and to symbolically cut ties with the old regime he moved his capital from Nanjing to the northern city of Beiping, present-day Beijing. There, in the span of only fourteen years, he built the imperial palace that became known as the Forbidden City.

The Forbidden City, so named because it was off-limits to the public, was a sprawling fortified compound that covered one hundred and eighty acres and

50 Great East Hall, Foguang Monastery, Mount Wutai, China, c. 857. Ornate wooden brackets support the wide eaves and tiled roof of this Tang dynasty Buddhist temple.

housed as many as ten thousand people—not only the royal family but a retinue of court dignitaries, scholars, craftsmen, eunuchs, concubines, guards, and servants. There were almost nine hundred buildings arranged in walled courtyards and surrounded by gardens. The private quarters were confined to a restricted area in the northern half of the compound, while the chief ceremonial buildings were arranged along a processional axis in the south.

Six centuries separated the Ming from the Tang dynasty, yet the main architectural features of the earlier period survived unchanged: one-story timber-frame buildings on stone platforms, large clay-tiled sloping roofs with curved eaves supported on ornate brackets, and bilateral symmetry in architecture and planning. The traditional layout followed a strict hierarchy: the main house was on the north side of the courtyard facing the sun, buildings for secondary uses were on the east and west sides, and the south end was reserved for children and servants. Larger residences added additional courtyards as needed. In palace and temple compounds, the buildings and courtyards were larger, but the relationships remained the same. The idea that a building was always part of a group set Chinese architecture apart from its European counterpart, as did the low horizontality of the predominantly one-story buildings.

Whether the buildings were large or small, they were built of timber using post-and-beam framing. The key to timber framing is the connection between columns and beams, and Chinese builders developed a variety of ingenious interlocking joints. They did not use roof trusses; rafters were supported either directly on columns or on multiple layers of crisscrossing beams. In important buildings, distinctive corbeled brackets called dougongs acted like capitals and distributed the weight of the rafters. The dougong, which was ancient and is prominent in the Great East Hall (see fig. 50), consists of superimposed corbeled layers. This is hardly the simplest way to build, but it creates a striking architectural effect, and over time the corbeled bracket developed into a decorative motif. Because wood had to be protected from the elements, Chinese buildings had large overhangs. Wood was painted or enameled to protect against rot and insects, and vivid polychromy was applied to doorways, windows, latticework, and ceilings.

The Greeks had started by building with wood but switched to longer-lasting stone for important buildings—why did the Chinese continue to use wood, which is susceptible to fire and decay? Chinese builders were familiar with masonry construction, which they used for fortifications, arched bridges, and vaulted tombs. The chief reason to use wood for habitable buildings was to counter the threat of earthquakes, which were a common occurrence throughout China. The walls of brick buildings tended to separate during earthquakes, leading the heavy tiled roofs to collapse, injuring and killing the occupants, whereas timber-frame structures held together during tremors. Frame construction imposed a rigid discipline on design: beams had to follow straight lines, columns needed to be regularly spaced, timber spans were limited to about twenty feet. The result was a modular approach to building based on repetitive bays. What is unusual is that this construction system was used for *all* buildings, irrespective of their function or status; interiors were left open or subdivided into rooms, as required. Using standardized components meant that buildings could be rapidly built and easily repaired, or even dismantled and moved. It also meant that when functional demands changed, these barnlike structures could be modified and reused.

Official visitors to the Forbidden City passed through five gates and crossed three large courtyards before arriving at the largest building in the palace, the Hall of Supreme Harmony (fig. 51). In Ming China, significant buildings were elevated

51 Hall of Supreme Harmony, Forbidden City, Beijing, 1420, rebuilt 1695–97. The hip type of roof with double eaves was reserved for palaces and temples.

on platforms—the more important the building, the taller the platform—and the primacy of the Hall of Supreme Harmony was indicated by its three-story platform of white marble. The hall housed a single immense throne room that served for state banquets and grand official ceremonies; a row of narrow rooms at each end contained private offices for court officials. The building, about two hundred feet long and one hundred feet wide, was eleven bays wide. The wider central bay was occupied by a raised dais on which stood the imperial throne—the Dragon Throne. Above the dais, the flat forty-foot wooden ceiling opened into a polygonal dome. The grid of beams supporting the ceiling, as well as the coffered ceiling itself, was painted with multicolored decorative patterns. The massive wooden columns, carved from single tree trunks and tapered, were lacquered red, the imperial color; the columns around the throne were gold-plated with dragon motifs. Only a year after it was completed the hall was struck by lightning and burned to the ground. It was rebuilt exactly as before, and over the years, this occurred several times—thus while the design of the building that we see today dates from 1420, the actual construction is from the end of the seventeenth century.

The two-hundred-foot-long facade consists of a columned loggia, with a row of latticed doors opening into the hall. The immense roof, covered with glazed yellow ceramic tiles, has curved hips and double eaves; the top ridge is decorated with imperial dragons. The eaves of imperial buildings were regularly adorned with mythical animal figures that were intended to protect the structure and its occupants from harm. The precise number and nature of the figures depended on the rank of the building, and because the Hall of Supreme Harmony was the most important building in the empire, it was unique in having ten colored-glass figures on each eave. The yellow roof tiles, the curved hips, and the double eaves were likewise reserved for special imperial buildings.

Imperial buildings were defined according to eight ranks, with different ranks accorded specific roof shapes, roof ornaments, platform heights, colors, and so on. The Chinese were remarkably conservative when it came to architecture. Despite a formidable spirit of innovation—after all, silk and porcelain production, papermaking, printing, the compass, and gunpowder were Chinese inventions—the design of buildings was governed by age-old conventions. As early as the twelfth century an official manual, *Yingzao fashi* (usually translated as Building Standards), was widely distributed in printed form. Its thirty-four illustrated chapters codified the correct way to build. The precise layout of buildings was also governed by the geomantic art of feng shui, which flowered during the Ming dynasty. Because architectural design was constrained by rigid custom and religious concerns, as well as superstition, Chinese builders were not expected—or even permitted—to invent new forms. Instead, they deployed standard solutions. Perhaps that is why there is no evidence that architects were accorded special status, even though poets, painters, and calligraphers were highly prized at court. Indeed, the word for "architect" did not appear in the language before the twentieth century. The Chinese character used to signify architecture was simply "construction."

Prominent Chinese buildings were radically different from their medieval European and Arab counterparts. Although Gothic cathedrals, town halls, and palazzos used similar columns, pilasters, arches, and moldings, different types of buildings had different forms and methods of construction; similarly, an emir's palace looked very different from a mosque. In fifteenth-century China, however, there was little difference in form and construction between a temple and an imperial hall, or even between a palace hall and a minor court dignitary's residence—they all used the same timber-frame method of construction. What distinguished different buildings were their details: the shape of the eaves, the color of the roof tiles, and the exact nature and amount of ornamentation. Interestingly, these differences communicated the rank of the building but not its actual function.

▪ ▪ ▪ ▪ ▪

The codified Chinese approach to architecture provided an admirable sense of continuity and consistency, but it precluded the flashes of individual brilliance that characterized Venetian Gothic and Islamic architecture. However, architectural inventiveness did manifest itself in one distinctly Chinese type of building: the pagoda. Pagodas were Buddhist commemorative structures that housed relics and sacred writings. Unlike a church steeple, the pagoda was not part of a larger building. The form originated in the sixth century as the Chinese version of a stupa, the mound-like structure of Buddhist India. The first wood pagodas were basically conceived as stacked buildings, hence the layers of eaves or pent roofs that became a characteristic pagoda feature. Timber pagodas sometimes had a central mast that reinforced the structure and extended into a spire. The design of pagodas was not regimented, and builders were free to explore a variety of plans—square, hexagonal, and octagonal; no two pagodas are alike. Because timber pagodas were susceptible to fire from lightning strikes, builders experimented with brick and stone. Masonry pagodas imitated the features of wood pagodas, such as steeples and pent roofs supported by dougong brackets, but were sometimes given tapered and curved profiles. Like the European cathedral builders, pagoda builders strove to build higher and higher; the tallest surviving ancient timber pagoda (built in 1056) is two hundred and twenty feet tall, slightly taller than the crossing tower of Durham Cathedral.

Masonry pagodas were susceptible to earthquakes, and many were destroyed over the years. The oldest example still standing, and also one of the most beautiful, is the pagoda of the Songyue Monastery on Mount Song, one of the sacred Taoist mountains of central China (fig. 52). Built in the sixth century, it is one hundred and thirty-one feet tall, although the fifteen pent roofs give the illusion of greater height. The tower, with a particularly elegant curving profile, is built of yellowish bricks laid in clay mortar. Unique among Chinese pagodas, it has twelve sides, making it appear almost circular. The walls of the two-story base are eight feet thick and have four tall arched openings oriented to the four points of the compass. The upper part of the base is heavily decorated with niches and ogee arches, as well as windowed niches decorated with relief carvings of teapots and lions. The decorations, as well as the pilasters with lotus leaf capitals, appear almost Byzantine (the pagoda is contemporaneous with Hagia Sophia). The upper levels of the tower have both actual and blank windows. The soffit of the pent roofs is curved, and the surface modulations suggest stylized dougong brackets. The tower is hollow, and traces of supports in the interior of the walls suggest that it originally had eight wooden floors, presumably linked by a stair.

52 Pagoda, Songyue Monastery, Mount Song, AD 523.

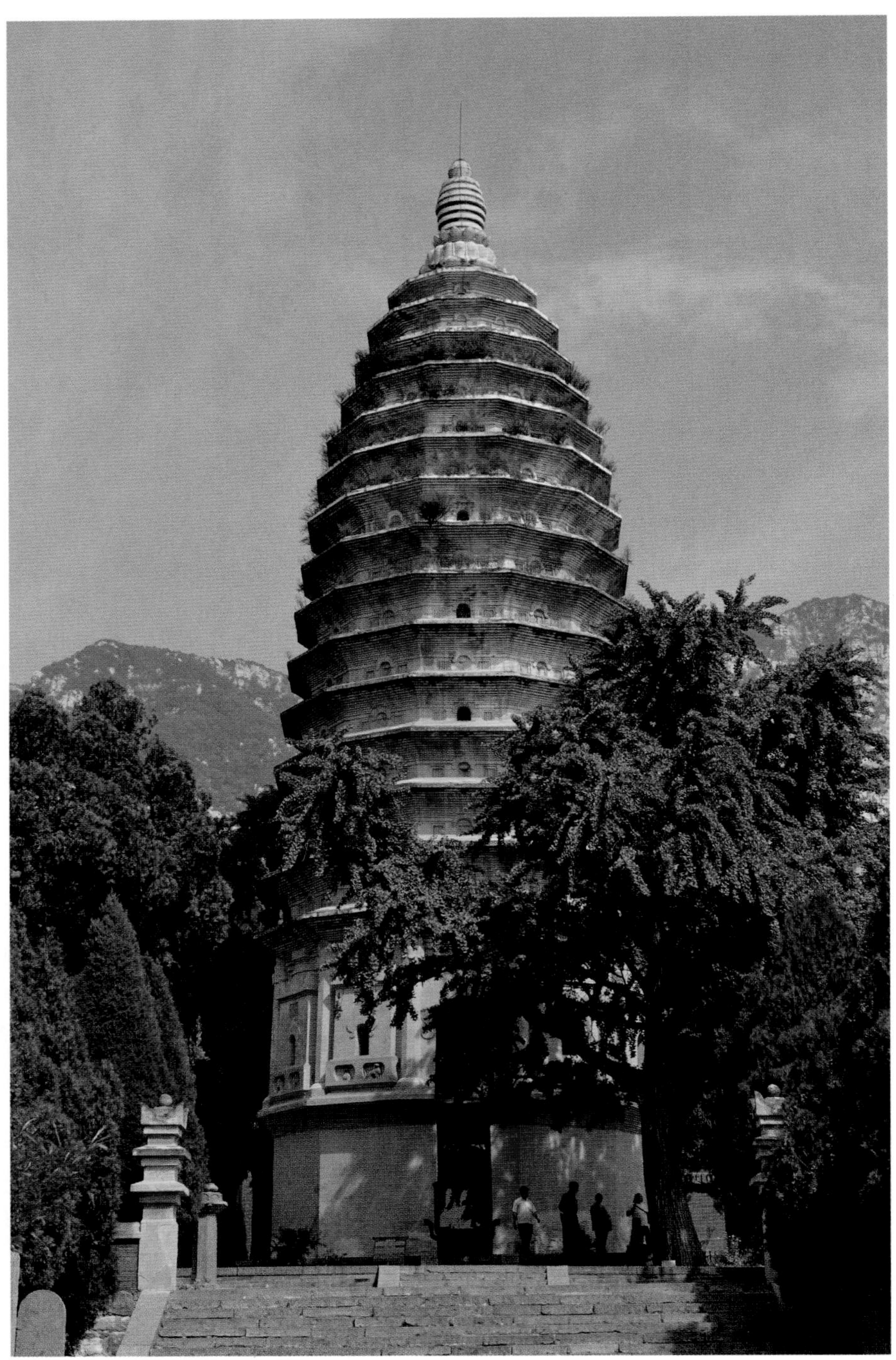

Pagodas were analogous to Gothic spires and bell towers, but because they were freestanding they were even more dramatic. This was especially true because the surrounding buildings were generally only one story high. Because many monasteries were in rural locations, the tall pagoda emerging from a forest landscape, or surrounded by hills, was a poetic image frequently depicted by Chinese painters. Not standardized at all.

III
A REIMAGINED WORLD

14

Glancing Back

Florence, fifteenth century

Charlemagne revived the architecture of a two-hundred-and-fifty-year-old church in order to evoke a connection with the old Roman Empire, but his reference to the past was too narrowly focused to have a widespread influence. On the other hand, a revival that began in Florence in the fifteenth century had consequences that were felt across Europe and beyond. I am referring, of course, to the Italian Renaissance. That event had three salient features. First, it involved an ancient Roman past that was considered a heritage rather than simply history. Second, it encompassed literature, philosophy, and painting, as well as architecture. Third, it looked back across a span of more than a thousand years, which required considerable imaginative conjecture because, while some ancient buildings, such as the Pantheon and the Colosseum, were intact or largely intact, most, like the Forum, the imperial baths, and the basilicas, existed only as fragmentary ruins. But whatever the state of the buildings, the imposing physical presence of ancient ancestral architecture was a reminder of what seemed to have been a golden age.

The first to systematically study the ruins of Roman antiquity was Filippo Brunelleschi (1377–1446). Born to a well-to-do Florentine family—the son of a notary—he was trained as a goldsmith, a craft that combined artistry and technique. In 1401 he entered a prominent competition for a new set of bronze doors for the Baptistery of San Giovanni, a beloved medieval building in the center of Florence. The jury awarded the commission jointly to him and to the goldsmith and sculptor Lorenzo Ghiberti (1378–1455). The hot-tempered Brunelleschi refused to collaborate and in a fit of pique abandoned the city; with his friend Donatello (1386–1466), who also had trained as a goldsmith, he moved to Rome. There the pair were drawn to the ancient ruins. These were not in a preserved state, as they are today, and the young enthusiasts scoured the rubble to turn up moldings, capitals, and other fragments, which they measured and sketched. Brunelleschi spent most of the next fifteen years away from Florence, and while he supported himself as a jeweler and clockmaker, his chief pastime was surveying and documenting the ruined architecture of antiquity.

Brunelleschi returned to Florence around 1417, where he became known for devising a geometrical method for constructing accurate perspectival drawings, a technique that revolutionized Renaissance painting. He entered another competition, this time to complete the dome of Santa Maria del Fiore, the city's cathedral. This Gothic building, begun more than a hundred years earlier, was intended to have an eight-sided dome over the crossing. With a diameter of a hundred and forty-three feet the dome would be larger than the Pantheon's—then the largest dome in the world—and, springing from a height of a hundred and seventy feet, it would be taller than any previous cathedral. It may seem odd for a goldsmith to become involved with building construction, but in the fifteenth century there was no organized architectural profession, no guild or apprenticeship system; a general background in the arts was a sufficient qualification. The competition finalists were once again Brunelleschi and his old rival Ghiberti. Ultimately, both were appointed *capomaestre,* or masters-of-the-works, although Brunelleschi ended up taking the lead thanks to his initiative and skill. He was extraordinarily inventive. During the construction of the dome he devised a new way of laying bricks that did away with the need for temporary formwork, designed an ox-powered crane, and built an amphibious fourteen-wheeled cart to transport marble up the Arno River. The last was a rare failure—for unexplained reasons, the mammoth barge came to grief and sank.

Brunelleschi was acclaimed for his perspectival experiments, which he demonstrated publicly, and his renown was increased by his participation in the dome competition and led to architectural commissions. One of the first was from the wealthy silk merchants guild, to which as a goldsmith he belonged. The building was a charitable project, the Ospedale degli Innocenti, or Foundling Hospital, a home for abandoned children. Brunelleschi skillfully organized the plan around two cloisters, but the building's most original feature was the loggia arcade facing Piazza Santissima Annunziata. The design of the great dome of Santa Maria del Fiore, with its ribs and pointed shape, had to be Gothic to suit the style of the building, whereas the architecture of the loggia gave Brunelleschi the opportunity to apply his antiquarian research. The long arcade takes up one entire side of the square: nine semicircular arches, each spanning nineteen feet and supported on columns nineteen feet tall. The square proportions are repeated on the interior of the loggia, which is roofed by a succession of square domelike

53 Foundling Hospital, Florence. Filippo Brunelleschi, 1419–24. The Corinthian capitals of the loggia are modeled on ancient precedents. The glazed terra-cotta roundels are original, but the infant sculptures, like the lunette fresco, were added decades later.

vaults. Instead of stocky Gothic columns with stylized capitals, Brunelleschi designed elegant Roman columns and engaged half-columns based on ancient models and complete with entasis and Corinthian capitals (fig. 53). He used the same arrangement in the interior cloisters.

The Foundling Hospital is not an archaeological re-creation—its graceful arches have no exact precedent in Roman antiquity. Brunelleschi was interested in learning from the past but he was not a historian, he was an artist. His slender arcades are oddly reminiscent of the Alhambra, although there is nothing remotely Arab or even Venetian in the austere and undecorated design, whose gray stone columns and moldings contrasting with the whitewashed plaster walls would become a Brunelleschi trademark. The one decorative touch is a series of roundels in the spandrels, or triangular areas between arches (see fig. 53). Roundels were a Roman motif—they appear in the Arch of Constantine—although placing them in the spandrel was Brunelleschi's idea. (The terra-cotta discs, originally blank, were filled around 1490 by charming glazed terra-cotta reliefs of infants in swaddling clothes sculpted by Andrea della Robbia.) Brunelleschi's monochrome color scheme emphasized proportion and geometrical rigor rather than surface ornamentation—that was new, too. This unfussy architectural minimalism appealed to Florentine tastes, and the style became known as *all'antica,* in the manner of the ancients.

54 Old Sacristy, San Lorenzo, Florence. Filippo Brunelleschi, 1419–29. Interior. An exercise in perspectival space that is defined by Roman orders.

At the same time as he was designing the Foundling Hospital, Brunelleschi was working on a high-profile commission for the powerful Medici family, the leading bankers and merchants in the city. Brunelleschi's project was an addition to the Basilica of San Lorenzo, the Medici parish church: a sacristy that also served as mortuary chapel for Giovanni di Bicci de' Medici and his wife, Piccarda Bueri. (The room is today known as the Old Sacristy, to distinguish it from Michelangelo's New Sacristy, built a hundred years later.) The room is a perfect cube, about forty feet on a side, surmounted by a dome supported on four large pendentives (fig. 54). The sarcophagus is in the center. The umbrella dome is divided into twelve segments by ribs, the spaces between spanned by brick vaults. Light enters through twelve small circular windows and a central oculus. On one side, in a square niche, stands the altar, surmounted by a smaller dome.

The wall containing the altar niche resembles a Roman triumphal arch, the linked curves of the pendentives forming a large semicircle that rests on an entablature supported by giant Corinthian pilasters. The pilasters are patterned on antique models, whereas the entablature is a series of terra-cotta roundels decorated with putti. The doors between the pilasters, which give access to a vestry and a stair, have pediments supported on small Ionic columns. The sculpted bronze doors, which depict scenes from the lives of the apostles and the martyrs, were the work of Brunelleschi's friend Donatello, who also sculpted the terra-cotta lunettes above the doors, the eight large polychrome stucco roundels that fill the pendentives and the arches, and the putti that decorate the entablature.

The sacristy, which was unlike a traditional Gothic interior, caused a stir even before it was finished. According to Antonio Manetti, who wrote a biography of Brunelleschi in the 1480s, "[The Old Sacristy] astonished all of the people of the city as well as foreigners who chanced to see it, for the novelty and beauty of its style. And so many people came continually to see it that it greatly disturbed the men who were working on it." Instead of being frescoed, as was the custom, the dome and walls were left blank, the white stucco contrasting with the gray-green stone of the Corinthian pilasters and the moldings. In earlier times, architecture had often been a framework for decorative art; here the framework *was* the art. Building on his perspectival research, Brunelleschi used the moldings to lead the eye, emphasizing the geometrical composition of the space. This was a crucial innovation, for it placed the human observer at the center of things. Together with the Foundling Hospital, the sacristy heralded the advent of a new kind of architecture, calm and ordered, glancing back to ancient Rome but stylistically innovative.

Brunelleschi was now the premier architect of the city. "His fame and reputation had grown to such an extent that anyone who needed to construct a building sent for him from great distances to obtain drawings and models prepared by the hand of such a great man," wrote Giorgio Vasari in his pioneering work of art history, *Lives of the Most Excellent Painters, Sculptors, and Architects* (published in 1550). "Fame" is not a word that had previously been attached to architects—medieval master builders labored in obscurity as anonymous members of a team. Brunelleschi became the first architect to be accorded the artistic status of a poet or a painter. "[Brunelleschi's] genius was so lofty that it might well be said he had been sent to us by Heaven to give a new form to architecture which had been going astray for hundreds of years," wrote Vasari, who disliked medieval architecture. "Filippo rediscovered the use of the ancient cornices and restored the Tuscan, Corinthian, Doric, and Ionic orders to their original forms." Notice the word *restored*. Like many revivals, the Renaissance was seen as the reinstatement and continuation of an earlier tradition.

The idea that a building, like a poem or a painting, could be the result of an individual imagination—or that the course of architecture could be altered by a single person—was a uniquely Renaissance concept. Not since ancient Greek times had architects been individually recognized as artists in their own right. That recognition changed the way that people looked at buildings, and it also changed the way that architects thought of themselves, placing on them the responsibility to live up to their new role. The term "architect" still described a position rather than a profession, but it was now a position of importance.

▪ ▪ ▪ ▪ ▪

Quattrocento architects and patrons who were interested in antiquity studied Roman ruins, but they had another source of firsthand information—a book. In 1414, Poggio Bracciolini, a Florentine scholar working in the library of the Abbey of Saint Gallen in Switzerland, came across a medieval parchment copy of an ancient Roman architectural treatise, the only work of its kind to survive from antiquity. Its author was Marcus Vitruvius Pollio (c. 80–15 BC), an otherwise unknown architect and military engineer. His book, *De architectura,* or On Architecture, was a detailed manual of building practice. The author also described the principles underlying Roman architecture, and for Quattrocento architects and their patrons *De architectura* could not have turned up at a more opportune moment. The precise meaning of the fragmentary Roman ruins was often elusive, and Vitruvius, who included information on the origin of the various Greek columns and the correct way to proportion and use them, helped to unravel their mysteries.

Vitruvius's book had been read throughout the Middle Ages, and it was known to fourteenth-century scholars such as Boccacio and Petrarch, but thanks to Bracciolini, handwritten copies of *De architectura* were soon circulating in Florence. The copies were in Latin, the lingua franca of Italian scholars and intellectuals (an Italian translation appeared only in 1521). Brunelleschi did not read Latin, although it is possible that his young friend Leon Battista Alberti translated passages for him. Alberti (1404–1472), the illegitimate son of an exiled Florentine banker, had studied canon law and lived in Genoa, Venice, and Bologna before coming to Florence. While there, he was befriended by Brunelleschi and wrote a book on painting and perspectival drawing, whose later Italian edition he dedicated to his mentor. Alberti subsequently moved to Rome, where he took holy orders and served as a diplomat in the papal court. The scholar-courtier-cleric was a prolific author, churning out books and pamphlets on a variety of subjects: sculpture, law, mathematics, agronomy, public speaking, the family, secret ciphers, even horsemanship and dogs.

When he was in his forties and already well known, Alberti became interested in architecture. It is a reflection of the degree to which the field had become an intellectual pursuit that it attracted the attention of such an eminent scholar. The result was a treatise, *De Re Aedifactoria,* usually translated as *On the Art of Building.* The book was modeled on Vitruvius, although Alberti found the Roman author wanting in several respects. "He wrote in such a manner that to the Latins he seemed to write Greek, and to the Greeks, Latin: but indeed it is plain from the book itself, that he wrote neither Greek nor Latin, and he might almost as well have never written at all, at least with regard to us, since we cannot understand him." The book was partly a handbook loaded with practical information about the minutiae of building construction and partly a scholarly treatise on the correct way to design using the language of antiquity. Alberti was opinionated; he was guided by Vitruvius in describing the four kinds of columns but added a fifth, which he called Composite, a combination of Ionic and Corinthian. Alberti's approach to architecture was intellectual; he wanted to give a rational underpinning to the subject. The cleric was a moralist, and he made it very clear that there was a right way and a wrong way to design.

Alberti was not only a student of architecture—he was often approached for practical advice on building design. One of his earliest clients was Giovanni Rucellai, a wealthy Florentine wool merchant and banker who was enlarging his town residence. The basic arrangement of the interior followed the conventions of the time: banking offices and work spaces on the first floor, reception rooms on the second floor, private family rooms on the third, and accommodations for the servants in the attic. Like all Florentine palazzos, the building came right up to the street, and the interior rooms surrounded a courtyard. Alberti designed the street facade using a pattern of pilasters and architraves (fig. 55). The architraves corresponded to the three floors, and the pilasters divided the hundred-foot-long facade into eight identical bays. He arranged the columns on the three floors according to the model of the Colosseum: Doric on the first floor, Ionic on the second, and Corinthian on the third. A prominent cornice terminated the composition. The flat pilasters, without flutes or entasis, were delineated by deep grooves. Arched windows were a traditional Florentine feature, but Alberti gave

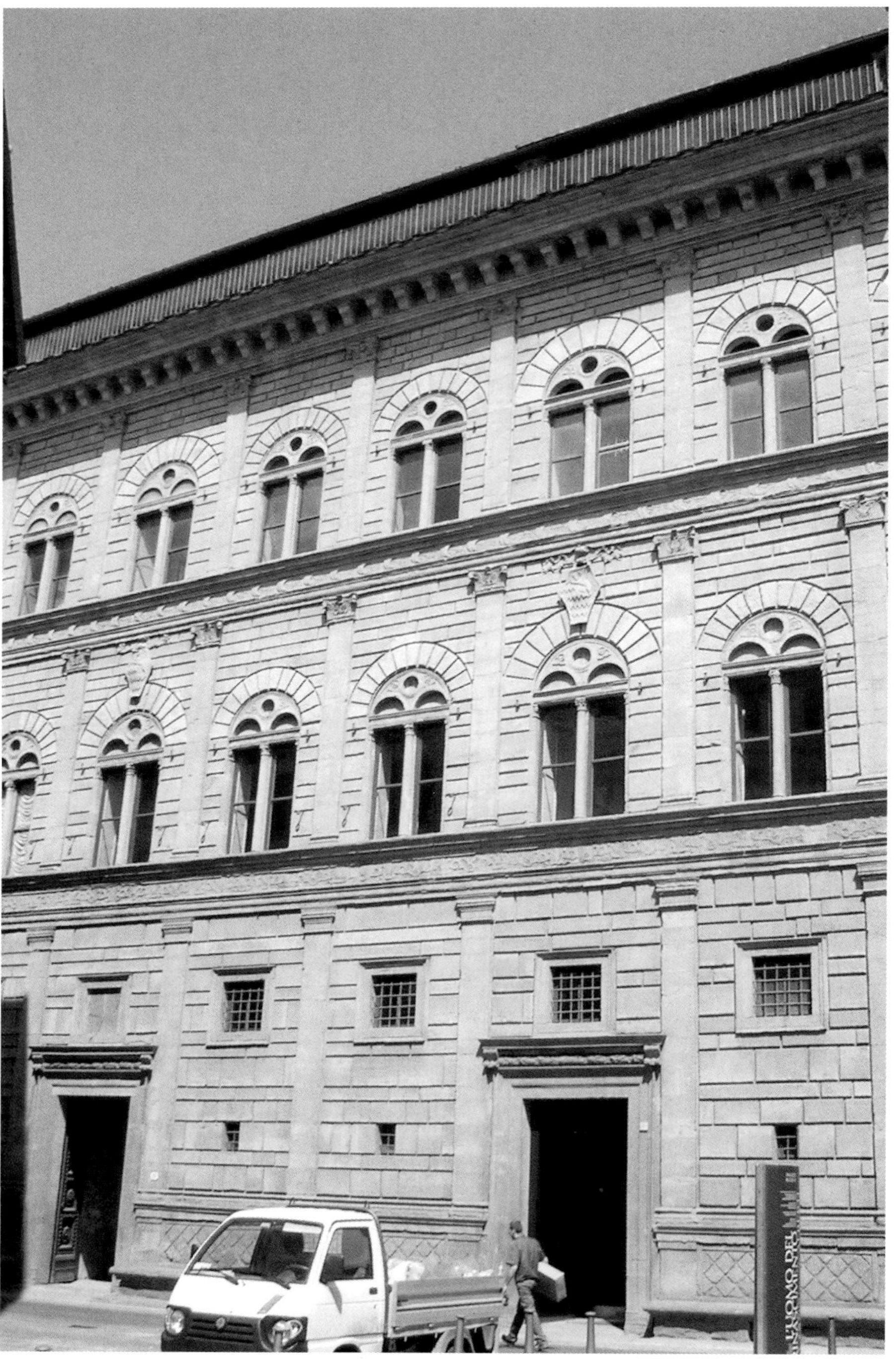

55 Palazzo Rucellai, Florence. Leon Battista Alberti, 1446–51. The hierarchic arrangement of the Roman orders in the facade pilasters was influenced by the Colosseum.

them a classical appearance by building the arches with wedge-shaped blocks called voussiors and adding roundels. The precisely chiseled facade was delicate compared to contemporaneous Florentine palazzos, which tended to be massive and resemble fortresses.

It took the best part of a decade for Rucellai to acquire all the necessary land, and it is likely that his house was built in phases, a process that would have been facilitated by the modular design of the facade (the eighth bay was never built). But Alberti's scheme was not simply a pragmatic solution to a practical problem, it was an exercise in applying columnar Roman architecture to a solid masonry wall pierced by windows. The pilasters and architraves had no structural function, they were merely symbolic. Alberti dealt with this apparent contradiction by making the classical elements so flat as to be almost diagrammatic. Nevertheless—or perhaps because of that—the Rucellai facade proved enormously influential.

Alberti's didactic scheme is architecture as the expression of an intellectual idea. To my eye, the result is rather stiff—a scholar's idea of architecture—and it lacks Brunelleschi's warm and lively grace. In some ways the two men represent the two faces of Quattrocento humanism: the intellectual and the intuitive. Alberti looked to Rome with cool calculation, aiming to rationalize the past and discover rules that could be applied to present-day building. Brunelleschi admired the past but approached it creatively rather than intellectually, open to interpretation and as ready to ignore rules as to follow them. He never explained his architectural ideas and was notoriously secretive—his early surveys of Roman ruins were written in a private code. But if asked to elaborate he might have answered gruffly, "Let the building speak for itself." Faced with a new problem, Brunelleschi resorted not to rules but to his own inventiveness. For Alberti, on the other hand, one senses that the intellectual concepts came first.

Alberti's *De Re Aedifactoria* was the first book on architecture to appear in printed form—in 1485; Vitruvius's *De architectura,* published the following year, was the second. (Like most scholars, Alberti wrote in Latin, and it was more than sixty years before an Italian edition appeared.) The invention of printing in the mid-fifteenth century allowed such architectural treatises to reach a wide audience, introducing ideas about ancient Roman architecture to many who had never been to Rome. Divorcing architectural concepts from built reality was novel. Architects had always had ideas, of course, but the ideas remained private, and they spread slowly, mainly through their assistants or through the evidence of built work. The Renaissance introduced a new ingredient to architecture: the written word. Books, printed in large numbers and easily transportable, assumed a life of their own. Moreover, once architectural ideas were put down on paper, they acquired a new potency—and a new intractability. In the process, architecture started to change, decisively and permanently, from a craft into an intellectual discipline.

15

Ancient and Novel

Rome, sixteenth century

Thus far in the story of architecture the most esteemed buildings were generally the largest and the grandest—palaces and cathedrals. In 1502, a building was erected in the cloister of the monastery church of San Pietro di Montorio in Rome that was neither large nor grand. It enclosed a space only fifteen feet in diameter, its practical function was almost nonexistent, and it stood on a cramped site in an out-of-the-way part of the city. Yet this diminutive pavilion became celebrated as one of the architectural exemplars of what is called the Roman or High Renaissance.

The architect was Donato Bramante (1444–1514). Bramante was a newcomer to Rome, having arrived in the city only three years earlier. He was born in modest circumstances in a small town outside Urbino and was trained as a painter in the court of the Duke of Urbino, a renowned patron of the arts. Bramante moved to Milan and spent twenty-five years in the service of Duke Ludovico Sforza, working first as a painter, then as an architect. The accreditation for his projects is not always clear, but it is evident that he was involved with large buildings. In 1499 Milan fell to the French, and the exile of his patron led to Bramante's departure for Rome.

When he arrived in the Eternal City, Bramante was fifty-five, and his years of experience had provided him with a solid grounding in humanist principles—one of his friends in the Sforza court had been Leonardo da Vinci. Bramante was familiar with Vitruvius's treatise, which was now available in printed form, and, like all architects coming to Rome for the first time, he was smitten by the ancient ruins. According to Vasari, "Within no great space of time he had measured all the buildings in that city and in the Campagna without; and he went as far as Naples, and wherever he knew that there were antiquities." Bramante was experienced in his craft, personable, a well-read conversationalist, and a skilled

56 Santa Maria della Pace, Rome. Donato Bramante, 1500–1504. Cloister. In this unusual design, the architect combined trabeated with arched construction, and columns with pillars.

lutenist. He was extremely ambitious, and in a city eager to take the artistic lead away from Florence and Milan, he quickly made his mark.

According to Vasari, Bramante's travels to Naples led to his first commission, rebuilding a cloister adjoining the monastery church of Santa Maria della Pace in Rome for an influential Neapolitan cardinal, Oliviero Carafa. The cloister was not large—less than fifty feet square—but Bramante made the most of the small commission. He modeled the lower arches and piers on a Roman triumphal arch, using flat Ionic pilasters on tall plinths and an entablature containing a frieze with a beautifully carved Latin inscription commemorating the cardinal's munificence (fig. 56). This elegant combination of arches and pilasters is a very early example of what would become a standard Cinquecento motif.

The height of the upper gallery of the cloister was limited by an adjoining building, which meant that Bramante could not use arches, so he substituted a simple entablature supported by alternating columns and piers. This small change broke several established conventions: there was no classical precedent for combining trabeated and arched construction in this way, nor for locating columns directly over the midpoint of the arches below. In addition, the Composite capitals of the columns were dissimilar from those of the adjacent piers. Bramante was too knowledgeable to make mistakes; he was intentionally breaking rules. Rather than simply incorporating ancient motifs in a scholarly fashion, as Alberti might have done, the irrepressible Bramante deployed the language of antiquity in an inventive manner. The result is that he turned the small cloister into a rich composition of varying rhythms, masses, and shapes. The experiment was not a complete success—the abbreviated corner piers are awkward—but, as Vasari observed, "although it was not a work of perfect beauty, it gave him a very great name, since there were not many in Rome who followed the profession of architecture with such zeal, study, and resolution as Bramante." The newcomer was getting noticed.

The San Pietro di Montorio project came to Bramante through another cardinal, the Spaniard Bernardino de Carvajal. Pope Sixtus IV had given the old monastery church of San Pietro on the Janiculum hill to a reforming order of Spanish Franciscans on the understanding that they would restore the ruined buildings. The royal patrons were the Spanish monarchs, Ferdinand of Aragon and Isabella of Castile, whose representative to the Holy See was Carvajal. San Pietro stood on what was then believed to be the site of Saint Peter's crucifixion, and Carvajal wanted to honor the exact spot of the apostle's martyrdom with a martyrium, or commemorative chapel. That was Bramante's commission. The constricted site was in the center of a small cloister next to the renovated church, and the architect proposed demolishing the cloister and rebuilding it in a larger circular shape to provide a more spacious setting. His suggestion was declined.

Bramante's martyrium resembles an ancient circular temple as described by Vitruvius and also draws inspiration from the circular Temple of Hercules Victor, the oldest surviving marble temple in Rome. Bramante used Roman spolia—Tuscan columns—and he added an entablature, the first appearance of a Doric entablature since antiquity; the entablature was historically accurate, although the metopes were decorated with papal insignia rather than pagan symbols. The soffit of the colonnade was divided into Pantheon-like coffers containing rosettes. The walls of the two stories were articulated with Tuscan pilasters that framed alternating windows and niches with half-domes in the form of conchs. The shell shapes were a rare decorative touch in what is otherwise an austere little building. The walls of the interior, a tall domed room, repeat the pattern of pilasters and niches; the crypt below is in the form of a grotto recalling an early Christian catacomb. The focus of the crypt, visible from above through an opening in the center of the chapel floor, is a square socket that marks what was believed to be the spot of the saint's crucifixion.

The classical motifs of the Tempietto (Little Temple), as the building came to be called, had their origin in antiquity, but the way that the drum of the domed

57 Tempietto, San Pietro di Montorio, Rome. Donato Bramante, 1502. This little building became a paradigm for combining antiquity with High Renaissance humanism. The lantern dates from 1605, when the dome was repaired.

building projected above the colonnade was unprecedented, as was the balustrade above the entablature, a device that would be copied in many Renaissance buildings (fig. 57). Bramante showed how to combine a "correct" classical colonnade with a Renaissance dome in a way that was both ancient and novel. The significance of this discovery was immediately recognized by his colleagues. According to Vasari, "Nothing more shapely or better conceived, whether in proportion, design, variety, or grace, could be imagined." The Tempietto was the perfect expression of High Renaissance ideals.

▪ ▪ ▪ ▪ ▪

The diminutive Tempietto revisited the age-old architectural obsession with centrally planned and domed places of worship. The idea had reemerged after Hagia Sophia in San Vitale and later in the Palatine Chapel. But because an elongated nave could more conveniently accommodate large congregations, the basilican plan remained the medieval standard, whether the church was Carolingian, Romanesque, or Gothic. Because the Renaissance was a conscious repudiation of the medieval past, it was perhaps inevitable that architects would revisit the centralized plan, especially as the Pantheon was a constant reminder of the powerful symbolism of a great dome covering the sacred space. The first centrally planned church of the Renaissance had been designed by that pioneer Brunelleschi. In 1434, late in his career, he was commissioned by the Medici family to build an oratory for the monastery of Santa Maria degli Angeli in Florence. His solution was an octagonal space covered by a dome supported on heavy piers. The fifty-five-foot dome with an oculus was modeled on the Pantheon. Niches were carved out of the thick walls. For unknown reasons, construction was discontinued after three years, and only the lower portion of the walls was completed.

In 1503, one of Bramante's early patrons, Cardinal Giuliano della Rovere, was elected pope. Strong-willed and heedless of tradition, Pope Julius II decided to replace Old Saint Peter's, which had been built by Constantine and was almost as old as Christianity itself but was in poor physical condition. He wanted a building that would be the grandest church in Christendom. The pope held a competition among several architects and picked Bramante's design (fig. 58). What appealed to Julius about the proposal was its scale. After building the smallest religious building in Rome, Bramante had gone to the other extreme: his immense design combined the cavernous space of the Basilica of Maxentius with the crowning dome of the Pantheon. Unlike Hagia Sophia, however, the plan was rigorously centralized: a giant Greek cross, with each arm terminating in an apse, and a very large dome over the crossing. The corners were marked by turrets. The four identical spaces between the arms of the cross were filled by four domed chapels, each in turn a Greek cross in plan, making for a perfectly symmetrical arrangement. The whole building measured almost five hundred feet a side, a larger footprint than Hagia Sophia. The huge dome, a hemisphere built of concrete in the Roman manner, would have surpassed even the Pantheon. Like the Tempietto, the dome sat on a drum surrounded by a colonnade. The most original aspect of the design, other than its unprecedented size, was the structure—all the domes were supported on very large piers rather than walls and columns. The piers, which were the size of small buildings, were modeled with carved-out niches and apses.

The surprise is not that Bramante designed a centrally planned basilica but that Pope Julius approved a plan that was such a radical departure from convention—not since Hagia Sophia had anyone built such a large centrally planned church. The lack of a nave was a serious drawback, but the willful pope—*il pontefice terribile,* the Romans called him—was not concerned with practicalities. He wanted a suitably grand setting for his tomb, a colossal freestanding structure with more than forty individual statues that he had commissioned from Michelangelo. Julius was sixty, and he was in a hurry. The cornerstone of the new building was laid in 1506, but only the lower part of the massive piers

58 Saint Peter's Basilica, Rome. Donato Bramante, 1506. Proposed plan.

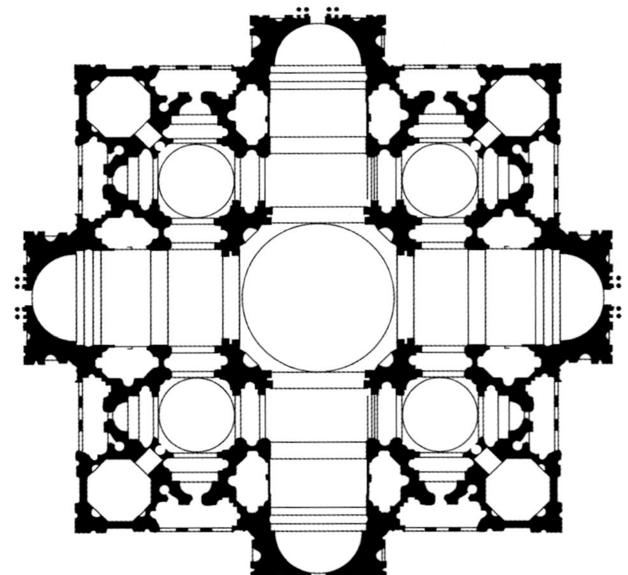

Opposite:
59 Laurentian Library, San Lorenzo, Florence. Michelangelo Buonarroti, begun in 1524. Vestibule. Antiquity is here filtered through a poetic and sculptural imagination.

and the coffered arches that connected them were completed at the time of his death in 1513. Bramante died the following year. As for the tomb, it was not completed until more than thirty years later, in a different location and in vastly reduced form.

Without Julius's drive and Bramante's genius, construction of Saint Peter's faltered; a succession of popes appointed a succession of architects who made little progress. In 1527, the mutinous troops of the Holy Roman Empire, which had invaded Italy in a war with the French, besieged, occupied, and pillaged the city. The so-called Sack of Rome had a calamitous effect on the arts, displacing artists and craftsmen and effectively marking the end of the High Renaissance. Work on Saint Peter's stopped altogether. Twenty years later, the capomaestro of Saint Peter's, Antonio da Sangallo the Younger, died. Pope Paul III's first choice as a replacement was Giulio Romano, a native Roman working in Mantua, but Romano unexpectedly died too. Paul then approached Jacopo Sansovino, who had left Rome and been appointed chief architect of the city of Venice, but Sansovino had no interest in returning. Finally, in 1546, the pope turned to the aging master Michelangelo Buonarroti.

Although Michelangelo (1475–1564) was primarily a sculptor, he was not without architectural experience. After Julius II's death, his successor, Pope Leo X, a Medici, had commissioned Michelangelo to design a facade for the Basilica of San Lorenzo, the family parish church in Florence, a building started by Brunelleschi. The facade was never built, but Michelangelo spent the following two decades in Florence working on various projects for San Lorenzo. In 1520, Pope Clement VII, another Medici, commissioned Michelangelo to add a library to house the family's large collection of manuscripts and books. The project included a vestibule that would be filled by a staircase leading up to the main reading room. This small space, only thirty-five feet square, was Michelangelo's first completed architectural commission, and as an established and celebrated artist he did not feel bound by convention. His interpretation of antiquity is so original as to be almost shocking. He designed the walls like the facade of a building, with full columns rather than flat pilasters. Constrained by existing foundations, he placed the columns inside niches and, as if to emphasize this unconventional solution, he doubled the columns and added pairs of oversized scrolled brackets (fig. 59). Like the moldings, these brackets are vigorously modeled. There are no frescoes or figural decoration, nothing to detract from the monochromatic architectural composition of columns, pediments, scrolled brackets, swags, and blank windows. This sampler of antiquity does not conform to Vitruvian, Albertian, or Bramantian rules, or indeed to any classical protocol.

Michelangelo, who had fallen afoul of the Medicis before the library was completed, fled to Rome in 1534. He devoted a good part of the following decade to frescoing the end wall of the Sistine Chapel, whose ceiling he had painted twenty-five years earlier. The last two decades of his life were spent working on several architectural projects, Saint Peter's Basilica chief among them. Michelangelo's immediate predecessor had proposed adding a short nave. Michelangelo abandoned that idea and returned to Bramante's original centralized concept, but he enlarged the piers—which needed strengthening—simplified the domed chapels, and eliminated the corner turrets, thus bringing the Greek cross concept to the fore (fig. 60). He added a deep entrance portico at the west end. The most radical change concerned the dome. Michelangelo replaced Bramante's shallow Pantheon-like dome with a tall double-skinned dome, and on the exterior, he surrounded the drum not with a colonnade but with sixteen pairs of giant freestanding Corinthian columns (fig. 61). The columns, which had no structural function, echoed the sixteen ribs of the ovoid dome. Michelangelo wanted a bright interior, and he filled the spaces between the columns with large windows.

Although the drum was completed by the time of Michelangelo's death, the dome itself was not finished until twenty-five years later in a slightly taller form.

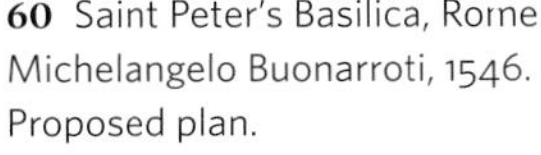

60 Saint Peter's Basilica, Rome. Michelangelo Buonarroti, 1546. Proposed plan.

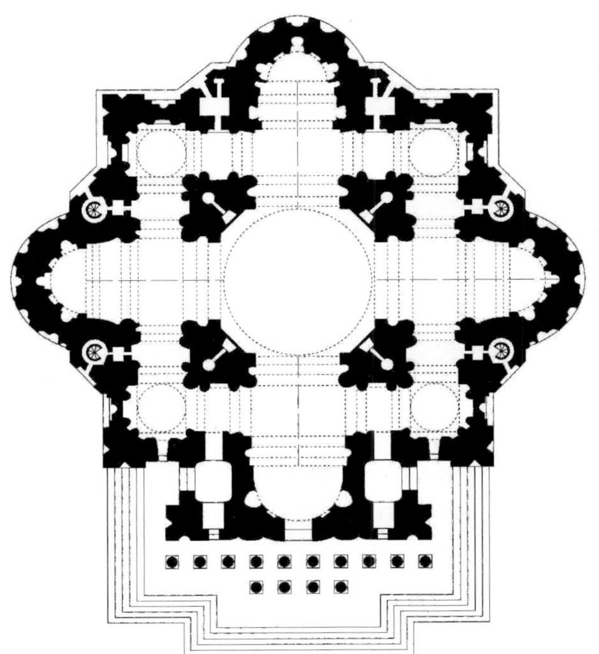

61 Saint Peter's Basilica. East end portrayed by Giovanni Battista Piranesi in an eighteenth-century etching. The massive scale of Michelangelo's syncopated rhythm of colossal paired Corinthian pilasters looms over the neighboring buildings.

There were other changes: the nave was lengthened to provide more space, and a rather banal facade was added to the front. But the east end of the building remains entirely Michelangelo's own: a lively composition of apses and angled walls overlaid by a syncopated rhythm of colossal paired Corinthian pilasters, ninety feet high. The composition of giant pilasters and wall piers mirrors the paired columns of the thrusting dome. It is a remarkable design. Despite the classical details, the undulating wall is not modeled on antiquity. Michelangelo pays obeisance to the ancient language that had been rediscovered by Brunelleschi, carefully defined by Alberti, and elaborated by Bramante, but he transcends his predecessors and turns it to his own expressive ends.

16

Villas

Venetian Republic, sixteenth century
Kyoto, seventeenth century

The revival of an ancient heritage was not the only architectural change that occurred in the sixteenth century. Thanks to Vasari, architects acquired greater authority and, following the example of Michelangelo, they were increasingly emboldened to depart from convention. At the same time, the popularization of printing ensured that architectural ideas circulated more quickly and more widely than before. These tendencies came together in the career and work of one remarkable individual. Andrea Palladio (1508–1580) stands apart from most of his contemporaries in several respects. He was trained as a mason and stonecutter, which meant that unlike most Renaissance architects, whose background was in the fine arts, he had a firsthand knowledge of construction. He did not make his name in Florence or Rome but in Vicenza, a small provincial city on the mainland of the Venetian Republic. And although he designed several notable churches at the end of his life, unlike Brunelleschi and Bramante his first commissions were not religious but domestic: not churches or cloisters but country houses.

Palladio came on the scene at an opportune time. Vicentine and Venetian nobles were investing in agricultural land, and they needed country residences commensurate with their social standing. That is what Palladio provided. The budding architect was fortunate in other ways. Living in Vicenza, he was not overly influenced by the latest fashions of Venice and Rome, and in any case grand architectural ideas did not apply to his rather modest commissions. He had the opportunity to visit Rome and study the ruins, and he pragmatically married classical details with the traditional construction methods of the Veneto mainland: plastered brick walls, timber roof beams, clay tile roofs.

Between 1540 and 1570, Palladio built more than thirty country houses. They varied in size—the smallest have only five primary rooms, the largest twenty or more—and most were on agricultural estates, though some were located in small towns and a few were suburban retreats. The villas varied in character, depending on the client. Palladio explained: "Therefore, as far as possible, one must pay particular attention to those who want to build, not so much for what they can afford as for the type of building that would suit them." His most refined clients were a pair of Venetian brothers, Daniele and Marcantonio Barbaro. Daniele, a highly placed cleric, was knowledgeable about architecture and published an Italian translation of Vitruvius for which Palladio provided the illustrations. The younger Marcantonio, a diplomat, promoted Palladio's career when the architect moved to Venice and was instrumental in securing some of his later religious commissions.

When their father died, the Barbaro brothers inherited the family estate in Maser, some thirty-five miles from Vicenza, and they jointly commissioned Palladio to build them a new house. As he did in several villas, the economically minded architect incorporated the existing house, in this case a medieval fortified *castello.* In addition to a new facade, he added two long residential wings that backed onto a steep slope, providing the second-floor rooms with direct access to a secluded terrace in the rear. Each of the brothers had a private suite—Daniele in the west wing, Marcantonio and his family in the east; the shared public rooms were in the existing central block. As in many Palladian villas, the farm functions were in close proximity to the residence: the lower floors of the new wings contained barns, wine cellars, and stables, while the pavilions at each end housed dovecotes; the south-facing arcade was used for drying grain. Barns with arcades, called *barchesse,* were traditional in the Veneto, and the novelty of Palladio's design was to connect the barchesse to the residence, partly for practical reasons but mainly to give the villa a more imposing presence.

Palladio's architecture is never shy. The central block of the Villa Barbaro is only forty feet wide, but the two spreading barchesse create an imposing facade that is more than one hundred and sixty feet across (fig. 62). Like all Renaissance architects, Palladio believed that just as symmetry was present in the human body, so should it govern building design. His villas are always bilaterally symmetrical in plan and elevation: the entrance is in the center and everything on the left is mirrored on the right. The result is a palpable sense of harmony and balance. On the interior, doors and windows are aligned. In the Villa Barbaro, the *sala,* or main living room, frescoed by Paolo Veronese (1528–1588), even included false doors that mirrored the real doors, thus preserving the symmetry of the plan.

The new temple-front facade that Palladio added to the old castello bears close examination. Why should a house resemble a temple? Palladio revered

62 Villa Barbaro, Maser. Andrea Palladio, 1554–58. The arcaded wings housed farm functions: barns, stables, wine cellars and, in the end pavilions, dovecotes.

antiquity, but because no actual Roman villas survived, and Vitruvius had little to say on the subject, there were no ancient residential models. Despite the lack of evidence, Palladio surmised—incorrectly, as it turned out—that Roman houses resembled temples, and he made a pedimented temple front the chief feature of all his villa facades. Sometimes the temple front was a projecting columned portico, sometimes it took the form of a recessed loggia, and in the Villa Barbaro it is merely suggested by Ionic half-columns and a flat pediment applied to the facade. The tympanum, or triangular face of the pediment, is filled with plaster sculpture like an ancient temple—most likely the work of Marcantonio, who was an amateur stuccoist. In addition to the family coat of arms there are two male figures—the brothers?—holding an ox skull, a common classical motif. Beneath the skull a garlanded cornucopia over arched balcony doors interrupts the entablature. By "breaking" the entablature, Palladio was consciously—and prominently—flouting a classical rule, perhaps to underline the unusual double nature of this villa. Michelangelo introduced rule-breaking and unexpected effects in the vestibule of the Laurentian Library. A taste for this kind of exaggeration, which is referred to as Mannerism, was a reaction against the strict formulas imposed by Alberti, and it was shared by many Cinquecento architects. But while Michelangelo's architecture is severe, almost forbidding, my main impression of the Villa Barbaro facade, the first time I glimpsed it from the road, was festive, a cheerful yellow and white celebration of country life.

The last villa that Palladio designed before moving to Venice, where he spent the final decade and a half of his life, was the Villa Almerico, popularly known as Villa La Rotonda (figs. 63, 64). His client was a cleric, Monsignor Paulo Almerico, who had been in the papal service in Rome and had retired to his native Vicenza. The plan of the villa, which is on the outskirts of the city, followed common practice: the lower level housed the kitchen, larders, storerooms, and servants' quarters, and the upper floor contained the main living spaces. The Almerico property was not a working farm, and the attic, which normally would have served as a granary, was here simply a "place in which to walk around the hall," in Palladio's rather vague description. The unusual plan is a function of the hilltop site, which offered views in four directions: a square house with a circular sala in the center surrounded by four identical two-room suites. The sala was for formal entertaining; the rooms were used indiscriminately for sleeping, working, and everyday dining. The four large rooms had fireplaces, while the smaller rooms and the sala were unheated. Symmetry was a Renaissance planning convention, but few architects were as rigorous as Palladio. The axes of the four porticos intersect in the center of the domed sala; doors and windows are aligned along secondary axes. The tall sala, with a gallery at the attic level, is lit by an open oculus. The resemblance to the Pantheon is unmistakable, and the use of a dome in a secular building, especially a private house, was a radical and somewhat daring departure from Renaissance convention.

Palladio's villas often have a pedimented entrance portico; La Rotonda is distinguished by having four identical Ionic porticos, one on each of its four facades. The six Ionic columns that support each portico rise the full height of the house, the two center columns being spaced slightly wider apart, as Vitruvius prescribed. Each portico is reached by a monumental stair whose scale would suit a civic building—another Mannerist exaggeration. As Vitruvius recommended, Palladio placed statues of human figures on the pediments and the stair abutments. All this is very grand, but it is accomplished with simple means. Palladio uses carved stone only for the column capitals and bases, the door and window frames, and the moldings; the rest of the exterior, including the shafts of the columns, is plastered brick; the roofing is common red clay tiles.

A large part of the charm of Palladio's villas lies precisely in the contrast between their lofty ambition and their down-to-earth execution. Not theatrical display at the price of practicality, but display *and* practicality. At the same time, for me there is something slightly contrived about La Rotonda. If a building is supposed to be designed in accord with the human body and the facade represents a face, what is one to make of a building with *four* faces? It is like the

63 Villa La Rotonda, Vicenza. Palladio, 1566–70. The hilltop villa has four identical Ionic porticos.

playfully spooky two-faced masks that Venetians wear during Carnevale, and it gives the house a slightly sinister presence.

The unusual La Rotonda eventually became widely known, not because people visited Vicenza, which is rather out of the way, but because they could read about the building in Palladio's book, *I quattro libri dell'architettura* (The Four Books on Architecture). He published the thick tome of 346 octavo pages in Venice in 1570, a decade before his death. The text was in Italian, not Latin, and the book was profusely illustrated with woodcuts based on own drawings. Palladio modeled the book on Vitruvius and Alberti, but *Quattro libri* is more like a builder's handbook than a scholar's treatise. By this time the design and use of five classical orders had been codified. Palladio devoted five pages to the Ionic order, for example, including dimensioned drawings of the capital, base, and architrave, accompanied by explanatory text and rules of thumb. The fourth book of *Quattro libri* contained reconstructions of Roman temples based on Palladio's surveys of the ancient ruins. He included Bramante's Tempietto, the only building by a contemporary that was illustrated in *Quattro libri*. Palladio explained: "Since Bramante was the first to make known that good and beautiful architecture which had been hidden from the time of the ancients till now, I thought it reasonable that his work should be placed among those of the ancients."

Palladio was not the first Renaissance treatise writer to include illustrations, but he was the first to illustrate a treatise with his own work. The second book of *Quattro libri,* which discusses residential architecture, contains more than forty of his villa and palazzo designs. Each building is described with a plan and an elevation and sometimes a cross-section; in some cases, an enlarged detail is included. The illustration of Villa La Rotonda, for example, pairs the floor plan with an ingenious drawing that combines an elevation and a cross-section and shows how the domed room rises the full height of the house (fig. 64). All the drawings are dimensioned, and the text on the facing page gives information about the client, the site, and the building program.

Palladio's treatise established an important precedent: books could be tools for disseminating not only scholarly information but also architectural designs. Understandably, the author presented his own work in its best light. For example, he did not differentiate between buildings that were completed, buildings that were as yet unfinished, and proposals that had not seen the light of day. In some

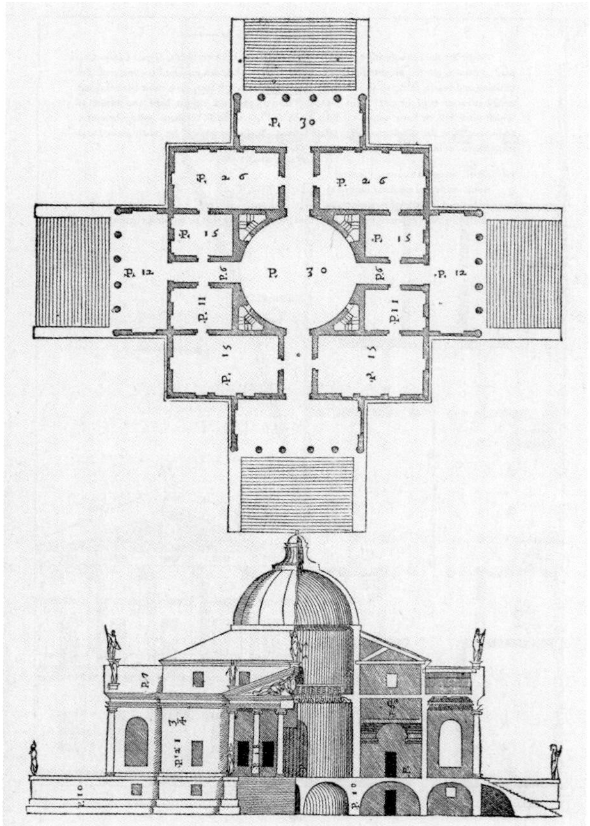

64 Villa La Rotonda. Palladio shows the house in a combined elevation and section in this drawing from *I quattro libri dell'architettura,* published in 1570.

cases, he modified the original designs, either for didactic purposes or because he had had a better idea. He did not discuss the ways that local conditions such as a client's demands or the budget had affected—or compromised—his original architectural intentions. On the building site, Palladio's creative freedom might be curtailed by forces outside his control; on the printed page he had an opportunity to document his ideal vision. Thus the illustrated book provided architects with a new speculative dimension. Not simply what was, but what could—or should—have been.

▪ ▪ ▪ ▪ ▪

Halfway around the world, another villa builder also looked to the distant past, although his inspiration was literary rather than architectural. Hachijō Toshihito (1579–1629), born the year before Palladio's death, was a prince of the royal family and the younger brother of the emperor. Toshihito lived in the ancient capital Kyōto, home of the imperial court, and when he was thirty-six he came into possession of a sixteen-acre parcel of land on the Katsura River outside the city. The location was famous as the site of a fictional mansion that featured in an eleventh-century masterpiece of Japanese literature, *The Tale of Genji,* and the prince set out to build a garden whose landscape features were modeled on passages from the book. The centerpiece of his garden was a manmade pond on which Toshihito took guests in a small roofed barge. Despite his exalted position, he was not wealthy, and the first structure he built was a rustic hut for tea ceremonies and informal get-togethers. The prince also organized moon-viewing parties inspired by the old book, whose author, the noblewoman Murasaki Shikibu, had written: "Far away, in the country village of Katsura, the reflection of the moon upon the water is clear and tranquil."

In due course, Prince Toshihito built a small villa to serve as a country retreat. In Japan, as in China, there were no architects in the Western sense, and Toshihito, who was skilled in the aristocratic arts—poetry, music, painting, calligraphy, and flower arranging—is sometimes credited with the house's design. More likely he gave general directions to the craftsmen-builders, who followed established traditions and current conventions. Japanese architecture was rooted in the sixth-century arrival of Buddhism, and although early temples and pagodas had followed Chinese models, over time the Japanese developed their own simpler and less elaborate way of building, an approach that was particularly influenced by the simple aesthetics of the Zen tea ceremony that had been established in the fourteenth century.

65 Katsura Imperial Villa, Kyoto. Hachijō Toshihito and Hachijō Toshitada, 1615–29, 1640–63. The first stage of the villa, including the moon-viewing platform, is on the right. Rough boulders serve as steps.

The naturalistic architecture of the teahouse and its surrounding garden achieved their full expression during the Edo period (1603–1868) and are visible in Toshihito's villa. Like most buildings in a country prone to earthquakes, the house was constructed of wood. The floor of the one-story post-and-beam structure was raised off the ground, and the exterior was ringed by verandas protected by large tiled roofs. A bamboo moon-viewing platform faced the pond (fig. 65). The exterior walls of the house consisted of wood and plastered panels, as well as screens—either solid (*fusuma*) or paper-covered (*shoji*)—that could be slid open to provide views of the surrounding garden. The interior was subdivided by similar sliding screens. The translucent paper screens allowed light into the house; as in China; window glass was unknown. The ceilings of Japanese houses were not particularly tall; unlike the Chinese, who developed sitting furniture, the Japanese sat or knelt on the floor, which was covered in woven rush mats (*tatami*). The dimensions of rooms were multiples of these mats, which were about three feet by six feet. Unlike Palladio's villas, whose geometric rigor often interfered with functional demands, the loose layout of the Katsura villa could accommodate a variety of different spaces suited to various activities—socializing, studying, making music, bathing, dressing, and sleeping. Built-in features included display shelves (*tokonoma*), niches, and storage cupboards.

Toshihito died less than fifteen years after building the villa. His son, Prince Toshitada (1620–1662), was only ten at the time. When the prince grew up, he married into a wealthy family, which allowed him to restore and greatly enlarge his father's building. Toshitada built a servants' wing as well as two additions, the second to accommodate a visit by the emperor. The resulting rambling structure was intentionally subordinated to the garden. The interiors were more elaborate than those built by Toshihito, partly because of the son's added wealth and partly due to changing taste. There was more embellishment in details, such as a comb-shaped window, colored screens, ornate door pulls, precious woods, and elaborate curvilinear cabinetwork. Toshitada also added several teahouses in the garden and built an arched bridge (no longer extant) whose balustrades were finished in red lacquer.

Red bridges were common in Chinese gardens, and while Japanese culture was greatly influenced by China, the architecture of Katsura is striking in the ways that it is *not* Chinese. The hip-and-gable roofs lack exaggerated curves, and the roof tiles are neither glazed nor brightly colored; there are no roof ornaments; asymmetry rather than symmetry is the rule; there are no monumental marble platforms, no painted and gilded columns, and no elaborate dougong brackets. The details are rather plain: square columns and beams, slatted wooden ceilings that conceal the roof trusses, austere interiors with rooms separated by simple paper screens. The unpainted cedar woodwork is allowed to weather and stain; the bases of columns often rest on rough boulders.

Seventeenth-century Japan isolated itself from commercial and cultural contacts with the West, and its low-key architecture was worlds apart from the grand monuments of Europe, Byzantium, and Persia. Not that there was no opulence. A villa such as Katsura provided a contrasting backdrop for the rich dress and elaborate rituals of the imperial court. The guiding aesthetic principle was *kirei-sabi,* which has been translated as worn elegance, refined rusticity, and even gorgeous humbleness. This mannered philosophy was a combination of sixteenth-century Zen Buddhism and the somewhat effete taste of the imperial court. It is particularly evident in the teahouses that Toshitada added in the garden. There are four of them, one for each season. The winter teahouse, Shokintei, is self-consciously rustic. The name was taken from *The Tale of Genji* and signifies the strumming of a *koto* (a plucked zither) and the wind whistling through pine trees. The veranda

66 Katsura Imperial Villa. Shokintei teahouse. The interior woodwork is unpainted cedar; the exterior columns are tree trunks with the bark left on. The floor is covered in tatami.

columns are made of tree trunks, the roof is thatched, and the walls are bamboo. These plain materials contrast with the conspicuous indigo and white checkerboard of the patterned shoji screens (fig. 66). The deceptively simple result is both naturalistic and studied, crude and sophisticated, imperfect and idealized. "My dwelling is but a rustic cottage," a monk tells Genji in Lady Murasaki's novel, "but still I should like you to see, at least, the pretty mountain streamlet that waters my garden."

17

The Art of Rhetoric

Rome, seventeenth century

Construction is expensive, and architecture is always dependent on economic circumstances. The Katsura villa, for example, was completed at the beginning of an extended period of prosperity following centuries of civil war. Societal changes are also a factor. By the beginning of the seventeenth century, the influence of the Japanese imperial family had declined and power was now in the hands of the Tokugawa shogunate, based in Edo (present-day Tokyo), thus Katsura represented a political as well as a personal retreat. The greatest societal change that affected European architecture in the late sixteenth century was the Counter-Reformation. To restore the moral authority of the Roman Catholic Church following the Protestant Reformation that had swept northern Europe, Pope Paul III convened the Council of Trent, which concluded in 1563 and pronounced on a host of doctrinal and liturgical issues. It also called for reforms in the arts, particularly those that affected the faithful: religious arts should encourage spiritual reflection and also reassert the predominance of the Church. For architects, the message was mixed: churches should be religiously uplifting with broad public appeal, and at the same time they should unabashedly express the ascendancy of the Church over competing faiths, that is, Protestantism.

The first major building to incorporate the teachings of the Counter-Reformation was Il Gesù, the Roman mother church of the Jesuit order. The architect was Giacomo Vignola (1507–1573), who added a traditional nave to Michelangelo's domed Greek cross, producing a plan that would influence many subsequent churches. Construction began in 1568, but Vignola died before the church was finished, and the facade (fig. 67) was completed in 1580 by his student, Giacomo della Porta (1532–1602), a Genoese sculptor and architect. Like Vignola, della Porta had worked under Michelangelo, and the master's influence is apparent in details such as the paired columns and pilasters, and the imposing

67 Church of Il Gesù, Rome. Giacomo Vignola, 1568–73. Facade by Giacomo della Porta, completed 1580. A hybrid of old and new, the architecture celebrated the Church triumphant.

scale—the pilasters of the lower half of the facade are as tall as the adjoining four-story building. The church seems even taller because the impact of the entrance is magnified by its two pediments, one inside the other. The pediments are supported on a mismatched pair of pilasters and engaged columns—a Mannerist detail. The niches contain statues of the two great Jesuit saints, Ignatius of Loyola and Francis Xavier, and the cartouche over the entrance contains the monogram IHS, the first three Greek letters of the name of Christ, which Loyola adopted for the Jesuit seal. The inscription across the facade commemorates the Farnese cardinal who funded the church.

Della Porta's hybrid facade combines Mannerist Michelangelesque motifs with giant scrolled brackets, which Alberti had introduced a hundred years earlier in a Florentine church. The most striking aspect of the facade is its assertiveness, which is the result of the vigorous modeling of the entablature, which casts jagged shadows across the receding planes of travertine. This dramatic quality anticipates a particular brand of theatrical classicism that would develop

68 Saint Peter's Baldacchino, Rome. Gian Lorenzo Bernini, 1623–34. Seventeenth-century engraving. The gilded bronze structure is almost one hundred feet high.

more fully in the next century and would be called Baroque, a term that was first applied—disparagingly—to seventeenth-century music and originally meant something needlessly complicated or even bizarre.

The leading architect of the Baroque period was Gian Lorenzo Bernini (1590–1680). Born in Naples, he was a child prodigy, widely hailed as the successor to Michelangelo. Handsome and glamorous, Bernini was primarily a sculptor, but he also painted, designed fountains and tombs, and wrote, produced, and even acted in plays. When his patron was elected Pope Urban VIII, the twenty-three-year-old Bernini received his first architectural commission: a monumental baldacchino, or canopy over the tomb of Saint Peter in Michelangelo's great church (fig. 68). The gilded bronze structure was more theatrical than the rather dry architecture of Vignola and della Porta, and it incorporated a profusion of dramatic ornament, leafy vines, and tassels, all cast in bronze. The four colossal spiral columns were intended to recall King Solomon's temple; the canopy itself consisted of four great volutes and resembles a crown. Angels,

69 Saint Peter's Square. Gian Lorenzo Bernini, 1656–67. The curved rows of colossal Doric columns create a constantly changing and endless vista.

twice life-size, stood at the four corners of the curving cornice, a hundred feet up in the air.

Bernini's magnificent canopy is located in the crossing of Saint Peter's Basilica, directly below the great dome. Michelangelo would have hated it, and not only because this was the place originally intended for Julius's tomb. Although Saint Peter's is today richly embellished with multicolored marble, painted stucco, and gilt, the original interior was stark and undecorated, similar to the Laurentian Library, making the modeled architecture and the majestic space the focus of attention. Compared to this severe vision, Bernini's dazzling concoction, which was calculated to appeal to his patron and to the public alike, was almost operatic. As happened before in the story of architecture—and would happen again—minimalism had been succeeded by maximalism.

Thirty years later, when the facade of Saint Peter's was completed, a subsequent pope, Alexander VII, commissioned Bernini to design an outdoor square in front of the basilica where crowds could gather to receive papal benedictions. Bernini's solution was both simple and grand: a trapezoidal space directly in front of the church, preceded by a vast oval plaza the size of the Colosseum. The plaza was defined by curved colonnades that Bernini described as arms welcoming the faithful. The colonnades consisted of four rows of giant marble columns, and were wide enough to contain a sixty-foot carriageway (fig. 69). Although

Bernini and the pope had considered a Corinthian order to match the pilasters of the basilica facade, they settled on the simpler Doric. Bernini, who had no interest in historical accuracy, made the column shafts more slender than convention dictated and added an Ionic frieze. He placed twelve-foot-tall statues of popes and saints on top of the entablature—"a cloud of witnesses," he called them.

As one moves along the curve of the giant colonnade, the constantly changing perspective creates a never-ending vista. There are two hundred and eighty-four travertine columns. The overlapping row after row of fifty-foot shafts recalls the giant halls of ancient Egypt. Authentically Egyptian is the four-thousand-year-old red granite obelisk that had been brought from Alexandria by the Emperor Caligula, and which Bernini relocated to the center of the plaza. The overall effect is spectacular.

▪ ▪ ▪ ▪ ▪

Unlike Michelangelo, who worked more or less alone, Bernini managed a large workshop. One of his architectural assistants, who worked on the Baldacchino, was the Swiss-born Francesco Borromini (1599–1667). Borromini, son of a stonemason and trained as a stonecutter, was a talented draftsman and, like so many Renaissance architects, he was a student of antiquity. He had none of Bernini's considerable social skills, however, being of a melancholy and somewhat neurotic disposition, and when the two men eventually became rivals, it was usually Bernini who came out on top. Borromini was thirty-nine when he received his first independent commission, a monastic complex on the Quirinal Hill for a community of Spanish monks, the Order of the Most Holy Trinity. The focus of the building, which included a cloister, was a small church dedicated to Saint Charles Borromeo, a leading figure of the Counter-Reformation. The church of San Carlo alle Quattro Fontane, which Romans refer to affectionately as San Carlino, demonstrates Borromini's creative genius—and how far architecture had moved from the prim geometry of the Quattrocento.

The nave of the church is shoehorned into an awkward corner site and is hemmed in by a staircase and hallway, a sacristy, and two small chapels (fig. 70). The rounded-off arms of the Greek cross plan consist of four apses containing the main altar, two side altars, and the entrance. A sinuous modeled entablature supported by sixteen giant columns surrounds the space. The engaged columns, which appear to be freestanding, are irregularly spaced and the order is nominally Composite but reconfigured by the inventive Borromini. Above the entablature, pendentives support a complex coffered elliptical dome topped by a tall lantern (fig. 71). It is a breathtaking composition, made all the more vertiginous by being squeezed into a tiny space—although the dome rises eighty feet, the nave is only about thirty feet wide. While Bernini used rich materials and a monumental scale to celebrate his grand patrons, Borromini, whose commission was more modest, achieved his spatial complexity by simpler means. The chaste interior of San Carlo was built with plastered brick—no multicolored marble and gilt. The entire interior, except for the painter Pierre Mignard's altarpiece, was stuccoed and painted white. As a result, the chief impression is of an ethereal space flooded by daylight from the tall windows and the lantern.

The impoverished Trinitarians ran short of funds and were unable to complete the facade of the church, and Borromini returned to finish the work twenty years later, shortly before his premature death (a lifelong depressive, he committed suicide). It is said that he forfeited his fee for San Carlo, so keen was he to build; in return, the Trinitarians gave him a free hand. The tiny facade, barely sixty feet wide, is a remarkable example of Baroque theatricality (fig. 72). The main elements are two superimposed giant orders. The four engaged columns are Borromini's fanciful interpretation of Corinthian below and Composite above. The entablatures are triple curves: convex-concave-convex on the lower level, and convex-convex-convex on the upper. The result is a kind of architectural syncopation. The giant columns enclose smaller orders—a motif borrowed from Michelangelo—that in turn support niches. A curious cylindrical temple-like

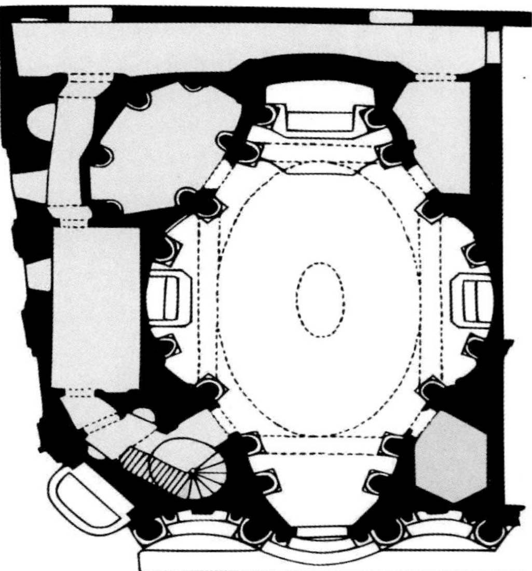

70 San Carlo alle Quattro Fontane, Rome. Francesco Borromini, 1638–46. Plan. The church is shoehorned into an awkward corner site.

71 San Carlo alle Quattro Fontane. Interior looking toward the entrance. The sinuous entablature supported on giant engaged Composite columns surrounds a rounded-off Greek cross plan.

form, or aedicule, in the central portion of the upper floor further enriches this composition. When I visited the church as a student and tried to sketch the facade I quickly got lost in the overlapping rhythms; it was like trying to unravel the intricacies of a piano riff by Art Tatum.

The facade is densely populated by figural sculpture. In the central niche, over the entrance, a statue of Saint Charles Borromeo is flanked by two angelic caryatids; in the niches on either side are the two Trinitarian founders, Saint John of Matha and Saint Felix of Valois. At the very top, two hovering angels support a giant medallion that originally contained a fresco of the Holy Trinity. As if that were not enough, the medallion interrupts the upper entablature and is capped by a curious ogee shape that comes to a point, echoing the pointed angels' wings below. The upper part of the facade is essentially a false front and was completed after Borromini's death by his nephew. The language of Baroque architects is oratorical compared to the measured tones of their Quattrocento predecessors, yet Borromini's work is not simply declamatory. Instead of theatrical gestures there is a sense of continuous and fluid motion in which the parts are always

72 San Carlo alle Quattro Fontane. Despite its constrained setting, the small facade, completed in 1667–70, is a remarkable example of Baroque theatricality.

subservient to the agitated gyrating whole. Standing in the narrow street, you are overwhelmed by the interlocking shapes and rhythms. Architecture is generally a reflection of the shared values of the day, yet on rare occasions it ventures into the realm of the deeply personal, which is the case with Borromini's restless and idiosyncratic creation.

18

Classicism

Paris and London, seventeenth century

In the late 1600s, Louis XIV began a major enlargement of the Louvre Palace, which had been the royal residence since the fourteenth century. The most publicly visible part of the new additions was a new wing on the east side that would feature an imposing facade five hundred feet long facing the Place du Louvre. To finesse the controversial selection of an architect for this important project, the king's chief minister and superintendent of building, Jean-Baptiste Colbert, decided to bring in a foreign star. Bernini, now sixty-six and the most famous artist in Europe, was the obvious choice. In 1664, Colbert sent a representative to Rome, and Bernini accepted the commission. In due course he sent drawings of his proposal, a highly modeled building with a round central pavilion and concave arcades. This, as well as a modified version, was rejected by Colbert because it would have required demolishing too much of the existing palace. The nonplussed Bernini, used to getting his way, nevertheless agreed to continue working on the prestigious commission and arranged to make a five-month visit to Paris. Once there, he modified his proposal according to his client's wishes. The final design consisted of a three-story facade with a giant order of engaged columns and pilasters on a rusticated base. The plan was accepted, a cornerstone was laid in a formal ceremony, and Bernini returned to Rome leaving an assistant to deal with the details.

Behind the scenes, Colbert was not happy. He considered the Louvre to be a political symbol as well as a royal residence, and he wanted the home of his monarch to publicly proclaim its occupant's regal authority. The problem was that Bernini's facade was distinctly unimpressive—as in an Italian palazzo, he reserved the grandest effects for the interior. There were also practical problems. Bernini was treated with great deference in Rome, and he had a difficult time with the insistent—and thrifty—Colbert. Moreover, the maestro was not used to dealing with mundane issues such as room sizes, daylighting, and sanitation. Nor did his imperious behavior help. Although Bernini established a friendly rapport with the young king, of whom he sculpted a splendid marble bust, his scornful pronouncements about what he considered the shortcomings of French art and architecture earned him many enemies at court. Colbert belatedly realized that he may have made a mistake in inviting the Italian master. Two years after Bernini's departure, his proposal was quietly but definitively shelved.

Colbert gave the responsibility for preparing a brand-new design to a three-man committee, the so-called Petit Conseil, whose members were Louis Le Vau (1612–1670), the royal architect who was coordinating the rebuilding of the Louvre; Charles Le Brun (1619–1690), the king's personal painter and decorator; and François Mansart (1598–1666), the country's leading architect, who had introduced Baroque classicism to France. When Mansart unexpectedly died, Colbert appointed Claude Perrault to take his place. Perrault (1613–1688) was neither an architect nor a painter but a physician. More to the point, he was the older brother of Colbert's trusted secretary, Charles Perrault (best remembered today as the author of the Mother Goose fairy tales). Claude Perrault belonged to the newly formed Academy of Sciences, and his wide interests included anatomy, botany—and architecture. Colbert had earlier entrusted him with the preparation of an annotated French translation of Vitruvius, a project that gave Perrault the opportunity to review not only various editions of Vitruvius but also to become familiar with the written work of Alberti, Palladio, Vignola, and others. At the time, French architects fell into two camps with respect to *classicisme* (the first use of the word in a European language): the so-called Ancients and Moderns. The former, who represented the architectural establishment, believed in strict adherence to the rules of antiquity as described by Vitruvius, whereas the latter held that modern times required an expansion of the ancient lexicon. In this quarrel, Claude Perrault sided with the Moderns, which appealed to Colbert.

The design of the East Front of the Louvre was produced and approved in only three months. The design was a groundbreaking departure from convention, an immense loggia fronted by a colonnade that was interrupted by a prominent central entrance and terminated by projecting bays (fig. 73). The entrance, which combines a temple front and a triumphal arch, is surmounted by a large pediment and contains an arched opening that is gracefully echoed by the windows of the end bays. While the bulk of the colonnaded front is relatively plain, the bays and the pediment are decorated with low-relief sculpture. The use of bays, or *pavilions,* as the French called them, was not unusual, but the design of the colonnade

73 East Front, Louvre, Paris. Louis Le Vau, Charles Le Brun, and Claude Perrault, 1668–70. This facade, designed according to a rational logic, is a prime example of French classicisme.

was novel: paired freestanding columns in the loggia, paired engaged columns in the entrance pavilion, and paired pilasters in the end pavilions. The giant columns were Corinthian with fluted shafts. Michelangelo had earlier introduced the idea of pairing columns, but no one had ever used them this way, in a colonnade. Perrault is often credited with the idea, although the entire facade is too accomplished to be the work of a novice and he surely benefited from the presence of the experienced Le Vau.

The East Front of the Louvre is considered one of the triumphs of French Baroque. Its grand scale is comparable to Bernini's colonnade at Saint Peter's, as is its dramatic impact, although the composition is more complex. The hierarchy of an entrance pavilion, two arms, and terminating pavilions recalls Palladio's Villa Barbaro, but with more pomp and circumstance—an orchestral work rather than chamber music. The giant order on a base, the flat roof, and the rooftop balustrades came directly from Bernini's proposal, but there the similarity ended. A residential building requires many windows, and whereas rows of repetitive windows were a prominent—and rather monotonous—feature of Bernini's proposal, Perrault's colonnade kept the windows literally in the background, behind the colonnade. Moreover, while Bernini's composition appears somewhat arbitrary, the new stately facade was rationally composed according to a logical hierarchy. In a word, it was French.

French architects were just as interested in antiquity as their Roman counterparts, but in not being surrounded by ancient ruins their approach was less influenced by precedent and more conditioned by theory. French classicisme was rational, disciplined, and balanced. In characteristic fashion, the whole enterprise was institutionalized in the rigorous curriculum of the Académie des

74 Queen's House, Greenwich. Inigo Jones, 1616–35. South facade. The first classical building in England was influenced by Jones's firsthand experience of Palladio, as shown in this 1715 engraving.

Beaux-Arts, which taught painting, sculpture, and architecture and which had been founded in 1648 by Colbert's predecessor, Cardinal Mazarin.

By the time that the Louvre facade was completed in 1680, Louis had moved his court out of the city to nearby Versailles. The king commissioned Le Vau and Le Brun (without Perrault) to enlarge what had been a hunting lodge into a full-blown palace. Later, Jules Hardouin-Mansart (1646–1708), the grand-nephew of the famous architect, expanded the palace into the largest royal residence in Europe, with a garden facade that is almost three times as long as the East Front. It is the size of the palace rather than its details that is most impressive, a suitably monumental home for the absolute monarch whom his subjects called Louis Le Grand.

■ ■ ■ ■ ■

Classicism arrived late in England. At the time that Italian architects were starting to explore Baroque, English architecture remained a conservative blend of fussy Flemish and Elizabethan styles. The man who single-handedly changed this was Inigo Jones (1573–1652). Jones, who started his career as a painter and designer of court masques, had lived in Italy and was intimately familiar with the buildings of the High Renaissance. He was not drawn to the Mannerism of Michelangelo and his followers, however, preferring the simpler designs of architects such as Palladio. This preference is apparent in the Queen's House in Greenwich, designed for Anne of Denmark, James I's queen and Jones's patron (fig. 74). This restrained little garden bijoux—the first classical building in England—was a radical departure from the elaborate Jacobean style that prevailed in Jones's day. He had visited several of Palladio's villas, and his severe design, with its rusticated base and plain second floor, is distinctly Palladian in its symmetry, the proportions of its rooms, and its balanced composition. There is a demure Ionic loggia on the south side, although no pediment.

Jones was Surveyor-General of the King's Works, or effectively the royal architect, and this position, the prominence of his commissions, and his exceptional talent ensured that classicism became the dominant national style. So much so that when Jones was repairing and remodeling London's venerable Saint Paul's Cathedral he grafted—somewhat awkwardly—a Corinthian portico to the Gothic west front. His influence on English architecture might have been greater had not the civil war put an abrupt end to his career. By the time of the Restoration, eighteen years later, Jones was dead and his austere Palladian version of classicism had fallen out of favor.

The Great Fire of 1666, which destroyed the entire center of London, was a momentous event that altered the course of English architecture. The responsibility for reconstruction of the destroyed religious monuments fell on the shoulders of Christopher Wren (1632–1723). Like Bernini, he was a prodigy, though not in the arts but in mathematics. His brilliance was recognized early, and at a young age he was appointed to a prestigious Oxford professorship in astronomy. When Wren was thirty-seven, Charles II named him assistant to the Surveyor-General of the King's Works, and eight years later Wren assume the post of Surveyor-General. As we have seen with the example of Claude Perrault, in the seventeenth century there was no hard and fast divide between architecture and science, and it was not unusual for a prominent scientist, especially a mathematician, to be given architectural responsibilities. Unlike Perrault, however, who remained an architectural dilettante, Wren became a full-fledged practitioner. He was responsible for the royal palace at Hampton Court, new military hospitals at Greenwich and Chelsea, and, after the Great Fire, no fewer than fifty parish churches in London.

Wren's great task was rebuilding Saint Paul's Cathedral, which had been severely damaged in the fire. There was talk of restoring the Gothic structure, which dated back to the eleventh century, but it was finally decided to replace it with an entirely new building in a modern—that is, classical—style. Wren's first proposal, which conservatively reused the old foundations, was judged to be too modest. He next produced a splendid centrally planned domed church whose Greek cross plan owed a lot to Bramante and Michelangelo. The king liked this proposal and Wren refined it, adding a short nave, an entrance portico at the west end, and a small dome over the narthex. He spent the next ten months building a large wood and plaster model—more than twenty feet long and large enough to stand inside. To his dismay, his proposal was rejected. The new building would take decades to build, and the cathedral clerics wanted a choir to be built first so that it could be used for services in the interim, which was impossible with a centralized plan. The clergy also wanted a traditional nave. Finally, there was a general feeling that the resemblance to Saint Peter's in Rome was inappropriate for an Anglican cathedral.

Wren's final proposal responded to all the objections: instead of a centralized plan he provided a Latin cross plan with an extended three-bay choir that could be built first, and a long five-bay nave. The tall crossing spire of the old cathedral had been a beloved landmark in the city, and Wren designed a tall lantern atop a low dome over the crossing. This proposal was approved, but Wren had a card up his sleeve. The king generously stipulated that the architect should have "the Liberty, in the Prosecution of his Work, to make some Variations, rather ornamental, than essential, as from Time to Time he should see proper; and to leave the Whole to his own Management." Wren interpreted this liberty very freely. This time he did not build a model, and he left the details of his design vague, allowing him to introduce modifications during construction. Chief among them was to replace the lantern, an odd structure that resembled a pagoda, with a magisterial dome almost three hundred feet high and more than a hundred feet in diameter.

The dome of Saint Paul's is Wren's great achievement (fig. 75). Although obviously influenced by Michelangelo's dome for Saint Peter's, which Wren had not seen, the structural solution was based on Jules Hardouin-Mansart's recently completed Dôme des Invalides in Paris, which Wren had visited. Like Hardouin-Mansart, Wren built a triple dome: a lead-covered wooden outer dome, a masonry inner dome that was viewed from inside the church, and, concealed between the two, a brick cone that supported the heavy stone lantern. The drum supporting Wren's dome was neither richly Baroque like the Invalides nor Mannerist like Saint Peter's. Instead, it looked further back—to Bramante's Tempietto. Wren surrounded the drum with a continuous colonnade of giant Corinthian columns standing well clear of the wall. The engaged columns are attached to short walls with arched openings that act as buttresses and resist the sideways thrust of the dome, with every fourth intercolumniation filled in to further strengthen the structure. Like Bramante's Tempietto, the colonnade is surmounted by a balustrade and a second smaller drum. The pilasters of this drum are not pronounced; neither are the shallow ribs of the dome itself. The beautiful lantern, on the other hand, which is as tall as the dome itself, is an exquisite aedicule, or little building, a miniature Baroque temple in the sky.

Wren was an empiricist; Saint Paul's has a Gothic plan, a High Renaissance dome, and a Baroque lantern. The west front is likewise Baroque (fig. 76). The

75 Saint Paul's Cathedral, London. Christopher Wren, 1668–1711. The design of the dome surrounded by a continuous colonnade recalls Bramante's Tempietto.

chief compositional devices of the two-story facade are paired columns and pilasters; tall Corinthian below and shorter Composite above. The columns and pilasters serve to organize the facade in a similar fashion to Il Gesù, although the columns of the deep portico are fluted in the manner of Perrault's Louvre colonnade. To express the transition from the wider nave-plus-aisles below to the narrow nave above, Wren and his talented assistant Nicholas Hawksmoor (1661–1736) did not use scrolled brackets but simply extended the lower entablature—a highly unorthodox solution but executed so skillfully that one scarcely notices the inconsistency. Statues adorn the pediment in Palladian fashion: Saint Paul in the center, flanked by Saint Peter and Saint James. The relief sculpture in the tympanum of the pediment portrays the conversion of Saint Paul. Twin towers had been a fixture of west fronts since medieval times, but their design here is a combination of curves and angles topped by gilded pineapples. The richly

76 Saint Paul's Cathedral, west front. Neither Mannerist nor Baroque, the facade is an empirical mixture of classical elements.

modeled towers are Borrominiesque, but there are no curves in the facade itself. The monumental scale, the paired columns, and the vigorous modeling of the portico are Baroque, although with little of that style's theatricality. Instead, the overall effect of this restrained classicism is balance and harmony.

In Catholic countries, the eminence of Rome ensured classicism's primacy, but thanks to the fame of Michelangelo and Bernini, classicism also took hold in the Protestant north. That was one of classicism's strengths; it could be adapted to suit different building traditions and different national tastes, even different religious beliefs. Seventeenth-century British classicism—many of its most skilled adepts were Scots—was different from the Italian and French versions. Its historical foundation was identical, however, and visiting the antiquities of Rome became an indispensable part of a British architect's education. For those unable to travel, the treatises of Palladio, Alberti, and Vitruvius provided useful tools for gleaning "the best of ye ansientes," as Inigo Jones put it. His own work had demonstrated the flexibility of classical rules. "The libberty of Composing wth reason is not Taken awaye," he wrote in his distinct orthography. That liberty was one of classicism's strengths, too.

19

The Square of the Map of the World

Isfahan and Agra, seventeenth century

Classicism dominated seventeenth-century Europe; elsewhere, other deeply rooted traditions prevailed. The homegrown Chinese way of building, which influenced Japan, dated back to the third century. The roots of Islamic architecture were more recent, an amalgam of Byzantine, Roman, and Persian influences. It is worth looking more closely at the last because Persian architecture began even earlier than Chinese, in the sixth century BC. At its height, the Achaemenid Empire of Cyrus the Great stretched from present-day Libya to the Indus River; it remained a potent force for a thousand years. The deeply rooted Persian culture—and its language—survived several incursions: the Arab conquest of the seventh century and the Mongol invasions of the thirteenth and fourteenth centuries. Following the 1501 founding of the Safavid dynasty, which established Shia Islam as the official religion, Persia regained its independence, and its sprawling multiethnic empire included not only present-day Iran and much of Iraq but also parts of Turkey, Afghanistan, and Pakistan.

The consolidation of the Persian Empire was the work of the fifth Safavid ruler, Shah Abbas I, known as the Great. In addition to being a successful military and political strategist, Abbas was a builder. In 1598 he moved his capital from the northern city of Qazvin to Isfahan, whose central location provided greater security from Persia's traditional enemy, the Ottoman Turks. The imperial city, which would grow to half a million, became one of the largest and most beautiful cities in the civilized world. The farsighted Abbas renovated the caravansaries and bazaars of the old town, turning Isfahan into an important stop on the Silk Road. He built a boulevard-like grand avenue with rows of trees and a central canal, linking the old city to a monumental bridge over the Zayandeh River. Abbas had a pragmatic approach to urban planning. He laid out a new residential district with a leafy grid of houses and private gardens but also preserved the

77 Maidan, Isfahan. Drawing by Pascal Coste, a French architect who visited Persia in 1839. The Maidan, built at the beginning of the seventeenth century, was the commercial, administrative, and religious center of Isfahan, the capital of the Persian Empire. The great Shah Mosque is in the center, the tiled dome of the smaller Sheikh Lotfollah Mosque is visible on the left, and the tribune of the royal palace is on the right.

traditional narrow, winding streets of the old quarter. The focus of his capital was an immense twenty-acre sand-covered rectangular square that was used for horse racing and polo, as well as for markets and festivals, and was surrounded by a two-story arcade containing shops (fig. 77). The square was called Maidan-e Naqsh-e Jahan, or the Square of the Map of the World.

The Maidan was Isfahan's commercial, administrative, and religious center. The four sides of the square were occupied by the entrance to the Grand Bazaar, the imperial palace, the private imperial mosque, and, at the far southern end, the Shah Mosque, the main mosque of the city. The Grand Bazaar was a mile-long vaulted market street linking the Maidan to the old quarter. The imperial palace was a sprawling complex of domestically scaled pavilions surrounded by gardens—somewhat similar to the Forbidden City. Only one building of this complex has survived, a six-story block facing the Maidan that includes a raised open-air tribune from which the shah and his retinue could watch sporting events. Opposite the palace across the Maidan was the Sheikh Lotfollah Mosque, named after a famous imam who was the shah's father-in-law. This building, which was for the exclusive use of the imperial household and was linked to the palace by an underground passage, is considered one of the masterpieces of Safavid architecture.

Persia had an ancient architectural tradition—the monuments of the powerful Achaemenid Empire, whose impressive ruins are still visible in Persepolis, predate the Parthenon—and Safavid architects were influenced by this tradition. The Maidan facade of the Lotfollah Mosque exhibits many characteristic Persian features (fig. 78). First, bilateral symmetry, both in plan and elevation: everything on the left is mirrored on the right. Bilateral symmetry was shared with European classicism, but there the similarity ends. There is nothing classical about Persian architecture—not a pilaster or column in sight. What are in evidence are pointed arches, both structural and ornamental. This shape emerged in Persia prior to the Arab conquest and predates the Gothic pointed arch by several hundred years. The inventive Persian builders also developed horseshoe arches and double-curve ogee arches that, like pointed arches, spread throughout the Muslim world and as far away as Venice. The facade of the Lotfollah Mosque is divided into panels and reminds me of a patchwork of prayer carpets. The flat walls contain three deep portals whose vaulted ceilings are covered by a honeycomb of muqarnas vaults constructed of plastered brick. Muqarnas vaulting, the ancestor of the Arab mocárabes, appeared in Persia as early as the tenth century.

The most striking aspect of the Lotfollah facade is the treatment of the walls. What would have been a richly modeled expression of structure in European classicism—pilasters, engaged columns, and entablatures—are largely flat surfaces. Flat but richly decorated in elaborate patterned tilework. Tiles were a consistent feature of Persian architecture since the Achaemenid period. Lacking a supply of good building stone, the Persians built in clay brick and covered the surfaces with glazed brick and mosaic tile. Persian carpet weaving also dates to this time and surely influenced the mosaic designs—or was it the other way around?

78 Sheikh Lotfollah Mosque, Isfahan. Sheikh Baha'i, 1603–19. The facade facing the Maidan is richly decorated with polychrome mosaic tilework that resembles a collage of prayer carpets.

Given its private function, the compact Lotfollah Mosque did not require minarets or an outdoor prayer court. The main hall, turned forty-five degrees to face Mecca, is a tall room about sixty feet square, covered by a dome and lit by grilled windows in the drum. The surfaces of the interior walls and the drum are covered in floral and geometric patterns: black, blue, green, and yellow mosaics in arabesque and floral patterns, as well as many inscriptions—Koranic extracts, Shi'ite sayings, and poetic verses. The dome is a sunburst pattern made with lozenge-shaped tiles that decrease in size as the dome rises, the glazed and unglazed tiles changing colors depending on the time of day. The sparkling exterior of the onion dome is also tiled: the drum is predominantly turquoise, the dome itself is buff colored with white, blue, and black arabesques. These complex multicolored patterns transform the dome into an object of ethereal and numinous beauty.

The architect of the mosque and the planner of Isfahan was Bahāʾ al-Dīn Muhammad ibn Husayn al-ʿĀmilī (1547–1621), known as Sheikh Baha'i. Baha'i, born in Ottoman Syria, was a scientist-architect in the mold of Christopher Wren, equally famous as a renowned astronomer and mathematician as for his philosophical writings. Like Wren, Baha'i was an empiricist, and the basic elements of his buildings—domes, pointed arches, muqarna—dated back hundreds of years. This is particularly evident in the Shah Mosque, the main mosque of the city that stands at the southern end of the Maidan.

The entrance to the Shah Mosque is through a monumental portal that interrupts the shopping arcade and frames a deep outdoor porch with a vaulted ceiling covered in muqarnas. The arched portal, or iwan, was a traditional device in Persian architecture that originated in the third century and was used in both secular and religious buildings. The portal was framed inside a richly patterned freestanding screen wall, and, like theater scenery, it was intended to be seen only from the front. The iwan of the Shah Mosque, flanked by two slender ornamental minarets, is oriented to the Maidan, but the mosque itself is turned forty-five degrees to face Mecca, and the plan adroitly handles this angular shift (fig. 79). After passing though the iwan, the worshipper enters a large paved courtyard with a central pool for ritual ablutions. The courtyard is surrounded by a two-story arcade of pointed arches interrupted on each side by a large iwan; this so-called four-iwan plan dates to the third century. The iwans on the east and west sides of the mosque lead to madrassas, or religious schools, each planned around a private courtyard and including a small prayer hall. The largest iwan marks the entrance to the main prayer hall.

The prayer hall of the Shah Mosque is very different from an Arab hypostyle hall. The square chamber is covered by a single large dome; two rectangular flanking halls that accommodate additional worshippers are each roofed by eight smaller domes. The pointed arches supporting the smaller domes rest on stubby octagonal columns with simplified capitals, but on the whole, Persian builders downplayed structure. Instead, they covered the surfaces of the walls and domes in complex tilework. Religious rules forbade the representation of human images, but thanks to calligraphy, the decorated surfaces were extraordinarily rich in meaning. In many respects, these multicolored graphic patterns *are* the architecture.

The chief architectural feature of the Shah Mosque is the prayer hall dome, seventy-five feet in diameter. Unlike the Arabs, the Persians were accomplished dome builders, and examples of large domes date back to as early as the third century. (The ancient Persians invented the squinch, which, like a pendentive, enabled domes to be combined with square rooms.) Monolithic domes, built of brick, were used in a variety of buildings: tombs, mosques, and bazaars. Persian domes did not have lanterns or oculi but ended in a point; illumination was through grilled openings in the drum. The Shah Mosque introduced the double dome, a tall,

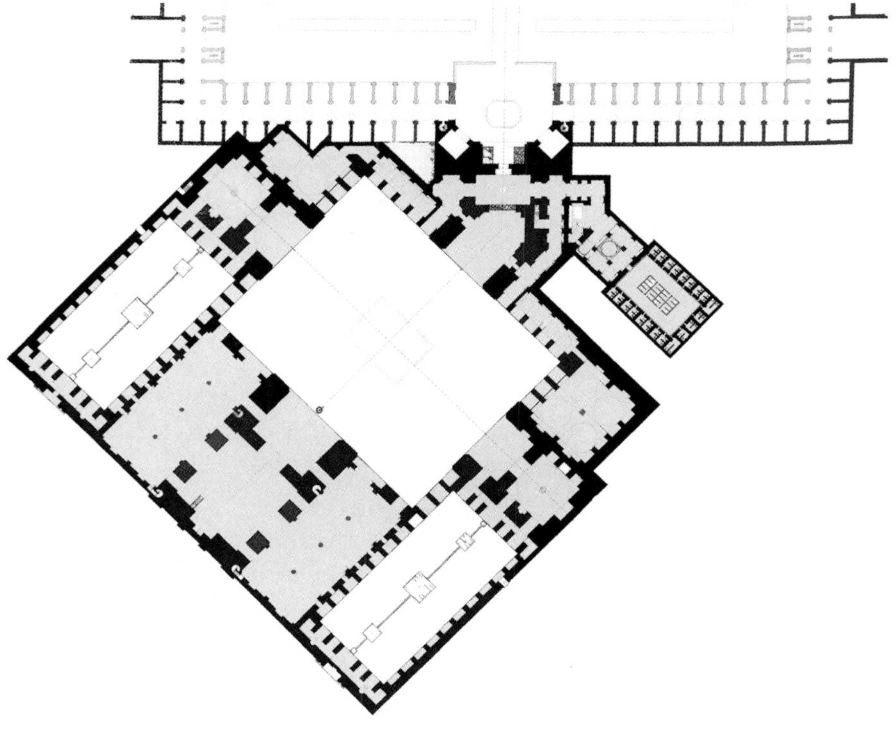

79 Shah Mosque. Sheikh Baha'i, 1611–29. Plan. The entrance to the mosque interrupts the shopping arcade that surrounds the Maidan. Four iwans, or portals, face the central courtyard; a large dome covers the main prayer hall which is flanked by smaller domed spaces.

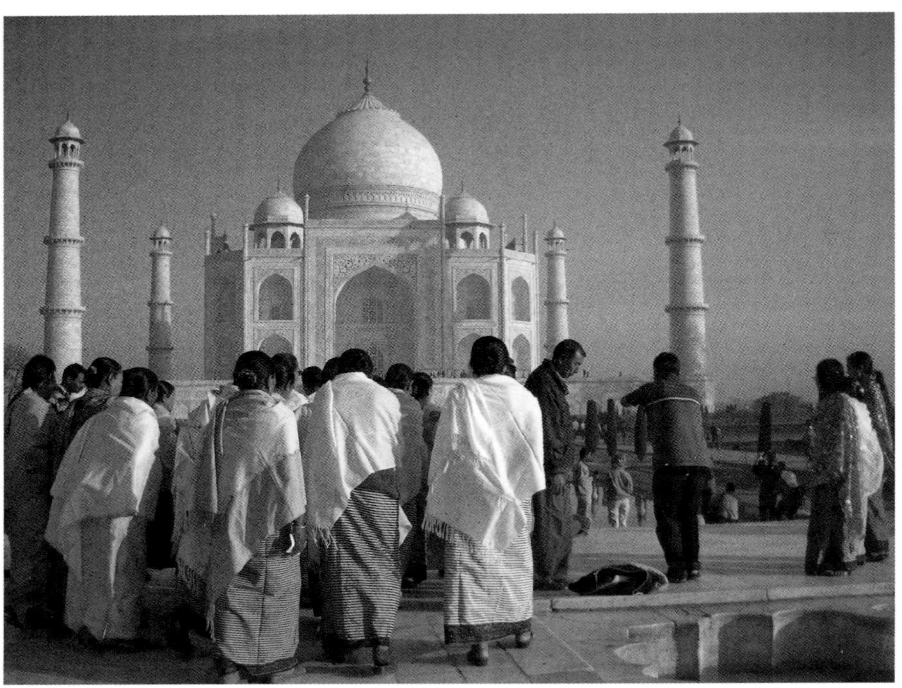

80 Taj Mahal, Agra. Ustad Ahmad Lahori, 1632–48. The mausoleum, which exhibits the Persian preference for symmetry, incorporates pointed arches, iwans, and a bulbous pointed dome.

bulbous-shaped onion dome on the exterior and a lower pointed dome within. The outside surface of the dome is tiled, like the interior, and is visible from anywhere in the city, a turquoise jewel-like form glittering in the dry desert air.

Persian architecture had a wide influence. As we have seen, decorative tilework influenced Byzantine builders, and pointed arches showed up in Islamic architecture. Elements of Persian architecture also migrated east, to the neighboring Mughal Empire. The Mughals were Islamic descendants of the Mongols, and beginning in the sixteenth century they invaded and occupied most of present-day India, Pakistan, and Bangladesh. The population of the Mughal Empire was largely Hindu, and perhaps for that reason, in addition to building fortified palaces, the Islamic rulers laid great store in erecting imposing mosques and tombs.

The pinnacle of Mughal architecture is the mausoleum that the emperor Shah Jahan built for his favorite wife, Mumtaz Mahal, a Persian noblewoman who died in childbirth. The Taj Mahal stands beside the Yamuna River in Agra, the capital of the Mughal Empire (fig. 80). The building was begun shortly after the Shah Mosque in Isfahan, and its architect, Ustad Ahmad Lahori, incorporated many Persian motifs, such as pointed arches, iwans, and a bulbous onion dome.

He used a double-dome construction: a very tall exterior onion dome on a drum, and a low shallow interior dome. The Persian preference for symmetry prevailed. Like the Villa Rotonda, the four-sided building is perfectly symmetrical; the domed room in the center contains the cenotaphs of the emperor and his wife (the actual tombs are in a crypt below). The building is elevated on a large platform whose four corners are defined by ornamental minarets topped by domed pavilions. Four similar pavilions stand at the four corners of the mausoleum.

Mughal architecture is sometimes referred to as Indo-Persian because it incorporates indigenous Indian building traditions. The kiosk-like domed pavilions, for example, called chhatris (literally umbrellas), were a traditional Hindu element often used in funerary sites. The interior of the mausoleum was decorated not with tiles but with inlaid precious and semi-precious stones such as turquoise, coral, onyx, carnelian, sapphire, amethyst, and lapis lazuli—another local technique. The exterior surfaces of the mausoleum were similarly decorated with stone and plaster carving and intricate stone inlays in the form of plant motifs and calligraphy. The most striking feature of the building is that the brick structure is entirely covered in gleaming ivory-white marble, brought from various sites in India, Afghanistan, Tibet, and China. Most Mughal buildings at the time were covered in red sandstone, with marble reserved for select interiors, and the unusual effect of the all-white mausoleum is magical. Whether the Taj is an undying symbol of an emperor's love or a "despot's monument to a woman, not of India, who bore a child every year for fifteen years" (as V. S. Naipaul acerbically put it), it remains one of the most beautiful buildings in the world.

IV
THE FIRST MODERNS

20

Architecture Meets Real Estate

Bath and Paris, eighteenth century

The European eighteenth century marked the beginning of what came to be known as the Industrial Revolution, and with industrialization came urbanization and a new type of architectural client, neither religious nor regal but commercial. The fastest-growing city in Europe was London, where the monied classes' demand for town homes created a flourishing property market. A common practice was for syndicates of wealthy landowners to pool their resources, build an attractive landscaped square—often to serve as a private garden—and lease the surrounding subdivided land to individual tenants. One of the first examples was Cavendish Square in the city's West End, laid out in 1719 on what had been a titled estate. The landowner was Edward Harley, the 2nd Earl of Oxford, whose wife, Henrietta Cavendish, had inherited the property. The new development, which attracted an upper-class clientele, was a financial success and became a model for other similar real estate ventures, such as Hanover Square, Portman Square, and Manchester Square.

Fashionable architecture was an important ingredient of these projects—Harley engaged James Gibbs, a leading Scottish-born architect who was a protégé of Wren's, to provide the requisite cachet, and Gibbs designed several houses on Cavendish Square, as well as a market building and a chapel. In addition to wealthy individuals who commissioned their own houses and mansions, groups of craftsmen sometimes banded together to build houses on speculation. The leader of one of these groups was a young carpenter named John Wood (1704–1754), the son of a small builder in Bath. Nothing is known of Wood's life before he arrived in London. He seems to have taught himself architecture, learning on the job—he built his first house on Cavendish Square when he was only eighteen. I have the impression of a brash, self-confident go-getter. In 1727, Wood returned to Bath. The hot springs had turned the city of seven thousand into a fashionable

81 The Circus, Bath. John Wood, father and son, 1754–68. The round shape and the three superimposed orders—Doric, Ionic, and Corinthian—recall the Colosseum but were actually influenced by Stonehenge.

spa and resort, and the resulting real estate boom offered many opportunities for the ambitious young builder.

After completing a number of private commissions, including several for the Duke of Chandos, a Cavendish Square client, Wood proposed a speculative London-type residential development to a group of investors. To bypass the restrictions posed by local politicians, the syndicate acquired land outside the city limits. The plan was to build a square—Queen Square—subdivide the surrounding property, and lease individual lots to builders who had two years in which to build before their rent increased. It was a pioneering venture for Bath, and when his investors got cold feet, Wood took over the project. To create a sense of prestige and to ensure a unified appearance, he required builders to follow his design for the facades (there were no constraints on the interiors or the backs). This was not the first example of such an approach—the Place de Vosges in Paris had been laid out with uniform house fronts in the early seventeenth century. Like most British architects of that time, Wood was a classicist, but unlike most he modeled his work on Inigo Jones's simplified Palladianism of the previous century, whose straightforward and standardized lexicon of pedimented windows, pilasters, and engaged columns was easily adapted to the financial constraints of commercial building.

Wood's development was a smaller version of Cavendish Square. One entire side of Cavendish Square had been enclosed by a mansion, and to achieve a similar effect, he designed the facades of the seven houses on the north side of Queen Square to resemble a single grand residence. The limestone front—two stories atop a rusticated first floor—has giant Corinthian pilasters, alternating segmental and triangular pedimented windows, pronounced end pavilions, and a central bay defined by a large pediment supported on engaged columns. According to Wood's own flowery description, "it stands upon rising Ground; faces those who come from the City into the Square; and soars above the other Buildings with a Sprightliness, which gives it the Elegance and Grandeur of the Body of a stately Palace." Only the presence of the multiple front doors in the rusticated base gave the game away. The facades of the row houses on the other sides of the square, which included Wood's own home, were more conventional.

After an interval of almost two decades, during which time he was busy with private architectural commissions in Bath and elsewhere, Wood returned to the site of his earlier project. A short distance from Queen Square he laid out a companion square that he called the Circus, a circular square more than three hundred feet in diameter and ringed by thirty houses. The continuous curved facade, interrupted by three streets, presents a unified appearance: three stories defined by three superimposed colonnades of paired engaged columns: Doric, Ionic, and Corinthian (fig. 81). This time, Wood made no attempt to imitate a palace; the columns march implacably around the square in an unbroken rhythm, the bays framing plain windows and doors. Nor did he distinguish the individual houses, which each occupied three bays, their identities remaining anonymous. The center of the square, today a treed lawn, was originally paved.

The Circus had no precedent in either ancient or modern architecture. The ring of houses has often been described as an inside-out Colosseum, but although the superimposed columns are Roman, the inspiration for the Circus was closer to home. Wood, who described himself as an "antiquarian," was fascinated by Celtic history and published a detailed archaeological survey of Stonehenge. He based the diameter of the Circus on the prehistoric monument, and the number of houses mirrored the number of megaliths. Wood adorned the roof parapet with Druidic symbols—sculpted acorns. The rather mysterious bas-reliefs on the metopes of the Doric frieze include serpents and grape clusters, as well as Masonic symbols, Freemasonry being another of Wood's obsessions.

Despite his eccentric interests and his lack of formal training, Wood was an accomplished architect. In Bath, he was responsible for two hospitals, a grammar school, and several country houses; in addition, he designed the city hall in Liverpool and mercantile exchanges in Bristol and Liverpool. But he was not merely a busy provincial professional. He exhibited a peculiar combination of hard-headed realism and idiosyncratic historicism, combining a willingness to adjust to modern market demands with a devotion to an often imaginary past. He was well read in the classics and published a number of books, including *The Origin of Building*, an architectural treatise in which he argued that the Greek orders originated in ancient Jerusalem and were, moreover, the result of divine inspiration. There is evidence that the three superimposed orders of the Circus were derived from what Wood imagined to have been the design of King Solomon's Temple.

Wood, never healthy, died at only fifty, three months after laying the cornerstone of the Circus; the work was completed by his architectural partner—his eldest son, known as John Wood the Younger (1728–1782). After completing the street that connects the Circus to Queen Square, the son set to work on the third phase of his father's visionary plan, a grand semi-oval of thirty houses facing a large greensward, built on high ground overlooking what was then countryside (fig. 82). As in the Circus, the lots were sold to private individuals and builders who were contractually obligated to follow a predetermined facade design. The overall conception of what was named the Royal Crescent was the father's, but the details were the son's, and they were more conventional—no Druidic or Masonic symbols. The four-story facade consists of a plain first floor, two main floors marked by giant engaged Ionic columns, and a set-back attic story (fig. 83). The houses were built in succession, starting at one end of the oval, until the five-hundred-foot-long curved terrace was complete. Despite its grand dimension, the overall effect of the Royal Crescent is almost picturesque rather than monumental.

Bernini's colonnade in front of Saint Peter's and Perrault's East Front of the Louvre extended architecture into the realm of urbanism, but the Woods went

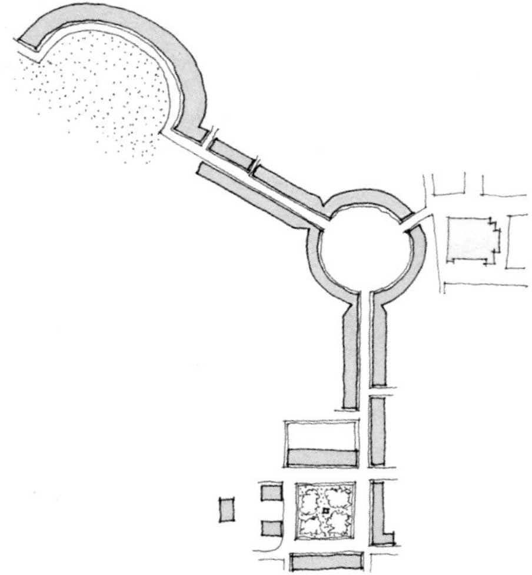

82 Queen Square, the Circus, and the Royal Crescent, Bath. Plan. John Wood, father and son, 1728–74. Queen Square, the first phase, is at the bottom of the drawing.

83 Royal Crescent, Bath. John Wood the Younger, 1767–74. Only the curved facade is uniform; the varied backs of the houses reflect the different individual house plans. The group of trees at the top of the photograph marks the Circus.

further. The Circus and the Royal Crescent showed how the language of classicism could be applied to anonymous housing. The unexpected combination of ordinary houses and monumental architecture presenting a dignified face to the street was unlike the dulling effect of rows of identical houses that characterized cities at that time, and it gave the impression of something grand, of a whole that was greater than the sum of its parts. Over time, the arrangement has shown itself surprisingly adaptable; today the Royal Crescent accommodates private residences, rooming houses, flats, offices, even a small hotel. The simplified Palladian-influenced architecture has proved amenable to repetition and permutation—the essence of good urban design. Similar terraces, circuses, and crescents became a feature of British eighteenth-century town planning, not only in Bath but notably in Edinburgh's New Town and London's West End.

▪ ▪ ▪ ▪ ▪

The Palais-Royale near the Louvre was the Parisian seat of the House of Orléans, whose descendants were princes of the blood—that is, next in line to the throne. While Louis XVI held court in Versailles, the Palais-Royale, which rivaled the Tuileries Palace and the Louvre in architectural splendor, was the center of Parisian high society. And not just high society; the large garden behind the palace was open to the public and was the most popular park in the city, a place for fashionable promenading as well as romantic trysts.

The current resident of the Palais-Royale was Louis Philippe Joseph, Duc de Chartres, the oldest son of the Duc d'Orléans. In 1780, the thirty-three-year-old Louis Philippe, a notorious libertine, found himself in serious financial straits thanks to his extravagant lifestyle and his gaming and horse-racing debts. A friend suggested an unorthodox solution: Why not capitalize on the current Parisian property boom and turn the seven-acre garden behind the palace into a commercial development? After convincing his father, and raising the vast sum of one million livres from Genoese bankers, Louis Philippe was ready to start. He chose as his architect Victor Louis, whom he had met several years earlier in Bordeaux, and whose wife was a friend of the Comtesse de Genlis, the governess of the duke's children and one of his many ex-mistresses.

Victor Louis (1731–1800) did not belong to the Parisian architectural establishment. The son of a Parisian master mason, he had a prickly temperament and had not been admitted to study at the Académie des Beaux-Arts. He must have shown exceptional promise, however, for he was permitted to take part in the school's competitions, whose capstone was the prestigious Prix de Rome. His entry was disqualified over a technicality, but he was awarded a special prize that enabled him to spend the next four years at the French Academy in Rome. After his return to Paris, Louis became a protégé of Madame Marie Thérèse Geoffrin, an Enlightenment intellectual and the hostess of the leading salon in the city. The architect's great opportunity came when he was commissioned to rebuild a theater destroyed by fire in Bordeaux, then the second-largest city in France. The Grand Théâtre de Bordeaux, which he completed in 1780, was celebrated as the largest and most modern theater in the country. Louis's innovations included a colonnaded facade (previously reserved for palaces), a grand staircase (which became the model for later theaters and opera houses), and the use of wrought-iron columns and beams to reduce the risk of fire.

The Duc de Chartres was a demanding client, and he rejected Louis's first two proposals. The final design was a five-story building surrounding the park, although the fourth side was never completed (fig. 84). There had been an uproar when the project was first announced, because the public was used to having free access to the garden, but the complaints died down once it became clear that the public garden would be maintained. To compensate for cutting down the large trees around the perimeter of the site to make space for the building, Louis planted rows of mature trees within the garden.

The new six-story building, more than two thousand feet long in all, was composed of a two-story shopping arcade; grand tall-ceilinged apartments above; and smaller apartments on the fourth floor, in the set-back fifth floor, and in the attic. The arcade faced inward, toward the garden. It was a garden of very earthly delights—some of the apartments were rented to *filles de joie,* high-class courtesans who became fixtures of the Palais grounds. Prostitution and gambling thrived because the duke forbade the city police from entering his property. In addition to gaming houses, the arcade contained music rooms, luxury shops, booksellers, and one of the first restaurants in Paris. There were many cafés, and, unlike British coffeehouses of that period, these were open to women. Additional attractions included a children's puppet theater and a larger theater (which would become the Comédie-Française), a wax museum, and a Turkish bath. The garden was surfaced in gravel with rows of manicured trees and a central octagonal water basin. In 1787, Louis Philippe, now the Duc d'Orléans, following his father's death, added a novel feature in the center of the garden: the Cirque. This long glass-roofed structure (long since demolished), partly buried to reduce its height, was originally intended for indoor horseback-riding and was also used for balls, banquets, and other festivities.

The glamorous arcades of the Palais-Royale were a resounding success. Although the urban poor were denied access, many classes of people rubbed shoulders: the bourgeoisie and the aristocracy, the military and tradesmen, the respectable and the demimonde. But the story of the developer-duke did not end happily. Despite his profligate lifestyle, the Duc d'Orléans was a committed Jacobin who supported the opposition to his cousin Louis XVI—the Palais-Royale was a favorite meeting place for radicals. As the Revolution unfolded, the duke dropped his title, becoming simply Philippe Égalité, and renaming the Palais-Royale the Garden of the Revolution. He further shocked his aristocratic friends when, as a member of the National Convention, he joined Robespierre

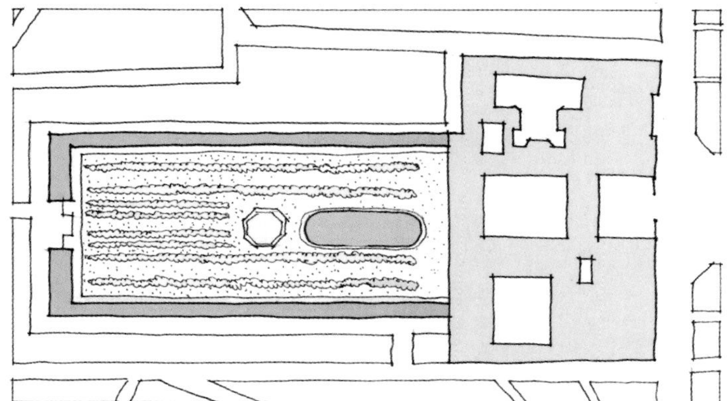

84 Shopping arcade, Palais-Royale, Paris. Victor Louis, 1781–84. Plan. The six-story residential building (left) that included a shopping arcade surrounds a public garden. The palace is on the right.

85 Palais-Royale. In the inner shopping arcade, Bramante's arch-and-pilaster motif is magnified and executed in the grand style of French classicisme.

in voting to execute the king. Nevertheless, in 1793, during the Reign of Terror, Citizen Égalité was accused of treason and fell victim to the guillotine.

The Palais-Royale remains one of the great accomplishments of French classicisme, architecture on an urban scale. Victor Louis modeled the garden facade on the side elevation of his recently completed Grand Théâtre. The combination of round arches and pilasters was inspired by Bramante, although the fluted Composite pilasters, which stand on plinths, rise a full three stories (fig. 85). Each of the exceptionally narrow bays, which mimic the arcades of the old palace, frames an arched opening and the tall French windows of the main apartments. There is no variety; the module simply repeats—more than two hundred times! This sounds dull, but when you are strolling down the arcade the effect is actually splendid, especially as the views of the facade are broken up by the tall trees of the garden. Louis's repetitive module recalls the colonnade of the Royal Crescent in Bath, although French classicisme is visually richer than the restrained Palladianism of Georgian England. The spandrels of the arches are filled with laurel swags; the tall French windows have stone balustrades below and bas-relief trophy medallions above; the entablature consists of a band that includes richly ornamented paired consoles supporting a cornice and the square windows of the fourth floor; and the cornice is topped by a balustrade with giant urns. An architecture once reserved for kings and popes has been made available, if not exactly to the masses, to a wide assortment of people. That, too, was part of the Duc d'Orléans's radicalism.

21

A Secular Temple

Berlin, nineteenth century

The same year that the Duc d'Orléans was guillotined, the Grand Gallery of the Louvre opened to the public. This immense wing of the palace, more than a thousand feet long, had been built in the seventeenth century to link the Louvre to the Tuileries. After Louis XIV moved his court to Versailles, the Grand Gallery became home to the royal art collection. Although the collection had occasionally been shown to the public, the revolutionary government decreed that the art belonged to the nation and opened the doors permanently. Six years later, the newly installed First Consul, Napoleon Bonaparte, turned the Louvre into a full-fledged museum. He appointed a director, ordered the building expanded, and renamed it the Musée Napoleon. "The Louvre can never be a comfortable residence," he declared. "I regard it as a kind of ceremonial palace in which we must store all our riches in the field of art and science, such as statues, bronze sculptures, paintings, books, archives, medals." The riches included not only the royal collection and other artworks confiscated during the Revolution, but also the paintings and sculptures that Napoleon had plundered while campaigning in Prussia, Italy, and Egypt. Thus was born the idea of a national gallery.

The Louvre may have been an uncomfortable residence, but it functioned reasonably well as a museum. The building had been designed to accommodate large numbers of people, the monumental staircase that led up to the main floor made for an appropriately impressive entrance, and there was a variety of different-shaped rooms. Among these were so-called galleries, long, narrow rooms with windows on one side and generous wall space on the other; these were originally intended for receptions, but the blank walls proved useful for hanging art. The palatial decor was imposing, of course. For most commoners, the experience of the Musée Napoleon was their first opportunity to see great works of art, and the grand setting was an integral part of that experience.

Napoleon was defeated at the battle of Waterloo in 1815. Although he was reviled in the rest of Europe, his idea of a national art collection took hold, and during the following decade national art galleries were founded in Madrid, London, Amsterdam, and Munich. And in Berlin, the capital of Prussia—King Friedrich Wilhelm III had been impressed by the Louvre when he visited the city to negotiate the Treaty of Paris. That treaty repatriated art looted from the Prussian royal collection, and in 1822 the king decreed that the restored art be displayed to the public. This would require a new building, and he appointed a special committee to study the matter.

The architect on the committee was the Prussian state's chief building surveyor, Karl Friedrich Schinkel (1781–1841). The son of a Lutheran pastor, he had been drawn to architecture after meeting David Gilly and his son Friedrich, both architects. As a boy, Schinkel was sent to Berlin to board with the Gillys and attend their private architecture school. He also worked in their office. Friedrich Gilly, who became Schinkel's mentor, died of tuberculosis—only twenty-eight—and left his incomplete commissions to his star pupil. Thanks to this income, Schinkel was able to embark on a two-year architectural Grand Tour that took him to Vienna, Prague, Venice, Rome, Naples, and Paris. In Rome he was befriended by Wilhelm von Humboldt, the noted Prussian philosopher and linguist who was serving as emissary to the Holy See.

Schinkel had returned to Berlin in 1805, shortly before Napoleon decisively defeated the Prussian army and occupied the city. It was not a propitious time to launch an architectural career, and Schinkel, who was a skilled draftsman, earned a living making architectural and landscape paintings, as well as creating large canvases for dioramas, the popular entertainments of the time that were forerunners of the cinema. This work brought him to the attention of Queen Luise, who, following a peace treaty with Napoleon, had returned to Berlin with her husband. She commissioned the young Schinkel to redecorate her apartment in the Charlottenburg Palace.

Despite this royal patronage, Schinkel had few private commissions, and in 1810, twenty-nine and newly married, he applied for a government job. With the Queen and von Humboldt's help he secured a position as chief building surveyor on the Royal Building Commission, which was in charge of all official construction in the kingdom. The peaceful decade following Napoleon's downfall saw a flurry of new building, and the busy Schinkel, now in charge of the Berlin office, was, in effect, the city architect. In addition to overseeing work by others, he was personally responsible for the Neue Wache, the royal guardhouse opposite the palace, and the Schauspielhaus, the main theater and concert hall of the city.

A severe Doric temple front dominated the guardhouse, and a monumental Ionic portico adorned the main facade of the theater; the inspiration for both was Greek rather than Roman. How did this ancient architecture, so long forgotten, reappear in the Prussian capital? Following the fall of Constantinople in 1453, the Byzantine Empire, which included most of mainland Greece, had come under Ottoman rule. By the eighteenth century, Athens was little more than a small town, and foreign travelers had few reasons to visit this provincial backwater; in any case, the Turks did not welcome infidel visitors. As a result, while ancient Roman ruins were intensively studied and documented, Athenian ruins remained largely unknown. Architects were aware of Greek temples, for there were surviving Doric ruins in southern Italy and Sicily, but these were considered merely archaic ancestors of Roman architecture and not worthy of study.

In time, travel restrictions in the Ottoman Empire eased, and in 1751 two intrepid British architects, James Stuart (1713–1788) and Nicholas Revett (1721–1804), received Turkish permission to study ancient sites in Athens and the vicinity. Stuart and Revett spent the next two years measuring and documenting the ruins, and nine years later they published the first volume of *The Antiquities of Athens,* which described five ancient buildings in great detail. Three additional volumes of their work were published posthumously. The large folio-size tomes contained views of buildings in their present ruined state, but the majority of the engravings were reconstructions—that is, meticulously drawn plans, elevations, and details that described the buildings as architecture rather than as archaeology.

The Antiquities of Athens appeared at an opportune time. The Greek struggle for independence had become a cause célèbre, and interest in Greece was high. For the first time, architects could appreciate the chaste beauty and sophistication of ancient Greek temples. Roman architecture had become associated with the Catholic Church and the Napoleonic Empire, so for Protestant Europeans the Greek examples, with their roots in an early democracy, offered an attractive alternative and sparked what became known as the Greek Revival. The style appeared in London and Edinburgh, Vienna and Saint Petersburg, and as far afield as Helsinki. In Germany, the Greek Revival style was especially popular in Berlin. As early as 1789, Carl Gotthard Langhans (1732–1808), Schinkel's predecessor on the Royal Building Commission, modeled the Brandenburg Gate on the Propylaea, and by the time that Schinkel appeared on the scene the Greek Revival had become the de facto official style of the Prussian capital.

Schinkel's first proposal for Friedrich Wilhelm's new museum involved adding two wings to the Royal Prussian Academy of Arts, one for art and one for science. This proved expensive, and it was decided to build only the art museum,

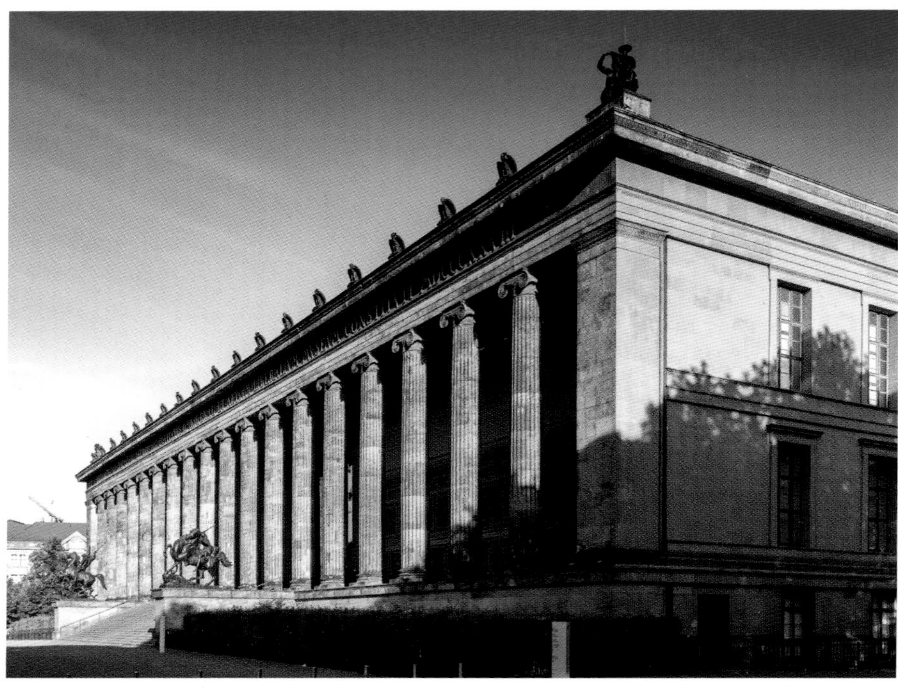

86 Altes Museum, Berlin. Karl Friedrich Schinkel, 1822–30. The entrance facade was modeled on a Greek stoa. The sides and back are considerably plainer.

and to locate the building opposite the royal palace on the Spreeinsel, an island in the Spree River. The museum was part of Schinkel's master plan to transform this key site in the center of the city. Schinkel and Alois Hirt, a professor of art history at the Academy of Fine Arts, were charged with developing a detailed program for the Königliches Museum, or Royal Museum (today the Altes Museum).

An architect designing a public art gallery in the early nineteenth century was faced with a challenging problem. In brief, what should such a building look like? Theaters and libraries had a long history, but there were no architectural precedents for an art gallery. Should a museum draw inspiration from the Louvre and resemble a royal palace? Or should it incorporate a temple front like the national galleries then under construction in Munich and London? Schinkel chose a different path. He modeled the long two-story front of his building on a Greek stoa (fig. 86). Ancient stoas, which had been documented by Stuart and Revett, were open-air porticos that faced a square or marketplace and provided a sheltered space for shopkeepers and craftsmen to display their wares. A stoa appealed to Schinkel because of its civic character, and also because a long colonnade would create an effective backdrop for the Lustgarten, the new public park between the museum and the royal palace. Eighteen giant fluted Ionic columns march across the almost three-hundred-foot-long facade, terminating at each end in antae, square pillars attached to short walls. It is bold design of the utmost simplicity.

Schinkel's novel plan for the museum skillfully resolved several practical issues. The visitor passed through the stoa into an open-air vestibule that contained a grand stair. This monumental staircase, with its views of the park, had a public character that contrasted with the more intimate galleries within. Each floor was divided into a variety of exhibition spaces: two small rooms in the front, two medium-size rooms on the sides, and a room in the rear that stretched across the full width of the building (fig. 87). These rooms were all of the gallery type, that is, long and narrow with windows along one side; Schinkel considered skylights, but these proved too expensive. In addition, there were six rooms for displaying smaller objects. The galleries, which surrounded two courts that functioned as light wells, formed a convenient circuit, and short corridors enabled the visitor to move directly from the entrance to the long gallery. The first floor was divided into aisles by two rows of columns and was devoted to sculpture; the second floor, whose galleries were column-free, was for paintings, which were displayed on wooden screens placed at right angles to the windows.

A building composed exclusively of exhibition spaces risks becoming a featureless storehouse. That was not what Schinkel wanted. "So mighty a building as the Museum will certainly be, must have a worthy center," he observed. This center was a domed rotunda rising the full height of the building and containing the royal collection of antique sculpture (fig. 88). Schinkel called the rotunda a "sanctuary" and envisioned the room as a sort of prologue to the museum, a contemplative space to put the visitor in the appropriate frame of mind. Light

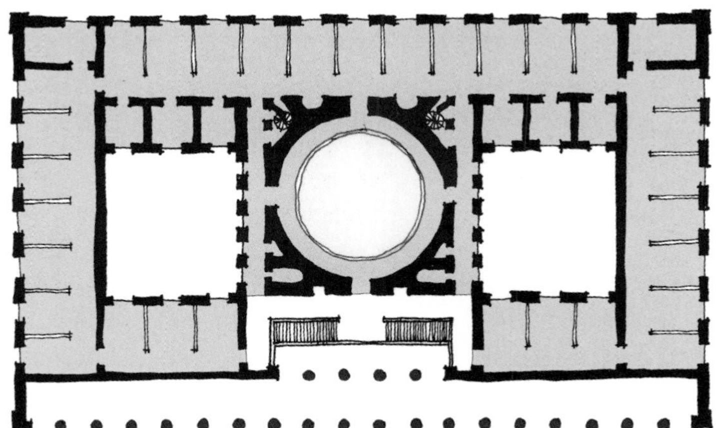

87 Altes Museum. Second-floor plan. The various-size galleries, organized around two light wells, form a circuit. Low screens at right angles to the windows served to display paintings; antique sculptures were exhibited in the central rotunda.

88 Altes Museum. Engraving, 1831, based on Schinkel's drawing of the rotunda. He called this room the "sanctuary" of the museum.

streamed in from an oculus, and a ring of Corinthian columns supported a balcony accessible from the second floor. The coffered dome and the oculus were modeled on the Pantheon. The symbolism was unmistakable: this museum was not simply a storehouse of artworks or a richly appointed palace, it was a secular temple. Schinkel was hardly the first nineteenth-century architect to find inspiration in the ancient Roman rotunda; Thomas Jefferson patterned the library of the University of Virginia on the Pantheon, and Sydney Smirke did the same in the circular Reading Room of the British Museum. A hundred years later, the American architect John Russell Pope took his cue from Schinkel and used the

Roman temple as a model for the great rotunda of the National Gallery of Art in Washington, D.C.

Schinkel and Hirt did not see eye to eye on the function of the museum. For Schinkel the main purpose of the building was to provide an aesthetic experience for the public; Hirt saw the museum as primarily a place where scholars would study the history of art, and he considered features such as the stoa and the rotunda to be a waste of space. The men also had different views about what should be displayed; Hirt wanted to emphasize chronology and comprehensiveness, whereas Schinkel, who had made study tours of museums in Paris and London, favored giving precedence to outstanding works and periods. His visit to the Louvre had convinced him that richly decorated interiors enhanced the experience of art, and he lobbied the king to increase the budget. Schinkel prevailed with regard to the building's design, which the king approved, but the matter of what to display was delegated to Wilhelm von Humboldt, who diplomatically steered a middle course between research and public edification. Hirt had the last word, however. He was responsible for the wording of the Latin inscription that adorns the entablature of the museum's facade. It reads: "Friedrich Wilhelm III dedicated this museum to the study of all kinds of antiquity and the liberal arts in 1828."

The Altes Museum is often described as an example of the nineteenth-century Greek Revival, and so it is, but Schinkel's expressed goal was more ambitious than mere replication. He aimed to "preserve the spiritual principle of Greek architecture, [and] bring it to terms with the condition of our own epoch." The stoa is Greek—Schinkel based the Ionic order on the north porch of the Erechtheion—but he was nothing if not pragmatic. The rotunda was inspired by the Pantheon, and on the exterior he concealed the Roman dome behind a Greek attic story. The spatial complexity of the switchback staircase, which recalls a grand palace stair, is Baroque, and the elongated galleries repeat a time-tested arrangement that originated in eighteenth-century palace planning. The capitals of the stone columns in the first-floor sculpture galleries are neither Greek nor Roman, and do not resemble any classical order. The sides and back of the building likewise defy stylistic definition (see fig. 86). Schinkel carried the stoa frieze around the building, added a matching frieze at the second-floor level, and placed rows of identical vertical windows between them, but he did not include columns, pilasters, or ornament of any kind. The king was notoriously parsimonious, so this simplicity suited the budget, but it also provided a contrast with the richly ornamented facade, for even as Schinkel stripped all conventional classical features from the sides and back of the museum he devised an elaborate iconographic program for the front: large sculptures on the attic roof and exterior steps, a row of cast-iron Prussian eagles lining the cornice. The back wall of the stoa contained murals on mythological themes, as well as panoramic paintings (all designed by Schinkel and no longer extant), which transformed the porch into a veritable outdoor gallery.

Schinkel was a rare combination of gifted artist and efficient administrator. Living at the time of Goethe and Beethoven, he was also a Romantic. He designed a series of country villas that beautifully exploit their natural surroundings and whose porticos, pergolas, and terraces extend the architecture into the landscape. He never lost his early love of Gothic, although he dispensed with flying buttresses, rose windows, and tall pitched roofs, and combined pointed arches with boxy brick buildings of a distinctly un-Gothic character. "The only act that qualifies as historical is that which in some way introduces something additional, a new element, in the world, from which a new story can be generated and the thread taken up anew," he wrote in the introduction to an architectural primer he produced for the Bauakademie, the architecture school whose curriculum—and building—he designed. *A new story . . . a thread taken up anew.* In this way Schinkel hoped to navigate the paradox facing all serious architects: how to reconcile novelty with tradition, how to look forward and backward at the same time.

22

Iron Monuments

London and Paris, nineteenth century

One of Schinkel's first public commissions was a monument honoring his patron, Queen Luise, who died unexpectedly at thirty-four. Erected in 1811 by the town of Gransee, the monument consisted of a replica of the royal sarcophagus under a canopy supported on delicate Gothic arches and extremely slender columns. The whole thing was made of cast iron. Iron had been cast into cannons since the Renaissance, but its use in construction was recent, thanks largely to the invention of the steam-powered blast furnace. Smelted iron ore combined with carbon and other additives had a relatively low melting point and could be inexpensively molded into a variety of shapes and decorative forms. Schinkel himself designed cast-iron stoves and outdoor furniture, and he used cast-iron columns as balcony supports in the Schauspielhaus. These extremely thin fluted colonettes are recognizably classical—as had happened before, the first use of a new material was an imitation of an older form. Cast iron would soon come into its own, however, and it would do so in a spectacular fashion in England.

In 1850, under the leadership of Queen Victoria's husband, Prince Albert, a royal commission was formed to plan an international industrial exhibition, the first of its kind. It was to be housed in a temporary hall in London's Hyde Park. The hall, which was to enclose eighteen acres, was the responsibility of a building committee that included Robert Stephenson, the famous locomotive and railway builder; the multitalented Isambard Kingdom Brunel, responsible for bridges, tunnels, and the first propeller-driven transatlantic steamship; and Charles Barry, the architect of the Palace of Westminster. The design and construction of the hall were the subject of a national architectural competition that attracted two hundred and forty-five entries. The committee awarded eighteen honorable mentions but did not declare a winner. Instead, it advanced its own design, which was largely the work of Brunel: an enormous sheet-iron dome attached to an unremarkable shed-like brick building. This proposal failed to garner public support, however, and only fueled the growing opposition to building anything in the park. Thus the Great Exhibition, which was scheduled for the following year, got off to a rocky start.

It was at this critical juncture that Joseph Paxton came on the scene. Paxton (1803–1865) was the head gardener and estate manager for the 6th Duke of Devonshire, for whom he had built what was then the largest greenhouse in the world, covering more than an acre. Paxton had achieved national renown by cultivating a giant waterlily, the *Amazonica regia,* named after Queen Victoria. The plant had been discovered in British Guiana, and numerous attempts to make it flower in the cold British climate had failed. But Paxton, a skilled horticulturist, succeeded, and personally presented a bloom to the queen.

Paxton cultivated the waterlily in a greenhouse whose delicate structure was distinguished by a flat roof built with his own patented "ridge-and-furrow" roofing system: glass gables supported on wooden beams that also served as gutters, with hollow cast-iron columns functioning as downspouts. The panes were manufactured by a glassworks in the English Midlands that had invented an inexpensive technique for mass-producing plate glass. Paxton believed that his glazing system, combined with a cast-iron structure, could be used to build the Great Exhibition hall, and that this standardized and prefabricated method of building would enable rapid construction at low cost. The structure in Hyde Park was to be temporary, and the fact that the materials could be reused would add to the building's economy.

Paxton shared his sketches with his friend Robert Stephenson, who introduced him to Prince Albert and the political backers of the exhibition. The prince, like Stephenson, was enthusiastic about the idea of a glass hall. Paxton shrewdly leaked his design to the *London Illustrated News,* which christened the structure the Crystal Palace, and the idea captured the public's imagination. The nonplussed building committee invited Paxton to submit a construction tender for both his own and Brunel's design. Paxton collaborated with a Birmingham engineer, Charles Fox (1810–1874), whose company was a leading builder of cast-iron bridges and railway stations. Fox guaranteed a firm price for building and removing the cast-iron and glass structure at one third the cost of Brunel's proposal, so the committee had no choice but to proceed with Paxton's scheme.

Paxton and Fox's design was a sort of basilica almost two thousand feet long with a nave-like central space flanked by aisles and galleries (figs. 89 and 90). At sixty feet, the hall was tall enough to enclose existing trees. Paxton's ridge-and-furrow glass roof was supported on a framework of cast-iron girders and columns,

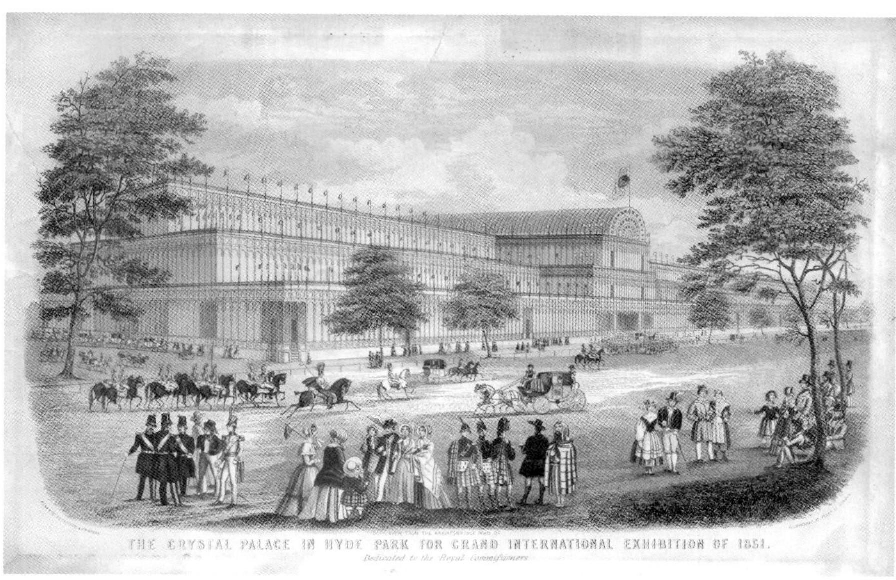

THE CRYSTAL PALACE IN HYDE PARK FOR GRAND INTERNATIONAL EXHIBITION OF 1851.
Dedicated to the Royal Commissioners

89 Crystal Palace, London. Joseph Paxton and Charles Fox, 1850–51. Lithograph of the exterior. The vast cast-iron and glass exhibition hall covered eighteen acres.

the hollow columns acting as downspouts to a network of underground drainpipes. The entire structure was bolted together, which enabled it to be disassembled when the Great Exhibition closed after twenty weeks. The radically simple linear plan was somewhat compromised when the building committee suggested adding a taller arched transept in the center to function as an entrance hall.

Fox personally prepared the construction drawings over seven intensive weeks; the actual construction took less than six months. This remarkable achievement was possible thanks to Paxton's highly standardized glazing system. The dimensions of the modular design were dictated by the size of the panes—ten inches by forty-nine inches; there were three hundred thousand of them. Once the twenty-four-foot-long cast-iron girders were in place, the U-shaped cast-iron beams that supported the glass and acted as gutters were erected eight feet apart. The beams served as rails for a wheeled trolley that carried the glazier team of two men and two boys who installed the panes; the trolley was roofed, so work could proceed even during rainy weather. Such ingenuity characterized the entire construction process. Wooden sashes for the glazing were produced in an assembly line on the site; the cast-iron beams, girders, and columns were drilled and punched after being delivered. The main structural material was cast iron except for the arches of the transept, which were laminated wood. The floor of the hall reused the wooden planks that served as the hoarding surrounding the building site.

90 Crystal Palace. Lithograph of the interior showing the nave overlooked by side galleries.

The Great Exhibition was opened by Queen Victoria on May 1, 1851. The writer Charlotte Brontë, who visited the Crystal Palace twice, found it a "wonderful place—vast, strange, new and impossible to describe." Despite—or perhaps because of—its basilican plan, the glass building was both familiar and alien. The columns had capitals, the transept used a barrel vault, and the sheer size of the building was as impressive as a cathedral. Yet the result was unlike conventional architecture, and not only because the walls and roof were glass. There was no craftsmanship in the traditional sense, nor was there any surface ornament or decoration, although the interior girders, columns, and trusses were painted vibrant colors: red for horizontal surfaces, yellow for projecting surfaces, light blue for receding surfaces, and white for verticals. The color scheme was the work of Owen Jones (1809–1874), an architect on the building committee who had developed a theory of color decoration based on his studies of the Alhambra. The barrel-vaulted transept vaguely recalled a Roman bath, but otherwise the modular glass hall stood largely outside architectural history.

By the middle of the nineteenth century, cast-iron and glass were not uncommon in shopping arcades and train sheds, although they were usually combined with conventional buildings. The spectacular iron and glass shed of Saint Pancras station in London, designed by the engineer William Henry Barlow, which opened in 1868, was mated to a red-brick Gothic Revival head house, designed by the architect George Gilbert Scott; the impressive iron trusses of the barrel vaults of the reading room of the Bibliothèque Sainte-Geneviève in Paris, designed by Henri Labrouste in 1843, were combined with a limestone Greek Revival exterior. Paxton and Fox's Crystal Palace was different. Assembled entirely from mass-produced parts, it dispensed with traditional architectural elements. The hall, which looked like it could go on forever, was purposeful but unexpressive, more like a work of engineering than a building. Such critics as the writer John Ruskin and the Gothicist Augustus Welby Pugin considered it to not be architecture at all.

Most of the six million people who visited the exhibition were uninterested in such distinctions; they saw the Crystal Palace as simply another triumph of the Victorian Age, like locomotives and steamships. The glass hall was built without a hitch, on time and within the budget. (The exhibition lasted five and a half months, after which the building was dismantled and moved to South London, where it stood until 1936, when it was destroyed in a fire.) What an audacious undertaking, a vast public building covered entirely in glass. Amazingly, the roof proved to be relatively watertight. During construction the building was subjected to winter gales and a severe hailstorm without sustaining any serious damage. Nor did the interior overheat as some critics foretold; it was protected by retractable calico sunshades that could be drawn over the nave when required. The story of architecture is full of failed, or at least half-baked, innovations. That was not the case with the Crystal Palace—Paxton had thought of everything.

■ ■ ■ ■ ■

Not to be outdone by the Great Exhibition, in 1855 the French organized their own Exposition Universelle. The second Parisian fair, held in 1867, sprawled over more than fifty acres on the Champs de Mars. The main exhibition hall was a huge oval iron-and-glass building that was intended to rival the Crystal Palace, although its design was rather pedestrian—the British had pioneered iron building, and it was taking the French time to catch up. Some of the iron arches in the exhibition halls were the work of Gustave Eiffel (1832–1923), a young engineer who had just opened his own office. Eiffel had studied chemical rather than civil engineering, but his first employer was a railway company and his knowledge of metallurgy proved useful since bridges and railway stations were predominantly built of cast iron. Eiffel early showed an ability for organization. When he was thirty-four he set up as an independent consulting engineer and in due course established his own foundry and construction company. By the 1880s, he was building iron bridges, viaducts, and prefabricated buildings not only in France but around the world; his work included the unique structural frame of the Statue of Liberty in New York.

In 1884, two of Eiffel's engineering staff, Maurice Koechlin (1856–1946) and Émile Nouguier (1840–1897) began working on a structure that they thought would make a striking centerpiece for the Exposition Universelle of 1889. Their idea was influenced by the 1853 New York international exhibition, which had included a 315-foot wooden observation tower; Koechlin and Nouguier's tower was iron and more than three times as tall, a thousand feet. Koechlin described their idea: "a great pylon, consisting of four lattice girders standing apart at the base and coming together at the top, joined together by metal trusses at regular intervals." Their conceptual sketch, which resembles a modern electrical transmission tower, was rather utilitarian. Eiffel was not impressed, and he encouraged them to refine the design. The pair sought the help of Stephen Sauvestre (1847–1919), who was in charge of Eiffel's architecture department. Sauvestre added nonstructural decorative arches to emphasize the tower's function as a gateway, as well as two observation platforms and such architectural embellishments as a domed cap. His contributions were important, and not only because they enabled Koechlin and Nouguier to gain the *patron's* approval. The arches visually solidified the base of the tower and gave it the "legs" that contribute so much to its anthropomorphic image (fig. 91). Eiffel threw the resources of his firm behind the project, and in the final design, the legs were moved farther apart and the upper half of the tower was made more vertical, shooting straight up in the air. An accomplished but somewhat stolid work of engineering had become an expressive work of architecture.

It took Eiffel two years to gain approval for the project. Thanks to his lobbying, the exhibition organizers accepted the idea of a thousand-foot observation tower as a centerpiece and held a competition, which the Eiffel entry—not surprisingly—won. Construction began in 1887 and took slightly more than two years. Building the tower was more complicated than erecting the Crystal Palace. Twice as much iron was involved, the connections were riveted rather than bolted (which required more skill), and because of its curved shape the structure was made up of more than eighteen thousand different parts. These came from Eiffel's foundry and were largely wrought iron, which had a lower carbon content and was stronger in tension than cast iron. Strength was important, because the tall structure had to resist not only gravity but also the considerable force of the wind.

91 Eiffel Tower, Paris. Gustave Eiffel, 1884–89. Photographed in 1889. The lowest platform, which housed four restaurants, would be altered in 1937.

The design of the elevators was especially challenging in the upper portion, where they had to travel a curved path. The two hydraulic cable lifts on rail tracks were built by the American company Otis. The elevators served an impressive number of amenities: four restaurants on the first platform; a patisserie and a bar on the second platform, which also housed the printing office of *Le Figaro*'s souvenir "Tour Eiffel" edition; and a wraparound observation platform at the top that included a post office and an apartment where Eiffel could entertain visiting dignitaries. Having financed the construction of the tower, he was effectively its owner (after twenty years ownership passed to the City of Paris), and he pocketed the admission fees, which were considerable; during the six months of the fair there were almost two million visitors.

Like the Crystal Palace, Eiffel's tower represented a way of building that was possible only because of advances made in engineering. The French profession was different from its British counterpart: British engineers were trained on the job, whereas French engineers received a formal education that underpinned their practical experience. Eiffel was a graduate of the École Centrale in Paris, which specialized in training engineers and industry leaders and was the most prestigious of the *grandes écoles* (elite schools) established after the French Revolution.

The structure—what people were calling the Tour de Monsieur Eiffel—had its critics. In February 1887 the leading Parisian newspaper, *Le Temps,* published a letter, signed by forty-six prominent writers, architects, painters, and composers, that described the tower as a "giant black factory chimney" and protested its "monstrous" intrusion on the beautiful Paris skyline. There was no official reply, probably because the tower's massive foundations on the Champs de Mars were already under construction. The letter is not particularly convincing, since many of the signatories later publicly expressed their admiration after visiting the tower, and the prime organizer of the letter was the architect Charles Garnier, a member of the commission that had unanimously approved Eiffel's design.

Garnier (1825–1898) was the dean of French architects, responsible for the Paris Opéra, completed a dozen years earlier. He was familiar with iron construction, having used cast-iron columns and wrought-iron beams and trusses in the Opéra, and having just completed the Nice Observatory, whose rotating wrought-iron dome was designed and built by Eiffel's company. But Garnier, who believed that engineering should always be the handmaiden of architecture, was right to be uneasy. For thousands of years, whether in Gothic vaults or Renaissance domes, engineering had played a subservient, sometimes even a concealed role. Now, in buildings such as the Crystal Palace and the Eiffel Tower, engineering had dramatically come to the fore.

23

A Personal Vision

Barcelona, early 1900s

In December 1895, a Franco-German art dealer, Siegfried Bing, opened a gallery devoted to the fine and decorative arts on the rue de Provence, not far from the Paris Opéra. In addition to Japanese prints, of which he was a pioneering importer, Bing sold contemporary paintings, posters, jewelry, glassware, fabrics, and furniture. He represented an international assortment of artists: William Morris, Aubrey Beardsley, Henri de Toulouse-Lautrec, René Lalique, Henry van de Velde, and Louis Comfort Tiffany. The Belgian architect Victor Horta advised Bing on the design of the gallery's exterior, van de Velde designed some of the rooms, and Tiffany provided stained-glass windows. The sign over the entrance read L'Art Nouveau.

Bing's gallery gave its name to an international movement. Art Nouveau was a response to the boredom and exhaustion that had befallen academic neoclassicism, as well as a reaction to the shabby, mass-produced domestic furnishings of the industrial age. Rejecting historical sources, Art Nouveau was influenced by the natural forms of plants and flowers. Luxurious, sophisticated, and decidedly metropolitan, the movement took root not only in the largest European cities but also in regional centers, such as Glasgow, Prague, and Helsinki. Art Nouveau influenced the design of houses, subway stations, and cafés, as well as posters, furniture, and furnishings, including women's fashions. Its reach was international—Chicago, Mexico City, and Buenos Aires—but this was not an international style; it took different forms in different places. Hardly monolithic, more like a shared taste, the reaction went under a variety of names: Art Nouveau in Paris and Brussels, Modern Style in London and Saint Petersburg, Jugendstil (Youth Style) in Berlin, Secession in Vienna and Budapest, and Stile Liberty and Stile Floreale in Milan. In the United States it was sometimes called the Tiffany Style, after its most prominent practitioner.

In fin-de-siècle Barcelona, Art Nouveau was called *modernisme*. The city had an unusual architectural heritage. The local historic buildings were Roman, Romanesque, and Gothic, and architects also had been influenced by the Islamic past of Andalusia. Barcelona was the most industrialized city in Spain, and modern materials—iron, steel, reinforced concrete—existed side by side with such regional building traditions as wrought ironwork and brick vaulting, to which the intensely nationalistic Catalans were strongly attached. In this environment, modernisme acquired a distinctly local flavor, especially in the hands of its most famous practitioner.

Antoni Gaudí i Cornet (1852–1926), descended from a long line of coppersmiths, was born in Reus, the second-largest city in Catalonia. His father was ambitious, and he sent his two sons to study in Barcelona, the older medicine, and the younger, Antoni, architecture. It took Gaudí almost ten years to complete his studies; he needed to take preparatory courses to enter the university, he took time off to fulfill his compulsory military service, and he also worked part-time to support himself. He was not an outstanding student, although he displayed an aptitude for mathematics. An ardent Catholic conservative, Gaudí was attracted to medieval architecture. He pored over the photographic collection of the school library, including the exotic architecture of Isfahan and Granada. This unusual combination of influences—a deep religious faith, ardent Catalan nationalism, and Orientalism—fueled the young architect's imagination. His first residential commission of note was heavily influenced by Andalusian architecture and included decorative tilework and a smoking room with a cardboard muqarnas ceiling.

Gaudí caught the eye of Eusebi Güell, a Barcelona industrial tycoon who became his patron, and for whom Gaudí undertook a series of increasingly larger commissions, including a mansion in the center of the city—the Palau Güell. This patronage was important not only because it provided the young architect an opportunity to build but also because it established his reputation among the Barcelona industrialists who would be his clients. The beginning of Gaudí's career coincided with the Renaixença (Renaissance), the intensely romantic Catalan cultural separatist movement of which modernisme was a part. Like his contemporaries, who saw modernisme as a means to create a uniquely Catalan architecture, Gaudí was a nationalist, but his nationalism was colored by an intense religious faith as well as a remarkable imagination. His clients shared his patriotic convictions, and they were open to his radical architectural expression of Catalan nationalism, whatever they thought of his often eccentric designs. They were also wealthy, which was important because Gaudí's painstakingly crafted buildings were expensive.

Gaudí's early commissions showed Islamic and Gothic influences, but by the turn of the century he had left such allusions behind. In 1904 he received a commission from the textile magnate Josep Batlló, who owned a twenty-five-year-old apartment building on the Paseo del Gracia, the city's most fashionable boulevard. Gaudí gutted the building, replanned the interior, added two floors, and rebuilt the facade. The owner's apartment occupied the entire second floor (the four upper floors were divided into private apartments). The interior of the Batlló apartment is astonishing: the grotto-like rooms have no right angles, and the whorls and swirls of the plaster ceilings morph into sculpted walls. The organic curves are echoed in the modeled wood paneling, the doors, the windows, the light fixtures, even the furniture, much of which was designed by Gaudí. His vivid imagination was tempered by practicality. For example, the doors between rooms are set into larger hinged panels that can be swung open for formal occasions or when moving furniture. The spirit of the building could be characterized as Baroque except that there are no historical allusions, nothing resembling columns, pilasters, or classical moldings. It is sui generis.

The Batlló property was hemmed in by its neighbors on two sides, and the old apartment building had a central light shaft that Gaudí enlarged, adding a glass roof, an open stair, and an elevator. He covered the walls in reflective cobalt-blue tiles, lighter colored on the lower floors, which had larger windows to let in more light, another example of the architect's practical side. The rooftop is a surreal landscape of sculpted chimneys whose warped surfaces are covered in fragments of broken tiles, a traditional technique called *trencadis,* revived by Gaudí (fig. 92). The facade facing the Paseo is covered in organic flowerlike patterns composed of similar multicolored iridescent tiles. In contrast to the delicate tiles, the upper window balconies have one-piece cast-iron balustrades that resemble masks or skulls. The openings of the lower floors are cavelike and incorporate limestone columns carved in the shape of human femurs, giving rise to the building's Catalan nickname Casa dels ossos (House of Bones).

The organic forms of Casa Batlló resemble Art Nouveau, but Gaudí was uninterested in international art trends, and his facade, a curious mixture of piety and patriotism, is an architectural allegory of the legend of Saint George, the patron saint of Catalonia, and the dragon. The garlic-shaped dome atop the spire, which carries the initials of the Holy Family, represents the tip of the lance that the saint used to dispatch the mythical beast; the ridge of the roof, with its scale-like roofing tiles, is the dragon's curved spine; and the skull-like balustrades and the femur-like columns symbolize the dragon's victims (fig. 93). Such architectural storytelling, somewhat akin to the facade of a medieval

92 Casa Batlló, Barcelona. Antoni Gaudí, 1904–6. The rooftop chimneys and spire are covered in broken tiles, a traditional technique revived by Gaudí.

Opposite:
93 Casa Batlló. Facade. The architecture symbolizes the legend of Saint George and the dragon. The main residence was on the second floor, with apartments above.

cathedral, was a distinctly unusual treatment for an early twentieth-century apartment building.

The Casa Batlló was an existing building, so the new facade did not carry any loads. The opportunity to design a fully fledged structure came to Gaudí in 1890, when Eusebi Güell relocated his textile mill in the suburbs of Barcelona where, in the paternalistic fashion of the time, he built a self-sufficient factory town for his employees: the Colònia Güell. The houses, as well as a clinic, a library, and other amenities, were designed by Gaudí's assistants, but the architect reserved the church for himself. He was familiar with reinforced concrete, but in his conservative fashion he decided to imitate the Gothic master builders and build in masonry. Gaudí did away with flying buttresses, which he dismissed as "crutches," and in the process invented an entirely original design method. He had a 1:10 floor plan of the church fixed to the ceiling. From this he suspended strings that represented the structural ribs of the roof. The hanging strings were weighted with little cotton bags filled with sand and buckshot to simulate the structural loads, and naturally assumed curved shapes. Gaudí had the string model photographed, and when the photograph was turned right-side up, the strings hanging in pure tension now represented catenary arches in pure compression. Masonry construction is strong *only* in compression,

CASA BATLLÓ
CASA BATLLÓ
P
taxi

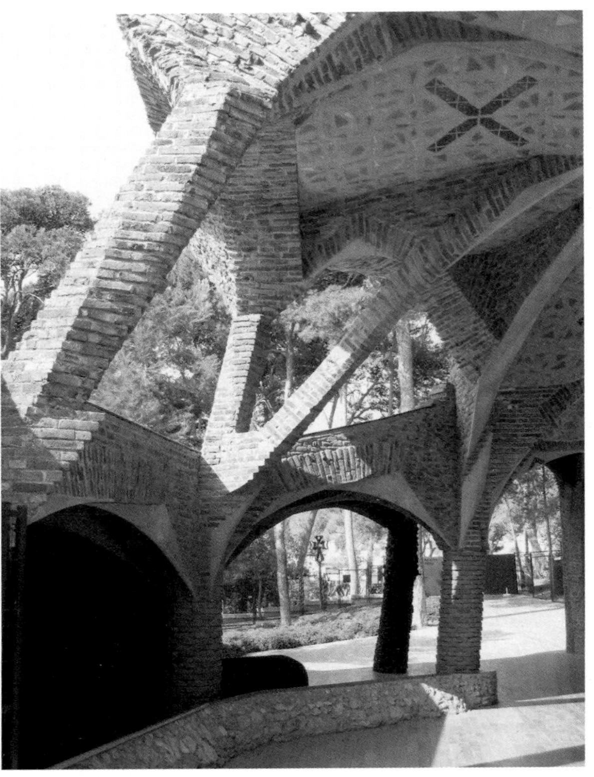

94 Crypt of the Church of Colònia Güell, Santa Coloma de Cervelló. Antoni Gaudí, 1908–18. The intersecting catenary arches create a remarkable space.

and the arches and angled columns effectively transmitted all the loads to the ground without the need for steel bars or buttresses. The twisted tilting columns and curving interlaced ribs supported thin Catalan brick vaults (fig. 94). Construction of the church was cut short by Güell's death in 1918, and only the crypt was completed. Nevertheless, the remarkable result is unlike anything that had been built before.

The project that allowed Gaudí to apply his structural ideas on a larger scale, and that occupied him for most of his life, was the Sagrada Família church. As early as 1882, only five years after graduating, he was approached by a conservative lay organization that was building a large Gothic Revival church in Barcelona: the Expiatory Temple of the Holy Family. The original architect had resigned over a disagreement, and they sought out the young Gaudí whose chief qualifications at that early stage of his career were his religious fervor, his interest in medieval architecture, and probably his willingness to accept a low fee. Gaudí's first proposal for the church was more or less conventionally Gothic, but after finishing the crypt that had been started by his predecessor, he radically changed the design to a soaring stone structure of catenary vaults and inclined columns.

Work proceeded extremely slowly. The cathedral-sized building, which was to accommodate nine thousand worshippers, had no official Church backing and was financed solely by alms and private donations, and over the years, funding slowed. In 1909, following a general strike and civil disturbances in the city, many of them intensely anticlerical, the central government forcibly suppressed Catalan nationalism. As the enthusiasm for the extravagance of modernisme waned, so did public support for the eccentric construction project. Yet Gaudí soldiered on, often contributing his own funds. Increasingly devout, isolated, almost hermit-like, and bereft of other commissions, he spent the last decade of his life focused on the great church. The slow pace of construction allowed him to further refine his ideas, and using weighted-string models he designed breathtakingly complex stone columns that branched out like giant trees. His design was replete with religious iconography—the three chief facades represented the Glory of Jesus, the Nativity, and the Passion, and the spires were named after the apostles (fig. 95). There would be no fewer than eighteen bell towers and spires; the tallest, over the crossing, was more than five hundred feet high. The circular bell towers, covered in broken tiles, were hollow and housed tubular bells that would effectively function as giant wind chimes.

When Gaudí died in 1926 at age seventy-three, struck down by a trolley, only a small portion of his great church was built. Work had yet to begin on the nave, one transept facade was only partially complete, and a single bell tower had been erected. Although Gaudí left models and drawings (which would be largely destroyed during the Spanish Civil War), these must be considered provisional because he tended to make decisions on the spot, changing and rebuilding as he went along. In any case, he assumed that, like a medieval cathedral, the great building would take scores of years to finish, and its design would evolve as subsequent architects made their own contributions.

As of this writing, Sagrada Família is still unfinished. Much of the later work has been in reinforced concrete rather than stone, which is controversial because many see it as compromising Gaudí's vision. Although in the past large buildings had been regularly altered over time—think of Durham Cathedral and Saint Peter's in Rome—today significant buildings have come to be seen as untouchable works of art. This attitude is partly the legacy of Gaudí's intensely personal architecture. Invention had been a feature of the work of such architects as Bramante and Borromini, but these Renaissance masters continued to use the classical vocabulary, even if sometimes in unorthodox ways. Gaudí

95 Sagrada Família, Barcelona. Antoni Gaudí, 1882–1926. The east transept with the Nativity facade. This postcard photograph of the unfinished church was taken in 1950, twenty-four years after Gaudí's death.

willfully dispensed with orthodoxy and imprinted his buildings with his own stamp. The Barcelona industrialists and entrepreneurs who were his private clients—there were no public commissions—did not feel constrained by convention and were willing to give their architect a free hand, and indeed were probably attracted by the novelty of his designs. Yet, unlike the buildings of Bramante and Palladio, Gaudí's personal and idiosyncratic work would have little influence on other architects. That was new, too. Since the Renaissance, the course of architecture had followed the models established by recognized masters—"the divine Michelangelo," "the great Wren." Paradoxically, as originality became more prized, its manifestations came to be seen as one of a kind, something to be admired but not necessarily imitated. This would increasingly be the pattern during the rest of the twentieth century.

24

Modern Life

Vienna, early twentieth century

Art Nouveau lasted several decades and involved some wonderfully inventive designers—not only Gaudí, but also Victor Horta and Henry van de Velde in Brussels, Hector Guimard in Paris, Charles Rennie Mackintosh and his wife Margaret Macdonald in Glasgow, Louis Comfort Tiffany in New York, and Louis Sullivan in Chicago (about whom more later). Perhaps the hottest hotbed of creative activity was Vienna. On May 25, 1897, a group of nineteen Viennese artists, led by the painters Gustav Klimt and Koloman Moser and the architects Joseph Maria Olbrich and Josef Hoffmann, "seceded" from the conservative Union of Austrian Artists. The so-called Secession was more like an arts club than a narrow orthodoxy, and it brought together a variety of individuals united in their dissatisfaction with the academic revival styles that characterized art and architecture in fin-de-siècle Vienna. The young firebrands—the leaders were all in their twenties and thirties—founded a magazine and organized exhibitions.

The following year, with the financial support of the steel magnate Karl Wittgenstein (the philosopher Ludwig Wittgenstein's father), the Secessionists built their own exhibition pavilion called the Wiener Secessionsgebäude, the Vienna Secession Building. Their brave motto, which appeared over the entrance, read "To Every Age Its Art; To Art Its Freedom." The building, designed by Olbrich (1867–1908), was a series of interlocking white boxes housing a skylit exhibition space. The white-painted plastered brick with gold trim was a striking contrast to the gray stone architecture of central Vienna. The severe rectangularity, influenced by the Mackintoshes, who were greatly admired by the Secessionists, was different from the organic forms of French and Belgian Art Nouveau, although the floral patterns painted on the walls were likewise influenced by Japanese woodblock prints. Nothing here suggested cultural nationalism: Vienna was simply too cosmopolitan, the capital of the Austro-Hungarian Empire that included

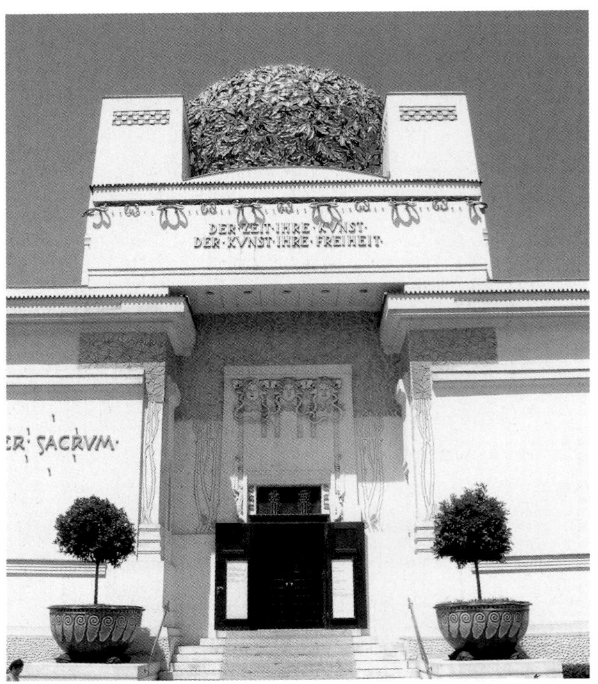

96 Secession Building, Vienna. Joseph Maria Olbrich, 1897–98. The boxy shapes and geometric ornament are characteristic of the Secession; the gilded leaves of the dome and the sinuous serpent frieze and floral pattern below recall Art Nouveau. The motto reads "To Every Age Its Art; To Art Its Freedom."

Magyars, Poles, Ukrainians, Slovaks, Croats, and Bohemians. Olbrich was born in Silesia, Hoffmann in Moravia.

The most striking feature of the Secession Building was a dramatic basket-like wrought-iron dome covered with gilded bronze laurel leaves (fig. 96). As in Schinkel's Altes Museum, the reference to the Pantheon was intentional—Olbrich called the pavilion a "temple of art." The laurel-leafed dome, which a Viennese wit christened the "golden cabbage," was not the only classical reference. Three Medusa heads in a bas-relief panel over the front door represented Painting, Architecture, and Sculpture; sculpted owls symbolized wisdom. On the other hand, a frieze of twisted serpents was Egyptian rather than Greek, as was the theme of a mural by Moser. The Secessionists wanted to evoke the spirit of the ancient past without using classical columns, capitals, and pediments, and the somewhat cryptic result combined romantic imagery with a severe minimalism. Klimt's poster for the opening of the building portrayed the goddess Athena as the liberator of the arts, as well as Theseus slaying the minotaur—that is, the Secessionists dispatching establishment art.

The shadow of an older architect loomed large over the Secession. Otto Wagner (1841–1918) had been Hoffmann's teacher, and he was also Olbrich's employer and mentor. Wagner, who came from a well-to-do Viennese family, had studied architecture in Vienna and Berlin and had a successful and lucrative practice developing and building handsome Renaissance Revival apartment buildings—"interest-bearing castles," he called them. When Wagner was in his mid-fifties, he experienced an architectural epiphany that coincided with his appointment as the professor of architecture of the prestigious Imperial Academy of Fine Arts. He addressed his students in a manifesto-like handbook titled *Moderne Architektur*. "One idea inspires this book," he wrote in the introduction, "namely that the basis of today's predominant views on architecture must be shifted, and we must become fully aware that the sole departure point for our artistic work can only be modern life." The sentence was capitalized.

Wagner pointed out that a Greek temple, a Gothic cathedral, and a Louis XV salon were not simply examples of different architectural styles but represented different ways of life and different tastes and customs. "A man in a modern traveling suit, for example, fits in very well with the waiting room of a train station, with sleeping cars, with all our vehicles," he wrote, "yet would we not stare if we were to see someone dressed in clothing from the Louis XV period using such things?" This was a roundabout way of saying that a Louis XV salon was not a suitable setting for a modern person—something different was required. *To Every Age Its Art*. In 1899, Wagner publicly joined his younger colleagues in the breakaway Secession movement, an unexpected gesture for a fifty-eight-year-old at the peak of his profession.

Wagner believed that the key to architectural expression lay in the manner in which buildings were built. "The architect always has to develop the art-form out of construction," he instructed in *Moderne Architektur*. He did not mean simply exposing the structure—architecture was not engineering—he meant *expressing* it, the way that the ancient Greeks did in their classical temples. Wagner considered modern construction to be different from what he called Renaissance construction, not because iron, steel, and reinforced concrete were industrially produced, but because these materials were assembled in fundamentally different ways. For example, unlike traditional masonry walls, the exterior cladding of a steel or reinforced-concrete frame building did not support heavy loads. Wagner believed that this new form of construction required a different form of expression. It is important to emphasize that he was not trying to reinvent architecture. To use the metaphor of spoken language, style was not about *what* you said, it was about *how* you said it.

At this time, Wagner was designing stations, bridges, and tunnels for the Wiener Stadtbahn, Vienna's new metropolitan railway. The station in the Karlsplatz,

97 Karlsplatz Stadtbahn Station, Vienna. Otto Wagner, 1898–99. Modern materials such as steel are combined with book-matched veined marble.

a prominent city square, represents his early attempt to devise a "modern" style (fig. 97). The small pavilion contained a ticket office, waiting room, and toilets; the platforms were on a lower level. The symmetrical composition was traditional—a vaulted central bay and two wings—but the construction method was not. The wooden roof was supported on a structural steel frame that was infilled with lightweight gypsum blocks, plastered on the interior and faced with polished Carrara marble on the exterior. The veined marble was cut into extremely thin (less than three-quarters of an inch) sheets that were book-matched and supported on a grid of steel angles. Thicker slabs of rusticated granite protected the vulnerable lower portion of the wall. The visible steel angles were painted apple-green—the Stadtbahn's corporate color. The verticals had decorative cast-iron scrolls at the bottom and gilded cast-iron brackets at the top. Ornament was an integral part of Wagner's modernism, whether it was applied to the surface, like the gold sunflowers and geometric patterns stenciled on the marble, or was three-dimensional, like the cast-iron organic plantlike forms on the parapet and the vaulted roof of the pavilion. The wrought-iron door grilles, which swirled in classic Art Nouveau fashion, echoed the floral theme. It was likely Wagner's assistant Olbrich who was responsible for the design of this exuberant decoration. More than a hundred years later, this delicate and beautifully designed pavilion remains cheerfully irreverent, standing in sharp contrast to today's crudely built mass-transit stations.

Wagner's was a multifaceted talent. He was active in city planning, and in 1892 he won an international planning competition organized by the City of Vienna and received a commission to replan the flood-prone Vienna River, which flowed through the center of the city. This involved designing bridges, weirs, and locks. The redirection of the river created a new boulevard that became the site of three apartment buildings that Wagner developed, designed, and built. Numbers 38 and 40 stand side by side on Linke Wienzeile (Left Vienna Row). Completed in 1899, they are straightforward six-story blocks with reinforced concrete frames and brick exterior walls. The two lower floors contain commercial spaces; the upper apartment floors are punctuated by rows of identical rectangular windows, reflecting the fact that, in Wagner's view, the elevator made all the floors equally desirable. As the developer, Wagner was free to innovate, and both facades were a dramatic departure from the heavy Baroque Revival style that was common in Viennese apartment buildings at that time. The facade of Number 38 is covered in white stucco and decorated with palm leaves, garlands, and other plant motifs painted in gold. The top row of windows is separated by prominent gilt medallions designed by Koloman Moser (1868–1918), and the cornice is adorned with human figures. Number 40 is even more striking. The entire facade is covered in glazed ceramic tiles whose rose patterns resemble a giant floral tapestry. The flatness of the tilework, emphasizing the wall's nonstructural character, is offset by a frieze of projecting lion heads and an elaborate multicolored cornice (fig. 98). The flowery ornament gave rise to the building's nickname, Majolikahaus, a reference to the colorful glazed Italian ceramic ware.

Wagner's use of ceramic tiles is analogous to Gaudí's broken tilework, although its flat, wallpaper quality produces a different effect. Unlike Gaudí, Wagner observed strict symmetry in the building's composition; vertical stacks of balconies frame the facade on each side; the prominent cornice recalls a Renaissance palazzo. In another nod to the past, he framed the openings but did so with leaves and garlands rather than pediments and pilasters. There is nothing abstract about the decorations; like Gaudí, Wagner wanted his architecture to have meaning.

In 1903, Wagner won a competition to design the headquarters of the imperial Austrian Postal Savings Bank, an important government institution. The seven-story office building, which covered an entire city block, occupied him for the next nine years. The design, which is contemporary with Gaudí's Casa Batlló, further highlights the differences between the two architects. The bank's entrance facade, a projecting bay facing a small square off the Ringstrasse, is axially symmetrical, with a solid-looking granite base and a projecting cornice; the central portion of the attic story is decorated with wreaths and statues (fig. 99). The structure is a combination of a reinforced concrete frame and load-bearing exterior brick walls that, like the Karlsplatz station, are faced with marble. Instead of being supported on steel bars, the thin slabs of Tyrolean marble appear to be anchored to the brick wall with iron bolts whose exposed heads are covered with aluminum caps to prevent rusting. The prominent bolt heads, which make a pattern on the facade, were Wagner's way of expressing the nonstructural character of the cladding. In addition, he decorated the exterior of the central bay with small aluminum blocks and made the marble slabs of the flanking portions slightly convex, creating a different texture. The cladding of the lower two floors is not marble but cambered granite slabs, whose countersunk anchor bolts emphasize the masonry's thickness.

Wagner was concerned with maintenance, and he commonly used glazed ceramic tile and polished marble as a cladding. For the same reason he adopted noncorrosive aluminum, a new material whose industrial production had been

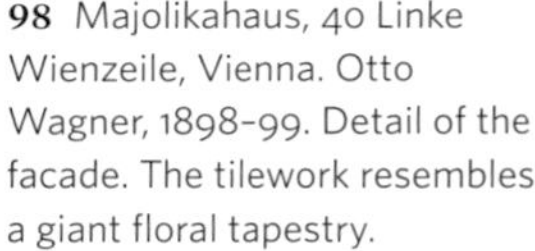

98 Majolikahaus, 40 Linke Wienzeile, Vienna. Otto Wagner, 1898–99. Detail of the facade. The tilework resembles a giant floral tapestry.

99 Austrian Postal Savings Bank, Vienna. Otto Wagner, 1903–12. The entrance facade is a combination of classical composition and modern construction. The marble and granite slabs are attached to the wall with bolts, whose aluminum-capped heads are exposed.

only recently perfected. In the Postal Savings Bank, he used cast aluminum not only for the bolt caps but also for door handles, lighting fixtures, heating grilles, and the colonettes that support the glass entrance canopy. Also cast aluminum are the fourteen-foot-tall angels that stand on the cornice, the work of Wagner's frequent collaborator Othmar Schimkowitz (1864–1947), who had been responsible for the statues on 38 Linke Wienzeile, as well as the carved Medusa heads in the Secession Building. Artists and architects working together was typical of the Secession and was another example of the compelling blend of modernity and tradition that marked the buildings of this period.

Like all large buildings at that time, the Postal Savings Bank was planned around large interior courtyards that functioned as light wells. The first floor of the central courtyard was also the site of the main public space of the building: the banking hall (fig. 100). This remarkable room is a classic basilican space but realized in industrially produced materials. A row of columns made out of riveted steel plates separates the two lower aisles from the central vaulted space. The ceiling is made of curved frosted glass panes supported on a steel grid suspended from the concealed greenhouse structure above. Part of the floor is constructed of glass blocks that allow natural light into the mail sorting room below. Wagner designed everything: patterned linoleum floors; columnar aluminum fixtures that distributed heated air; lighting fixtures; even the bentwood stools manufactured by the Thonet company of Vienna. The harmonious result is an accomplished example of a Secessionist *Gesamtkunstwerk*—a total work of art.

100 Austrian Postal Savings Bank, banking hall. The space is flooded with natural light from the suspended glass ceiling. The grilled aluminum columnar fixtures distribute heated air.

The Postal Savings Bank featured wide, naturally lit corridors, a pneumatic messaging system, a built-in vacuum cleaner system, and movable partitions in the work areas. The glass of the greenhouse roof over the banking hall was heated to melt the snow. "Something impractical cannot be beautiful," Wagner wrote in *Moderne Architektur,* and he worked hard to fulfill this dictum. But practical did not mean minimal; Wagner was no functionalist. The walls are enlivened by stenciled geometric patterns. The grilled columnar fixtures in the banking hall have beautiful flared bases, ornamental spheres, and grilles that resemble a medieval knight's helmet. Throughout the building, industrialization never displaces old-fashioned craftsmanship. Wagner's aim was not to undermine the traditional architectural values of solidity, permanence, and—in the case of the bank—gravitas, but rather to achieve them by different means.

Art Nouveau in its various guises, especially in Vienna, represents the beginning of a new chapter in the story of architecture. Since the Renaissance, architects had been guided by historic precedents, either Greek, Roman, or medieval. Now architects were looking elsewhere: in the case of Gaudí, turning inward to personal and spiritual visions; in the case of Wagner and his young colleagues, combining old values with new materials and techniques. Meanwhile, on the other side of the Atlantic, another young architect was pushing this tendency in an even more radical direction.

25

The New World

Buffalo, early twentieth century

Turn-of-the-century Buffalo on Lake Erie, in the northwestern corner of New York State, was hardly Habsburg Vienna. Less than a hundred years old, the small city was a third the size of the imperial capital. Yet thanks to the Erie Canal and to inexpensive hydroelectricity produced by the Niagara River, Buffalo had become a thriving commercial hub, a shipbuilding and industrial center, a shipping port for Midwestern grain, and a jumping-off place for immigrants heading west. The busy downtown may not have had a royal palace, but it did boast the world's largest office building. The Ellicott Square Building, which was completed seven years before the Austrian Postal Savings Bank, likewise occupied a full city block and had a similar glass-covered concourse in its central court. The two-story base containing shops was surmounted by eight floors of offices, and at ten stories the building was taller than any European office building. Built in only twelve months using a structural frame of rolled steel, Ellicott Square had a dozen elevators (the Austrian Postal Savings Bank was served primarily by stairs) and included the Vitascope Theater, which presented Edison's marvelous invention and was the world's first cinema.

The architect of Ellicott Square was Charles B. Atwood (1849–1895), who died unexpectedly before the building was completed. Atwood, a partner of Daniel H. Burnham (1849–1912), whose large Chicago firm was an acknowledged leader in commercial buildings, was born in Boston and educated at Harvard, and had been the architect-in-chief of Chicago's World's Columbian Exposition. A talented classicist, he wrapped the steel frame in an architectural skin of granite, brick, and terra-cotta (fig. 101). The style of the four identical facades is usually referred to as Beaux-Arts, after the French school that many leading American architects (though not Atwood) attended. The top floor resembled a giant frieze and was topped off with a prominent cornice featuring a row of Medusa heads.

101 Ellicott Square Building, Buffalo. D. H. Burnham & Company, 1895–96. This postcard view shows the building in 1900. The ornamented granite, brick, and terra-cotta exterior conceals a steel frame.

The terra-cotta and cast-iron decorations included cherubs, grotesques, bell-flowers, and laurel wreaths, and the two arched entrances incorporated reclining statues of Nike and Hermes flanked by pairs of heavily rusticated and banded columns. The resplendent effect was of an oversized Renaissance palazzo.

Only a block away from the Ellicott Square Building, on the corner of Church and Pearl Streets, stood the Guaranty Building, completed the same year and designed by another Chicagoan. Louis Sullivan (1856–1924) was also born in Boston; he attended MIT for a year, worked in Philadelphia, and eventually moved to Chicago. He found time to spend a year studying at the École des Beaux-Arts in Paris, and in 1879 he came to the attention of Dankmar Adler (1844–1900), a German-born engineer who recognized the young architect's talent. Their successful partnership's most prominent project was the spectacular Auditorium Building, completed in 1889, which housed Chicago's opera house and whose seventeen-story office tower was the tallest building in the Loop.

Like Otto Wagner, Sullivan was dissatisfied with the historicist character of contemporary architecture. Unlike Wagner, he believed the solution lay in expressing a building's purpose rather than its construction. "Form ever follows function," he wrote in an 1896 essay titled "The Tall Office Building Artistically Considered." Sullivan described the commercial office building, which was an Adler & Sullivan specialty, as a crude combination of technology (steel construction and elevators) and real estate economics (maximizing rentable space on a building lot). What was the appropriate architectural expression for this new type of building? Sullivan's answer was to divide the building into three parts: base, shaft, and capital, analogous to a classical column. The base was the lowest two floors, which related visually to the street and usually contained shops. "Above this, throughout the indefinite number of typical office tiers, we take our cue from the individual cell, which requires a window with its separating pier, its sill and lintel, and we, without more ado, make them look all alike because they are all alike," Sullivan wrote, describing the shaft. He finished off the top of the building—the capital—with an attic floor, a frieze, or a projecting cornice to indicate a definite ending to the tiers of office floors.

Like the Ellicott Square Building, the Guaranty Building consisted of a structural steel frame covered by a nonstructural masonry skin. There the similarity ended. In contrast to Atwood, who organized the facade in horizontal layers, somewhat like Alberti's Palazzo Rucellai, Sullivan chose to emphasize the vertical—the piers between the windows shot to the top of the building without interruption, and the spandrels beneath the windows were recessed to emphasize this upward movement (fig. 102). At fourteen stories the Guaranty Building was the tallest building in the city. Moreover, it *looked* tall; people called it a "skyscraper."

The identical double-hung windows, many of which had retractable canvas awnings (this was before air-conditioning), were separated by piers of brick-red terra-cotta tiles. Sullivan made no attempt to express the hidden structural frame; only every second pier corresponded to a steel column, and the piers terminated in nonstructural arches. Like the Secessionists, Sullivan dispensed with classical motifs; the cast terra-cotta piers and spandrels incorporated intricate floral patterns, an American version of Art Nouveau, of which he was a master. While Atwood distributed his ornament in a somewhat scattershot fashion, Sullivan smoothly integrated the decoration into the design, making it appear all of a graceful piece. The only references to antiquity were the round columns at the base of the building, although their richly modeled capitals, which incorporated the building's initials, did not correspond to any known classical order. They were Sullivan's invention.

▪ ▪ ▪ ▪ ▪

One of the employees in Adler & Sullivan's sixteenth-floor office in the tower of the Auditorium Building was a young draftsman named Frank Lloyd Wright (1867–1959), whom Sullivan had taken under his wing and in short order made his assistant. After five years, shortly before the Guaranty Building commission, Sullivan fired his protégé after discovering that Wright was designing private residences on the side, which violated the terms of his contract. Although only twenty-six, Wright was ready to strike out on his own. And despite having no formal architectural education he had a natural talent for design, as Sullivan recognized. Others reached the same conclusion. A few years later, Daniel Burnham, seeking to replace the deceased Atwood, offered to send Wright to Europe to

102 Guaranty Building, Buffalo. Adler & Sullivan, 1895–96. Detail of the facade showing the rich ornamentation of the terracotta cladding that emphasizes the verticality of the design.

study at the École des Beaux-Arts and spend two years in Rome if he would join the Burnham firm as a design partner. The ambitious young architect demurred.

Handsome, charismatic, and flamboyant, Wright had no difficulty attracting clients, and in his first ten years of practice he completed more than fifty commissions, mostly private residences. The first houses were conventional, but he soon developed his own style. By both temperament and background, the self-taught Wright was hostile to academic classicism. He had learned a lot from Sullivan, and through the British journal *The Studio,* a mainstay of Art Nouveau, he was familiar with Mackintosh, Olbrich, and Wagner. Like them, he sought to design buildings that would provide a suitable setting for modern life. Unlike them, he was no cosmopolitan and rather saw modernism as a means to a distinctly national—that is, American—architecture.

In 1903, Wright received a commission for a new headquarters office from the Larkin Company, a national soap and toiletry mail-order business based in Buffalo. The Larkin Administration Building was designed seven years after the Guaranty Building, and it shows how far Wright had moved from his mentor. No color photographs exist (the building was demolished in 1950), but the dark-red brick and red sandstone trim are comparable to the red terra-cotta of the Guaranty Building. That is the only similarity. The five-story Larkin Building had solid brick walls and reinforced concrete floors supported on concrete-encased steel beams. The site was adjacent to the company's factory in an industrial district, and Wright designed monumental brick forms that were intended to hold their own in the sooty surroundings. The windowless boxy corners and the heavy massing recall the Vienna Secession Building, as do the sculptural figures and globes atop the brick pylons (fig. 103). Like Olbrich's pavilion, the somewhat forbidding Larkin Building projects an air of temple-like mystery.

Inside, five open floors surrounded a tall, skylit atrium. There were no private offices; the executive work spaces were in the atrium, which was overlooked by the surrounding floors. Larkin was a progressive company, and the building provided a dining room (where executives and clerks ate side by side), a lounge, a conservatory, a classroom, and branches of the Buffalo Public Library and the YWCA (most of the office staff were women). The atrium also included a giant pipe organ that provided lunch-hour concerts for the benefit of the "Larkinites." The interior was finished in lightly glazed buff-colored brick, and the piers of the atrium were adorned with highly stylized capitals of white terra-cotta, between which were terra-cotta panels incised with inspirational phrases, such as "Generosity Altruism Sacrifice" and "Imagination Judgement Initiative." Like Wagner in the Austrian Postal Savings Bank, Wright designed everything, including the light fixtures, desks, and office chairs.

103 Larkin Administration Building, Buffalo. Frank Lloyd Wright, 1903–6. Photographed shortly after completion. The almost brutal massing of the building was a reaction to its industrial setting.

104 Darwin D. Martin House, Buffalo. Frank Lloyd Wright, 1904–5. The horizontal composition, bands of windows, and cantilevered roofs are hallmarks of the Prairie Style.

The Larkin Building is estimated to have cost $4 million, a very large sum at the time (the Ellicott Square Building cost $3.5 million). Fortunately for Wright, he had the strong support of a leading Larkin executive, Darwin D. Martin. Martin persuaded the company head, John D. Larkin, who had initially considered Sullivan for the commission, to choose Wright instead. Martin's brother William, who lived in Oak Park, outside Chicago, had just built a Wright-designed house. Darwin Martin, who would become a lifelong friend and supporter of Wright's, was impressed, and he not only backed Wright for the Larkin job but commissioned him to design his own house in Buffalo. The result is an early example of what came to be known as the Prairie Style.

The Martin House represented a radical departure from convention. Most houses, even Wright's early houses, were conceived as boxes; this house was the opposite. The exterior was defined by windmilling brick piers rather than by flat walls, and instead of traditional openings in a wall, the windows were organized in long rows that continued around corners, which further undermined the box (fig. 104). Another change was equally radical. Classical buildings used columns and pilasters to establish vertical rhythms—in the Martin House, everything was horizontal: the dramatic cantilevers, the long rows of windows, the continuous concrete and limestone trim, even the elongated Roman bricks. Wright claimed that the emphasis on the horizontal suited the Midwestern prairie, which was a rationalization since the Martin House, like most of Wright's residential commissions, was in a city—and northwestern New York State was hardly the prairie. Nevertheless, the stretched-out, ground-hugging house did strike what seemed to many a particularly American chord.

A visitor to the Martin house arrives under a porte-cochère. Several steps and a short path lead to the hidden front door. The entry vestibule, which provided discreet access to Darwin Martin's private study, connects to a reception room whose dominant feature is an arched brick fireplace. This room opens into a hallway that merges with the living room, which in turn extends in three directions, inward into the dining area and the library, and outward onto a large porch that is an open-air extension of the interior (fig. 105). A massive two-sided fireplace anchors this cruciform arrangement. The hallway behind the fireplace looks down a hundred-foot-long pergola that leads through a flower garden to a conservatory whose focus is a plaster replica of the Winged Victory of Samothrace. (Wright used a copy of the Greek statue in the reception area of the Larkin Building, as well as in his own studio.) The conservatory is attached to a carriage house and stable. Opposite, Wright designed a house for Martin's sister and her husband, its cruciform plan a smaller version of the larger house.

In the open plan of the Martin House, where one space flows into the next, Wright went further than his Secession contemporaries in creating an architecture unconstrained by conventions. The interior details were equally unorthodox. The supporting piers were exposed brick with gilded mortar joints; the low ceilings were animated by wood moldings and slight changes of level. Although portieres curtained off the dining room and the library, there were no window treatments; the long rows of bare windows were enlivened by geometrically patterned stained glass. Like Sullivan and the Secessionists, Wright favored floral motifs—wisteria on the first floor and the Tree of Life on the second. Other than the art-glass windows, the main decorative element in the living room was a mosaic mural over the fireplace, depicting wisteria branches, leaves, and blossoms. Most of the furniture in the living spaces was designed by Wright: barrel chairs in the style of Olbrich and slatted dining chairs that recall Mackintosh. Wright carried *Gesamtkunstwerk* further than Wagner, even designing a dress for Isabelle Martin, who is said to have disliked it because it made her blend into the decor.

The Martin House was a luxurious and expensive mansion, but the Prairie Style was adaptable to smaller residences, as Martin's sister's charming house demonstrates. The term Prairie Style is misleading, for Wright went further than the Secessionists, changing not only the architectural mode of expression but also its content. He designed buildings that looked different because they *were* different—differently planned and differently built. Perhaps too differently. The Martin house was an expensive combination of concrete slabs, brick walls, and wooden rafters, and the dramatic cantilevers required structural steel beams. The heavy construction and unconventional atrium of the Larkin Building were likewise expensive, which discouraged commercial builders. Nor was Wright offered any significant public work; no libraries, courthouses, or city halls came his way at this time. Politicians and public servants were wary of his bohemian individualism, and his clientele was limited to those rare middle-class professionals and businessmen, like Martin, who shared his unconventional taste. In standing outside the establishment, Wright was following in the footsteps of Gaudí, a visionary and self-reliant loner going his independent way.

105 Martin House. Plan. The long pergola leads to a conservatory. The carriage house and stable are on the top left of the plan. Martin's sister and her family lived in the small house at top right.

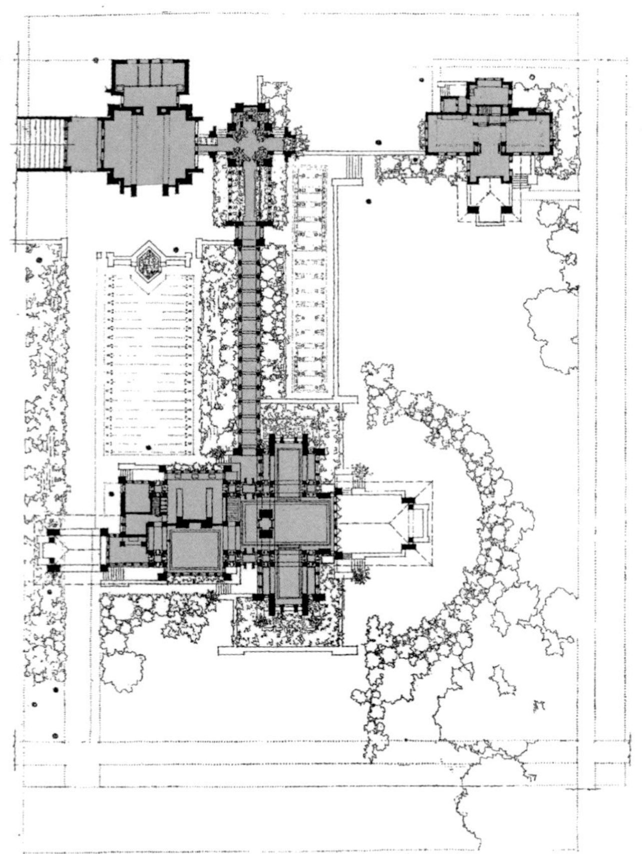

26

The Enduring Past

Washington, D.C., early twentieth century

Wright's efforts to establish a new architectural style had little effect on the American mainstream. Museums and libraries continued to be built in the Beaux-Arts style; the Gothic Revival dominated the design of cathedrals, churches, and educational institutions; and American Colonial, a version of English Georgian, remained popular for private residences, large and small. State and federal government buildings favored Greek and Roman classicism, following the lead of Washington, D.C., where, ever since 1836, when Robert Mills had modeled the entry porch of the Patent Office on the Parthenon, columns and pediments dominated the official architecture of the federal capital.

Washington was laid out in 1791 by the Frenchman Pierre Charles L'Enfant, but his ambitious Baroque plan had been severely compromised over the intervening century. In 1901, on the occasion of the centennial of the founding of the capital, Senator James McMillan from Michigan, who chaired the Senate committee on the federal district, decided it was time to remedy the situation. He assembled a four-man advisory panel composed of Daniel Burnham, by then nationally famous for overseeing the planning and construction of the fabulously successful 1893 Chicago World's Columbian Exposition; the landscape architect Frederick Law Olmsted, Jr. (1870–1957), the son of the great park builder; the architect Charles Follen McKim (1847–1909) of the prominent firm McKim, Mead & White; and the celebrated sculptor Augustus Saint-Gaudens (1848–1907). Burnham, McKim, and Saint-Gaudens were confirmed classicists who had worked together on the Chicago Exposition, whose plan was the work of Olmsted père.

A year later, the panel issued its report, which included a detailed blueprint for the city's monumental core, the so-called McMillan Plan. Under Olmsted's leadership, the fussy Victorian gardens that covered the National Mall were transformed into a broad greensward, and an intrusive railroad station was

106 Rashtrapati Bhavan (Viceroy's House), New Delhi. Edwin Lutyens, 1912–29. Baroque classicism in the grand manner is combined with Mughal motifs.

moved to another location and rebuilt—by Burnham—as Union Station. The new plan extended the Mall beyond the Washington Monument in the form of a long reflecting pool that terminated at the Potomac River with a proposed memorial to Abraham Lincoln. The report included an illustration of McKim's vision for the memorial: a large Doric portico forming a backdrop to a statue of the president.

McKim and his colleagues took it for granted that classicism was the appropriate style for the memorial. At the beginning of the twentieth century, no matter the continued popularity of the Gothic Revival, the current fashion for Beaux-Arts, and the new directions pursued by Art Nouveau experimenters like Sullivan, only Greek and Roman classicism conveyed the authority and gravitas required by national monuments. This was true not only in America. In 1912, when Edwin Lutyens (1869–1944) was commissioned to design the grand Viceroy's House in the replanned Indian capital of New Delhi, he adopted—and adapted—the classical language. Lutyens had made his name designing Arts and Crafts country houses and was considered by many the greatest British architect since Wren. Later in life he favored a rich, Baroque version of classicism, and in the New Delhi building he added Mughal features, such as deep overhanging eaves, chhatris, stone screens, carved elephants, and special column capitals that included bells and lotus blossoms. The copper-clad reinforced concrete central dome of the Viceroy's House has a Pantheon-like oculus, but its tall silhouette resembles a Buddhist stupa (fig. 106). Lutyens's work in New Delhi, which included a war memorial in the form of a Roman triumphal arch, demonstrated the adaptability of classicism.

In Washington, D.C., the McMillan Plan did not have the force of law but it garnered the enthusiastic support of President Theodore Roosevelt and became a template for the future. It took the better part of a decade for Congress to approve the proposed site for the Lincoln Memorial and to authorize funds for its construction. The federal Commission of Fine Arts, newly formed to oversee the implementation of the McMillan Plan, recommended Henry Bacon for the commission. Bacon (1866–1924), a contemporary of Frank Lloyd Wright's and likewise a Midwesterner trained through practice rather than formal education, had apprenticed with McKim, Mead & White and worked on such major projects as the Boston Public Library, New York's Pennsylvania Station, and the Chicago exposition. As a protégé of McKim, who had died unexpectedly two years earlier, Bacon—now in independent practice—was considered the ideal person to realize his mentor's vision.

Joseph G. Cannon, the recently retired Speaker of the House, disagreed. The powerful Illinois congressman was not a fan of the Senate's McMillan Plan, and he engaged the architect John Russell Pope to study alternative sites for the Lincoln Memorial. When this initiative failed, Cannon insisted that Pope be considered for the memorial commission. Pope (1874–1937), almost a decade younger than Bacon, came from an established New York family. A prodigy, he had graduated from Columbia University and likewise apprenticed with McKim, Mead & White. He was the first architect to win the Rome Prize (cofounded by McKim), which enabled him to travel to Italy and Greece and to study in Paris at the École des Beaux-Arts, whose challenging program he completed in only two years. What brought Pope to Cannon's attention was his recently completed memorial in Lincoln's Kentucky birthplace. The severe Greek Revival building, a sort of mausoleum, housed a replica of the log cabin in which Lincoln was born.

Pope and Bacon submitted competing proposals for the Lincoln Memorial. Following McKim's lead, both included a statue of the president and a marble structure using the Doric order. Both men were classicists, but their designs are very different. To Pope, the nearby Washington Monument was the main constraint. "To hold its own with the Monument a Lincoln Memorial first must possess this vital quality of bigness and of dignity," he wrote. "It cannot compete with the Monument vertically, therefore it must horizontally." To that end he located the statue in the center of a giant circular colonnade that was Roman in scale and majesty. Bacon took a different approach, placing the statue inside a relatively small freestanding building based loosely on the Parthenon. "The power of impression by an object of reverence and honor is greatest when it is secluded and isolated," he explained.

Pope's bold proposal, whose sweeping theatricality recalls Bernini, found favor with the public, but the architectural profession and the Commission of

Fine Arts, whose members included Burnham, Olmsted, and Saint-Gaudens, came out strongly in favor of Bacon's understated solution. In 1911, a bipartisan Congressional committee charged with overseeing the memorial voted in favor of Bacon's proposal. The classical temple solution did not please everyone. One critic described it as "a few columns and an entablature for a lid." Opponents of Bacon's design charged that classicism and the homespun Lincoln did not belong together. The opposition was strongest in Illinois, where Lincoln had spent much of his life and where the proposal was seen as yet another example of an overbearing Eastern establishment—despite Burnham's prominent role and Bacon's Midwestern background. "Architecture, be it known, is dead," fulminated Louis Sullivan. Frank Lloyd Wright called the idea of commemorating Lincoln by a Greek temple a "depravity." The Chicago chapter of the American Institute of Architects passed a resolution condemning Bacon's design as "purely Greek and entirely un-American."

But was classicism really un-American? Classical columns and entablatures were certainly not homegrown, but neither was the English political tradition, and both were integral to the young American republic. Of the first four presidents, three—Washington, Jefferson, and Madison—designed their own homes, and all—Mount Vernon, Monticello, and Montpelier—were in the classical style. Washington handpicked a Palladian design for the President's House; Jefferson modeled his designs of the Virginia statehouse and the library of the University of Virginia on ancient Roman precedents; and Jefferson appointed Benjamin Henry Latrobe, a Greek Revivalist, to be the architect of the Capitol. Classical Greek architecture in particular appealed to the young republic's founders since it was associated with the birthplace of democracy, and the style remained popular in private residences as well as public buildings, producing a second Greek Revival in the first half of the nineteenth century.

Bacon's Lincoln Memorial consists of a cella surrounded by Doric columns, all built of Colorado Yule marble, but it is not exactly a Greek temple. The roof is flat and topped by a Roman attic (fig. 107). The attic conceals a glazed greenhouse roof that covers a ceiling made of thin sheets of marble that allow a diffused light into the interior. In another departure from tradition, Bacon turned the building ninety degrees and located the entrance in the long wall—an unconventional solution for a Greek temple. There is no door, just a forty-five-foot-wide opening. In one way, Bacon did follow Greek precedent to the letter: the fluted columns have entasis and are slightly inclined to the center, the walls of the cella and the attic are sloped inward, and the base is not flat but very slightly convex. Few visitors to the memorial are aware of these optical refinements but, as in ancient

107 Lincoln Memorial, Washington, D.C. Henry Bacon, 1911–22. This aerial view shows the attic story concealing skylights that illuminate the interior, a novel idea for a Greek temple.

Greek architecture, they humanize the architecture, making the giant marble temple majestic but not overwhelming.

Like Lutyens in New Delhi, Bacon introduced iconographic elements to express the building's function. Instead of triglyphs and metopes, he substituted a frieze symbolizing the Union: intertwining wreaths of Northern laurel and Southern long-leaf pine. The wreaths alternated with the names and admission dates of the thirty-six states that existed at the end of the Civil War. The states admitted to the Union after 1865 are named on the east front of the attic story below a frieze of wheat garlands and rampant eagles. The memorial is raised almost forty feet on a grassy mound reached by a broad outdoor stair that is flanked by tall Roman tripod braziers decorated with eagles, corn cobs, and pinecones; the base contains bas-reliefs portraying lictor's rods, the Roman symbols of authority, and eagle-headed tomahawks. In these ways Bacon Americanized the classical idiom.

The author of the bas-reliefs on the upper frieze was Daniel Chester French (1850–1931), since Saint-Gaudens's death the leading American sculptor.

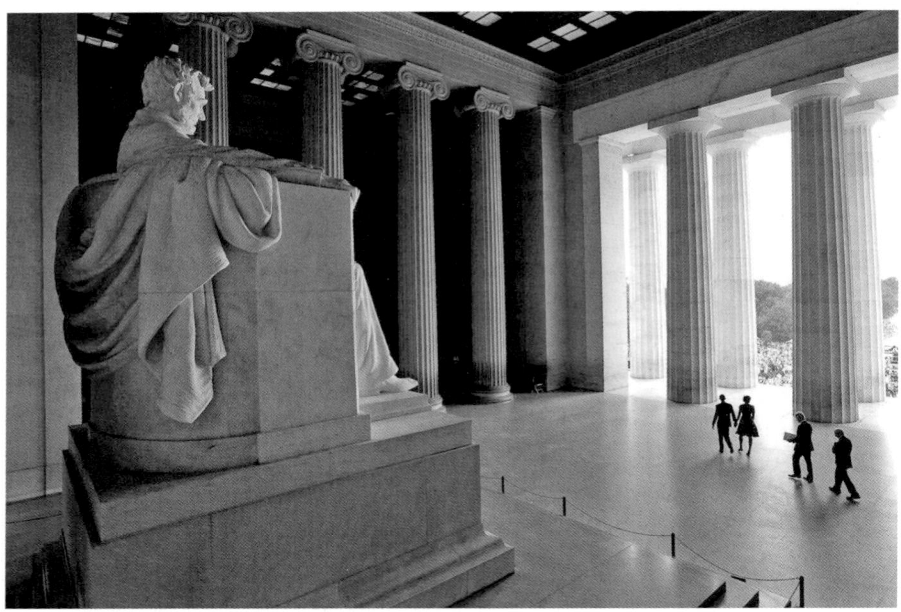

108 Lincoln Memorial. The colossal statue of the president dominates the interior. Beyond the Ionic colonnade is a wall tablet with Lincoln's Second Inaugural Address. This August 28, 2013, photograph shows President Barack Obama and First Lady Michelle Obama, followed by Presidents Bill Clinton and Jimmy Carter, at an event commemorating Martin Luther King, Jr.'s "I Have a Dream" speech, which was delivered at the memorial in 1963.

French, who was Bacon's close friend and frequent collaborator, is responsible for the marble statue of Lincoln inside the building. The statue of Athena in the Parthenon was erect, but French chose to portray a seated president. Although a chair carries the unrepublican connotation of a throne, there is nothing regal in the figure's demeanor—Lincoln looks almost weary. "Work over, victory his," was how French succinctly described the figure. The exact size of the sculpture gave French and Bacon trouble, and after testing a ten-foot-tall mock-up in the finished building they increased the height to nineteen feet, which enabled people to catch a glimpse of the statue as they climbed the stair.

The interior of the memorial is divided by two Ionic colonnades (fig. 108). The central space contains the colossal statue; the rooms on either side are devoted to Lincoln's two great speeches, the Gettysburg Address and the Second Inaugural, reproduced in their entirety on wall tablets. Above the tablets are two sixty-foot-long murals. *Emancipation of a Race* above the Gettysburg Address portrays the Angel of Truth releasing Black slaves from bondage. On the opposite side, *Reunion* shows two female figures representing the North and South holding palm fronds, and other figures representing the arts and sciences of peaceful prosperity. The murals are the work of Jules Guérin (1866–1946), an architectural artist whose evocative watercolor renderings had helped Bacon win the Lincoln Memorial commission.

Architecture is an art, and it should be judged as such, but when it is a public art the criteria are different than for a commercial building or a private residence. Bacon is not well known today—certainly not as famous as his contemporary Frank Lloyd Wright—yet with the Lincoln Memorial he created something remarkable: an enduring national icon that spoke to succeeding generations of his fellow citizens. Despite its name, the Lincoln Memorial does not commemorate Lincoln's life, his presidency, or his tragic death; it is essentially a war memorial—but of an unusual sort. It neither celebrates victory nor pays tribute to the more than six hundred thousand dead of that bloody conflict. Bacon created an architectural metaphor for a nation reunited after a harrowing civil war. That required presenting Lincoln both as a man—the tired leader—and as a national symbol, not deifying or canonizing him, but raising him to an almost mythic level. That is where classical architecture proved invaluable. The ancient art still resonated, even as it was adapted to present-day circumstances.

Architects such as Bacon and McKim, and artists such as French and Saint-Gaudens, were part of what is sometimes called the American Renaissance. The art historian and critic Bernard Berenson, a contemporary of Bacon's, wrote of that period: "We ourselves, because of our faith in science and the power of work, are instinctively in sympathy with the Renaissance . . . the spirit which animates us was anticipated by the spirit of the Renaissance, and more than anticipated. That spirit seems like the small rough model after which ours is being fashioned." In other words, the American Renaissance saw itself as more than a revival—it was a continuation. That self-confident spirit, combined with technological know-how and unequaled material resources, produced a spate of remarkable urban buildings: not only memorials, but also civic centers, concert halls, museums, libraries, and railroad stations.

In April 1943, twenty-one years after the Lincoln Memorial was inaugurated, President Franklin D. Roosevelt dedicated another presidential memorial in the national capital, this one to Thomas Jefferson. The lyrical marble rotunda on the Tidal Basin was the last work of John Russell Pope, who loosely modeled the memorial on the Pantheon, a building that Jefferson admired. Pope completed the design just before his death, and both events signaled the end of the American Renaissance. For even before that moment, a radically new chapter in the story of architecture was opening elsewhere.

V
NEW BUILDING

27

Starting Over

Rotterdam, Dessau, and Breslau, 1920s

During the 1920s, unusual-looking buildings with flat roofs and stark white walls appeared simultaneously in Vienna, Berlin, Paris, and Rotterdam. What happened? Simply put, the architects of the Secession had opened a Pandora's box. While Wagner and Olbrich cautiously explored an architectural expression that was different from—but not divorced from—what had come before, the succeeding generation of architects wanted to cut all ties with the past. This desire was reinforced by the calamitous Great War, which shattered the verities for European architects no less than for other artists. The luxurious materials and effervescent decorations of Art Nouveau now seemed frivolous, if not downright immoral. In any case, frills were expensive in an impoverished postwar Europe—better to get rid of them. The laborious handwork of the Arts and Crafts movement had proved an ineffectual alternative to industrialization, so why not set craftsmanship aside and embrace mass production and standardization instead?

Everywhere the old order was crumbling; change was in the air. "Modern life demands, and is waiting for, a new kind of plan, both for the house and the city," announced the Swiss-French firebrand Le Corbusier (about whom more later). Architecture is by nature conservative, and such radical rhetoric found expression almost exclusively in paper schemes that appeared in obscure little magazines such as Le Corbusier's *L'Esprit Nouveau* (The New Spirit), published in Paris in the 1920s, and the Dutch journal *De Stijl* (The Style). De Stijl, founded in Leiden in 1917, championed a new spare aesthetic based on ahistorical abstraction, asymmetry, and primary colors. Like the Viennese Secession, De Stijl brought together artists and architects; its members included the polymath Theo van Doesburg, the abstract painter Piet Mondrian, the furniture maker Gerrit Rietveld, and a young architect named Jacobus Johannes Pieter Oud. J. J. P. Oud (1890–1963) was largely self taught; he designed his first house (for his aunt) at

109 Terrace housing, Hoek van Holland, Rotterdam. J. J. P. Oud, 1924–27. The plain housing blocks include shops with curved display windows and cantilevered canopies.

sixteen. After dropping out of the Technical University of Delft and working for several architects, he set up on his own at twenty-three. Oud's early work was traditional: sturdy brick houses with gable roofs and picturesque chimneys. It was only after he joined De Stijl that his architecture changed. He was introduced to Frank Lloyd Wright's work, which was much admired in Holland, and to the radical ideas being explored in Vienna, Paris, and Berlin.

In 1918, Oud joined Rotterdam's housing department, which was responsible for addressing the city's postwar housing shortage. As the department's chief architect, he oversaw the design and construction of social housing, and dealing with budgets, building regulations, and municipal politics gradually distanced him from his more theoretically minded De Stijl colleagues. Unlike them, he was not building villas for wealthy aesthetes but housing for workers, which was, after all, the progressive modernists' stated ideal. Oud was committed to the creation of a new architecture. Brand new. "All in all it follows that an architecture rationally based on the circumstances of life today would be *in every sense* opposed to the sort of architecture that has existed up till now," he wrote (emphasis added). Despite this provocative statement, Oud was not doctrinaire, and his stripped-down housing was intended to serve its occupants. "I long for a house that will satisfy every demand for comfort," he observed, "but a house is not for me a living machine." This barb was aimed at Le Corbusier, who had proclaimed that "a house is a machine for living in."

One of Oud's early social-housing projects, designed in 1924, was in the seaside village of Hoek van Holland, newly annexed by the city of Rotterdam. The project consists of two long terraces containing identical three-bedroom flats on the first floor and two- and three-bedroom flats on the second. Although the budget did not allow for full bathrooms, the compact dwellings were equipped with indoor toilets, as well as built-in clothes closets. The upstairs flats each had a large balcony off the living room and a service balcony off the kitchen. The cantilevered balconies were reinforced concrete, as were the floor and roof slabs; the supporting walls were brick. In addition to forty-one flats, the project included a neighborhood library, two small warehouses, and four shops. The shops were located in the rounded ends of the terraces, distinguished by cantilevered concrete canopies shading curved display windows with thin steel frames (fig. 109). The solid balustrade of the balconies formed a continuous horizontal line—shades of Wright. The portion of the walls up to the windowsill was yellow brick, and the upper plastered portion was painted sandy beige. "The light-bleached color takes its cue from the dune landscape," Oud explained. The blue doors and metal balcony screens, and the red lamp posts, were colorful De Stijl accents.

Despite Oud's statement that modern architecture should be "in every sense opposed to the sort of architecture that has existed up till now," the two long terraces were symmetrical and the library was located in the center, giving the buildings a classical sense of repose. As in the Royal Crescent at Bath, the individual dwellings were subordinated to the overall building. Oud's spare architectural style suited the limited budget, but the unadorned plastered walls, flat roofs, and ribbon windows were not simply the result of economies but were an early example of a new, austere approach to architecture. One senses that the Hoek van Holland neighbors were not enthralled with the plain appearance, which they compared unfavorably to an Arab casbah. Oud's colleagues were more appreciative. "Best of all are those Hoek van Holland workers' dwellings," wrote Rietveld in a congratulatory letter. "I think it's the best I've seen yet."

▪ ▪ ▪ ▪ ▪

Thanks to the De Stijl movement and the work of architects such as Oud, the Netherlands found itself in the forefront of what the German avant-garde called the Neues Bauen (New Building), and in 1923 Oud received a lecture invitation from a progressive German art school in Weimar. The Grand-Ducal Saxon Art School had been founded by the Belgian architect Henry van de Velde, who also designed the Art Nouveau building. When the Great War broke out, van de

110 Bauhaus, Dessau. Walter Gropius, 1926. In the foreground, the classroom wing (left) and the workshop wing (right), are connected by the teachers' offices, which span the road; the tall block houses dormitory rooms.

Velde was obliged to return to Belgium, and he recommended an up-and-coming Berlin architect, Walter Gropius (1883–1969), to be his successor. Gropius, who took over in 1919, renamed the school the Bauhaus—the Building House. In his Bauhaus lecture, Oud described the new architecture of the Netherlands, including the work of the De Stijl group and his own housing projects. The lecture was published by the school in its book series, the first title by a non-Bauhaus author. Oud included a photograph of the Hoek van Holland housing and paired his project with white-cube buildings in Germany and France by Gropius and Le Corbusier. He referred to the buildings as "international architecture"—one of the first uses of this term.

Oud's lecture was published as *Holländische Architektur* in 1926. By then the Bauhaus was no longer in Weimar. After losing state funding, Gropius had relocated the school to the small industrial city of Dessau in the Free State of Anhalt. The Bauhaus remained in Dessau only seven years—the school moved to Berlin in 1932 and closed a year later. Nevertheless, thanks to its illustrious faculty, which included the painters Paul Klee, Wassily Kandinsky, and Lyonel Feininger; the artists Josef and Anni Albers; the furniture designer Marcel Breuer; and the graphic designers Herbert Bayer and László Moholy-Nagy, the school acquired an outsized reputation and became a symbol of the New Building movement. Gropius had cautiously organized the original Weimar curriculum with a medieval emphasis on traditional crafts, but when the Bauhaus moved to Dessau he adopted a more radical slogan—"Art into Industry"—and redirected the teaching away from craft and toward industrial design, focusing on consumer products, furniture, graphics, and textiles—architecture was introduced a year later. History was not taught, nor was easel painting, despite the presence of Klee and Kandinsky.

The new industrial emphasis was evident in the Bauhaus's striking home. The Dessau municipal government had agreed to underwrite the construction of a new building and provided a site on the outskirts of the city. Designed by Gropius in 1926, the school was composed of several connected wings, each containing a different function (fig. 110). Two three-story blocks housed the classrooms and the workshops, which included facilities for furniture-making, pottery, weaving, metalwork, and sculpture and were distinguished by their facades—ribbon windows for the classrooms and all-glass walls for the workshops. The two wings, located on two sides of a street, were connected by a bridge containing the teachers' offices, with the director's office in the symbolic center. A low wing containing the school canteen and an assembly hall was connected to a six-story block that housed dormitory rooms for students and junior faculty (senior faculty lived in Gropius-designed houses nearby). The construction was similar to an ordinary industrial building: floor slabs made of flat-arch clay tile and reinforced concrete supported on concrete frames. The exterior walls were either glass or plastered brick.

The Bauhaus had all the hallmarks of the New Building movement: boxy forms, flat roofs, white plastered walls, ribbon windows, and utilitarian details, such as factory-sash windows and pipe railings. Traditional architectural ornament was entirely missing. The most dramatic feature of the building was the glass wall of the workshop wing (fig. 111). Before the war, Gropius and Adolf

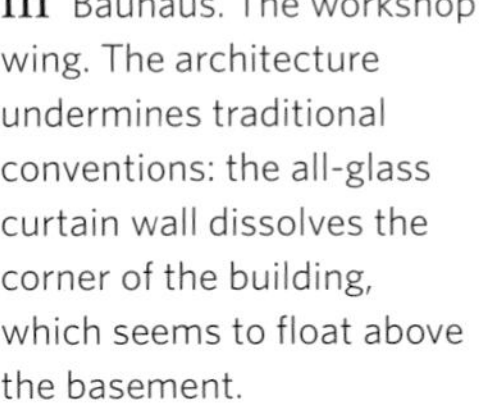

111 Bauhaus. The workshop wing. The architecture undermines traditional conventions: the all-glass curtain wall dissolves the corner of the building, which seems to float above the basement.

Meyer, who would become his office manager and partner, had designed a striking all-glass facade with thin metal mullions for the Fagus shoe factory in southern Germany. They elaborated that concept in the Bauhaus, attaching the glazing to the outside of the cantilevered concrete structure like a three-story-high glass curtain.

Many of the interior fittings of the Bauhaus building were fabricated by the students: industrial-looking metal lighting fixtures, painted colored accents on the walls and ceilings, tubular steel and canvas furniture in the assembly hall, and tubular steel stools in the canteen. Although the no-frills architecture was referred to as "functionalist," the building had functional shortcomings: the flat roofs leaked, the plate glass provided cold comfort in the winter, and, because the all-glass workshop wall faced west, the interior overheated in the summer.

The parallels between the Bauhaus building and the Hoek van Holland housing are obvious, but Gropius was far more doctrinaire than Oud. The design of the Bauhaus building was not simply the expression of an industrial aesthetic, it was a conscious repudiation of the past. Unlike Oud, Gropius avoided symmetry, scale, and axial composition; the pinwheeling wings resemble an abstract De Stijl sculpture—the iconic view of the building is from the air. There is no front or back; there are three entrances, none more important than the others. Traditional buildings had solid corners; Gropius made the corners glass. Traditional buildings sat on the ground; he cantilevered the workshop walls so they seemed to float above the basement. Traditional windows emphasized the thickness of walls; he made the white walls appear paper-thin. Traditional educational buildings incorporated pedagogic symbols; he designed a building that looked like a factory. The result was an architectural world turned upside down.

■ ■ ■ ■ ■

The most celebrated New Building practitioner in Germany was Erich Mendelsohn (1887–1953). Four years younger than Gropius, born in East Prussia, Mendelsohn likewise studied architecture in Berlin and Munich, and his career was similarly interrupted by the Great War—both men saw wartime service. Unlike Gropius, Mendelsohn was a gifted draftsman—his first exposure to the public was a gallery exhibition of his wartime sketches, visionary fantasies of imaginary buildings. He burst upon the architectural scene in 1921 with a remarkable building, the Einstein Tower in Potsdam, an astrophysical observatory built to test Einstein's theory of relativity (fig. 112). The building, whose expressionistic, sculpted forms recall Gaudí, was intended to demonstrate the

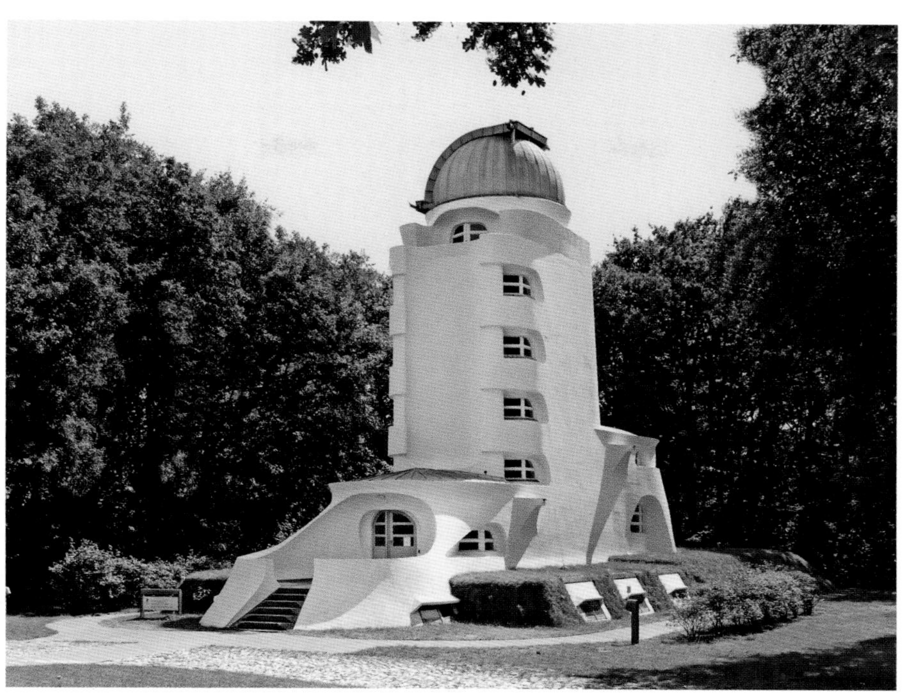

112 Einstein Tower, Potsdam. Erich Mendelsohn, 1920–21. The sculpted form is as much a monument to the new theory of energy and matter as a piece of scientific apparatus.

plastic possibilities of reinforced concrete, although due to postwar shortages, and much to Mendelsohn's chagrin, it was built of brick, plastered and painted white. The design—dynamic, expressive, exciting—was as much a monument to the new theory of energy and matter as a piece of scientific apparatus. It seemed to surprise even Mendelsohn. "It will always remain a strange building," he wrote to his wife. "How did it come to me?"

Thanks to the Einstein Tower, and to its connection with the celebrated German-born physicist who had just received the Nobel Prize, Mendelsohn became an overnight sensation. His practice, which specialized in commercial buildings, expanded rapidly. One of his early high-profile commissions was the renovation and expansion of Mossehaus, the Berlin headquarters of Rudolf Mosse's publishing empire. In 1924, Mosse sent Mendelsohn on a tour of the United States on behalf of *Berliner Tageblatt,* another Mosse publication and the city's leading liberal newspaper. The architect stopped in New York, Detroit, and Chicago and spent three days in Buffalo, where he visited the Larkin Administration Building and the Darwin D. Martin House. He admired American skyscrapers—no such buildings existed in Europe—as well as industrial buildings such as grain elevators, steel mills, and Henry Ford's mammoth automobile plants. He was shocked by the scale of American cities, their frenzied growth, and their lack of planning. After Mendelsohn's return Mosse published a collection of the architect's own photographs and pithy observations as *Amerika: Bilderbuch eines Architekten* (America: Picture Book of an Architect). Mendelsohn's photographs included the backs of buildings, fire escapes, ventilators, and elevators. "Surprisingly simple, monumental in effect, this machinery," he wrote. Of the Gothic Revival Woolworth Building in New York, a dozen years old and still the tallest building in the world, he observed: "This romantic combination is splendid and grotesque at the same time." *Amerika* was a popular success—Bertolt Brecht called it the best book of the year—and contributed further to the architect's celebrity.

Like all European modernists, Mendelsohn was interested in industrial buildings—he himself designed several factories—but the key to his success were his commercial designs: office buildings, department stores, and cinemas. These pointedly did *not* resemble factories; far from being austere, the curvy shapes and luxurious materials captured the excitement and dynamism of the Weimar Republic. Although his architecture was just as ahistorical as that of Gropius and Oud, Mendelsohn embraced and even celebrated the emerging consumer society with its flashy advertising and fast pace. This attitude, as well as his colleagues' jealousy over his success—his large office employed as many as forty people—distanced Mendelsohn somewhat from his Bauhaus contemporaries, as did the fact that he was Jewish (as were many of his clients).

A typical Mendelsohn commission of that period is the Kaufhaus Rudolf Petersdorff, an expensive department store for ladies' fashions in the Silesian capital of Breslau (today Wrocław in Poland). Mendelsohn's commission was to enlarge an existing corner building, add several floors, and rebuild the facades. The new construction was in steel, which allowed Mendelsohn to create a dramatic fifteen-foot curved cantilever at the corner (fig. 113). The two facades are different: one is covered in travertine panels with a grid of discrete square windows, the other consists of alternating bands of travertine and glass. The horizontality was characteristic of Mendelsohn's work at that time, although its purpose was different than Wright's Prairie Style. "Modern man, amidst the excited flurry of his fast-moving life, can find equilibrium only in the tension-free horizontal," Mendelsohn wrote. Like Oud, whose work he admired, Mendelsohn used curves, but he did so in a more pronounced way that, a decade later, would be called streamlining. That distinguished the Petersdorff store from the Bauhaus building, as did its luxurious materials: bronze and travertine. Mendelsohn designed department stores that featured large signs, but the Petersdorff store needed no such identification—the entire eye-catching glass

113 Kaufhaus Rudolf Petersdorff, Breslau. Erich Mendelsohn, 1927–28. The dramatic facade of glass, bronze, and travertine functions as a billboard.

facade was a billboard. At night, special illumination turned the wall into a "glowing curtain," in Mendelsohn's words.

Like Otto Wagner, Mendelsohn saw construction as the key to a new architecture. "After the load-equilibrium of antiquity, after the upthrusted loads of the Middle Ages, comes the dynamic tension of reinforced concrete construction . . . thereby it rises to its own expression, makes possible activity, great eloquence and transcendental qualities," he observed in a 1919 lecture. The last phrase is key. Eloquence and transcendence were traditional architectural aspirations. Mendelsohn saw new materials as opening a door to the next chapter of the continuing story of architecture. "So much is clear," he observed in the same lecture, "out of the specialized techniques of purely functional and industrial building, a decisive artistic achievement seems to be growing to maturity." But where would it lead?

28

On the Wings of Tradition

Lincoln, Nebraska, 1920s
Washington, D.C., and Château-Thierry, France, 1920s

The farthest west that Mendelsohn traveled during his 1924 American trip was Spring Green, Wisconsin, where he spent a convivial weekend as a guest of Frank Lloyd Wright at Taliesin, the architect's rural estate. Mendelsohn originally had planned to go to California but underestimated the distance involved. Had he gone, his train from Chicago to San Francisco would have made a stop in Lincoln, Nebraska, where he would have seen the new state capitol under construction. He could hardly have missed the building, which towered above the prairie landscape. What would he have made of it? It was definitely not an example of European New Building, but it was hardly traditional either.

The design of the Nebraska capitol was the result of a competition. Among the seven prominent architects invited to participate were the ubiquitous John Russell Pope; the well-regarded Paul Cret of Philadelphia; Bertram Goodhue, who was designing the National Academy of Sciences in Washington, D.C.; McKim, Mead & White, which was responsible for the Rhode Island State House; and Egerton Swartwout, a McKim protégé whose firm had built the imposing Missouri state capitol.

Like many state capitols, those of Rhode Island and Missouri were smaller versions of the U.S. Capitol in Washington, D.C., and most of the Nebraska competition entries featured prominent classical domes. This was not the case with the winning design, however, which was the work of Bertram Grosvenor Goodhue (1869–1924), one of the most creative architects of his generation. Born into a distinguished but impoverished New England family, he was apprenticed at fifteen to the New York architect James Renwick, Jr., known nationally for his Gothic Revival churches. Goodhue's precocious talent was recognized early. When he was only twenty-two and still in Renwick's employ, he won a national competition for an Episcopal cathedral in Dallas. Goodhue left Renwick and moved to Boston, where he formed a partnership with the gifted Gothicist Ralph Adams Cram (1863–1942). Theirs was the leading Gothic Revival firm in the country, responsible for numerous cathedrals and churches, including the Cadet Chapel of the U.S. Military Academy in West Point, whose campus Cram and Goodhue also designed. Their collaboration lasted twenty years; the prominent Saint Thomas Episcopal Church in Manhattan was their last joint project. Cram, who would go on to design the Princeton University Chapel and the Cathedral of Saint John the Divine in New York, was committed to Gothic architecture, but the irrepressible Goodhue wanted to explore other styles. He built the Byzantine Saint Bartholomew's Church on Park Avenue, and he was the lead architect of the 1915 Panama-California Exposition in San Diego, which introduced the Spanish Colonial Revival style to California. The exposition led to more work in the West, including the Spanish mission–style California Institute of Technology (CalTech) in Pasadena. Goodhue received commissions as far afield as Hawaii: "Simple white-walled buildings with tile roofs and no, or practically no, ornamental features whatsoever would be the rightest thing for them," he prescribed.

The Nebraska capitol is in the center of Lincoln. Goodhue described his concept: "a vast though rather low structure from the midst of which rises a great central tower which, with its gleaming dome of tiles, would stand a landmark for many miles around." The plan of the low portion was a square donut surrounding a Greek cross, the simple geometry echoing the regular street grid of the spread-out city. The square donut—four hundred feet a side—housed offices; the slightly taller arms of the internal cross contained a nave-like foyer, a wing leading to the Supreme Court, and the legislative chambers. The four landscaped courts between the arms of the cross were treated like cloisters. Rising from the center was a four-hundred-foot tower with a rotunda in its base, offices in the shaft, and a domed Memorial Hall at the top (fig. 114). Goodhue had provided a dome and a rotunda, which people expected in a state capitol, just not in their usual places.

In the early 1900s, Goodhue had spent six months traveling on horseback through Egypt, Persia, and the Arabian Peninsula, and the influence of that trip is visible in the monumental battered walls that recall the pylons of a pharaonic temple, and in the tower that resembles a minaret. The tower is topped by a tall octagon surmounted by a gold-tiled dome—shades of Isfahan—which is crowned by a twenty-foot bronze statue not of Columbia or a Greek goddess but of a barefoot farmer, pants rolled up, seed bag on his shoulder, casting seed for planting. *The Sower* was by the German-born sculptor Lee Lawrie (1877–1963). Goodhue, who had worked with Lawrie for more than two decades, put a high value on artistic collaboration. "I should like to be merely one of the three people to

114 Nebraska State Capitol, Lincoln. Bertram Grosvenor Goodhue, 1920–32. This 1934 photograph shows the powerful composition of bold abstract forms.

produce a building, i.e., architect, painter, sculptor. . . . I should like to do the plan and the massing of the building; then . . . turn the ornament (whether sculpture or not makes no difference) over to a perfectly qualified sculptor, and the color and surface direction (mural pictures or not as the case may be) to an equally qualified painter," he observed.

In the statement accompanying his Nebraska competition entry, Goodhue had written, "So, while the architectural style employed may, roughly, be called 'Classic,' it makes no pretense of belonging to any period of the past." He disliked the Beaux-Arts conventions that dominated American architecture at that time. Most leading architects studied at the École in Paris and apprenticed with McKim, Mead & White; Goodhue had done neither. He was temperamentally unsympathetic to the strict rules of classicism, and he generally refrained from using the Greek and Roman orders. "All rules in architecture save absolutely basic ones are outside the subject," he once said. "And the 'five orders' are entitled to no more veneration than all other good constructive form." There were no classical columns or pilaster in the Nebraska capitol; the massive Indiana limestone forms were rendered in abstract relief. But that did not mean the building was unadorned. The plain walls were enlivened by Lawrie's low-relief sculpture, which was integrated into the architecture in a highly original fashion. Look at the detail of the south facade: the low-relief sculptures of ancient lawgivers emerge seamlessly from the wall like figural pilasters (fig. 115). The quotation from Aristotle—"Political Society Exists for the Sake of Noble Living"—becomes a sort of frieze.

Goodhue was concerned that the Nebraska State Capitol reflect its Midwestern location as well as its legislative function. In addition to Lawrie, he engaged a young New York mural painter and designer, Hildreth Meière (1892–1961), to create wall paintings, tapestries, floor mosaics, and ceremonial door panels. She was also responsible for the mosaic ceilings of the foyer and the rotunda. Meière, who would later design the evocative roundels on the 50th Street facade of Radio City Music Hall in New York, had a lively sense of form and color. Although the decorated surfaces of the capitol interior owe a debt to Persian and Byzantine buildings, the iconography is strictly Nebraskan and includes symbols of the Great Plains—Native Americans, homesteaders, bison.

European modernists such as Gropius had done away with ornament and decoration, and in doing so they lost the opportunity to provide their buildings with *meaning*. There is nothing in the Bauhaus building that says "school" or "art"; all that the building communicates is "This is how I am built." Goodhue

115 Nebraska State Capitol. Detail of the south facade. The sculptures, fully integrated into the architecture, portray the lawgivers Solomon, Julius Caesar, Justinian, and Charlemagne. The room behind the arched windows houses the Supreme Court.

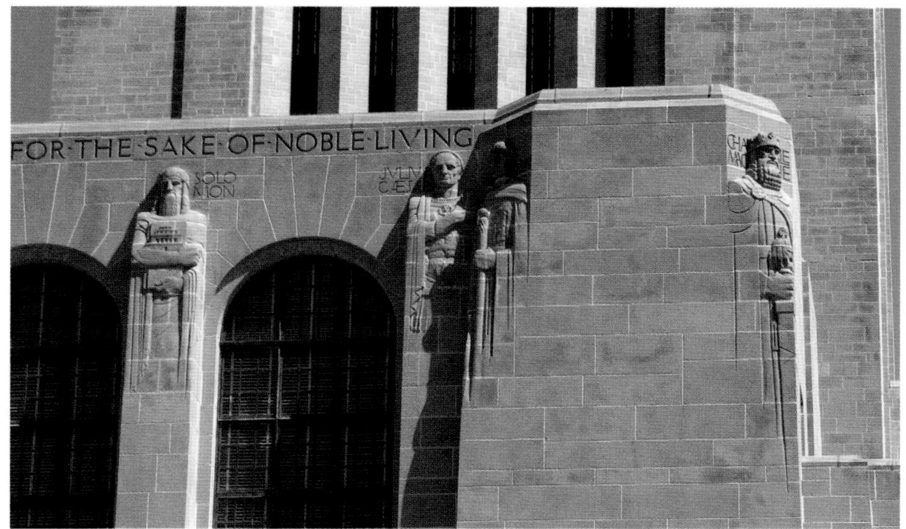

was uninterested in structural expression. He was a romantic for whom the experience of architecture was emotional, however it was built. For example, he conceived the massive Nebraska tower as a load-bearing masonry structure, and when his engineers persuaded him to use a steel frame clad in stone, he agreed but did not change the exterior design. The low building, on the other hand, was built of load-bearing masonry and used structural Guastavino tiles for the dome of the rotunda and the vaults of the foyer.

No less than Gropius and Mendelsohn, Goodhue was interested in creating a new architecture for the modern age, but unlike them he was not ready to jettison the past. "I feel that we must hold tradition closely, it is our great background; as a matter of fact, good technique is born of tradition," he wrote in a 1916 magazine article. "We cannot start each generation at the beginning in our mastery of workmanship. The big universal progress in art moves on the wings of tradition." *We cannot start each generation at the beginning.* Goodhue had put his finger on the conundrum of European modernism: If every age deserved its own unique art, where did that leave the architect? Was it necessary for every generation to start over, to reinvent the wheel? How was that even possible? Goodhue's answer was firm—not possible and not necessary.

The celebrated Nebraska capitol, with its original use of sculpture combined with stark astylar architecture, was Goodhue's crowning achievement. It was also his last project. He died of a heart attack in 1924, before the building was complete. His unexpected death—he was only fifty-four—struck many as particularly tragic. "If he had but lived another ten years the vitality of his design and the dynamic force of his personality might well have wrought an architectural revolution that would have averted the debacle of contemporary modernistic art," wrote his friend and former partner Ralph Adams Cram.

▪ ▪ ▪ ▪ ▪

It would be hard to find two men more dissimilar than Bertram Goodhue and Paul Philippe Cret (1876–1945): a Connecticut Yankee and a French immigrant, a self-taught romantic who rarely set foot in a university and a distinguished École des Beaux-Arts graduate who was a lifelong teacher. Yet there are similarities: both came from somewhat impoverished backgrounds and were obliged to make their own way professionally, both were exceptionally talented designers, and both received a rare distinction, the Gold Medal of the American Institute of Architects (Goodhue posthumously). The diffident Cret had none of Goodhue's flamboyance. His entry in the Nebraska competition similarly dispensed with a classical dome, relied on pronounced massing, and used a Great Plains symbol atop the building—a group of bison. But Cret's compact design was determinedly low-key compared to Goodhue's bold tower.

"I have had, and I have, a high regard for Goodhue's talent. I feel, however, that the recent hero-worship has been somewhat far-fetched," Cret wrote in 1929, five years after Goodhue's death. "Starting from Gothic Romanticism, he was attracted to Classicism by that element of the picturesque found in minor works, such as Spanish Colonial architecture, and did not live long enough to come to understand the real greatness of classical forms. Classicism is a discipline which requires a certain humility, an abandonment of too much personality or, as we moderns put it, an abandonment of the modern exasperated 'self expression.'" Cret's respectful interpretation of classicism was conditioned by his background. He was born in Lyon. His parents were not well off, but a wealthy relative financed his education. A prizewinning student at the École des Beaux-Arts, Cret came to the United States in 1903 immediately after graduating, with an invitation to head the senior design studio of the University of Pennsylvania's school of architecture. He was free to pursue his own career, and in the next decade he realized three prominent commissions: the Pan American Union Building in Washington, D.C., the National Memorial Arch at Valley Forge, and the Indianapolis Central Library. After the interruption of the Great War (he served with distinction in the French army) Cret built the Detroit Institute of Arts as well as three outstanding small museums, the Rodin Museum and the Barnes Foundation in Philadelphia, and the Folger Shakespeare Library in Washington, D.C.

The Folger Library houses the large collection of Shakespeareana amassed by Henry Clay Folger, a Standard Oil executive. Folger originally wanted an Elizabethan-style building, but he was advised that the prominent site on Capitol Hill beside the Library of Congress required a classical design (he got his way in the interior, which is Tudor and Elizabethan). Classical is what Cret delivered—up to a point. The Beaux-Arts plan is a biaxial scheme with the public theater on one side and private administrative offices on the other, linked by an exhibition gallery in the front and a reading room for scholars in the rear. The white marble facade is classical in spirit and in its symmetrical composition—the public entrance is on the left, the private on the right; a row of tall windows signals the presence of the exhibition gallery. But there is almost no classical ornament: the windows are separated by highly stylized pilasters that are simply fluted panels (fig. 116); above the windows is a delicately carved frieze of what look like thistles; and the attic story is finished with a molding that suggests stylized dentils. The geometric patterns of the aluminum grilles over the windows

116 Folger Shakespeare Library, Washington, D.C. Paul Philippe Cret, 1929–32. Detail of facade. The bas-relief panels beneath the windows depict scenes from Shakespeare's plays: *Macbeth, Julius Caesar, King Lear,* and *Richard III.*

and the entrance doors are not classical but were influenced by Art Deco, a Parisian style that appeared just before the Great War and grew in popularity in the 1920s. Americans, whose everyday life had not been disrupted by the Great War, embraced Art Deco and its glamorous interpretation of modernism, which reflected their general faith and optimism surrounding technological progress.

Like Goodhue, Cret understood that the ability of architecture to communicate meaning was limited—there is only so much that a building can say with abstract forms—and he too regularly collaborated with sculptors and painters. John Gregory (1879–1958) was responsible for the nine bas-relief panels beneath the windows, which depict scenes from Shakespeare plays, including *Macbeth, Julius Caesar, King Lear,* and *Richard III.* Brenda Putnam (1890–1975) sculpted the statue of Puck in the west garden. The attic story carried inscriptions about the Bard, chosen by Folger, from Samuel Johnson, Ben Jonson, and John Heminges and Henry Condell (two actors in Shakespeare's troupe).

Cret characterized the architectural style of the Folger Library as New Classicism. He was a confirmed classicist, but unlike some of his contemporaries—classicists as well as modernists—he was pragmatic and recognized that architecture was too complex to succumb to a narrow creed. He believed that buildings had to adapt to the needs and tastes of the modern world, and New Classicism largely dispensed with columns and pilasters while preserving a classical sense of proportion, balance, and symmetry. The two largest examples of this approach, commonly known as stripped classicism, were realized late in Cret's career: the Eccles Building, the headquarters of the Federal Reserve in Washington, D.C., and the National Naval Medical Center in Bethesda, Maryland (popularly known Walter Reed).

Cret's first stripped classical project was designed in the late 1920s. The Château-Thierry American Monument in northern France was one of several American First World War battlefield memorials. The Château-Thierry monument, which commemorates the American Expeditionary Force's role in the Second Battle of the Marne, occupies a hilltop overlooking the Marne River valley. Cret's concept was extremely simple: a roofed double colonnade, fifty feet high and one hundred and fifty feet long, standing on a broad terrace (fig. 117). The two sculpted figures that represent the United States and France are the work of Alfred-Alphonse Bottiau (1889–1951), a French sculptor who collaborated with Cret on several war memorials. The architecture of the Château-Thierry monument is austere. The square piers, without capitals or bases, are lightly scribed to suggest fluting. The architrave, which merely continues the plane of the piers, is engraved with the names of individual battle sites. The Doric frieze—palm leaf triglyphs symbolizing victory over death, alternating with oak leaf metopes symbolizing longevity—is the only overtly classical motif. The piers are so close together that the voids are barely wider than the solids, and the result is more like a massive wall with slots than a colonnade; from a distance it resembles a bulwark—or a line of soldiers standing fast. Cret wrote that the architectural style "although inspired by a Greek simplicity of treatment is not, however, an archaeological adaptation but follows, rather, the American traditions of the post-colonial period, and develops them in the spirit of our own times." The Château-Thierry Monument was completed only a decade after the Lincoln Memorial, but compared to Bacon's literal interpretation of the past, Cret's subtle historical allusions give the monument a severe modernity.

Cret's version of modern classicism was influential in the United States, as evidenced by the many stripped classical federal buildings built during the 1930s. The austere, undecorated style suited the post-Depression era, and it appeared in Canada, Britain, France, Sweden, and Poland; in parliament buildings in Helsinki and Canberra; and in the new headquarters of the League of Nations in Geneva. Stripped classicism also took root in Nazi Germany. In 1935, three years after Château-Thierry was completed, the architect Albert Speer (1905–1981) built a grandstand for party rallies on the Zeppelinfeld, outside Nuremberg. Speer based his design loosely on the Altar of Pergamon, a reconstruction of which was displayed in a Berlin museum. "Loosely" because while the Hellenistic monument is about a hundred feet wide, the Nuremberg grandstand, which could seat sixty thousand, extended over twelve hundred feet and included a massive central tribune that contained a rostrum for dignitaries (fig. 118). The white travertine double colonnade was composed of unadorned square piers rather than Ionic columns. The superficial resemblance to Cret's colonnade is striking, and Speer was likely aware of the American monument. The Zeppelinfeld grandstand (demolished in 1967) was the first of several large projects that Speer built for the Nazi regime, including the New Reich Chancellery, a building in a stripped classical style that extended over a Berlin city block.

For the Nazis, as for American New Dealers, stripped classicism represented a reinvented and simplified modernity with ties to the past. The similarity ends there, however. Cret's stripped version of classicism was in the service of democracy, and while it could be monumental, it was never grandiose, and it was always colored by the architect's rational humanism and considered reticence. "Classicism is a discipline which requires a certain humility," he had written. Humility is hardly a totalitarian virtue. Speer used similar stripped classical elements, but the purpose of his architecture was radically different. The oversized buildings were calculated to impress and awe. The endless vistas, the mind-numbing repetition, and the inhuman scale all conspired to create a

117 Château-Thierry American Monument, Aisne. Paul Philippe Cret, 1926–32. The 1930s photograph shows the First World War memorial commemorating the Second Battle of the Marne. The two sculpted figures represent the United States and France.

118 Grandstand, Zeppelinfeld, Nuremberg. Albert Speer, 1935. Postcard, 1930s. The Nazi grandstand was a vastly expanded version of the Altar of Pergamon.

menacing and even bullying atmosphere. Indeed, Speer later described his work as an "intimidating display of power."

The contrast between the Zeppelinfeld and the Château-Thierry Monument underlines an important architectural distinction: the difference between *form* and *content*. For example, medieval Gothic forms could be used to build a village parsonage or a doge's palace, a college quadrangle or a robber baron's mansion, a whimsical royal castle or a democratic parliament building. Similarly, classical columned porticos could indicate a merchant's villa in the Veneto, a plantation house in the American South, an orphanage in Philadelphia, and an art museum in London. A rustic cabin could house a sharecropper's shack, a president's birthplace, or an imperial teahouse. Although certain architectural forms are associated in the public's mind with a particular historical period or a particular culture—or in the case of stripped classicism with a particular political regime—architectural history suggests otherwise. As in language, the same words can be used to say many different things.

29

The Vertical Dimension

New York, 1930s

The Woolworth Building, whose Gothic design Erich Mendelsohn described as both splendid and grotesque, was built less than two decades after Louis Sullivan's Guaranty Building, but it was five times as tall. Compared to the squat thirteen-story Guaranty, the soaring fifty-five-story Woolworth was a colossus. Height made all the difference. Skyscrapers represented a particular design problem: What should these distinctly untraditional buildings look like? Some architects followed Sullivan's formula, while others looked to historic precedents and designed Gothic spires, Renaissance campaniles, and vertical palazzos.

In 1922, the *Chicago Tribune* announced an international competition to design a new headquarters tower for the newspaper; it should be "the most beautiful office building in the world." More than two hundred and fifty architects from two score countries threw their hats in the ring. The newspaper seeded the competition by commissioning entries from ten leading American firms: five from Chicago, four from New York, and one from San Francisco. Bertram Goodhue was one of the New Yorkers. Although he had never built a commercial office building, he had experience with tall buildings and recognized that skyscrapers, like bell towers and church steeples, were experienced from a distance—that is, on the skyline. To that end, he designed a distinctive thirty-story silhouette that stepped back at intervals as it got taller. As his expressive drawing shows, the masses of masonry, the planar surfaces, the chamfered corners of the upper portion, and the columnar window arrangement, were all calculated to draw the viewer's eye to the pyramidal top, whimsically crowned with the statue of a newsboy (fig. 119). Goodhue's astylar design was not Gothic like the winning scheme, nor could it be described as modernist; it was quite different from Walter Gropius and Adolf Meyer's utilitarian entry, which resembled a vertical factory. Nor was it classical—there were no pilasters or moldings, and the windows were

119 Chicago Tribune Tower competition entry. Bertrand Goodhue, 1922. The planar surfaces, stepped masses of limestone, and window arrangement all emphasized a skyward thrust. The crowning statue was of a newsboy.

simply rectangular apertures cut out of the limestone. Ornamented friezes in colored mosaic were limited to the top of the building. The overall effect was apparently too severe for the judges, who gave it only an honorable mention.

Goodhue died two years later and he never had a chance to build a commercial skyscraper, but because the premiated entries to the Chicago Tribune competition were widely published and exhibited, his design, which anticipated the Art Deco skyscrapers of the 1930s, was influential. The most prominent of its progeny, because it was the tallest, was the Empire State Building. The architect was William Frederick Lamb (1883–1952) of the New York firm Shreve, Lamb & Harmon. Lamb and Richmond Harold Shreve (1877–1946) had been partners at Carrère & Hastings, the leading Beaux-Arts firm in the city, responsible for the New York Public Library. In 1924, the pair left to start their own practice, intending to specialize in tall commercial buildings. Lamb, a Brooklyn native who was a graduate of the École de Beaux-Arts, was the designer; the Canadian-born Shreve, who had attended Cornell, saw to the business side of the practice. Five years later they were joined by Arthur Loomis Harmon (1878–1958), a Cornell graduate who had apprenticed with McKim, Mead & White and was experienced in high-rise apartment buildings and hotels.

The Empire State Building was not a lavish corporate headquarters like the Chicago Tribune Tower, but a speculative office building. This affected the design in several ways. To begin with, the architect was expected to maximize the amount of rentable space. Lamb explained: "The logic of the plan is very simple. A certain amount of space in the center, arranged as compactly as possible, contains the vertical circulation, mail chutes, toilets, shafts and corridors. Surrounding this is a perimeter of office space twenty-eight feet deep. [Twenty-eight feet was roughly the distance that daylight penetrated an office floor.] The sizes of the floors diminish as the elevators decrease in number. In essence, there is a pyramid of non-rentable space surrounded by a greater pyramid of rentable space." A speculative office building needed to be built quickly because an economic return was realized only when tenants moved in, and the Empire State Building was completed in only twenty months. To that end, the design and construction needed to be highly standardized. Lastly, the developers, headed by the financier John J. Raskob and Alfred E. Smith, a former governor of New York, were intent on marketing the building as the tallest in the city—that is, the tallest in the world—which meant it had to be taller than the Chrysler Building, which was then under construction. Lamb designed a fifty-story tower, but as the competing Chrysler grew taller, he was obliged to increase the number of floors to sixty, finally to eighty.

The Empire State Building consists of a frame of riveted steel columns and beams clad in Indiana limestone. The evocative stepped-back forms were the result partly of New York City's 1916 zoning regulations, which required tall buildings to have setbacks to avoid a "canyon effect" on the street, and partly of Lamb's desire to create a striking silhouette (fig. 120). The Empire State has major zoning setbacks at the five-story and twenty-story levels, and several purely architectural setbacks higher up. The overall effect is to visually buttress the main shaft of the tower. Like Goodhue, Lamb emphasized the vertical dimension, both in the pyramidal massing and in the details. He provided the identical double-hung windows with spandrel panels of cast-aluminum (cheaper and lighter than stone) and arranged them in paired columns separated by shiny stainless-steel mullions and wide limestone piers. The distinctive vertical stripes were accompanied by

120 Empire State Building, New York. Shreve, Lamb & Harmon, 1930–31. The distinctive profile is the result of building design and zoning regulations.

Art Deco details: spandrels adorned with zigzag geometrical patterns, stainless-steel mullions terminating in sunburst motifs, and a pair of stylized eagles on fluted columns framing the entrance. Art Deco motifs continued in the lobby, whose marble ceiling was rendered in aluminum and gold leaf, representing the starry night sky; whose elevator doors were geometrically patterned in black and silver; and which contained a marble mural with duralumin and bronze inlays depicting the building itself with rays of light radiating from the rooftop mast.

The mast was not part of the original design. Although the office floors reached eighty stories, the developers, concerned that their building might be overtaken by the Chrysler Building, demanded more height, and Lamb added a two-hundred-foot spire to the roof. The tapered stainless-steel clad cylinder with streamlined buttresses, which included an indoor observatory, brought the building's total height to 1,250 feet. The pinnacle of the spire was optimistically advertised as a mooring mast for Zeppelin dirigibles, although no airship ever docked at the Empire State Building. Yet the spire was a fortuitous addition. With its distinctive silhouette, the skyscraper became an icon—New York's Eiffel Tower—standing both for the city and for modernity itself.

▪ ▪ ▪ ▪ ▪

A year after the Empire State Building was completed—1932—ground was broken on what many consider the premier skyscraper of that golden age of skyscrapers: the RCA (Radio Corporation of America) Building. The building was the centerpiece of Rockefeller Center, a commercial development in midtown Manhattan that encompassed three city blocks and included Radio City Music Hall, a landscaped pedestrian street, a sunken plaza, and fourteen office towers. The leader of the architectural team was Raymond Mathewson Hood (1881–1934).

Hood's extraordinary career resembles a delayed starburst. Although well educated (Brown, MIT, the École des Beaux-Arts) and talented, Hood languished in obscurity until achieving fame at the ripe age of forty-one. In the following dozen years he built five outstanding skyscrapers before dying at only fifty-three of rheumatoid arthritis. His meteoric rise began with the 1922 Chicago Tribune Tower competition. John Mead Howells (1868–1959), a socially prominent architect and son of the famous novelist William Dean Howells, was one of the four New Yorkers invited to compete, and he asked Hood, whom he had met years before at the École, to be his partner. Their entry was a Gothic Revival skyscraper with an elaborate buttressed crown modeled on the fifteenth-century Butter Tower of Rouen Cathedral. The details of their collaboration are unclear, although Hood, who as a young man had worked for Cram and Goodhue on the Gothic Saint Thomas Church, seems to have been responsible for the bulk of the work. Their entry was awarded first prize.

The Tribune Tower, which was completed in 1925, propelled Hood—at first with Howells and later with others—into the limelight, resulting in several prominent office building commissions in Manhattan. These designs had the expressive verticality of the Gothic Tribune Tower but increasingly relied on the abstract volumetric approach pioneered by Goodhue. One of the earliest examples was the thirty-six-story Daily News Building, the home of the largest-circulation newspaper in the country. This was a time before air-conditioning, when office buildings relied on natural ventilation, which produced facades composed of hundreds of double-hung windows. In the Daily News Building, Hood

121 Daily News Building, New York. Hood, Fouilhoux & Howells, 1929–30. Colorized postcard, 1941. Raymond Hood stripped the tall commercial office building to its bare essentials.

arranged the windows and their dark brick spandrels vertically between glazed white brick piers that shot straight up the full height of the building (fig. 121). The striped pattern continued to the top of the building, screening the unsightly water tanks and elevator penthouses on the roof. Contrary to Sullivan's dictum, Hood made the building all shaft—there were no base and no capital; at the top, the stripes simply stopped without any architectural fanfare. The mass of the building was modulated by several pronounced setbacks, some required by New York's zoning, others of Hood's own making. The result was neither Gothic nor classical. "That's not architecture," proclaimed one architecture critic. "So much the better," snapped the irascible Hood.

The Daily News Building windows were equipped with red Venetian blinds that at night turned the building into a huge glowing Chinese lantern. Like

Mendelsohn, Hood realized that large commercial towers could be effective corporate billboards—the Daily News did not need to display its name in lights. Hood had stripped the tall commercial office building to its bare essentials, but he did so with such a sense of style that the result did not look in the least utilitarian. "I do not feel that the Daily News Building is worse looking than some other buildings, where plans, sections, exteriors and mass have been made to jump through hoops, turn somersaults, roll over, sit up and beg—all in the attempt to arrive at the goal of architectural composition and beauty," he observed with characteristic bravura.

The RCA Building (popularly known as 30 Rock) was Hood's masterpiece. That project presented him with a problem of an entirely different scale: a sixty-six-story building that occupied the length of half a city block, making it a slab rather than a spire. The building was in the center of the block, so it was not subject to zoning setbacks; nevertheless, Hood gave it pronounced setbacks. According to him, these were the result of reducing the number of elevators as the buildings rose. "As each elevator shaft ended, we cut the building back twenty-seven feet from the core of the building to the exterior walls," he explained. "By so doing we have eliminated every dark corner." Form follows function? Not exactly. The building has many purely architectural setbacks on the narrow end facing the sunken plaza, as well as large setbacks on the lower levels to accommodate roof gardens. The facade is striped, like the Daily News Building, but the piers are gray Indiana limestone rather than brick, and the spandrel panels are cast aluminum. The stepped-back forms reach a kind of crescendo toward the top.

Hood incorporated dramatic outdoor floodlighting. A 1933 nighttime photograph shows the massive slab whose clifflike setbacks resemble a stunning geological formation, endlessly repetitive and yet oddly organic (fig. 122). "The view of Rockefeller Center from Fifth Avenue is the most beautiful thing I have ever seen ever seen ever seen," wrote Gertrude Stein. A common description of skyscrapers is "soaring" or "thrusting." In reality, tall buildings do exactly the opposite: they carry heavy loads down to the ground and resist the sideways force of the wind—the upward movement exists only in the mind's eye. In that sense the RCA Building resembles a Baroque church steeple—it is not designed according to a set of abstract or engineering principles but with the human observer in mind. Hood's slab, despite its overriding real-estate function, its riveted steel frame, its industrial materials, and its functionally determined banks of elevators, is a humanist creation. It soars.

Although Hood often baldly insisted that the appearance of his buildings was simply the result of practical considerations, he was speaking—as he often

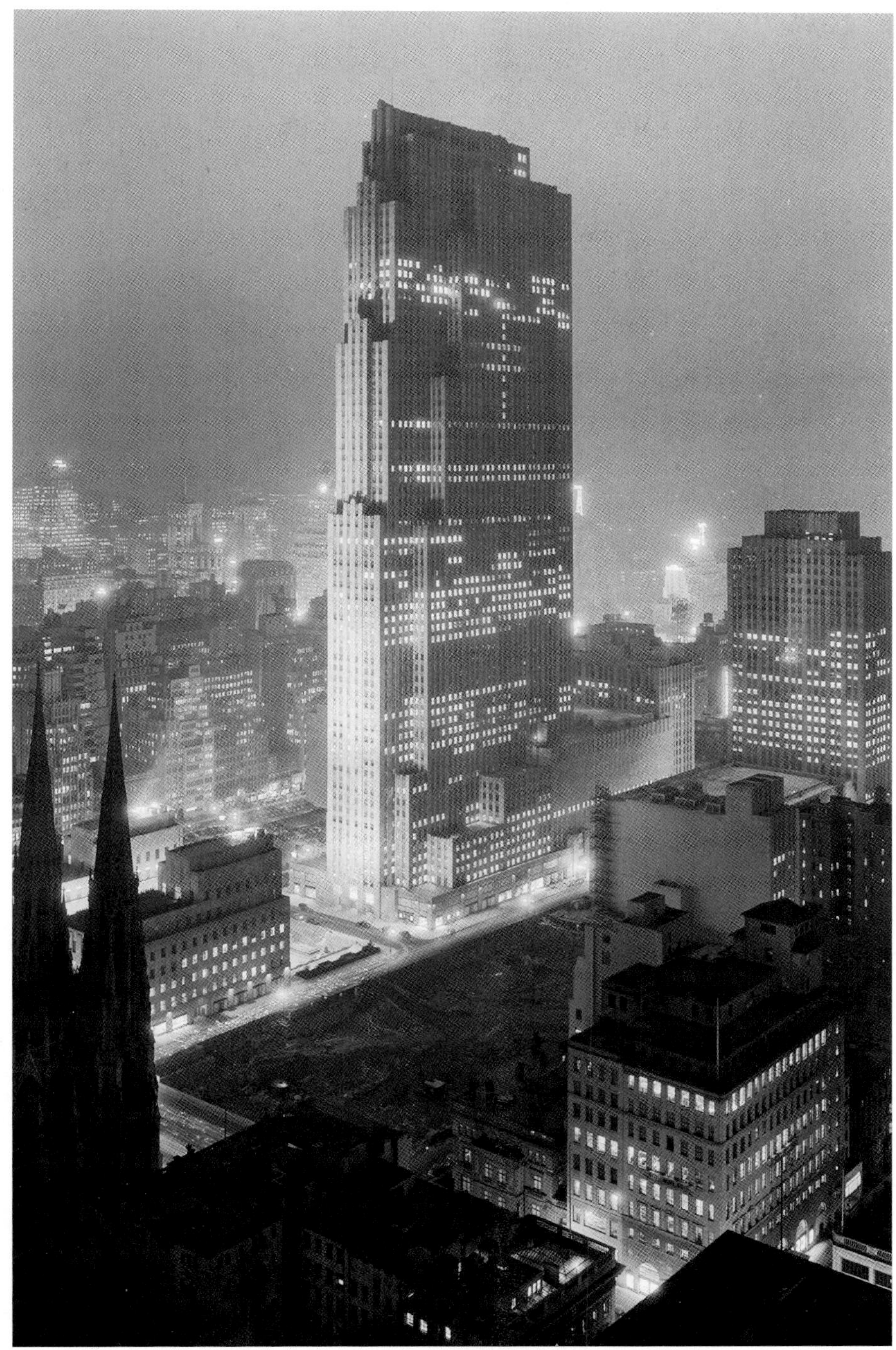

122 RCA Building, 30 Rockefeller Plaza, New York. Hood, Godley & Fouilhoux, with Corbett, Harrison & MacMurray, and Reinhard & Hofmeister, 1932–33. The massive slab, with its clifflike setbacks, resembles a geological formation.

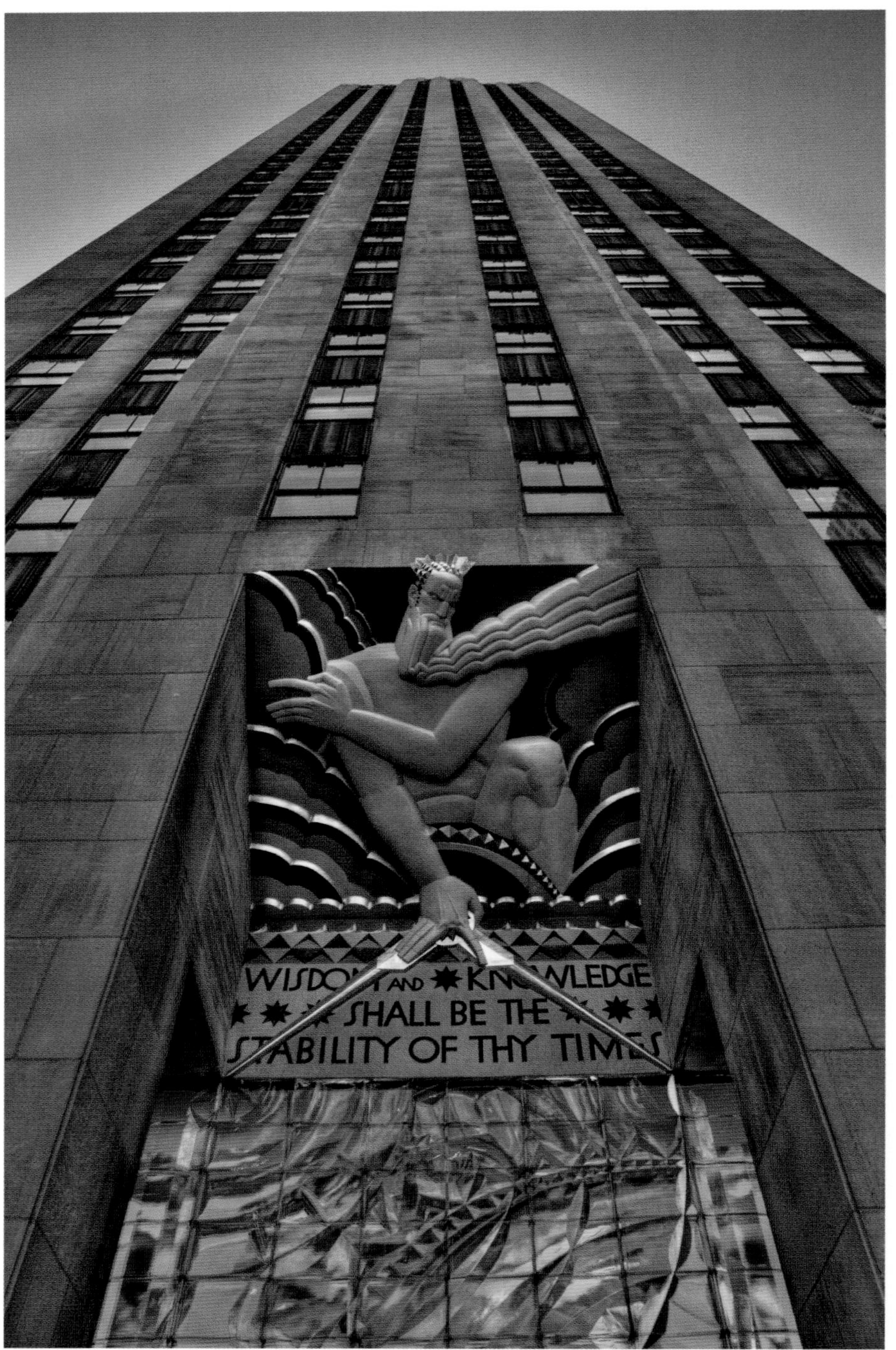

123 *Wisdom: A Voice from the Clouds,* Rockefeller Center, New York. Lee Lawrie, 1933. Art and architecture are integrated in this Jazz Age portal as intimately as in a Gothic cathedral. The biblical quote is from Isaiah. Above, limestone piers separate columns of windows and cast aluminum spandrels.

did—with tongue in cheek. In truth, he was as involved with aesthetics as any Renaissance master. He once observed of the typical office tower: "For the client it is a chance to get a return on his money, for the manufacturer a chance to sell his products, for the contractor a chance to make a profit. There remains the architect, the building's only friend." Hood was greatly concerned with the nonpractical aspects of his designs. The red and black brick spandrel panels of the Daily News Building were intricately designed, especially at the lower levels, where they are seen close-up. The aluminum spandrels of the RCA Building were cast in a variety of Art Deco patterns: stepped ridges, leaf clusters, and interlaced pointed arches. Like Goodhue and Cret, Hood regularly collaborated with artists. One of them was the sculptor René Paul Chambellan (1893–1955), who also made the large clay study models that were an integral part of Hood's design method. Chambellan's three-story-high gilded limestone bas-relief panel above the main entrance of the Daily News Building portrays a procession of office workers, flappers, and construction workers; Hood called it a "small explosion or architectural effect." The explosion over the entrance to RCA Building needed to be proportionately larger. The three main doorways are adorned with gilded and painted limestone bas-reliefs, the work of Lee Lawrie, whom Hood had met when he was working in Goodhue's office. Figures representing Sound and Light flank the large central figure of Wisdom, a bearded god holding thunderbolts above a backlit screen made of cast-glass blocks (fig. 123). It is the Jazz Age equivalent of a Gothic portal.

The presence of art in a building that is otherwise as astylar as the RCA Building underlines the difference between American and European conceptions of architectural modernity. Skyscrapers such as RCA and the Daily News Building are just as minimalist as the factory-like Bauhaus building—and technologically much more sophisticated—but they exhibit a kind of joyful self-confidence that is entirely different. The European modernists, with the exception of an outlier such as Mendelsohn, had a stern Calvinist idea of modernity; they were concerned with the correct way to do things, and many of them saw design as a series of moral choices: form had to follow function, structure should be expressed, ornament was a crime. Hood disliked such orthodoxy. "I am sorry that there grows up around modern architecture these rules, such as Palladio and Vignola made for the Renaissance," he told a symposium on the occasion of the Museum of Modern Art's 1932 exhibition *Modern Architecture*. "For the moment we put a cast-iron frame on this International Style, that we're all working at, this fine, marvelous movement will turn into a tight, hard, unimaginative formula, just as did colonial architecture." Prophetic words.

30

Volte-face

Chicago and Marseille, Ronchamp and New York, 1950s

A week before Christmas Day 1949, on a prominent site along Chicago's Lake Shore Drive, construction began on a pair of apartment towers. Passersby could see the steel frame going up. Nothing unusual about that, but what happened next was unexpected; instead of brick or stone, the twenty-seven-story steel frame was wrapped in glass. There were no setbacks, no patterned spandrels, no art; instead of an evocative spire or a geological formation, it was—a box. Coming only a dozen years after the RCA Building, this was a remarkable development; neither an evolution nor a refinement, almost a reversal.

What happened? There were several factors that produced such a radical volte-face. First, there was the coincidence of the decade-long Great Depression followed by the Second World War, which meant that with the exception of such government buildings as the Federal Reserve headquarters or such privately funded projects as Rockefeller Center, building construction in the United States was effectively halted for a decade and a half. The long-term outcome for architects was disastrous. The networks of craftsmen, artists, manufacturers, and builders unraveled; skills were lost as firms went out of business; individual architects retired early or changed professions. Older practitioners, such as William Lamb and William Van Alen, the designer of the Chrysler Building, saw their careers wither; young architects had few opportunities for apprenticeship and little chance to learn their craft. By 1945, the old masters, such as Raymond Hood, Cass Gilbert (the architect of the Woolworth Building), John Russell Pope, Ralph Adams Cram, and Paul Cret, were dead. But where were their replacements? The normal course of architectural apprenticeship and succession that ensured a measured transfer of knowledge and skills from one generation to the next was rudely and irrevocably interrupted.

Prosperity and pent-up demand set the stage for a postwar construction boom. At the same time, technological advances such as nuclear energy, space exploration, and the invention of the transistor created a heady atmosphere of innovation and the public expected something commensurately new on the building front. It was too late to revive Art Deco; Hood's Moderne style seemed dated; and Cret's stripped classicism was too closely associated with the disgraced Nazi regime. But "something new" was precisely what European avant-garde architects had been advocating—with limited success—for more than twenty-five years. Here another coincidence intervened. In the late 1930s, when Hitler acceded to power and National Socialism became firmly established, many German scientists, intellectuals, and artists—both Jews and non-Jews—fled the country, and of these most ended up in the United States (Albert Einstein, Thomas Mann, Bertolt Brecht, Arnold Schoenberg, Bruno Walter, Otto Preminger, Fritz Lang). Among these émigrés were several members of the Bauhaus circle, including Walter Gropius, Marcel Breuer, and Ludwig Mies van der Rohe. Erich Mendelsohn fled Germany too, and after spending time—and building projects—in England and Palestine, he ended up in San Francisco, although his American work never achieved the heights of his Berlin ascendancy.

Gropius and Breuer were invited to teach at Harvard University and established a joint practice on the East Coast. Mies van der Rohe (1886–1969) accepted a job directing the architecture program of the Armour Institute (today the Illinois Institute of Technology) in Chicago. With that position came the commission to design the institute's new campus and the opportunity to open an architecture office. One of his early commercial clients was Herbert Greenwald, a young Chicago developer. Greenwald thought that a noted architect would add value to his apartment projects. Greenwald approached Mies after being turned down by Frank Lloyd Wright, Eliel Saarinen, and Walter Gropius.

Mies van der Rohe was hardly a household name. When he arrived in America in 1937 he was fifty-one. He had been a leading figure in the German architectural avant-garde, had served as the last director of the Bauhaus, and had designed distinctive furniture and several striking unbuilt competition entries. But he had built relatively little—an exhibition pavilion in Barcelona and a private villa in Brno, Czechoslovakia, were his most prominent works. Nevertheless, in an impressively short time Mies absorbed the rudiments of American high-rise construction: standardized steel frames of columns and beams fireproofed with concrete, reinforced concrete floor slabs, and central cores containing elevators and fire stairs bracing the steel frame. The two Lake Shore Drive

124 860/880 Lake Shore Drive, Chicago. Ludwig Mies van der Rohe, 1949–51. The twin apartment towers were a combination of conventional American high-rise construction with a radically new architectural expression: steel and glass.

towers—Greenwald and Mies's third collaboration—incorporated all these features, but their all-glass exteriors were distinctly unconventional. The choice of glass was partly aesthetic—German modernists had always been fascinated by *Glasarchitektur*—and partly pragmatic. Greenwald's construction budget was not lavish, and glass was cheaper than masonry. More important, an all-glass facade seemed like the right expression for a forward-looking postwar America. Greenwald marketed his project as The Glass House.

In the Lake Shore Drive towers Mies transformed American steel construction into an architectural language that he referred to as "skin and bones." Unlike Art Deco skyscrapers, which emphasized verticality, the gridded facades of the Lake Shore Drive towers gave equal importance to the horizontal (fig. 124). The glass panes went from floor to ceiling (the lower portion of the windows was openable because the building was not air-conditioned)—there were no spandrels. The mullions that supported the aluminum window frames were off-the-shelf steel I-beams. The regular rhythm of structural bays and the pilaster-like I-beams recalls the neoclassical rationalism of Karl Friedrich Schinkel, an architect whom Mies admired. The I-beam mullions and the metal-covered structural frame were painted black, which gave the impression of an industrial building. By contrast, the lobby floors and elevator cores, like the outdoor plaza, were finished in creamy travertine. This matter-of-fact combination of luxury and utilitarianism would become a Mies trademark.

The twenty-six-story Lake Shore Drive towers have no crowns; they simply stop. The buildings could have been shorter or taller, it wouldn't have changed their design. This is somewhat similar to Hood's Daily News Building, but there is nothing soaring about Mies's boxy towers, whose implacable structural grid is interrupted only at the base by a two-story high lobby whose setback creates a colonnade around the building (see fig. 124). The asymmetrical arrangement of the two buildings at right angles to each other and connected by a canopy resembles a De Stijl painting. Parking is in an underground garage.

A *Life* magazine article that featured the Lake Shore Drive towers approvingly quoted Mies: "Alone, logic will not make beauty inevitable. But with logic, a building shines." But is a building clad entirely in glass really logical in the American Midwest, with its brutally hot summers and cold, windy winters? (In later apartment towers Mies used tinted glass and air-conditioning to somewhat mitigate the environmental drawbacks.) "It is not functional to provide in our climate and with city conditions twice as much glass surface as is usable," Paul Cret observed twenty years earlier. Cret was skeptical about the modernists' functionalist claims. "I unfortunately lack the strong faith of the modernists in the 'functionality' of their architecture. Looking at it with a critical eye, I cannot see in it anything but the age-old method which consists in being logical, truthful and functional in design as long as it is convenient, and being decidedly less so when certain aesthetic results are wanted."

The aesthetic result that Mies wanted was obvious; he had just completed a weekend house outside Chicago that was walled entirely in large sheets of glass. Even before the Farnsworth House was built, it was the subject of a Museum of Modern Art exhibition. "Architecture is the will of an epoch translated into space," Mies had written in 1924. Did the epoch really demand glass walls? Whatever the practical drawbacks of glass buildings, the new architectural language did seem to many to suit its time. As the *Life* article put it, "[The] severely geometric, unembellished buildings have been designed to express in purest forms a technological concept of our technological age." Like Bramante's Tempietto, the stripped-down glass towers on Lake Shore Drive changed the course of architecture.

▪ ▪ ▪ ▪ ▪

At the same time that Mies van der Rohe was building the two towers in Chicago, another leading European modernist was building a high-rise apartment block in Marseille. Charles-Édouard Jeanneret (1887–1965), a French citizen born in Switzerland who adopted the name Le Corbusier, was an almost exact contemporary of Mies. Both men were the sons of artisans; Mies's father was a stonemason, Le Corbusier's an enameler of watchcases. Both architects were largely self taught—neither attended architecture school—and they had apprenticed in the same Berlin office, though not at the same time. Temperamentally, however, the two were opposites. The taciturn Mies rarely explained his work, whereas Le Corbusier was an outspoken propagandist who churned out a stream of manifestos, magazines, and books. While Mies patiently developed and refined his ideas, the irrepressible Le Corbusier frequently changed course. In the 1920s, they had both designed prominent houses in the prevalent International Style—flat roofs, white walls, ribbon windows—but since that time their work had developed in very different directions.

The apartment block that Le Corbusier built in Marseille was commissioned in 1947 by the French government as part of a postwar reconstruction program. The twenty-story building was five hundred feet long—a massive slab. Halfway up was a two-story corridor—Le Corbusier called it an interior street—lined with shops, a post office, a café, and other amenities. The rooftop contained a nursery, a children's wading pool, a gymnasium, and a running track. Le Corbusier called the building a Unité d'habitation—Dwelling Unit—and intended it as a prototype for a new form of vertical urban living, an alternative to conventional neighborhoods of streets and family houses. He imagined a city consisting of ranks of Unités in a natural landscape—towers in a park.

The Marseille Unité d'habitation was designed to accommodate roughly sixteen hundred residents in three hundred and thirty-seven apartments of various sizes. The apartments were influenced by Le Corbusier's visit to a fourteenth-century Carthusian monastery in Florence, where each two-story cell was effectively a little house with its own private garden. The Marseille apartments did not have gardens, but they did have loggias as well as two-story-high living rooms. The long and extremely narrow (twelve feet!) apartments extended the full sixty-foot depth of the building to enable cross-ventilation. This arrangement was achieved by an ingenious interlocking cross-section that resulted in corridors only on every third floor. The interiors were equally unconventional. The double-height living room was overlooked by a loft containing either the parent's bedroom or a kitchen-dining area; glazed folding doors opened the narrow living room into the loggia. The two children's bedrooms, which were on a different floor, had their own loggias and were divided by a partition that could be slid open in daytime.

Le Corbusier had previously built apartment buildings with steel structures and glass facades in Geneva and Paris, but the Marseille building was

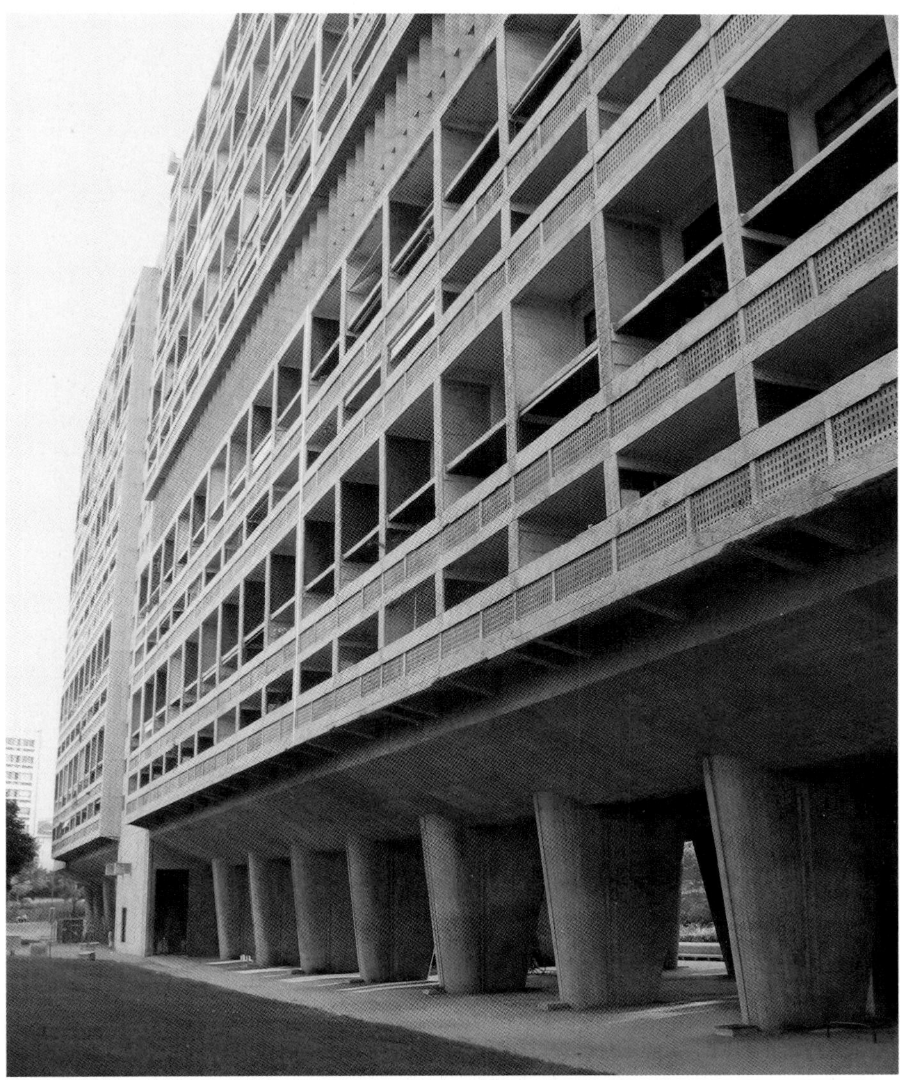

125 Unité d'habitation, Marseille. Le Corbusier, 1947–52. The rough exterior is a combination of cast-in-place and precast concrete. The building is raised up on massive piers that resemble ancient megaliths.

primarily reinforced concrete. Portland cement concrete reinforced with steel bars was invented in the mid-nineteenth century and by the early 1900s was in common use. The concrete was sometimes exposed in industrial buildings, but more commonly it was covered by brick or stone. In Marseilles, Le Corbusier left much of the concrete in full view (fig. 125) and exploited two of the material's unique qualities: it could be cast in a variety of shapes, and the shuttering, or wooden formwork, left its imprint on the surface. This appealed to Le Corbusier.

"Exposed concrete shows the least incidents of the shuttering, the joints of the planks, the fibers and knots of the wood, etc. But these are magnificent to look at, they are interesting to observe, to those who have a little imagination they add a certain richness." Magnificent or not, concrete cast this way had some of the roughness and texture of wood.

Le Corbusier would go on to build four more Unités—three in France and one in West Germany. He had earlier coined the phrase "A house is a machine for living in," yet these apartment buildings were not machinelike at all. Although they included factory-made elements, such as prefabricated kitchens, the rough concrete provided an overall impression that was almost rustic. While Mies made refined details the heart of his architecture, Le Corbusier tried, as much as possible, to eliminate detail. Rather than a "technological concept of our technological age," the Marseille building seemed more like a rough *antidote* to the machine age. Roughcast concrete is called *béton brut* in French, which gave rise to the English term "Brutalism," which also conveys something of this new architecture's coarse monumentality.

Monumentality had been a part of architecture since ancient times; important public buildings were meant to last and to incorporate lasting values, and they were intended to impress the onlooker with these qualities. The early modernists at first rejected monumentality in favor of functionality. The writer and critic Lewis Mumford spelled this out in a 1937 essay: "The very notion of a modern monument is a contradiction in terms: if it is a monument, it cannot be modern, and if it is modern, it cannot be a monument." Le Corbusier's Marseille apartment building challenged this view. Although the mammoth slab was not a public building, Le Corbusier gave it distinctly monumental qualities. The massive tapered concrete piers that quixotically raised the building three stories off the ground resembled ancient megaliths; the concrete ventilation stacks on the roof were like colossal biomorphic funnels. Few architects copied the Unité's complicated cross-section and extremely narrow apartments, but its coarse monumentalism proved a popular alternative to Mies's guarded steel-and-glass vocabulary.

The building in which Le Corbusier decisively broke with the International Style was completed in 1955: Notre-Dame du Haut in Ronchamp in eastern France, a pilgrimage chapel on a mountaintop. "It's the most revolutionary work of architecture for a long time," he wrote to his mother. For once Le Corbusier was not exaggerating. The curved shapes of the walls and the sweeping concrete roof that resembles a seashell or a nun's coif were pure sculpture (fig. 126). Instead of emphasizing lightness and transparency, the architecture was heavy, or at least it looked heavy—the roof and some of the thick walls were actually hollow. The

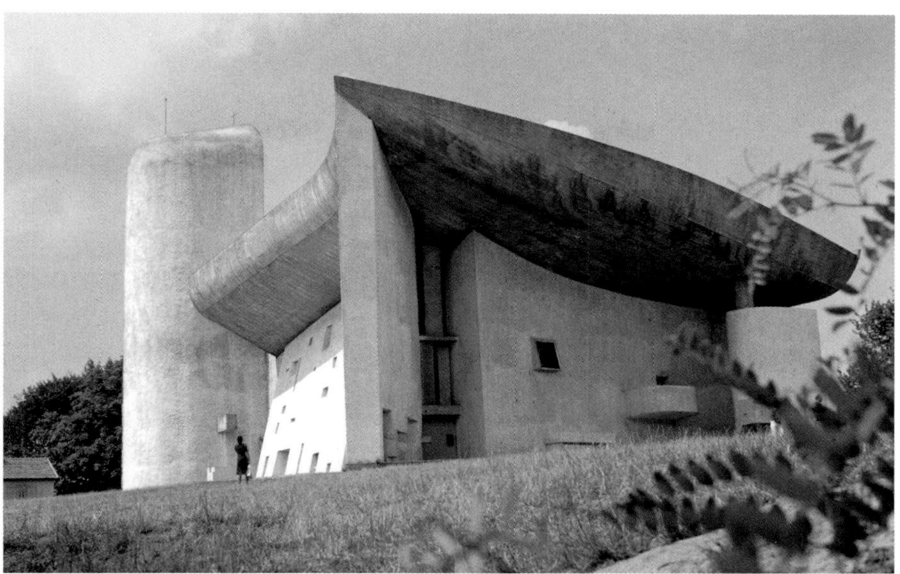

126 Notre-Dame du Haut, Ronchamp. Le Corbusier, 1953–55.

roof resembled a shell but it was actually carried on hidden concrete girders, and the hollow walls concealed reinforced concrete frames. Hiding rather than expressing the structure was a radical departure from modernist orthodoxy. The roughly textured material of the curved walls was gunite, a thin cement skin sprayed onto wire mesh. In addition, Le Corbusier incorporated ornament in the form of an enameled door and hand-painted stained-glass windows. This was a new and different sort of modernism that had nothing to do with industrialization—indeed, the rough walls and the dark, cavelike interior looked ancient. The Marseille Unité had included sculptural elements, but here the entire building was a sculpture. The iconoclast who had once upset traditional conventions had now upended the orthodoxies of the International Style.

Meanwhile, Mies van der Rohe was pursuing his own vision. He treated the economic language of steel and glass like the classical orders, which he would adapt to a variety of buildings, such as apartment towers, office blocks, and campus buildings, and to a variety of building locations, rural as well as urban, subtropical as well as temperate. Hood might have called it a formula; Mies would have disagreed. "One doesn't invent a new architecture every Monday morning," he said.

Three years after completing the Lake Shore Drive apartments, Mies began work on an office building on Park Avenue in New York. The Seagram Building was thirty-nine stories, and it was on a busy downtown street, not a lakefront, but it was clearly a descendant of the Chicago towers (fig. 127). A metal and glass

127 Seagram Building, New York. Ludwig Mies van der Rohe, 1954–58.

skin was wrapped around a structural frame in such a way that the structural columns were entirely concealed, except at the base, where the two-story lobby was set back behind a colonnade. The generous budget allowed Mies to indulge his taste for luxury: the lobby floor and the elevator cores were travertine, the large plaza in front of the building was paved in granite, and the mullions and the spandrels of the exterior were not painted steel but bronze (the mullions, which looked like standard I-beams, were actually custom-made T-shapes). The traditional materials, as well as the symmetry and regularity of the design, even the vertical striations on the lobby columns that suggested, however faintly, fluting, emphasized Mies's connection to the classical past.

The silky bronze tower and the rough pilgrimage chapel dominated architecture in the 1950s. As a young architecture student I visited and admired them both. I don't think I gave much thought to the contradictions implicit in two such different—almost diametrically opposed—approaches. One appealed to Cartesian logic, the other to Mediterranean romanticism. Clearly modernism had traveled far from its International Style roots. Could it successfully embrace such conflicting visions? After Seagram and Ronchamp, modernist architects would struggle mightily to find the answer.

31

In-Between

Paimio, 1930s
Säynätsalo, 1950s

If Mies van der Rohe and Le Corbusier represent two poles of the modern movement in the postwar era, the Finnish architect Alvar Aalto occupies a complex position somewhere in between. A decade younger, Aalto (1898–1976) was university trained in Helsinki, and, precociously talented, he opened his own office when he was only twenty-three. His early work was classical in the Nordic manner, but after European travel and contacts with Swedish modernists, he was drawn to the International Style.

In 1928, Aalto and his wife, Aino (1894–1949), also an architect, entered a competition for a tuberculosis sanatorium in a remote forested location near the city of Turku in southwestern Finland, where they lived. In its deliberations, the competition jury sought the advice of three medical experts, who unanimously recommended the Aaltos' proposal. The sprawling complex—the pair's first large commission—incorporated all the hallmarks of the New Building movement: flat roofs, white plastered walls, horizontal openings, ribbon windows, and roof terraces (fig. 128). Designed only three years after the Dessau Bauhaus, the building was similarly organized into functional wings: a six-story slab for the patients' rooms; an adjacent six-story wing of outdoor balconies for open-air sunning (then the prescribed treatment for tuberculosis); a communal wing for the dining hall, library, chapel, and lounge, as well as physicians' offices; a separate wing for an operating theater; and a low service wing for the kitchen, bakery, laundry, and heating plant. Houses for the staff were scattered in the surrounding forest. Unlike the Bauhaus building, the plan did not follow an abstract geometry. Instead, the wings were oriented to optimize solar orientation: the sunbathing balconies faced due south, as did the social spaces; the patients' wing was turned slightly southeast to increase morning sunlight; and the operating theater and the service wing were placed on the sunless north side

128 Tuberculosis Sanatorium, Paimio, Finland. Alvar and Aino Aalto, 1928–33. South facade. The wing containing the patients' rooms is turned slightly eastward to capture the morning sun. The cantilevered concrete balconies at right were originally open-air sunning balconies.

of the building. Three of the wings formed a U-shaped entry court on the west side of the building.

The Aaltos were not doctrinaire. The patient wing of their winning proposal was four stories high, and when the number of rooms was increased following the competition, they simply added two more floors. They varied the column spacing of the largely concealed concrete structural frame to suit the functions of the different wings. Exposing concrete to the harsh elements did not make sense, and the only place where the sanatorium's structure was visible was in the open-air sunning balconies, which were dramatically cantilevered (see fig. 128). The modernists of continental Europe were frequently cavalier when it came to building details, but the severe Finnish climate demanded careful construction, including proper insulation and double-glazing.

The Aaltos were responsible for the design and furnishing of the interior. Although they favored a minimalist aesthetic—no ornament, no decorative frills, no art—the clinical atmosphere was a functional choice, and the occupants' well-being was their paramount concern. "The room design is determined by the depleted strength of the patient, reclining in his bed," wrote Aalto. "The color of the ceiling is chosen for quietness, the light sources are outside the patient's field of vision, the heating is oriented towards the patient's feet, and the water runs soundlessly from the taps to make sure that no patient disturbs his neighbor."

The ceilings were painted a restful dark green and the linoleum floor was brown. Brighter colors were used in public areas: the rubber-coated floors of the stairs and hallways were pale yellow; doors were teal green. The south-facing windows of the social wing were shaded by colorful canvas awnings. In a rare theatrical gesture, the patients' wing was served by a panoramic glass elevator.

The design of the sanatorium was functionalist, but not in a heavy-handed manner. This was not the effete aestheticism of the Bauhaus. The standardized interiors were softened by curvilinear elements. Ingeniously designed details included baffled openable windows to reduce drafts, door handles designed to not catch on doctors' lab-coat sleeves, patients' wardrobes that were raised off the floor to facilitate cleaning, and desk lamps that could be clipped to the headboard for nighttime reading. There was a variety of furniture: stools, dining chairs, and easy chairs, as well as laboratory and doctors' office furnishings, all designed by the architects. Modernist furniture tended to be tubular steel, but the Aaltos preferred wood, which was less mechanical-looking, was warm to the touch, and was lighter and easier to move. To that end they developed innovative techniques for steam-bending wood and molding plywood. Opting for a traditional material such as wood was unusual for International Style architects—this was modernism with a deliberately human face.

▪ ▪ ▪ ▪ ▪

In 1948, Aalto won another competition (Aino was ill and would die the following year). The building was a town hall in Säynätsalo, a recently founded industrial community on a heavily wooded island in central Finland. The concept was simple: a building organized around a courtyard. "In government buildings and town halls, the courtyard has preserved its primal significance from the days of ancient Crete, Greece, and Rome, through the Middle Ages and the Renaissance," Aalto explained. Three sides of the square courtyard contained the town offices and residential apartments, and the fourth side was defined by a freestanding wing housing a public library, with shops and a post office on the lower level (fig. 129). The library was accessed from the courtyard, which was raised up one floor, both to provide a sense of civic occasion and to make the space sunnier. There were two entrances to the courtyard; a granite stair on one side and a set of grassy sitting steps made of split tree trunks and sod on the other (fig. 130).

The idea of a courtyard was markedly traditional, and the building deviated from modernist orthodoxy in other ways. The walls were red brick, not smooth and machinelike but made of rough clinker brick, deliberately chosen for its imperfections. The ten-inch-thick brick walls supported reinforced concrete floors and wooden roof beams. Aalto used concrete columns and beams in the larger spaces, such as the library, but he did not highlight the structure—for example, he concealed the concrete lintels over openings. On the other hand, he left the brick exposed on interior walls and floors. Flat roofs were a signature feature of modernist buildings at that time, yet Aalto made the roof of the town hall sloping, covered in traditional galvanized metal and copper.

Le Corbusier coined the term *promenade architecturale* to describe an orchestrated movement through a building. The promenade that Aalto devised for the town hall is an effective example. It begins outside, with broad granite steps that lead to the raised courtyard. After passing under a wooden pergola and making a sharp right turn, the visitor arrives at the entrance. The door resembles a rustic wooden gate with wide vertical boards whose gaps are filled by strips of glass. The door handle is cast bronze wrapped in leather—a little piece of old-fashioned handicraft. After entering the foyer and making a sharp U-turn, the promenade continues up a brick stairway that becomes progressively narrower as it turns yet another corner, until finally reaching the council chamber.

The scale of the Säynätsalo council chamber is unexpectedly monumental. "The world's most beautiful and most famous town hall, that of Siena, has a council chamber sixteen meters high," Aalto told his client. "I propose that we build one that is seventeen meters [almost sixty feet]." He designed a room that was a cube—the ideal Renaissance proportions—with brick walls and a high clerestory window. The sloped wooden ceiling is supported by two unusual butterfly trusses whose wooden members resemble the spokes of an umbrella (fig. 131).

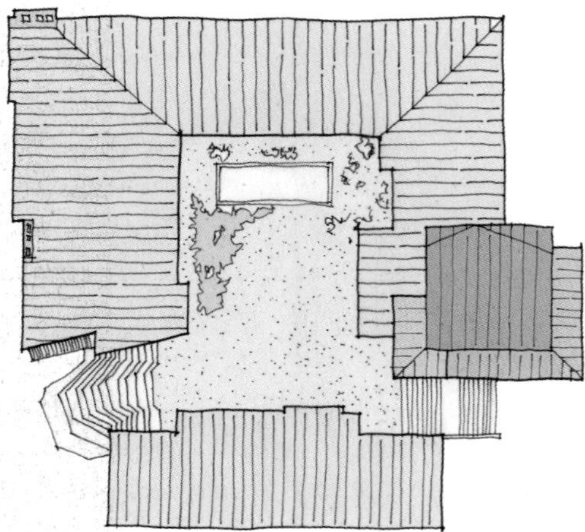

129 Town Hall, Säynätsalo, Finland. Alvar Aalto, 1948–52. Roof plan. Town offices surround the raised courtyard on three sides; the freestanding building at the bottom houses a public library. The shaded square on the right is the council chamber.

130 Town Hall, Säynätsalo. View from west. The sitting steps lead up to a courtyard that is dominated by the tall mass of the council chamber.

Exposing structure, as Gropius had done in the Bauhaus building, tends to look utilitarian—that is not the case here. The radiating trusses are as evocative as a Gothic fan vault.

While the Säynätsalo town hall is neither machinelike nor Brutalist, it is identifiably modernist, just not *completely* modernist. The composition of brick volumes was inspired by the hillside villages that Aalto had seen on his Italian travels, as were the imperfect brick walls; the overgrown grassy courtyard recalls a traditional Finnish farmstead. The building is full of such oblique references. Yet despite the use of traditional materials and rustic-looking details, the architecture does not literally represent the past; it is as abstract as the buildings of Mies and Le Corbusier—or a painting by Cezanne. Aalto's idea of abstraction was complicated and highly personal. "Abstract art at its best is the result of a kind of crystallization process," he wrote in a 1947 essay. "Perhaps that is why it

131 Town Hall, Säynätsalo. Council chamber. The butterfly trusses are as evocative as a Gothic fan vault.

can be grasped only intuitively, though in and behind the work of art there are constructive thoughts and elements of human tragedy. In a way it is a medium that can transport us directly into the human current of feelings that has almost been lost by the written word." At Säynätsalo, the "intuitive current of feelings" is sparked by the memories of farmyards and sloping roofs, by the visual experience of rough brick, and by the touch of a leather-wrapped door handle.

32

Variety and Richness

Bremen and Montreal, 1960s

Architects had been responsible for royal palaces since ancient times, and during the Renaissance they built urban palazzos and country villas. The profession's involvement with commercial residential buildings, whose occupants were more like customers than clients or patrons, began in the eighteenth century, with housing terraces for the well-to-do in London, Bath, and Edinburgh. In the late 1800s, architects designed not only apartment houses for bourgeois Parisians, Viennese, and New Yorkers, but also worker housing in British and American model factory towns. In due course, architects became involved with social housing, which was at the heart of the International Style modernists' agenda. The early work J. J. P. Oud was extended by Le Corbusier, who promoted a radically new urbanism based on high-rise living.

Alvar Aalto designed garden apartments for middle-class families, as well as low-rise housing terraces for factory towns, but he stood apart from his modernist colleagues in his skepticism about tall buildings. "High-rise apartments must be regarded, both socially and architecturally, as a considerably more dangerous form of building than single-family houses or low-rise apartments," he sensibly warned in 1946. "A badly planned private house or a less successfully planned block of modest low-rise flats disturbs a housing area much less than a badly planned and constructed group of high-rise buildings." What would a well-planned high-rise building look like? A dozen years later, Aalto was given the opportunity to provide an answer. Neue Vahr, a new district in the port city of Bremen, was the largest postwar social housing development in West Germany. The district consisted predominantly of two- to eight-story buildings, and the master plan called for a tall apartment tower in the town center to serve as a landmark. This was Aalto's commission.

Instead of adopting a conventional arrangement with an elevator core surrounded by apartments, in the manner of Lake Shore Drive, Aalto created an unusual fan-like plan with all the apartments facing the preferred view, of the River Weser and the church steeples of the old city, with the compact elevator and stair core facing away (fig. 132). The apartments were intended for individuals and couples. Each of the identical twenty-one floors contained seven wedge-shaped studio apartments, one apartment with an alcove, and a larger apartment with a separate bedroom. The narrow end of a typical apartment contained the entry, a storage room, a bathroom, and a kitchenette overlooking the main living space. A year earlier, Aalto had completed a low-rise apartment building in Berlin with partially enclosed loggias instead of projecting balconies, and in Bremen, he provided each apartment with a small loggia—in effect, an outdoor room. The unusual plan had a number of advantages. The glazed loggias brought more light into the deep apartments, whose wedge shapes made them feel less tunnel-like. At the same time, the fan-like plan enabled the public corridor to be shorter. The corridor was flooded with daylight thanks to a south-facing public sitting area at one end, and windows overlooking a communal airing balcony at the other. The stair landings that provided access to the elevators likewise had windows. The daylight, the compact arrangement, and the angled walls produced a domestic atmosphere.

The heavy concrete walls that supported the building provided sound separation between the apartments. The first floor contained an entrance lobby, as well as small shops and offices; the top floor housed a common room and a rooftop terrace. Aalto provided occasional decorative touches to the rather modest interiors: custom-made ceramic wall tiles and a wooden ceiling in the entrance lobby, slatted wood screens in the public areas in the upper floors, and teak window frames in the apartments. Neither luxurious nor crude—no travertine or

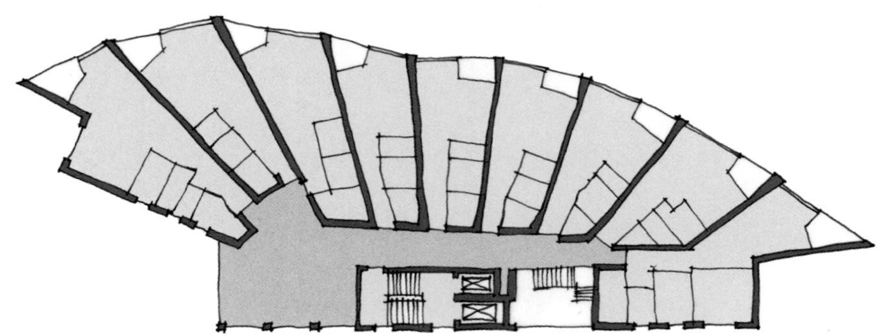

132 Apartment Tower, Neue Vahr, Bremen. Alvar Aalto, 1958–62. Typical floor plan. All the apartments are oriented to the view; the stairs, elevators, and an airing balcony are grouped in the rear and provided with natural light.

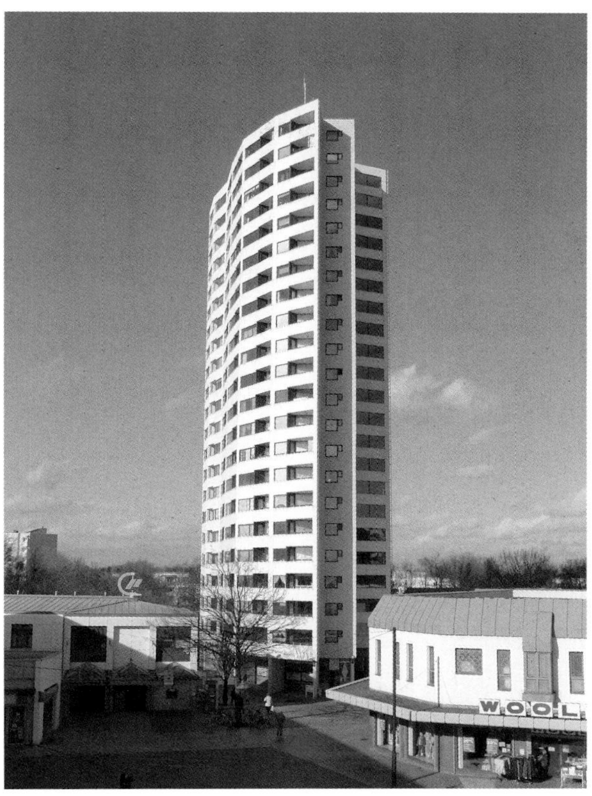

133 Apartment Tower, Neue Vahr, Bremen. The building is located in the town center. The irregular faceted curve of the facade produces an organic, naturalistic impression.

rough concrete here—the simple and thoughtfully designed interiors radiated uncomplicated bourgeois comfort.

Aalto's apartment building has an everyday quality that sets it apart from his civic architecture. There is nothing monumental about the undramatic facade; the identical floors are pragmatically stacked one on top of the other. At the base, the radiating concrete walls create deep recesses. The spandrels of the facade are unostentatious precast concrete panels, and the chiseled profile of the rather utilitarian rear is punctuated by windows and airing balconies; part of the rear wall is covered by a metal trellis—not that plants could grow on a building this tall, but the garden feature serves to soften the facade. Seen from the side, the stepped-back, sharply angled forms of the tower create a slender profile (fig. 133). The Bremen tower was Aalto's conscious attempt to escape the impersonal architecture that characterized most mass-produced housing at that time. He espoused what he called "flexible standardization." "The purpose of architectural standardization is thus not to produce types," he wrote in 1941, "but to create variety

134 Habitat 67, Montreal. Moshe Safdie, 1964–67. The stepped arrangement of concrete boxes, which resembles a hillside village, was a reaction to anonymous high-rise apartment buildings.

and richness which could, in the ideal case, be compared with nature's unlimited capacity to produce variation." Variety and richness are apparent in the mixture of materials and the organic plan of the Bremen tower, in the unusual combination of tower and slab, and in the irregular—almost whimsical—faceted form, which resembles a rocky escarpment as much as a building.

▪ ▪ ▪ ▪ ▪

Variety and richness were at the heart of another housing design of the 1960s. Moshe Safdie (b. 1938), a Canadian architect, was a member of a team working on the master plan for the 1967 Montreal world's fair. The fair site—manmade islands in the Saint Lawrence River—included a disused pier that Safdie proposed be used for a housing exhibit. He illustrated the idea with his own student thesis, completed only a few years earlier. Against all odds, his suggestion was accepted, and Safdie found himself—at twenty-six—setting up an independent office to design and build his first commission.

Safdie's McGill University thesis had been inspired by Le Corbusier's original idea for the Marseille Unité, which was to prefabricate the apartments in a factory, transport them to the building site, and slip them into a structural frame—like "bottles in a wine rack," in his memorable phrase. Although the Unité was constructed conventionally, the image of dwellings produced in a factory became part of architectural lore, and Safdie's thesis resurrected the idea, arranging prefabricated boxlike modules in a multistory structural frame. What he built for the Montreal fair was a modified version. Habitat, as the project came to be called, was made up of three hundred and fifty-four precast concrete boxes, roughly one hundred and fifty apartments. The apartments consisted of one, two, or three boxes, combined horizontally and vertically. There was no structural frame; instead, boxes were stacked, with the roof of the lower box acting as a terrace for the unit above (fig. 134). The twelve-story pyramidal stack was supported by elevated pedestrian walkways that spanned between stair and elevator towers. All the precast concrete elements—boxes, roofs, terrace railings, and walkways—were fabricated in a concrete plant located at the end of the pier adjacent to the building site. After the freshly cast box was removed from a giant mold and the concrete had cured, the box was moved to the site and lifted into place. There the interior was completed, including the installation of prefabricated kitchens and bathrooms. The dimensions of the box—forty feet long and eighteen feet wide—were standardized, although the size and location of windows and doors varied.

Safdie's design was a reaction to the standard solution of anonymous high-rise apartment buildings. Aalto had been right: high-rise housing was dangerous. Le Corbusier's concept of vertical living had produced rows of identical slabs and an environment of mind-numbing uniformity. Habitat, in contrast, used mass-production to create a sense of individual identity. The pile of concrete boxes has some of the qualities of a Mediterranean hillside town—Safdie was born in Haifa and was sixteen when his family immigrated to Canada. But Habitat is a manmade hillside that is both porous and hollow, so that you can see through it and even walk under it. This was not a building in the traditional sense—there are no facades, no roof, no front or back—and the stacked arrangement of the house boxes could be extended indefinitely in different directions. It is this organic quality, and a sense of unlimited variation, that sets Habitat apart. Each house has its own front door, either directly off a public walkway or reached by a private stair. Thanks to the stacking arrangement, each dwelling also has one or two private terraces. The terrace is the key to the project. "Habitat was, above all, about the theme 'for everyone a garden,'" Safdie wrote, "a metaphor for making an apartment in a high-rise structure into what connotes 'house'—a dwelling with its own identity, openness in a variety of orientations, and adjacent personal garden space set within a community."

33

Form Follows Imagination

New York, 1950s
Sydney, 1960s

Modernist architecture produced some strikingly original buildings, such as the Bremen tower and Habitat, yet cutting itself off from the past had disadvantages. Designing without the benefit of historical models was challenging, and few architects were as thoughtful as Aalto or as adventurous as Safdie. It proved difficult to invent a brand-new architectural language; unadorned walls, flat roofs, and ribbon windows were exciting at first, but the novelty soon wore off. Mies had his followers, but by the end of his career his work had become repetitive, and the limitations of his approach had become obvious—there was only so much you could do with I-beams and plate glass.

Le Corbusier was not the only architect to turn to sculptural form as an alternative. Frank Lloyd Wright's career had suffered setbacks since its auspicious beginning, but he had returned to prominence in the 1930s with Fallingwater, an unusual house in rural Pennsylvania with dramatically windmilling cantilevered terraces over a waterfall. This was followed by the Johnson Wax headquarters in Racine, Wisconsin, a striking streamlined building with concrete columns that resembled giant lily pads. In 1943, Wright was approached about a commission in New York City. He was seventy-six and had never built a prominent building in a major American city, so this was literally the opportunity of a lifetime. The request came from Hilla Rebay, a German baroness, connoisseur, and artist who was advising Solomon R. Guggenheim, a wealthy retired businessman who had amassed a formidable collection of modern art. The commission was to design what she and Guggenheim called a "Museum of Non-Objective Painting."

The most prominent American private collections at that time were housed in distinctly traditional buildings: Isabella Stewart Gardner's Venetian palazzo in Boston; Albert Barnes's neoclassical villa outside Philadelphia, designed by Paul Cret; and Henry Clay Frick's Beaux-Arts mansion on Fifth Avenue, designed by Carrère & Hastings and converted into a museum by John Russell Pope. Modernist museums were rare. The recently built Museum of Modern Art in New York, designed by Philip L. Goodwin and Edward Durell Stone, was a six-story Bauhaus box with ribbon windows and anonymous loft-like galleries. There was no question that the architecture of Guggenheim's museum would be modernist, but Rebay wanted something much more expressive. "Functionalism does not agree with non-objectivity," she announced in her introductory letter to Wright. "I want a temple of spirit, a monument."

Wright's first idea was a one-story building, and he tried to persuade Guggenheim to buy a large piece of land overlooking the Hudson River in the Bronx. When it became clear that his client was set on a midtown Manhattan location, which meant a more compact site, Wright switched to a multistory solution. He sent Rebay and Guggenheim a drawing of a ten-story building resembling an upside-down ziggurat. "A museum should be one extended expansive well-proportioned floor space from bottom to top," he advised them, adding a distinctly odd metaphor: "a wheel chair going around and up and down, *throughout*." Wright's unconventional idea was to display the paintings along a continuous spiraling ramp, the ultimate promenade architecturale. Like Karl Friedrich Schinkel, who made a rotunda the spiritual center of the Altes Museum, Wright was influenced by the ancient Romans—he once referred to the Guggenheim as "my Pantheon."

It would be thirteen years and many redesigns later before construction actually began. There were several obstacles to overcome, not least the fact that initially no site had been chosen. That did not stop Wright from developing alternative versions, round and hexagonal, both upside-down and right-side-up ziggurats. The building lot, on Fifth Avenue facing Central Park, was not acquired all at once, and Wright was obliged to modify his plans several times. America's entry into the Second World War further postponed the project, as did Guggenheim's death—he was eighty-eight—and construction did not get under way until 1956, which was roughly the time that Le Corbusier completed his sculptural chapel in Ronchamp.

The circular ramped museum was entirely reinforced concrete—it could hardly have been built otherwise. Wright envisioned a sort of nautilus shell, with the exterior skin, the internal partitions, and the floor forming a seamless whole. The ramp was cantilevered from structural fins and stiffened by the curved and tilted exterior walls, which were made of sprayed gunite. This was the same material that Le Corbusier used at Ronchamp, but Wright had no interest in roughness—quite the opposite, he wanted the surfaces to be as smooth as possible, inside and out. Postwar construction costs had risen, which required him to

135 Solomon R. Guggenheim Museum, New York. Frank Lloyd Wright, 1943–59. Interior.

pare back—the final exterior finish was painted concrete rather than the polished red marble he had originally intended.

When construction commenced, Wright encountered another obstacle. The Guggenheim heirs, who did not get along with Rebay, replaced her as museum director with James J. Sweeney, a professional curator previously at the Museum of Modern Art. Sweeney had firm views about displaying art, and he and Wright quickly became adversaries. Wright, who still had the support of some of the family, was given the last word on the exterior, but Sweeney prevailed inside. For example, he shrouded the rotunda's oculus skylight and introduced artificial lighting (Wright preferred natural light, even direct sunlight), he closed off the upper part of the ramp to use as storage, and he insisted that the interior be painted stark white rather than the off-white that Wright favored. The architect's proposed method of exhibiting the paintings was another source of disagreement. Wright's unconventional idea was to display frameless Kandinskys, Arps, and Miros directly on the slanted walls as if they were leaning on an artist's easel; Sweeney insisted on keeping the paintings vertical, which required attaching a special hanging mechanism to the slanted wall.

Wright, a connoisseur of Japanese prints, was no lover of modern art. But whatever the limitations of his unusual museum—and they are considerable—I am always impressed by the extraordinary experience of being on a ramp surrounding

136 Solomon R. Guggenheim Museum, New York. Exterior. The painted concrete form stands in sharp contrast to its urban surroundings. The windowless block on the left is a 1992 addition.

a skylit rotunda (fig. 135). The Guggenheim ramp is usually described as a spiral; in fact, it is a conical helix whose diameter increases as it ascends. The ramp leans outward, but the structural fins that transfer its weight to the ground and support the central skylight lean in. Thanks to the use of monolithic concrete, the floors, walls, and structural fins form a continuous surface. The eye is not distracted by details because there aren't any. The helical balustrade is a simple concrete parapet with a rounded top; there are no changes of material, no joints, no baseboards, no moldings, none of the fussy precision so beloved by modernist architects.

On the exterior, the elephantine monolith stands in sharp contrast to its urban surroundings; indeed, it would appear out of place anywhere (fig. 136). Like Gaudí, the elderly Wright exhibited a creativity that was both inexhaustible and idiosyncratic. Not for him Le Corbusier's crude roughness, Mies's machined rigor, or Aalto's naturalistic palette. Nor does the museum incorporate any of Wright's early Arts and Crafts details. It is as if he has stripped away all inessentials; what is left looks both ancient and futuristic. In a 1908 essay Wright speculated that in the future, architecture would "grow more truly simple: more expressive with fewer lines, fewer forms; more articulate with less labor; more plastic; more fluent, although more coherent; more organic." With the Guggenheim Museum, that future had arrived.

■ ■ ■ ■ ■

Wright devoted his last sixteen years to the Guggenheim project—he died six months before the official opening. On the other side of the world, another unusual building likewise took sixteen years to complete, and its architect likewise did not attend the opening—although for a different reason. That building was the Sydney Opera House in Australia, and the architect was Jørn Utzon (1918–2008). The design of the opera house was the subject of an international competition that took place in 1956 and attracted more than two hundred entries from twenty-eight countries. Unlike the other entrants, many of whom designed International Style boxes, Utzon took full advantage of the spectacular site, a narrow spit of land sticking into Sydney Harbor. He placed the two large auditoria required by the competition side by side on top of a stepped plinth. The auditorium seating was carved out of the plinth, which extended to become a stepped entry plaza (fig. 137). Above the plinth hovered a series of overlapping concrete shells that resembled billowing sails—Utzon, the son of a naval architect, was an enthusiastic yachtsman. In his accompanying statement he imagined "opening up the halls, foyers and public areas towards open-air during intermission whenever weather permitting and presents to the audience the full sensation of the suspended shells while moving through the foyers commanding the beautiful view of the harbor." It was a compelling image.

"I don't want to be interesting. I want to be good," Mies van der Rohe told an interviewer in 1955, but after Ronchamp and the Guggenheim Museum it was not enough for new important buildings to be good, people expected them

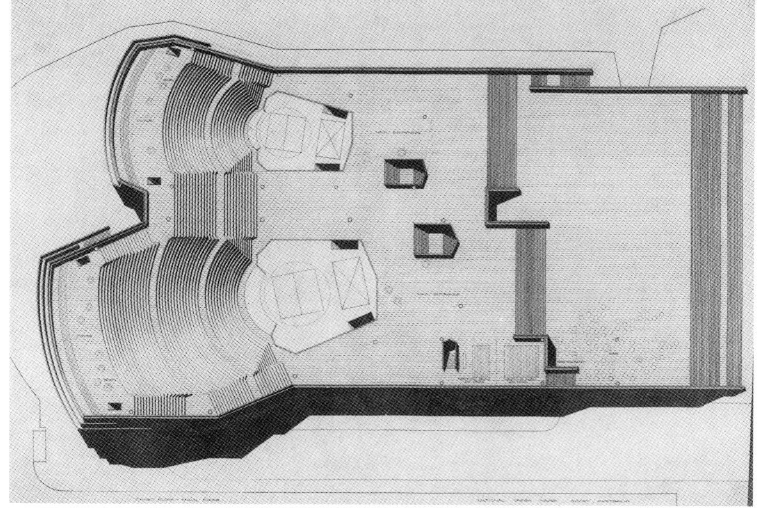

137 Sydney Opera House, Australia. Jørn Utzon, 1957–73. Plan. Utzon's original competition drawing showing the amphitheater seating for the two halls carved out of a stepped plinth.

to be interesting, too. Utzon understood that. A Dane, he had graduated from Copenhagen's Royal Academy of Fine Arts in 1942 and spent the war years in Sweden. He worked briefly for Alvar Aalto and spent a year on a scholarship traveling in the United States and Mexico, visiting Frank Lloyd Wright and working on an archaeological site in Yucatán. He opened his own small office in 1950. Utzon, a late bloomer, was thirty-eight when he entered the Sydney competition; his chief built accomplishment to date was his own house. As many young architects do, he entered competitions partly in the hope of winning a commission and partly as a design exercise. The Sydney competition seems to have been chiefly the latter—his last-minute submission was incomplete and did not scrupulously adhere to the program.

The great stepped plinth of Utzon's winning scheme was influenced by his experience of Mayan architecture, but the concrete shells were unprecedented in his work, or indeed in anyone else's. Architects and engineers in Italy, Spain, and Mexico had pioneered extremely thin reinforced concrete shells in such long-span structures as stadiums and exhibition halls, but Utzon's shells were different—the free-form shapes were not self-supporting. Indeed, it was far from clear how they could be made to stand up. The answer was provided by the engineer Ove Arup (1895–1988), a transplanted Dane based in London who joined Utzon on the project. Arup's large firm was a leader in reinforced concrete construction and was known for its successful collaboration with architects. The Arup engineers devised a way of building the roofs using precast and post-tensioned concrete ribs rather than smooth shells, and making the different shells segments of the same sphere, which enabled the use of standardized formwork. The ribbed roofs were pointed, like fragments of Gothic vaults, and were covered with white glazed ceramic tiles inspired by the mosques that Utzon had seen during a trip to Morocco.

The large building was designed and built in three separate phases: first the plinth (which housed backstage facilities, such as rehearsal rooms, recording studios, dressing rooms, and workshops), then the shell roofs, and lastly the interior halls. The Australians were in a hurry, so construction of the shells began before the design of the halls was finalized. That is when the troubles began. Some of the problems were due to the original competition program, which called for the larger hall to be used both for opera and symphonic music, even though an opera hall requires a fly loft, extensive space for scenery, and shorter reverberation times than a symphony hall. Another problem was Utzon's design; simply put, his concert hall did not accommodate the required number of seats and he had to add two balconies, which compromised the simplicity of his original concept.

138 Sydney Opera House. Exterior. The striking building was the first postwar work of architecture to achieve the status of an urban icon.

Utzon had a very small office in Denmark with a young and inexperienced staff, and he had difficulty producing the vast number of drawings required by the mammoth undertaking. In addition, he had the temperament of an artist and lacked the diplomatic skills necessary to manage such a complicated public project. Arup's firm, which was much larger and more experienced, picked up most of the slack, but because Utzon insisted on having the last word, tensions arose between the architect and the engineers. "I wonder whether you really are master of the situation and can manage without help except from sycophantic admirers," an exasperated Arup wrote him. "I have often said that I think you are wonderful, but are you all that wonderful?" The final straw concerned the budget; thanks to poor coordination, delays, and last-minute changes, by 1965 the estimated construction cost had grown more than sixfold. The following year a newly elected Australian government demanded that Utzon associate himself with a large local firm and take a secondary role. Utzon refused and threatened to resign, but the government was unyielding and the architect returned to Denmark. There were futile attempts at reconciliation, and the interior of the building was finished without the Dane's involvement and not according to his design: the larger hall was turned into a multipurpose auditorium for symphonic concerts and musical performances, and opera was relegated to the smaller hall. When the building was finally completed, seven years later, Utzon, who had devoted nine years to the project, chose not to attend the opening ceremony and never returned to Australia.

The ill-fated Opera House had all the ingredients of a fiasco, yet even though imperfectly realized, Utzon's artistic vision of sail-like forms in Sydney Harbor turned out to have enormous public appeal (fig. 138). His building became an icon, one of the most recognizable urban structures in the world, comparable to the Eiffel Tower and the Empire State Building. It was the first work of postwar architecture to achieve that elevated status. There were several reasons for this popularity. Utzon was an uncompromising modernist in his use of asymmetry, abstraction, and lack of ornament, yet the building exhibited a Scandinavian sense of craftsmanship: where the concrete was exposed, as in the vault ribs, it was mirror smooth; the concrete plinth was clad in earth-toned, reconstituted granite; the roofing tiles gleamed like traditional mosaic. Not that the building techniques were traditional. "I like to be at the edge of the possible," Utzon said. The construction process involved innovation; the precast concrete ribs were joined using epoxy, and the specially developed glazed ceramic tiles were a novel combination of clay and crushed stone.

Even as it was identifiably modernist, the Sydney Opera House was iconoclastic. The shells were built thanks to the ingenuity of the Arup engineers, but the basic shapes did not follow structural logic. Otto Wagner taught that the "architect always has to develop the art-form out of construction," yet Utzon's evocative sail-like forms had little to do with the way they were built—they were the product of his imagination. Nor did Utzon follow Louis Sullivan's dictum that "form ever follows function"; there was no functional rationale for the overlapping shells, which had nothing to do with the freestanding halls beneath. Asked his opinion of Utzon's design, Frank Lloyd Wright responded, "This circus tent is not architecture."

Wright meant his characterization to be derogatory, but the truth is that people like circus tents, and they loved Utzon's opera house. The gleaming roofs conjured up popular images that were both intelligible and cheerfully multivalent: sails, clouds, cathedral vaults, seashells, turtles. Like so many great buildings of the past, the opera house's beauty appealed to the senses rather than the intellect. The public, which had admired and enjoyed prewar Art Deco buildings, had never warmed to postwar modernism—whether starkly minimalist steel-and-glass or rough Brutalism. The Sydney Opera House was different.

Only thirty-one years separate Utzon's building from Walter Gropius's Bauhaus, yet the two buildings were worlds apart. The Sydney Opera House was modernist in its abstraction, its ahistoricism, and its avoidance of traditional architectural motifs. At the same time, the design broke many modernist conventions: the architecture did not express its structure or its construction, the form did not follow its function, and the effect of the shell roofs was decidedly playful. It all signaled that after only three decades the severe and dogmatic New Building episode had come to a definite end. Architecture was moving on.

VI
AFTER MODERNISM

34

The Seesaw

New Haven, 1950s
Dhaka, 1960s and 1970s

Paul Cret once characterized the history of architecture as an up-and-down cycle. "In Art there are two broad groups—the Classic and the Romantic—and in the seesaw balancing between them which is recorded in the history of Art, it is now one, now the other, which is on the high end. The ascendancy group believes in good faith to have discovered the one and only Truth, and to have forever vanquished its adversary, until the limit of its ascent having been reached, there appears what they will call a Reaction, and the opposite group, a New Tendency, and the vanquished of yesterday become the victors of today." The "limit of its ascent" to which Cret was referring represented the moment when the creative answers to a particular aesthetic problem had been exhausted and all the permutations and combinations had been explored. This was the time when architects often switched gears, so to speak: from sturdy Romanesque to airy Gothic, from Gothic to disciplined Renaissance, whence to expressive Baroque, orderly Greek Revival, and so on. The shifts were not preordained and they had different causes, but the story of architecture roughly follows Cret's seesaw metaphor.

Cret made his observation in 1930, when the International Style was beginning its ascent—interestingly, he considered this attempt to step outside history and remake architecture as fundamentally a romantic quest. This was especially true in the late work of Le Corbusier and Wright, as well as in Utzon's idiosyncratic opera house. Cret was right that a reaction would inevitably set in. By 1950, Mies's skin-and-bones architecture was moving—albeit tentatively—in the classical direction. In 1953, a small building appeared that seemed to square the circle, being both classic *and* romantic.

The building in question was an addition to the Yale University Art Gallery, a Romanesque Revival building on New Haven's Chapel Street designed in 1928 by Egerton Swartwout. The new addition housed architecture studios and

139 Yale University Art Gallery, New Haven, Connecticut. Louis I. Kahn, 1951–53. The gallery is next to Egerton Swartwout's 1928 Romanesque Revival museum.

printmaking workshops, as well as museum galleries. The four floors were free-span spaces, designed so that when the teaching functions moved out, galleries could take their place. The identical spaces were divided by a central core of elevators, stairs, and utilities. The functional layout resembled a conventional office building, but instead of acoustic tile, the ceiling was an exposed eggcrate of rough concrete. Equally unexpectedly, the stairs were housed in a concrete cylinder that resembled a silo. The modernist exterior ignored its revivalist neighbor—that was not unusual—but unlike many museum buildings at that time it was self-consciously undramatic; no cantilevers, no unusual forms, no structural gymnastics. The flat windowless south wall along Chapel Street was gray-brown brick relieved only by bluestone stringcourses indicating the floor levels (fig. 139). The north wall, overlooking a sculpture court, was all glass; the east and west walls were likewise delicate grids of steel and glass.

Just as Brunelleschi's Foundling Hospital had done hundreds of years earlier, the Yale museum set the architectural world on its ear. The building was definitely modernist, but it had a new quality—character. Or, rather, several characters. The prim brick wall with stringcourses looked traditional, the glass curtain walls were Miesian, and the rough concrete on the interior recalled Le Corbusier's Brutalism. The heavy ceiling—a tetrahedral space frame—was clearly influenced by engineering, except that the massive concrete looked archaic and crude rather than technical. As for the monumental stair-silo, it was like something out of a Piranesi engraving. Altogether, an unexpected combination of influences.

The architect of this collage was a fifty-year-old design critic in the Yale architecture department whose work until that point had attracted little attention. The story of architecture has prodigies, such as Bernini, Goodhue, and Wright; Louis I. Kahn (1901–1974) was not one of them. His career was constrained by both personal and external circumstances. Born in Estonia, he was brought to the United States as a child by his parents, who settled in Philadelphia. He graduated in 1924 from the University of Pennsylvania. Kahn's lowly status as a poor Jewish immigrant (as a student he supported himself by playing piano in a silent movie house) shaped his early career. Lacking social contacts, he was obliged to partner with established practitioners. Like other architects, his career was adversely affected by the Depression and the Second World War—except for some wartime housing projects, most of his early designs remained unbuilt.

Kahn was the product of a Beaux-Arts education—Paul Cret was his teacher and one of his early employers. Nevertheless he was drawn to modernism and developed a local reputation as a committed modernist with an artistic bent. In 1947, at forty-six, he opened his own office. That same year, the Yale University department of architecture, which was installing a modernist curriculum, invited him to be a visiting critic. Kahn turned out to be a popular teacher, and he became a regular, commuting between Philadelphia and New Haven. In 1950, George Howe (1886–1955), celebrated as the codesigner of the Philadelphia Saving Fund Society Building, an early International Style skyscraper, was appointed chair of the Yale department. Howe and Kahn had earlier worked together, and Howe appointed his friend a permanent member of the faculty. Also thanks to Howe, Kahn was invited to be a resident at the American Academy in Rome. Kahn had made architectural trips to Europe before—in 1928, to Britain and France—but the three-month stay in Rome and the opportunity to see Greece and Egypt opened his eyes to the ancient architectural monuments and sparked an enduring interest in masonry construction. While he was in Rome, Kahn received an unexpected offer. Yale had decided to extend its Art Gallery—the addition would be the first modernist building on the largely Collegiate Gothic campus. The commission had originally been offered to Eero Saarinen (1910–1961), a Finnish-American architect who was also a visiting critic at Yale. Saarinen, who had

140 Yale University Art Gallery. Interior before installation of the gallery. The impression of the massive concrete structural ceiling is archaic rather than technological. The stair/silo is visible on the left.

recently won a national competition for the Gateway Arch in St. Louis and was occupied with the General Motors Technical Center, suggested Kahn—the two were friends—and with Howe's support, Kahn was offered the job. It was his first major commission.

The design that Kahn produced shows the extent to which his recent travel had prompted him to move away from orthodox modernism. The tetrahedral ceiling is an example. Saarinen had recently built a steel tetrahedral space frame in his General Motors project, and Kahn translated this form into concrete (fig. 140). Influenced by a visit he had made to Le Corbusier's unfinished Unité d'habitation in Marseille, Kahn left the concrete rough. He admired the simplicity of ancient architecture, which was not disfigured by plumbing, heating ducts, and mechanical equipment, and in the Yale gallery he ran the ducts and utilities within the deep ceiling, and he grouped the stairs, elevators, and bathrooms in what he called "servant spaces." Kahn's approach to design distinguished him from his contemporaries. Instead of inventing new forms, he sought to discover what he considered the building's essential character. "What does this building want to be?" he would ask his students.

▪ ▪ ▪ ▪ ▪

The Yale Art Gallery opened in 1953, and the following decade was a busy one for Kahn. He built a medical laboratory at the University of Pennsylvania, where he now taught, with freestanding brick stair shafts and vent stacks that resembled medieval towers. The highly original building was the subject of a special exhibition at the Museum of Modern Art and brought him national renown—and more work: a research institute for Jonas Salk in La Jolla, California, a Unitarian church in Rochester, New York, a student dormitory for Bryn Mawr College, and an unbuilt proposal for a U.S. consulate in Angola. An unbuilt monumental synagogue in Philadelphia, whose large cylindrical forms acted as light wells, signaled a further move away from mainstream modernism.

In 1962, Kahn received two major commissions outside the United States. The first was a new campus for the Indian Institute of Management in Ahmedabad; the second, which would occupy him for the rest of his life, was a large parliamentary complex in Dhaka, East Pakistan. Pakistan had been created as a result of the partition of British India in 1947, and the bifurcated Islamic country consisted of the Punjab in the west and Bengal in the east. The capital city was Islamabad in the Punjab, and a second capital was planned for Dhaka, the largest city in Bengal. The Pakistanis engaged European and American architects to design the Islamabad parliament buildings, and for Dhaka they first approached Le Corbusier, who was too busy with other projects, then Alvar Aalto, who declined because of poor health. A leading Bengali architect who had studied at Yale suggested Kahn, and he was offered the commission.

The eight-hundred-acre site of the new administrative capital was on the outskirts of Dhaka. In addition to a three-hundred-seat assembly hall, the government complex was to include offices and housing for the members of parliament and their staffs (who would travel between the two capitals), as well as the supreme court, a museum, a school, recreational facilities, and a medical center. The national assembly and the associated housing and offices were to be built first. It was two years before construction could begin, a delay caused by the size of the project and its changing programmatic requirements, as well as by Kahn's travel schedule and his measured pace of work. On the other hand, the half dozen trips that the architect made to Bengal during that period enabled him to become familiar with the place and its people.

Kahn visited Chandigarh, the new state capital that Le Corbusier was building in the Indian portion of the Punjab, and although he found the architecture beautiful, it seemed to him "out of context"—the modern concrete buildings could have been anywhere. Like Lutyens, Kahn was impressed by the ancient Mughal architecture of India and Pakistan. Imitating domes and minarets did not interest him, but he did want his building, which would be an important national symbol, to have local meaning. "What I'm trying to do is establish a belief out of a philosophy I can turn over to Pakistan so that whatever they do is always answerable to it," he observed somewhat cryptically.

Kahn rejected the modernist planning of Mies and Le Corbusier, and his strictly geometrical arrangement of cubes and cylinders in the Dhaka National Assembly reflected his Beaux-Arts education as well as his experience of the ancient buildings of Rome and Egypt. The entrance to the ten-story octagonal National Assembly was from a raised plaza on the north side. The roughly circular assembly chamber, a Pantheon-like space lit from the top by clerestories, was surrounded by a tall ambulatory, a sort of interior street that was lined by four large halls: an entrance hall with a grand stair on the north; a prayer hall (slightly turned to face Mecca) on the south; ministerial lounges on the west; and a dining hall on the east. In between, four rectangular blocks housed the members' offices (fig. 141). To give a sense of place to the flat, featureless site, and to control flooding, Kahn surrounded the assembly building with a manmade lake, lining the two arms of the lake with the houses for parliamentary secretaries, members of parliament, and ministers (fig. 142). The two-story residential buildings, originally to be built of concrete, were made of local brick at the client's insistence. The houses, arranged along two diagonals, opened onto private gardens. The gardens and the water basin were conscious references to the Persian-inspired Mughal architecture of the Indian subcontinent.

Kahn referred to the parliamentary complex as a citadel, and the monumental building is as massive as a Norman keep. The unbuilt U.S. consulate in Angola had what he called glare walls: external screens with large openings. In Dhaka,

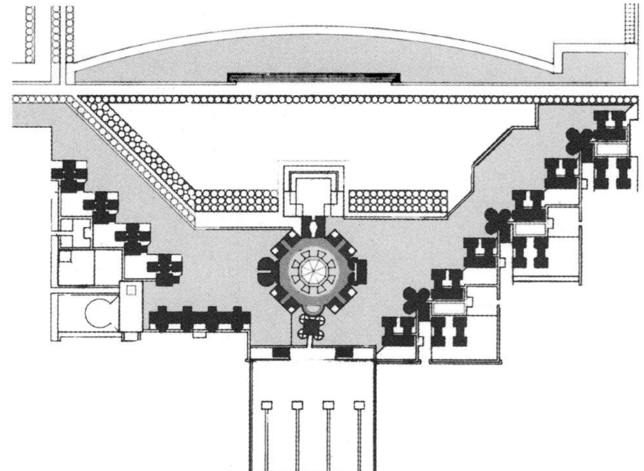

141 National Assembly, Dhaka, Bangladesh. Louis Kahn, 1962–83. Site plan. The area around the octagonal assembly building included a manmade lake lined by housing for members of parliament (right), parliamentary secretaries (left), and ministers (bottom left).

142 National Assembly, Dhaka. The massive parliamentary complex (right) resembles a concrete citadel; the clerestories of the assembly chamber are visible on the roof. The brick housing (left) is for members of parliament; the cylindrical forms house dining halls.

the apertures in the glare walls are large circles, semicircles, and triangles enclosing deep verandas that provide protection from the piercing sun and the monsoon rains. Kahn favored monolithic construction, and the assembly building is built entirely out of cast-in-place concrete. As in the interior of the Yale Art Gallery, the concrete is exposed. Kahn referred to concrete as "molten stone," and in Dhaka he treated it like smooth masonry, very different from Le Corbusier's *béton brut*. The walls are divided into horizontal panels by strips of white marble (fig. 143). Kahn rationalized the strips as delineating the limits of daily concrete pours, but they are clearly meant to relieve the large expanses of concrete. The decorative marble accents are another reference—albeit subtle—to Mughal tradition.

Construction proceeded slowly. Pakistan was a poor country, cement and reinforcing steel had to be imported, and cranes and construction machinery were scarce—the work was carried out largely by hand. In 1971, just as construction of the roof was beginning, East Pakistan, which considered that West Pakistan was unfairly dominating the government as well as the military, declared its independence. A brutal civil war ensued. After nine months of fighting, which claimed as many as half a million Bengali lives, Bangladesh, as the new country was called, prevailed (with Indian assistance). Although Dhaka was bombed, and the assembly buildings were used as temporary army barracks, the parliamentary complex emerged unscathed—it is said that the West Pakistan pilots thought the buildings were ancient ruins. Construction resumed on what was now a national capitol. The master plan was modified to accommodate additional government offices,

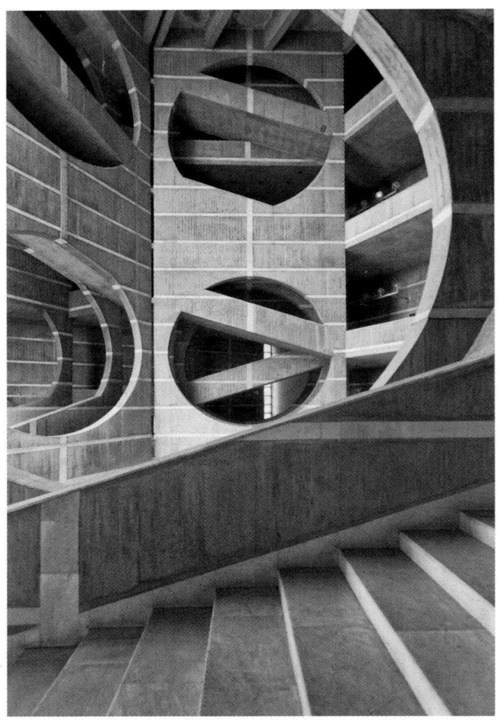

143 National Assembly, Dhaka. Interior. The entrance hall contains a grand stair. The cast concrete surfaces are relieved by strips of white marble.

and Kahn designed a long nine-story secretariat building across the water basin from the National Assembly.

Kahn died unexpectedly of a heart attack in 1974 while returning home from site visits to Ahmedabad and Dhaka. It took nine more years to complete the parliamentary complex, although neither the secretariat nor the supreme court buildings were built. Many consider the Bangladesh project to be the architect's greatest achievement, not only because of its scale and complexity, but also because of the way that it incorporates regional traditions. In its classical sense of repose, the National Assembly building bears comparison to the Shah Mosque of Isfahan, and even to that seventeenth-century masterpiece of Mughal architecture, the Taj Mahal. Kahn's brooding and severe design is much more austere than the ancient monuments, which reflects his own taste as well the limited resources of his client, one of the poorest countries in the world. Paradoxically, Kahn was approached because he represented—in Bengali eyes—American know-how and modernity, but what he delivered was neither particularly American nor particularly modern. "Timeless yet of its time" was how he put it. In that sense, he truly had squared the circle, looking forward and back at the same time.

35

The Industrial Gene

Paris and Norwich, 1970s

Despite the spectacular examples of Paxton and Eiffel, early modernist architects generally kept technology at arm's length. Le Corbusier declared that "a house is a machine for living in," but he had neither the inclination nor the ability to follow through, and, especially after Ronchamp, his architecture was increasingly unmachinelike. To the untrained eye, Mies van der Rohe's architecture looked like engineering, but it was structurally conservative; and Aalto preferred preindustrial materials and handcrafted details. As for Utzon and Kahn, technology remained a distinctly background issue, a means to an end but not a central architectural concern, such as form or space.

Nevertheless, industrialized building was an important strand in modernism's DNA—think Gropius and Meyer's all-glass wall at the Bauhaus and Mendelsohn's department store facades—and while deeply buried, the strand occasionally surfaced. One place it appeared was in postwar Southern California, notably in the work of Charles and Ray Eames. Charles (1907–1978), an architect, and his wife Ray (1912–1988), an artist, were interested in how things were made; for example, they developed a technique for molding plywood for a variety of wartime applications, which they later applied to groundbreaking plywood shell furniture. Their own home and studio in the Pacific Palisades neighborhood of Los Angeles showed a similar inventiveness. The overall forms were simple: two boxes. Like a Unité apartment, the double-height space of the house had a sleeping loft (fig. 144). The steel-framed building was pragmatically assembled from a variety of industrially produced off-the-shelf components: steel decking, open-web steel joists, skinny pipe columns, and fiberglass panels. Begun in 1947, two years before Mies's Lake Shore Drive apartments, the Eames house and studio demonstrated a very different sensibility. Whereas many of the "bones" in Mies's towers were concealed, the Eames's house exposed structural details, such

144 Eames House, Pacific Palisades, California. Charles and Ray Eames, 1947–49. Interior. Assembled unselfconsciously—and delicately—the architecture is distinctly unmonumental.

as X-shaped cross-bracing and the corrugated underside of its steel roof deck, which created an industrial appearance. At the same time, because the parts were assembled unselfconsciously and delicately, compared to Mies's architecture the house was distinctly unmonumental. It was "as light and airy as a suspension bridge, as skeletal as an airplane fuselage," in Charles Eames's words.

Despite its origins in the work of the Eameses and other Southern California architects, what might be called Lightweight Modernism did not take root in the United States, where heavy concrete prevailed in the work of leading architects, such as Kahn and Marcel Breuer. Instead, the industrial gene reemerged a decade later, on the other side of the Atlantic. Architectural innovation is often the result of a serendipitous interaction between architects, their clients, and the cultural milieu. This cross-pollination often functions best in the hothouse atmosphere of a city: Renaissance Florence, fin-de-siècle Vienna, Jazz Age New York. In the 1960s, it blossomed in Swinging London, which fostered a youthful, antiestablishment counterculture focused chiefly on music (the Beatles) and fashion (Carnaby Street). The city was also a breeding ground for architectural innovation. Reacting to the grim Brutalist concrete buildings of postwar Britain, iconoclastic young architects explored lightweight construction and adaptable and flexible buildings, such as tents, inflatables, space frames, and geodesic domes. Much of this work was the result of collaboration with like-minded engineers. Architects and engineers worked together everywhere, but the British collaboration was creative as well as professional—the engineers were interested in architecture, and architects saw the discipline of engineering as a valuable framework for creative design.

Edmund Happold (1930–1996) was an engineer in charge of one of the divisions of Ove Arup & Partners. In 1971, he came across an announcement for an international competition for a mixed-use cultural center on a prominent site in the heart of Paris. Because the announcement stipulated that teams be headed by an architect, he approached Richard Rogers, a young London architect with whom Arup had collaborated on an earlier competition. Rogers (1933–2021), born in Florence of an established Anglo-Italian family but raised in England, had recently formed a partnership with Renzo Piano (b. 1937), an Italian architect based in Genoa who shared Rogers's interest in building technology. With fewer than a dozen employees in two cities, Piano & Rogers was a very small firm, and the opportunity to work with one of the largest consulting engineering firms in the world was hard to resist.

In addition to offering an opportunity for architects and engineers to gain a commission, a competition was an opportunity to collaboratively explore new ideas. Piano's and Rogers's previous work had all the hallmarks of Lightweight Modernism: spidery steel frames, factory-produced components, a functionalist aesthetic, and, above all, flexible plans. These interests dovetailed with Arup's engineering expertise. The Parisian cultural center was intended to house a public library, a cinematheque, and an industrial design center, as well as a museum of contemporary art. Piano & Rogers's concept was to accommodate the different uses in a loose and informal way that would allow for future change. Their basic design was simplicity itself: a six-story box that occupied half the site, leaving the other half as an open plaza for outdoor events. The structural material was steel. The loft-like floors were entirely column-free and spanned by one-hundred-and-fifty-foot trusses that allowed for maximum freedom in planning. The Arup engineers developed an innovative lifting mechanism that would enable the floors to move up and down, thus creating different ceiling heights. To achieve this extreme flexibility, all the services and movement systems were moved to the exterior of the building: ducts, plumbing, and freight elevators in the rear, covered walkways and escalators on the side facing the plaza (fig. 145). The steel framework of the plaza facade was covered in giant electronic billboards carrying images and text. The competition narrative, written by Rogers, described the building as a "Live Centre of Information." By a vote of eight to one, the competition jury awarded the Piano

145 Centre Pompidou, Paris. Renzo Piano and Richard Rogers, 1971–77. The public circulation—covered walkways and escalators—is on the exterior of the building, supported by a lightweight framework of steel.

& Rogers project first place and all the prize money—there were no second- or third-place winners among the more than seven hundred entries.

The Centre Pompidou, as it came to be called, took six years to design and build, but unlike the Sydney Opera House there were no crises or resignations; the building was completed on time and within an acceptable margin of the projected cost. Not that there weren't changes and modifications: the abbreviated construction schedule prevented the development of the unusual floor-lifting system; the electronic billboards were eliminated for budgetary reasons; and many of the design features that animated the plaza were likewise deleted. The Arup team was led by Peter Rice (1935–1992), an Irish structural engineer who had been site engineer on the Sydney Opera House. Rice had a particular idea that he wanted to explore. "I had been wondering for some time what it was that gave the large engineering structures of the nineteenth century their special appeal," he wrote in his autobiography. "Like Gothic cathedrals, they exude craft and individual choice. The cast-iron decorations and the cast joints give each of these structures a quality unique to their designer and maker, a reminder that they were made and conceived by people who had labored and left their mark." The modern equivalent of cast iron is forged steel, and Rice designed massive

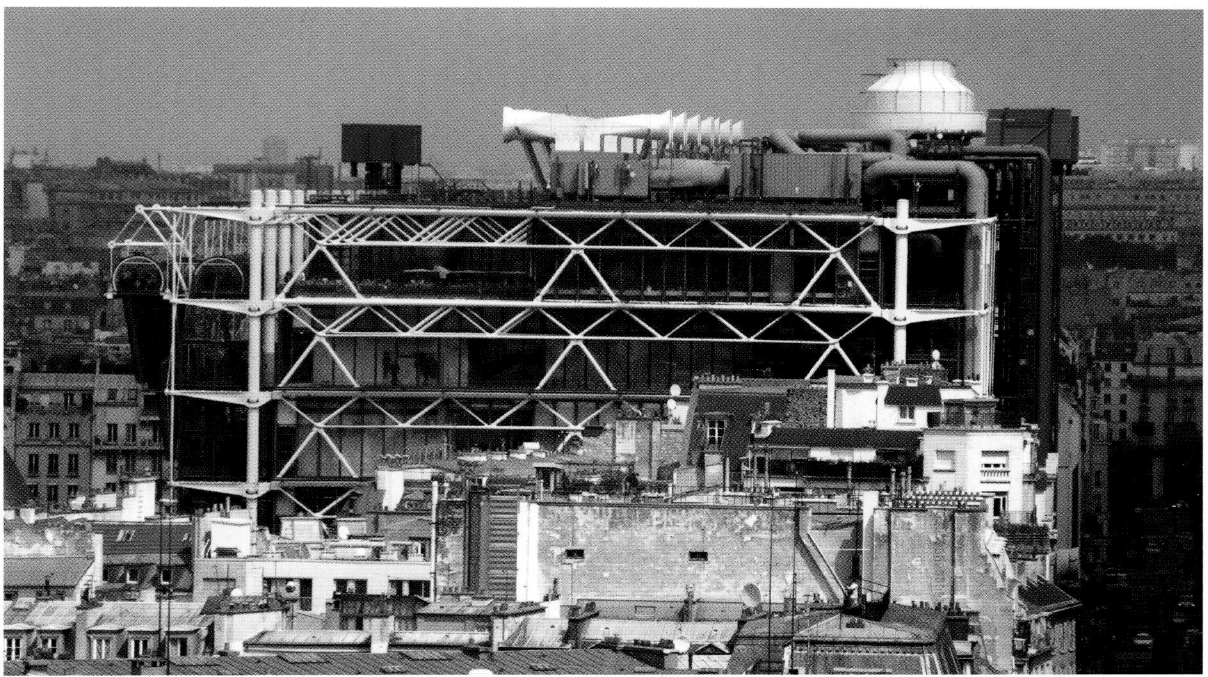

146 Centre Pompidou. The view of the southern end shows the long trusses spanning the column-free floors, and the forged steel outriggers cantilevered on each side. The services are on the exterior of the building: the ducts, plumbing, and freight elevators on the right, public galleries and escalators on the left.

forged-steel outriggers, called gerberettes, which cantilevered from the columns and also supported the trusses. The sculpted outriggers provided the individuality that he wanted (fig. 146).

The site of the Centre Pompidou is Plateau Beaubourg, an old neighborhood not far from Notre-Dame Cathedral. I remember my first visit. My chief impression was the startling contrast between the new architecture and the old buildings. The most striking visual aspect of the former, in addition to its heroic structural elements, was the spider's web of pipes and ducts that was exposed on the exterior rather than being concealed inside the building. The service components were cheekily painted bright colors: blue for air-conditioning ducts, green for plumbing, yellow for electrical systems, and bright red for elevators and the escalators that snaked across the facade. The structural elements were off-white. There were echoes here of the painted cast iron of the Crystal Palace. And like the Palace—and the Eiffel Tower—the Centre Pompidou had its critics, who likened the architecture to an oil refinery, although Piano & Rogers's industrial components were as carefully designed and composed as any classical building.

Piano and Rogers were irreverent functionalists—according to them, a thing should look like what it was, nuts and bolts and all. That is why exposing pipes and ducts appealed to them. The unconventional appearance of the building complemented the unconventional planning. The Centre Pompidou was the functional opposite of a traditional art museum: unmonumental, nonhierarchical, accessible from all sides. Piano described their intentions. "After the 1960s, museums were a fantastic place, but they were only for the elite. Nobody really went to the museum except people in love with art. So, as bad boys, we thought, 'We must bring art to anybody, even people who don't care about art.' So we had to break that sense of intimidation, break the monumental—like stone, like marble, like steps, like cold. We thought, 'Maybe we do something that looks more like a factory, an open space, accessible.' Someone would stand there and say, 'It's a factory.' And we were very happy about that, because that's much better than a monument. This was the idea that a museum must be a place for people."

▪ ▪ ▪ ▪ ▪

Before he teamed up with Piano, Richard Rogers had another partner, Norman Foster. They had met at Yale, where both were scholarship students in the graduate architecture program. Foster (b. 1935), raised in Manchester, from a working-class background, and shy rather than outgoing, was temperamentally Rogers's opposite. But the pair discovered a shared interest in design economy and advanced technology, and after returning to London they opened an office together in 1963. Their most notable project was Reliance Controls, a suburban electronics factory whose light steel architecture recalled the Eames House—which both men had visited and admired. After four years, owing to a lack of commissions, Rogers and Foster amicably parted ways. Foster and his wife, Wendy (1937–1989), also an architect, founded Foster Associates. The struggling young firm carved out a niche for itself in a neglected field, suburban industrial buildings. Their factories and warehouses were distinguished by refined design and precise construction.

Foster Associates' first opportunity to build a major public building came in 1974 at the University of East Anglia, one of the postwar universities. The Sainsbury Centre for Visual Arts was to house the art collection of Robert and Lisa Sainsbury, who personally picked Foster on the strength of his refined industrial work. The Sainsburys wanted their collection to be integrated into the life of the university, and in addition to galleries and a museum café, the new building would house the university's art history department, a research library, a faculty club, and a student cafeteria. Foster's planning strategy was similar to that of Piano & Rogers: accommodate different uses in adaptable nonhierarchical spaces that could be changed over time. The result was a vast interior that resembled an aircraft hangar. The anonymous space was subdivided into galleries, classrooms, and offices. Lighting was provided chiefly by skylights shaded by louvers (fig. 147). Unlike the Centre Pompidou, mechanical systems and structure were kept in the background, and the color scheme was predominantly gray and white.

The smooth metal hangar was a stark contrast to the rather grim 1960s-era Brutalist concrete buildings of the surrounding campus. Like the Crystal Palace, of which it is a direct descendant, the Sainsbury Centre was assembled rather than built. The lattice columns and hundred-foot trusses were fabricated in a factory and arrived on the building site fully assembled and painted; erection of the entire structural frame took only three weeks. The walls and roof were covered in aluminum panels bolted to the structural steel frame. The standardized and interchangeable panels were set in neoprene gaskets—a technique adapted from the automobile industry. This was only one of the building's many innovations. The fully glazed ends of the five-hundred-foot-long building consisted of very large sheets of glass braced by structural glass mullions, the largest self-supporting glass wall in Britain at the time (fig. 148). The end walls revealed the triangulated crisscrossing thin metal pipes, which are similar in conception to Louis Kahn's tetrahedral Yale gallery ceiling, except that here they appear light as a feather.

147 Sainsbury Centre for Visual Arts, University of East Anglia, Norwich. Foster Associates, 1974–78. Interior. Skylights shaded by movable louvers illuminate a monochrome interior that resembles an elegant aircraft hangar.

148 Sainsbury Centre for Visual Arts. Exterior. The glazed ends of the metallic tubes reveal the lightweight steel structure of the column-free building. The reclining figure sculpture at right is by Henry Moore.

Foster was an enthusiastic glider pilot, and there is something aeronautical about his single-minded approach to design, quite apart from the Sainsbury Centre's resemblance to an aircraft hangar. Like Piano and Rogers, Foster broke down building design into a series of functional problems to be solved individually, although Foster's solutions tended to be more integrated. For example, the overhead trusses not only support the fixed and movable louvers that shade the skylights, they also carry lighting fixtures and gangways so that the spotlights can be adjusted without disturbing the exhibitions below.

Although the architecture of the Sainsbury Centre, like that of the Centre Pompidou, is often referred to as High Tech, Foster saw industrialized building methods as a tool, not an end in itself. Yet there is something implacably self-sufficient about the metallic hangar; in that sense it is like a machine. Although Foster was not insensitive to the experience of a building, like Piano and Rogers he showed little interest in architectural history or in traditional architectural concerns, such as fitting a building to its setting. The minimalist abstraction of the shed-like Sainsbury Centre communicated nothing about its contents. But for other architects, such abstraction was not enough. The desire to say more, and to say it in a more nuanced fashion, was at the root of a recessive strand of the complicated modernist gene that likewise emerged in the 1960s.

36

Expanding the Language

Portland, Stuttgart, and London, 1980s

Ever since Alberti and Palladio, architects had been disseminating their ideas—built and unbuilt—through books. In 1966, at the same time as the young partnership of Richard Rogers and Norman Foster was developing an industrialized version of modernism, an unknown Philadelphia architect published a polemical book that pointed architecture in a different direction. Robert Venturi (1925–2018) based *Complexity and Contradiction in Architecture* on a course that he taught at the University of Pennsylvania. Although he described the book as a "gentle manifesto," he was unequivocal in his critique of orthodox modernism. "I am not intimidated by the puritanical, moral language of modern architecture," he wrote in a 1965 magazine article. "I like forms that are impure rather than 'pure,' compromising rather than 'clean,' distorted rather than 'straightforward,' ambiguous rather than 'articulated,' allusive rather than simple, perverse rather than impersonal, accommodating rather than excluding." Venturi was not exactly arguing that modernism was wrong, rather that in its reformist zeal it had oversimplified things.

When Le Corbusier published his 1923 manifesto *Vers une architecture* (Toward an Architecture), a battle cry for a radically new approach to building and city planning, he included photographs of racing cars, ocean liners, and dirigible sheds. This reflected the unspoken modernist assumption that modern problems were unprecedented and required brand-new solutions—the past was irrelevant. *Complexity and Contradiction* was illustrated almost entirely with photographs of old buildings: Baroque basilicas, High Renaissance palazzos, Victorian churches. Venturi was not interested in the social or even the functional aspects of these buildings, only in their formal qualities. This led him to compare a Byzantine chapel to a church by Christopher Wren, or to pair a palazzo by Bramante and a building by his colleague Louis Kahn—one of the few contemporary architects, other than Alvar Aalto, who were included in the book. Venturi's message was clear: architecture was an expressive language, and it could be enriched by learning from the past.

Venturi considered himself a practicing architect, not a historian, although at forty-one he had built little. He included several of his own mostly unrealized projects and unsuccessful competition entries in *Complexity and Contradiction*. His work was distinguished by a modest flouting of modernist orthodoxies and included pitched roofs, prominent chimneys, windows with mullions, and the occasional molding. It was left to another architect to incorporate historical motifs in a more dramatic fashion. In 1982, Michael Graves (1934–2015) built a municipal office building in Portland, Oregon, that shook the architectural world not simply because it incorporated classical decoration, but because it did so in a particularly flamboyant manner.

Like Venturi, Graves was a struggling practitioner who was also a teacher—at Princeton. He shared Venturi's dislike of abstract modernism and aimed to "re-establish a language of architecture and values that are not a part of modernist homogeneity." His competition-winning design for the Portland Building was a fifteen-story cube that filled an entire city block (fig. 149). The building sat on a two-story stepped-back base with an arcade covered in ceramic tile; instead of a steel-and-glass facade, the wall above was plastered concrete with square windows, and instead of being monochrome, the building was vividly colored: the ceramic tiles were teal green, the body of the building was a creamy yellowish color with large areas of terra-cotta brown, and the penthouse was light blue. According to Graves, a talented painter, the colors were chosen for their associations: green for the garden, terra-cotta for the earth, and blue for the sky. The clearest statement of the architect's intentions was a large sculpture above the main entrance. The hammered bronze statue, thirty-eight feet tall, portrayed a woman holding a trident. The figure of Portlandia came from the city's seal, but the sculptor Raymond Kaskey (b. 1943) chose to depict her in a modern pose, not standing but kneeling, with one hand outstretched in a gesture of welcome.

Graves incorporated such classical motifs as keystones and pilasters in the facade, but he magnified and stylized them in a highly idiosyncratic manner. The pilasters were abstracted and huge—seven stories high. The capitals were wedge-shaped blocks. A decorative frieze of ribbons and medallions on the side of the building was blown up to a giant scale and flattened, which gave it the appearance of a cartoon. It was hard not to see Graves's gift-wrapped box as a calculated provocation, a cheeky send-up of classical as well as contemporary conventions, which is certainly the way it was received by mainstream modernists.

▪ ▪ ▪ ▪ ▪

149 Portland Building, Portland, Oregon. Michael Graves, 1979–82. Symmetrical, multi-colored, and ornamented, the design was a calculated provocation to established modernism.

The Scottish-born James Stirling (1926–1992) was another architectural provocateur. Like Graves and Venturi, he was dissatisfied with the constraints of modernism. He achieved prominence in the 1960s with a trio of academic buildings: an engineering building at the University of Leicester, a history library at Cambridge, and a student residence for an Oxford college. The striking designs were modernist but neither International Style nor Brutalist. The buildings incorporated a lot of glass, à la Crystal Palace, and were industrial looking, although not in the sleek High Tech manner that Foster and Rogers would explore. Instead, the gritty red-brick structures seemed to draw on early precedents, such as Victorian factories.

Stirling's university buildings were a prelude to an even more radical departure from modernist orthodoxy. In the mid-seventies, he was invited to participate in three German museum competitions, in Düsseldorf, Cologne, and Stuttgart. All three projects were located in historic districts—the Cologne site was adjacent to the famous Gothic cathedral. Fitting new buildings into old urban settings had always been challenging for modernist architects. Most, like Frank Lloyd Wright at the Guggenheim, simply ignored their surroundings, and the best that could be said about Kahn's Yale Art Gallery and Piano & Rogers's Centre Pompidou was that they provided a sharp contrast with their older neighbors. This was not good enough for Stirling. A new museum should be "both a twentieth-century container for contemporary works of art and an integral element in historic Düsseldorf," he wrote in one of his competition entries. "It is hoped to achieve an architectural appearance that is as individual as the older buildings in contrast to the oversimplified appearance and overblown scale associated with modern architecture (i.e., the box, the slab)."

Stirling was unsuccessful in Düsseldorf and Cologne, but he won the Stuttgart competition. The result is what many consider his finest building. The Neue Staatsgalerie (New State Gallery), which includes a library, a chamber theater, and a music school, as well as art galleries, is a large addition to a mid-nineteenth-century neoclassical building that had been restored in the 1950s after being badly damaged in the Second World War. Stirling's design is the opposite of an anonymous container, such as the Centre Pompidou and the Sainsbury Centre. He described the Stuttgart museum as a "sequence of well-defined and well-proportioned gallery 'rooms' avoiding 'endless flexible space' or gymnastic roof sections." Instead of elaborate skylights, Stirling used the time-tested nineteenth-century solution of greenhouse roofs over milky glass ceilings. He aligned the doorways of the galleries to create a continuous vista—an enfilade, another nineteenth-century convention. A separate L-shaped wing that mirrored the old museum and had its own entrance off a new town square contained the chamber theater and the music school. The U-shaped gallery building surrounded an open-air rotunda containing a sculpture court (fig. 150). Shades of Schinkel.

"If it is modern, it cannot be a monument," Lewis Mumford had proclaimed. "We hope that the Staatsgalerie is monumental, because that is the tradition for public buildings, particularly museums," countered Stirling and his partner Michael Wilford (b. 1938) in their competition submission. "We also hope that it is informal and populist—hence the anti-monumentalism of the meandering footpath, the voided center, the coloring and much else." I visited the museum the year after it opened, and if the animated crowd of predominantly young visitors was anything to go by, Stirling's mixture of monumentality and populism was a success. Monumentality informed the rotunda, the enfiladed galleries, and the exterior materials—travertine and sandstone. At the same time, monumentality was everywhere undermined. The open-air Schinkelesque rotunda contained an encircling ramp that mimicked the spiral of Wright's Guggenheim Museum. On closer examination, the solid-looking travertine and sandstone walls revealed themselves to be merely a thin facing with open, unmortared joints. Nor was there anything proper about the outrageous hot pink and electric blue sausage-like handrails of the entrance plaza, or the lime-green twisty steel-and-glass lobby wall that looked to me like Mies on acid (fig. 151).

Stirling had obviously moved a great distance away from his early red-brick designs. When the Staatsgalerie opened, many critics judged it to be an outright rejection of modernism. The overt classical references included coved eaves in the gallery wings, travertine walls, and the rotunda. This particularly upset German architects, who associated neoclassicism and monumentality with the Nazi regime. The traditional gallery planning was certainly reactionary—or perhaps merely common sense—but Stirling and Wilford's design also included modernist allusions: the entrance canopy's multicolored steel I-beams suggested

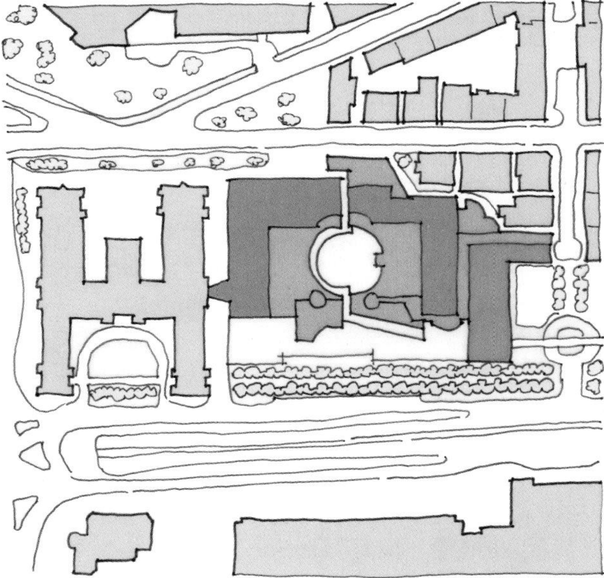

150 Neue Staatsgalerie, Stuttgart. James Stirling and Michael Wilford, 1979–84. Site plan. The new addition is fitted into the old city fabric. The nineteenth-century museum is on the left; the new galleries are organized in a U-shape around an open rotunda. The L-shaped music school, at right, defines a new urban square.

151 Neue Staatsgalerie, Stuttgart. The pink and blue sausage handrails, a multicolored steel canopy, and a warped lime-green Miesian glass wall contrast with traditional travertine and sandstone.

De Stijl; the music school facade, with stuccoed walls and horizontal strip windows, was International Style; and the bright blue oversized funnel air vents seem to have been lifted directly from the Centre Pompidou. As for the pink sausage handrails, these had no architectural lineage—they simply looked flashy and commercial, suggesting that vulgarity was part of modern life, too.

Stirling was critical of conventional modernism. "The language itself was so reductive that only exceptional people could design modern buildings in a way that was interesting," he told an interviewer. In Stirling's view, architecture had reached an impasse. "It got stuck and it will have to unstick itself to move on," he said. Like Graves, Stirling wanted to use history to do the unsticking. "Architects have always looked back in order to move forward," he declared. Stirling was not a conventional revivalist, nor was he an eclectic. The Neue Staatsgalerie is more like a Cubist collage containing scraps and fragments, knowing references to the distant and the not-so-distant past. The newly expanded Staatsgalerie, previously not particularly well attended, proved to be enormously popular with the public, as I discovered during my visit. Stirling's informed and good-natured provocations were hard to resist.

▪ ▪ ▪ ▪ ▪

Stirling and Venturi, who were almost exact contemporaries, were moving on parallel tracks, but in 1986 in London, those tracks intersected. Four years earlier, the National Gallery in London, which occupies a prominent site on Trafalgar Square, had held an architectural competition for an annex to house its collection of early Renaissance paintings. All the short-listed entries, which included one by Rogers, were modernist, and they bore no relation to the existing neoclassical museum designed by William Wilkins in 1833. Prince Charles, speaking at a gala evening of the Royal Institute of British Architects, sarcastically described the winning design as "a kind of vast municipal fire station, complete with the sort of tower that contains the siren." He allowed that a modernist building might be suitable if one were rebuilding the entire square in that style, but "what is proposed is like a monstrous carbuncle on the face of a much loved and elegant friend."

The prince's venture into architectural criticism was controversial—members of the royal family traditionally did not speak out in this manner—but while disparaged by the architectural profession, his remarks struck a chord with the public. The chastened National Gallery set the winning scheme aside and held a second—invited—competition that required the addition to be a sympathetic neighbor to the old museum. Among the six British and American architects were James Stirling and Robert Venturi.

By all accounts, the final choice came down to Stirling and Venturi. Stirling's proposal was a monumental limestone pavilion fronting a simpler block that contained skylit galleries arranged on each side of a central hall. The combination of monumentality and informality resembled the Neue Staatsgalerie, but without the historical allusions and the garish gestures—no pink sausage handrails. Stirling chose not to make any explicit reference to his neoclassical neighbor, probably because while the existing National Gallery building may have been a "much loved friend," it was not a particularly distinguished work of architecture. Wilkins, a proponent of the Greek Revival, had been constrained by an inadequate budget, and the result was a building whose porticos were too large, whose domes were too small, and whose low facade made an unsatisfying backdrop to Trafalgar Square.

Venturi's proposal, designed with his wife, Denise Scott Brown (b. 1931), responded explicitly to the existing National Gallery. Although the brick back and sides of their design were unremarkable, the side facing Trafalgar Square duplicated Wilkins's giant Corinthian pilasters, blank attic windows, dentilated cornice, and rooftop balustrade. The new facade was not an exact replica of the old, however; the classical elements started off conventionally, then were increasingly jammed together, until finally seeming to fade away entirely. A single giant fluted column, mimicking Nelson's Column in the square, marked the corner of the new wing. Venturi described this scenographic tour de force as a billboard. It is said that the curators and the gallery trustees preferred Stirling's design but that the selection committee and the donors (a different branch of the same family that had built the Sainsbury Centre in East Anglia) leaned toward Venturi, and he was announced the winner.

The plan of Venturi and Scott Brown's submission is ingenious. Instead of squaring off the building on the awkwardly shaped site, as Stirling had done, they followed the site's irregular outlines and squared off the interior instead. This planning technique was derived from Renaissance palazzos, which were often shoehorned into odd-shaped urban sites. The sixteen galleries were arranged in three rows; the four larger and taller enfiladed rooms of the central row formed a kind of spine, while smaller galleries lined the two sides. All the galleries were top-lit by traditional clerestories.

The promenade architecturale at the National Gallery begins in the entrance lobby. We are led to the galleries up a grand stair—just as in a nineteenth-century museum. A modern all-glass curtain wall on one side overlooks the old museum. At the top of the stair, a bridge in the form of a circular room connects to the old building, and it is on an axis that draws us into the new galleries, whose decor is neither entirely modern nor entirely traditional. The doorways are framed by squat Tuscan columns of pietra serena, the same gray Florentine sandstone commonly used as trim by Renaissance architects. The progressively narrower doorways create an exaggerated vista similar to that of the narrowing grand stair. Called diminishing perspective, this was a favorite device of Baroque architects.

Venturi and Scott Brown coined the term "duck" to distinguish buildings, such as the Sydney Opera House, whose architectural impact was the result of their overall form, from "decorated sheds," buildings that relied on applied decoration for their impact. The pair favored the latter, of which the new wing of the National Gallery was an example. Its overall form was simply the expedient product of an irregular site, while its architectural impact was the result of decoration—the Corinthian pilasters—applied to the surface (fig. 152). That sounds simple, but the design of the new wing is also informed by Venturi's predilection for "complexity and contradiction." For example, immediately around the corner

152 Sainsbury Wing, National Gallery, London. Venturi, Rauch & Scott Brown, 1985–91. Exterior. The classical elements, copied from the old gallery, seem to fade into the Portland stone wall until they disappear altogether. A portion of a glass curtain wall is visible at right.

from the classical "billboard" is a modern glass curtain wall, and the entrances to the building are not doorways with classical moldings but rather rectangular apertures pragmatically sliced out of the limestone. On the side wall, the openings are framed by polychrome cast-iron columns that seem to have migrated from some Art Deco building. Such odd juxtapositions abound. For example, no attempt is made to hide the plainly visible rooftop clerestories. On one of the rear walls, a large limestone plaque engraved with the name of the museum is unceremoniously squeezed between two metal ventilator grilles. Inside, the grandeur of the Baroque staircase is undermined by painted aluminum arches that are suspended from the ceiling and appear like a flattened cartoonish version of Victorian steelwork. Such unexpected effects, visual trickery, and ironic contrasts are generally associated with Mannerism. Venturi was a great admirer of Cinquecento Mannerism, and he included buildings by Michelangelo and Borromini in *Complexity and Contradiction*. Mannerism is an intellectual approach to architecture, and its presence distinguishes Venturi's work from that of a sensualist like Stirling, whose Stuttgart museum is definitely a duck or, rather, a duck *and* a decorated shed, for Stirling was never one to be constrained by consistency.

Graves, Stirling, and Venturi are often called Postmodernists. This loose term encompasses a variety of late-twentieth-century architects who shared a dislike for abstract modernism and, to different degrees, looked to historical examples for inspiration. Venturi, for one, rejected the characterization. But in a general way his work definitely represents a departure from—and a reaction to—orthodox modernism. That is, it is *post*-modern. The same could be said of the other architects who were trying to "unstick" architecture, in Stirling's words: Kahn and his revival of monumental archaic forms, and Foster, Rogers, and Piano and their embrace of industrial technology and industrial imagery. In the case of Graves, Stirling, and Venturi, the unsticking took the form of selectively incorporating historical elements in their designs. But the use of historical motifs raised a tantalizing question: What if instead of referring to the past in fragmented and ironic fashion, architects embraced the past more fully, in the manner of an Edwin Lutyens or a Henry Bacon? Was it too late to turn back the clock?

37

Turning Back the Clock

Cambridge and London, Chicago and Tuscaloosa, 1980s & 2000s

Turning back the architectural clock and retrieving the pieces of the classical past was the goal of the English architect Quinlan Terry (b. 1937). In the 1960s, as a freshly minted graduate of the Architectural Association in London, he found himself dissatisfied with modernist architecture. Seeking an alternative, he became an apprentice of Raymond Erith (1904–1973), an architect who worked exclusively in a premodernist idiom. Erith had been a student at the Architectural Association in the 1920s, when the curriculum was part traditional, part modernist. He had gravitated to the former, and in the postwar years he established his practice in rural Essex, concerned mainly with small houses and additions to village buildings, although in the late 1950s Prime Minister Harold Macmillan commissioned him to renovate and extend 10 Downing Street. As the British economy revived, so did the demand for traditional domestic architecture, and in 1969, Erith and Terry, now partners, were responsible for King's Walden Bury in Hertfordshire, one of the first large Palladian country houses of the postwar era.

Erith and Terry's commitment to tradition was more than a question of style—there were advantages to building in a time-tested manner. Modernist architects favored innovation and experimentation, but unproven materials had shown themselves to be problematic. Reinforced concrete was inexpensive and could be cast in a variety of interesting shapes, but when exposed to the weather it stained and cracked and did not age as well as stone and brick. Not only did concrete discolor, rubber gaskets failed, caulking dried up, and plastics faded. The useful lives of significant buildings had traditionally been measured in centuries; in contrast, many of the buildings constructed with new materials and novel methods lasted only a few decades before requiring overhauls. For example, the Centre Pompidou, completed in 1977, was closed for several years for maintenance in 1997, and again in 2020.

153 Howard Building, Downing College, Cambridge. Quinlan Terry, 1986–89. A modern Baroque building with Mannerist touches.

During the 1980s, economic prosperity resulted in a renewed demand for private houses, and Terry, on his own after Erith's death, completed a number of large residential commissions, both rural and urban. In 1986, on the basis of his expertise in traditional building, he was approached by Cambridge's Downing College about adding to its nineteenth-century campus. It was understood that the new building would be traditional in both appearance and construction. The original architect of the college, founded in 1800, was William Wilkins, the designer of the National Gallery. He had built two buildings in a severe Greek Revival style, and in 1930 a central building with a matching Ionic portico completed the quadrangle. Terry's project, the Howard Building, was the first addition to Downing College since a small Georgian quad was built in the 1950s.

The Howard Building is used for public lectures and musical events. The two-story boxy building with a pitched slate roof and a central pediment houses a foyer with a bar on the first floor and an assembly room on the second. Simple in conception, it is hardly simple in execution. Terry did not attempt to match Wilkins's dry archaeological style—he chose Baroque instead. The facade is adorned with pilasters standing on plinths (fig. 153). The elaborate entrance, marked by two engaged columns and a broken curved pediment, includes the coat of arms of the college. Ornamental urns decorate the roof. The pilasters, columns, and trim are white Portland stone, which contrasts with the wall cladding of pale brown Ketton limestone, a common material in Cambridge. There are

Mannerist touches, such as the broken pediment, a cartouche molding around the door frame, and two rusticated end bays, which correspond to the interior stairs. Equally Mannerist is Terry's unorthodox decision to incorporate all five classical orders: Corinthian for the pilasters on the facade, Composite for the engaged columns flanking the entrance, Doric for a colonnade on the back of the building, Tuscan in the foyer, and Ionic in the assembly room itself. The highly original overall effect is festive, as befits the building's function.

Unlike Venturi, Terry was not a modern architect making ironic references to the past but rather a modern architect who chose to walk in the footsteps of past masters—and to say something new with the old language. He was committed to proven methods of construction and resolutely avoided modern building materials, using lime mortar rather than Portland cement mortar, and thick load-bearing masonry walls rather than a steel frame with a thin stone veneer. Terry did not see anything anomalous in adapting age-old ideas to modern problems. "How can you, some ask, expect airports, multi-storey car parks, factories and office blocks to be part of the classical tradition?" he wrote. "I will admit that the architect has no ready-made answer and will have to do a lot of thinking. But had Bramante not thought hard about the juxtaposition of the circular pagan temple with an early Christian basilica, we might not have known the Renaissance church typified by Saint Peter's. Bramante approached a new problem along the well travelled lines of classical principles and he produced an entirely new and highly successful type of building. Is there not an opportunity and a challenge today to approach each new problem from old principles rather than from a childish desire to produce an elevation hitherto unknown?" Terry did not have the opportunity to design an airport, but he did build several office blocks. The largest of these, and one of the first modern examples of traditional design applied to a large urban site, is in the London suburb of Richmond.

Richmond, a historic town on the River Thames, grew up in the sixteenth century around Richmond Palace, the long-since demolished royal residence built by Henry VII. Terry's four-acre site facing the river included three listed historic houses as well as a disused nineteenth-century town hall. Over the previous fifteen years, there had been several proposals by developers for large office buildings that the municipality rejected as being out of scale with the old town center. Terry's design is different. Instead of two large office blocks, the required square footage is accommodated in fifteen individual buildings of different sizes organized around three courts (fig. 154). The largest court, on the right side of the plan, is above an underground parking garage. The town hall, a large building with corner turrets, has been renovated and turned into a museum. The three buildings on the left edge of the plan face a narrow and secluded court and contain flats. Most of the office buildings have shops on the first floor.

Terry adopts a variety of historic styles. The style of the new brick building with a central pedimented bay and plastered corner quoins, on the left in the row facing the river in the accompanying photograph, is Georgian (fig. 155). The roof has a widow's walk and a cupola that serves as an exhaust for the air-conditioning system; the rusticated stone base contains a restaurant. The five-bay brick Heron House next door was built in 1716. Next to it is a new building patterned on one bay of Palladio's fifteenth-century Basilica in Vicenza, the arched gateway serving as an entrance to the courtyard beyond. The remainder of the row consists of renovated historic houses dating from the nineteenth century. The new four-story building with a pedimented and pilastered central bay, on the extreme left of the photograph, is a simplified version of an unbuilt eighteenth-century design for Richmond Palace. Not visible is a building facing the river and containing a restaurant that was also inspired by Palladio, this time by a convent in Venice.

Richmond Riverside includes Venetian Gothic, Baroque, and Greek Revival styles. The mixture mirrors the restored historic buildings of the town center. Terry made no architectural distinction between new buildings and old, but the assortment is not a make-believe stage set. This is not a large building pretending to be something it is not; the separate facades belong to separate buildings, built with load-bearing brick walls and twenty-foot spans, and rented to separate

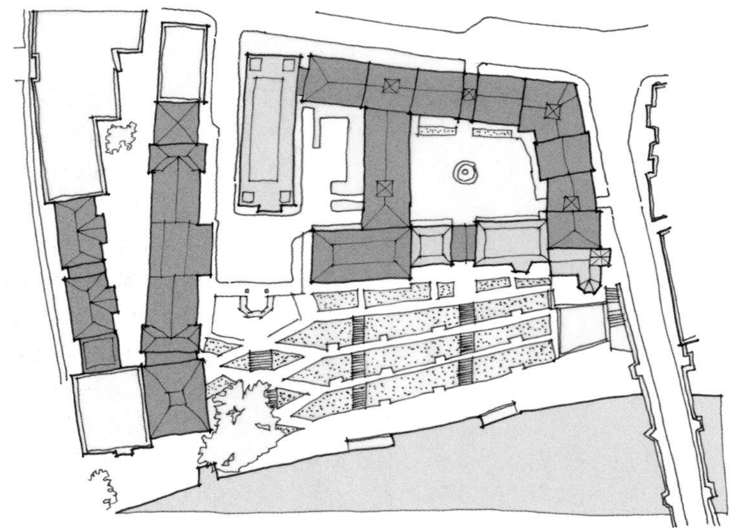

154 Richmond Riverside, Richmond, Surrey. Quinlan Terry, 1985–87. Site plan. The commercial development includes new construction (dark gray) as well as four eighteenth- and nineteenth-century buildings (light gray). The buildings surround enclosed courts and overlook landscaped terraces facing the River Thames.

155 Richmond Riverside, Richmond, Surrey. The row of office buildings facing the Thames is a seamless mixture of historic buildings and new construction. The large brick building on the left was built in 1987; its neighbor on the right, Heron House, dates from 1716.

tenants. It is true that behind the residential facades are commercial offices with all the modern conveniences, but in that regard these buildings are no different from many old residential buildings in European cities whose interiors have been altered and modernized over the years—and will presumably continue to be upgraded in the future.

▪ ▪ ▪ ▪ ▪

In 1987, the year that Richmond Riverside was completed, the City of Chicago held a competition for an ambitious new central library, a building that was to be the largest municipal library in the country. Unlike the other entries, the winner was neither modernist nor Postmodern. Like Louis Sullivan's Guaranty Building, the boxy building had a clearly defined base, shaft, and top. The two-story base was granite, the shaft was red brick, and the top was unexpectedly glass (fig. 156). The architect of the library, Thomas H. Beeby (b. 1941), called it a "building of memories." The rusticated granite base recalled the Rookery, a famous Chicago office building designed by Daniel Burnham's firm in 1888, and the massive brick walls referred to a nearby Burnham office tower, the Monadnock Building. The arched entrances were based on Adler & Sullivan's Auditorium Building, and the massive pediments of the glass roof were a version of the classical architecture of the Art Institute, a Beaux-Arts landmark on Michigan Avenue. These

156 Harold Washington Library Center, Chicago. Hammond, Beeby & Babka, 1987–91. The building fills the block, and, like Louis Sullivan's Guaranty Building, it has a clearly defined base, shaft, and cap.

architectural memories referred to nineteenth-century buildings, but there was also a more recent memory: the rear of the library consisted of an Miesian steel-and-glass curtain wall. Stirling's Neue Staatsgalerie was a building of memories too, but here the memories were assembled into an integrated design rather than a collage.

Beeby's concept for the library was simple: the six levels of book stacks and reading areas were organized like an old-fashioned department store, with escalators serving each floor. As in a department store, the loft-like floors allowed for a variety of changeable layouts. Three sides of each floor were lined with windowed alcoves that resembled the study carrels of a traditional library; the back (with the Miesian glass wall) contained offices, book sorting, and other back-of-the-house functions. The top floor housed special collections as well as a publicly accessed winter garden that was also used for galas and other civic events. The arched steel structure of the winter garden enclosed an airy space overlooked by the pedimented windows.

At the time of the competition, Beeby, who is a native of Oak Park, the Chicago suburb where Frank Lloyd Wright had built his first Prairie Style houses, was serving as the dean of Yale's School of Architecture. Like Venturi and Graves, he was a scholarly architect with an interest in history, but unlike them he did not play fast and loose with the past. In many ways the Chicago library is an old-fashioned building built with old-fashioned sturdiness. The rusticated base is Napoleon red granite surmounted by an elaborate chain-patterned band of cast stone called a guilloche; the front doors are bronze; the interior partitions are hand-laid plaster; the book stacks are lit by handsome hanging glass pendants rather than fluorescent strips; and the reading areas are equipped with courthouse armchairs of solid maple.

Beeby's traditional approach extended to the use of full-blown figurative ornament: cast-stone festoons (garlands) between the windows; medallions with puff-cheeked cherubs drolly personifying the Windy City; window spandrels decorated with Midwestern sheaves of cornstalks that terminated in a head of Ceres, the Roman goddess of agriculture; and a bas-relief ribbon with Chicago's motto, "Urbs in Horto" (City in a Garden). There is nothing ironic or tongue-in-cheek about this allegorical decoration. While only a few of the visitors to the library are likely be familiar with the Roman references, the medallions and corn stalks have another function. Modernist buildings are effective seen from afar, but close-up their blank surfaces and utilitarian details (seams, gaskets, caulking) hold no interest. By contrast, the festoons and medallions of Beeby's library are intimate and visually meaningful.

The most dramatic decorations in the Chicago library are the work of Raymond Kaskey, the sculptor of the Portlandia statue in Michael Graves's building. Huge cast-aluminum barn owls, traditional symbols of wisdom, are perched on the eaves of the library, and a large horned owl hovers at the top of the main facade. Such decorations are called acroteria, and in a Greek or Roman temple they often took the form of palm leaves or statues. Because the rooftop of the Chicago library is much higher than an ancient temple, Kaskey's acroteria are larger—the great horned owl has a twenty-foot wingspan. This magnification is as close as Beeby and Kaskey get to a Pop Art sensibility, although the great bird clutching a book in its talons suggests Beatrix Potter more than Andy Warhol.

▪ ▪ ▪ ▪ ▪

The pioneers of modernism took it for granted that modern life requires a brand-new architecture. But because buildings last a long time, much of modern life

157 United States Federal Building and Courthouse, Tuscaloosa, Alabama. Hammond Beeby Rupert Ainge, 2006–10. The Greek Revival central portico is modeled on the Greek Temple of Zeus at Nemea.

contentedly takes place in buildings that are hundreds of years old. People no longer sail in clipper ships or drive four-in-hands, but they still worship in Saint Peter's in Rome, live in the Royal Crescent in Bath, and shop in the Palais Royale in Paris. People are used to these old buildings; they understand and like them, and they do not see a disconnect between today's life and yesterday's buildings. This issue came to the fore in 2006 in a new federal courthouse in Tuscaloosa, Alabama. Beeby's firm was brought in after a proposed modernist design was rejected by the clients. "People need to have the sense they're coming to a place of justice, not an office building," observed one of the dissatisfied judges. Beeby and his staff prepared three alternative designs using different architectural styles based on local precedents: Greek Revival, which had been especially popular in the antebellum South; Federal, which dated from the early days of the newly founded United States and had been used in the original 1829 Tuscaloosa state capitol; and the omnipresent Georgian. Although all three options incorporated pedimented entrance porticos, the plans varied considerably: the Greek Revival scheme consisted of three connected parallel wings clad in stone; the brick Federal scheme had two flat-roofed cupolas; and the three-story Georgian alternative, capped by a steeple, was planned around a forecourt. The clients chose the Greek Revival option.

The Tuscaloosa courthouse is not "about" classicism; like Terry's Howard Building it *is* classical—in its planning, its design, and its details. The most prominent architectural feature is the monumental entrance portico, whose giant fluted Doric columns and pediment are modeled on a fourth-century BC Greek temple, the Temple of Zeus in Nemea (fig. 157). On the other hand, the side elevations, with flattened and simplified Doric pilasters and engaged Greek piers, or antae, recall Paul Cret's stripped classicism. The structure is a combination of concrete and steel: cast-in-place concrete with an Indiana limestone veneer for the walls, and steel framing for the roof. The limestone veneer looks solid because it is solid. Instead of extremely thin stone sheets attached to a concrete back-up wall—a conventional contemporary solution—the stone veneer is an eight-inch-thick self-supporting wall. The columns and entablature of the portico are likewise solid limestone, as are the door and window lintels. These traditional details are combined with modern materials, such as aluminum roofing. The acroteria and the antefixes—the decorated blocks that terminate the tile roofs of classical temples—are cast aluminum; the central acroterion on top of the pediment acts as a lightning conductor.

The Tuscaloosa courthouse contains several federal agencies and congressional and senatorial offices, as well as courtrooms and judges' chambers. The two-story building is bisected by a long atrium, which is naturally lit by a clerestory and provides access to the courtrooms. The decorative moldings are gilded, and the entrances to the courtrooms are framed by columns patterned on the Ionic columns of the Erechtheion. The sixteen wall panels between the pilasters—nine feet by fourteen feet tall—carry murals, the work of Chicago-based artist Caleb O'Connor (b. 1979). The representational art depicts scenes from local history: the University of Alabama in flames during the Civil War, a Depression-era farm, a civil rights scene from the 1960s, the effects of a destructive 2011 tornado. Murals were common features of Works Progress Administration (WPA) government buildings of the 1930s, and their presence here imparts a sense of occasion to what might otherwise have been an anonymous hallway. The formal atrium complements the strong sense of order created by the symmetrical and axial planning and helps people to orient themselves and find their way around. That is, it helps them to recognize their place in the world.

38

Starchitects

Bilbao, Beijing, and Baku, 2000s

The story of architecture does not always unfold smoothly. Occasionally iconoclastic buildings such as Michelangelo's Laurentian Library, Piano & Rogers's Centre Pompidou, and Graves's Portland Building upset the apple cart. Something like that happened in 1997. A remarkable building appeared on the site of a former shipyard on the south bank of the Nervión River in the old Basque industrial city of Bilbao, in northern Spain. Although the architecture was undeniably modernist, it departed radically from prevailing orthodoxy. There was no front or back, or even top or bottom; the walls twisted and turned without apparent reference to construction or function; and there was no clear expression of structure—what looked like a tower turned out to be a false front. Part of the museum slid under an adjoining bridge and another section loomed dramatically over a reflecting pool (fig. 158). The chaotic collision of forms had no architectural precedent. To complicate matters further, the whole thing—walls, roofs, tower—was covered in shining titanium. This was not a duck in Venturi's sense, it was a silverplated peacock.

The building in question was the Guggenheim Museum Bilbao, and its architect was Frank O. Gehry (b. 1929), a Canadian-born Angeleno. Like Louis Kahn, Gehry was a late bloomer—he was forty-seven when, after an unexceptional career, he attracted attention with an unusual work that defied categorization. Remodeling his own house, a 1920s Dutch Colonial bungalow in Santa Monica, he encased it in a collage of raw plywood, corrugated metal, and chain-link fencing. This was defiantly untraditional, but the prosaic materials and casual approach to architectural composition were not conventionally modernist either, and it set Gehry apart from his contemporaries. The difference was exaggerated in subsequent projects that incorporated startling forms and materials put together in a rough-and-ready

158 Guggenheim Museum Bilbao, Bilbao, Spain. Gehry Partners, 1991–97. The chaotic collision of forms covered in titanium had no architectural precedent.

fashion. Following two decades of increasingly international work—in Paris, Prague, and Germany—he was invited to participate in the competition for the new Guggenheim museum in Bilbao. His design edged out the two other entries.

Gehry's talent is evidenced by his fertile imagination; his skill lies in his ability to reconcile the unruly forms he imagines with the functional demands of his client. The Bilbao museum looks like a sculpture, but the orchestration of spatial experiences is distinctly architectural. A long outdoor staircase leads from a plaza to the entrance. After passing through a modest lobby, the visitor enters a soaring atrium that offers a view over a reflecting pool to the river and manages to be vertiginous, awesome, and carefree, all at the same time. The architecture looks slapdash, but there is nothing haphazard about the museum plan, which incorporates three types of exhibition spaces. The galleries, which display the permanent collection of early modern art, are surprisingly conventional, with enfiladed and skylit rooms. Eleven smaller galleries, each with a distinct character, provide more individualized settings. Last, a large, anonymous loft-like space houses temporary exhibitions. The entrances to these various spaces are conveniently clustered around the atrium.

Bilbainos referred to the museum as the Artichoke, which comes close to describing it, if you can imagine a giant artichoke made of gleaming titanium. This was the first major application to building construction of this light, strong, and corrosion-resistant material, previously used chiefly in aviation. Gehry exploits new materials and advanced computing techniques, but his building does not glamorize technology. There are no refined details and machined precision of the sort that are hallmarks of High Tech architecture. Gehry keeps the engineering in the background; the structure is there simply to support the architecture, not to define it. Nor is he a functionalist: the expressive forms have very little to do with what goes on inside. Instead, he manipulates space like a Baroque architect, combining the imagination of a Borromini with the showmanship of a Bernini. As a result, the Guggenheim Bilbao achieves something that had eluded severe modernists, such as Mies and Kahn. The cheerfully iconoclastic building is both resolutely avant-garde and immensely popular with the general public.

▪ ▪ ▪ ▪ ▪

The Eiffel Tower and the Empire State Building are urban icons, that is, they represent their cities in the same way that Big Ben represents London and the Brandenburg Gate represents Berlin. The photogenic Sydney Opera House achieved a similar status, the first work of postwar modern architecture to do so. The Guggenheim Museum in Bilbao aimed to duplicate that feat and in the process transform the city into a tourist destination. "They needed the building to do for Bilbao what the Sydney Opera House did for Australia," Gehry told an interviewer. This his striking design accomplished. For international tourists the Guggenheim Bilbao became the built equivalent of Niagara Falls and the Grand Canyon—a place that you had to visit at least once. And millions did.

The distinctive architecture of the Guggenheim Bilbao put the city on the map, and the worldwide publicity associated with the museum also put its architect on the map. Ever since Brunelleschi, leading architects had achieved a certain level of public recognition, but what happened to Gehry was different, at least in degree. The global reach of modern media and the popularity of international travel meant that almost overnight the startling titanium artichoke and its heretofore little-known architect became world famous. Thanks to globalization and a media that valued novelty, Gehry—and soon other architects—would enjoy the sort of international recognition previously reserved for star entertainers.

This newfound celebrity had an economic aspect. Just as a Hollywood star could ensure that a movie was "bankable," an international architectural star brought real economic value to a building project. The building had to deliver too, of course, but widespread name recognition meant that a designer label could attract visitors to a museum, tenants to an office building, and buyers to a condominium tower. Marketers referred to this phenomenon as brand recognition.

Globalization created new opportunities, but it also imposed constraints. In the past, architects were familiar with the places in which they built and with the people they built for—and the people they built for knew them. Globalization meant that the most famous architects regularly built in far-off places and for people with whom they had only a passing acquaintance. This was different from Jørn Utzon spending nine years working on the Sydney Opera House or Louis Kahn devoting the last twelve years of his life to the Dhaka capitol. Those buildings had become national icons. Christopher Wren once wrote, "Architecture has its political Use; publick Buildings being the Ornament of a Country; it establishes a Nation, draws People and Commerce; makes the People love their native Country, which Passion is the Original of all great Actions in a Common-wealth." The Bilbao Guggenheim notwithstanding, could hurriedly designed foreign implants, which often seemed like international trophies, really become the "ornament of a country"?

Another effect of globalization was the desire to replicate what was being called the Bilbao Effect. This meant that the overarching demand of clients—and the expectation of the public—became: Surprise me. What happens when the demand for originality trumps other considerations? History suggests that noted buildings are generally the result of ideas that have been percolating over time. Copying and refining the work of previous masters was the basis for the accomplishments of the Renaissance: Palladio learned from Raphael as well as from the ancient Romans, Inigo Jones learned from Palladio, and Wren learned from Jones. Today, this has changed. Craig Webb, a partner of the Gehry firm, succinctly described the situation in a filmed interview: "I think we [in our office] have two unwritten rules. One of them is, if it looks anything like something anybody else has done: No. And the second rule is, if it looks anything like anything *we've* done: No." Decades earlier Bertram Goodhue had pointed out that "we cannot start each generation at the beginning in our mastery of workmanship." Yet that seemed to be exactly what architects practicing on the global stage increasingly felt obliged to do.

The term starchitect was first applied to Frank Gehry, but it soon spread to other practitioners whose names were recognized globally. One of this select group was the Dutch architect Rem Koolhaas (b. 1944). Koolhaas had been a filmmaker and journalist before studying architecture in London. Unlike Gehry, who rarely explained his work, Koolhaas was an energetic proselytizer in the mold of Le Corbusier, writing books, editing magazines, and issuing manifestos. His Rotterdam-based firm, the Office for Metropolitan Architecture, became known for large urban buildings distinguished by their iconoclastic interpretation of the program and their tough, stylish designs. A new Koolhaas building was an eagerly anticipated event—that was Corbusian, too.

In 2001, Koolhaas's firm was invited to take part in an international competition for the Beijing headquarters of CCTV (China Central Television), the state broadcasting network. The huge building—almost five million square feet—housed studios and broadcasting facilities as well as offices. "The planned new CCTV building can not only represent the new image of Beijing, but also express, in the language of architecture, the importance and cultural nature of the TV industry," instructed the competition organizers, obviously hoping to duplicate the Bilbao Effect.

The new CCTV building was part of a plan to animate the skyline of Beijing in time for the 2008 Olympic Games, and most of the competitors, which included some of the leading American commercial firms, assumed that this meant an extremely tall skyscraper. It was a measure of Koolhaas's reputation that he was invited to compete despite never having actually built a high-rise building. Nor did he and his partner Ole Scheeren (b. 1971) produce a conventional skyscraper. Their winning design was tall—fifty-one floors—but it was not a tower; it has been variously described as a three-dimensional loop, a deformed donut, and an architectural Möbius strip. Two tapered and leaning towers of unequal height were connected by an L-shaped cantilevered section at the top, and a similar wing at the bottom (fig. 159). The architects' rationale for this unusual form was that it would encourage communication between the various departments of the mammoth media organization. Whether a continuous loop building really fosters human interaction is debatable, but the tall leaning legs and the dramatic cantilevers definitely produced an unusual skyline profile. The exterior was curiously scaleless because the uniform tinted-glass walls of the building lacked the usual grid of mullions and spandrels and instead were crisscrossed by a spider's web of structural members that corresponded to the stresses and strains exerted by the tilted and cantilevered forms.

The Arup engineers who were part of the design team produced an ingenious solution to a difficult problem, but the leaning towers and the two-hundred-and-fifty-foot cantilevers required more than twice as much structural steel as a

159 CCTV Building, Beijing. Office for Metropolitan Architecture, 2002–12. The fifty-story skyscraper has been variously described as a three-dimensional loop, a deformed donut, and an architectural Möbius strip.

conventional high-rise. In addition, the vertical elevator shafts rising through the leaning towers resulted in distinctly odd-shaped interiors. Perhaps for these reasons, the unorthodox high-rise did not "kill the skyscraper," as Koolhaas foretold. Although the CCTV Building is as unusual as the colliding silvery forms of the Guggenheim Bilbao, its appeal is intellectual rather than emotional. Indeed, there is something forbidding about the hulking shape and its dark, scaleless appearance. If Gehry is the "smart man from Hollywood," as he was once described, Koolhaas is the humorless man from the Low Countries.

■ ■ ■ ■ ■

Koolhaas's firm served as a training ground for young architects from all over the world. The most prominent of these was Zaha Hadid (1950–2016). Born in

160 Heydar Aliyev Cultural Center, Baku, Azerbaijan. Zaha Hadid Architects, 2007–12. The curvilinear building, which houses a concert hall, a museum, and a national library, contains blurred boundaries and merging surfaces—space appears endless, floors become walls, walls become ceilings, inside becomes outside.

Baghdad into a prominent family, she studied architecture in London, where Koolhaas was her teacher, and after graduating in the late 1970s went to work for him in Rotterdam. Hadid was a singular talent—Koolhaas described her as a "planet in her own inimitable orbit"—and he offered to make her a partner, but after a year she left to establish her own practice in London. Her idiosyncratic, angular, and fragmented designs were difficult to translate into actual buildings, and in two decades she realized only one major commission. Fiercely independent, she persevered, and thanks to her imaginative drawings and her uncompromising if unbuilt designs, she acquired an outsize reputation in the architectural world.

At the end of the 1990s, Hadid's career took off. Part of her success is owed to the computer. Architects can sketch any sort of shape, but they must document this shape in such a way that builders are able to construct it. This was easily done with rectangular shapes, but free forms such as Hadid designed were difficult to communicate. New computer software enabled Gehry to translate the indeterminate forms of the Bilbao museum into digital instructions that could be transmitted directly to builders and fabricators. The same software allowed Hadid to realize the sort of smooth organic forms and fluid space that recall the visionary wartime sketches of Erich Mendelsohn, an architect whom she admired.

Hadid became the quintessential globetrotting starchitect. In short order she built a museum in Cincinnati, a science center and an office building in

Germany, a museum in Rome, and an opera house in China. A cultural complex in the Caucasus is a good example of her later work. The striking building is in the center of Baku, the Azerbaijani capital on the Caspian Sea. The undulating white shapes house a concert hall, a museum, and a national library. A promenade architecturale threads through the building and connects the lobbies of the different uses. If the Guggenheim Bilbao is about unexpectedly colliding forms, this curvilinear building is about blurred boundaries and merging surfaces—space appears endless, floors become walls, walls become ceilings, inside becomes outside (fig. 160).

As in the Guggenheim Bilbao, the structure is there to serve the architecture. Although the roofs look like shells, they are actually space frames supported by steel trusses. This complicated structure is concealed behind a skin of fiber-reinforced concrete panels. The surfaces tuck, fold, and curve. The fluid organization of the building does not depend on hierarchy or axes, and the scaleless architecture is largely devoid of details. The thousand-seat concert hall, also used for opera and ballet, is finished in American oak and contrasts with the white, ice-cave lobbies. In the hall, as elsewhere in the building, the floors, walls, and ceiling form single continuous surfaces.

This unusual architecture has little to do with Baku, a city of Soviet-era high-rise apartment slabs and older neoclassical buildings dating from imperial Russia. But the startling appearance of the cultural center is consistent with other recent buildings designed by foreign architects. The political regime that rules this energy-rich republic, independent since 1991, is determined that Azerbaijan present a contemporary image to the world. The Heydar Aliyev Cultural Center, named after the previous president and father of the current president, is part of this architectural makeover.

"I think there should be no end to experimentation," observed Hadid, who died of a heart attack in 2016, only sixty-five. In her case, the experimentation was almost entirely formal—the same family of organic shapes might be an urban complex, a building, a piece of furniture, or even a pair of designer shoes. Hadid's designs represent a personal vision of the world no less than the buildings of Gaudí, although in her case the vision was underpinned not by religious zeal or structural inventiveness, but rather by a personal and highly developed sense of fantasy.

39

A Grounded Art

Abu Dhabi, Anandpur Sahib, and Houston, early 2000s

At the time of the construction of the Heydar Aliyev Cultural Center, Zaha Hadid's office was entering about thirty architectural competitions a year. Competitions had become the favored method for picking an architect—even a starchitect. Clients like competitions because they garner publicity and raise public awareness of their projects. First the competition is announced, in due course the finalists' designs are exhibited and winnowed down to a short list, and finally, with great fanfare, a winner is proclaimed. Competitions have sometimes been an opportunity for unknown talent to be recognized, as was the case with the Sydney Opera House and the Centre Pompidou, but they are not necessarily popular with established architects, for whom they represent a significant drain on time, energy, and resources. Competitions can also feel demeaning, like inviting a Hollywood star to do a screen test. Koolhaas has called competitions a "form of torture . . . where somebody can tell you, 'I really respect you, I think you're an exceptional human being, so can you collaborate or participate with nineteen other architects that are similarly amazing.'" Competitions can also have an adverse effect on the design process, and not just because they privilege the flashy proposal that catches the eye of the competition jury. Competitions put the architect in the position of having to guess what is wanted—or needed—which is very different from the intensive dialogue that usually takes place between client and architect. This dialogue can have a significant effect on the outcome, allowing different alternatives to be explored—or discarded—and enabling modifications to the program and even to the building site.

In 2007, when the government of Abu Dhabi, the capital of the United Arab Emirates, embarked on an ambitious plan to diversify the country's oil-rich economy by creating a cultural district on an island at the city's edge, it did not hold an architectural competition. Instead, the authorities chose individual architects for selected projects: Gehry for another branch of the Guggenheim Museum, Hadid for a performing arts center, and Foster for a national museum. "All cities, when they reach their golden age, construct for their people and for their culture, to bear witness to their epoch. It's perfectly logical," observed the French architect Jean Nouvel, who received a commission to design a "museum of world civilizations," an art museum that was to be established and operated with the collaboration of the Louvre.

Nouvel (b. 1945) came to international attention in 1987 with a competition-winning design for the Institut du Monde Arabe (World Arab Institute) on the Left Bank in Paris. The building included a glass curtain wall covered by a metallic grid of light-sensitive lenses that opened and closed and whose geometry resembled an Arab *mashrabiya,* or lattice screen—an imaginative fusion of tradition and technology. Nouvel went on to design major buildings in France, and then farther afield: an office tower in Barcelona, a concert hall in Copenhagen, a theater in Minneapolis. Even though these projects included innovations in construction and design, in some ways Nouvel is the most traditional of the starchitects. His evocative and often theatrical designs are usually driven by a powerful concept, and they tend to vary in appearance according to their setting—there is no Nouvel style.

Asked about the Louvre Abu Dhabi, Nouvel answered: "I wanted a strong symbol, an immediate dialogue, a powerful spiritual dimension. I then wanted an architecture that resonates with the history of the place by providing a direct echo in Arab architecture, but one that equally addresses universality. It is this synthesis that must be found." His design has two key features. The galleries, a children's museum, and temporary exhibition space, as well as related functions, such as a cafeteria, auditorium, and administrative offices, are housed in individual white buildings—fifty-five of them—separated by spaces that resemble alleyways and squares. This arrangement suggests a town, and this is the first echo of Arab architecture. The second echo is a perforated metallic parasol roof that shades the entire complex and whose intricate latticework reminds me of the facade of the Institut du Monde Arabe, although without the mechanical gadgetry—no moving parts (fig. 161).

The mammoth six-hundred-foot-diameter dome rises one hundred and twenty feet. The steel structure is a space frame sixteen feet thick consisting of eight filigree layers—four of stainless steel and four of aluminum. The layers filter sunlight and create dappled shadows and shifting starburst patterns on the floor and walls below. The low dome, supported on four concealed piers, seems to float over the museum. Like Stirling at the Neue Staatsgalerie, Nouvel kept the theatrical element—the dome—separate from the galleries, thus maintaining the intimate experience of looking at art. The two dozen galleries, many of which

161 Louvre Abu Dhabi, United Arab Emirates. Ateliers Jean Nouvel, 2006–17. The perforated parasol roof is a highly abstracted version of a tiled Islamic dome, and the irregular arrangement of galleries recalls a crowded Arab medina.

have skylights, follow established norms for museum display. The calm interiors vary in size, materials, and details and are designed to suit the different types of objects exhibited: paintings, sculptures, drawings, and precious artifacts.

Starchitect-designed buildings sometimes appear like alien intruders, imposed from outside—*parachutés,* as Nouvel scornfully put it. The Louvre Abu Dhabi building is not like that. The museum, which is reached by a bridge, is surrounded by water, and canals penetrate selected areas beneath the dome. Sea breezes off the Persian Gulf cool the shaded space. A museum under a parasol would not make much sense in Paris, but on the Arabian Peninsula shade is a potent symbol, as is water. Nouvel is too much of a modernist to include literal references, but he does connect his architectural language to local traditions. The perforated parasol is both a mashrabiya and a highly abstracted version of a tiled Islamic dome, and the irregular arrangement of minimalist white boxy buildings that compose what the architect calls a "museum city" suggests a crowded Arab medina, with its crooked alleys and intimate squares. The result is an architecture that is technological though not High Tech, nodding to tradition without being itself traditional.

■ ■ ■ ■ ■

Moshe Safdie had moved on after Habitat and developed an international practice that included libraries, museums, and institutional buildings in Canada and the United States, as well as Singapore, China, and his native Israel. He had built the National Gallery of Canada in Ottawa, the United States Institute of Peace in Washington, D.C., and the Yitzhak Rabin Center in Tel Aviv. In Jerusalem he expanded Yad Vashem, the national memorial to the victims of the Holocaust, adding a museum and a children's memorial. The latter had so impressed a visiting Indian politician, the chief minister of the northern state of Punjab, that he approached Safdie with a major building commission: a museum of the Sikh people.

The Khalsa Heritage Centre was to be in Anandpur Sahib, one of the sacred places of Sikhism and the site of several important temples and pilgrimage sites. After spending several days walking about the town, Safdie concluded that the proposed site on the outskirts was not ideal because most visitors would be arriving on foot, and he suggested that his clients consider a more central location. Together they selected a lyrical and hilly seventy-five-acre site traversed by a ravine. Safdie dammed the stream to create a series of reflecting pools, and located the museum on both sides of the ravine.

The library, an auditorium, and a gallery for temporary exhibitions are clustered near the entrance, and a long pedestrian bridge over the water leads to the museum. The entry to the museum proper is marked by a circular memorial gallery, surrounded by five drum-like towers representing the five Sikh virtues. Farther on are the galleries, arranged in a quarter circle and containing exhibits on Sikh and Punjabi art, literature, and history. Like Nouvel, Safdie is a modernist, and there are no literal references to the past, no domes or archaic Sikh motifs. The massive windowless tower-like galleries—cylindrical, rectangular, and triangular in plan—are clad in local honey-colored sandstone and give the impression of an ancient citadel. Their prominent roofs, seen against the foothills of the Himalayas, are double curvature spherical segments and are covered in gleaming stainless steel (fig. 162).

Before he designed Habitat, Safdie had worked for Louis Kahn. This was when Kahn was designing the Dhaka National Assembly, and the massive masonry drum-like towers of the Khalsa Centre owe a debt to Kahn's monumental geometry. According to Safdie, the masonry forms were inspired by the ancient fortress towns of Rajasthan and the mysterious eighteenth-century sundials and astronomical gnomons of Jaipur. Safdie sometimes favors dramatic structural effects in his projects, but here he kept engineering in the background. The spiky forms of the roofs reflect neither structure nor function; instead, they appeal directly to the senses, like the swirling forms of Baroque architects. The gleaming Khalsa roofs resemble hands open in prayer and are oriented to nearby Gurudwara Sri Anandpur Sahib, a Sikh temple that is the city's principal pilgrimage site.

162 Khalsa Heritage Centre, Anandpur Sahib, India. Safdie Architects, 1998–2011. The massive windowless tower-like galleries—cylindrical, rectangular, and triangular in plan—are clad in local honey-colored sandstone, and their prominent stainless-steel roofs are double curvature segments of a sphere.

The towers, the bridge, the pools, and the courtyards of the Khalsa Centre carry echoes of ancient architecture and create a complex set of orchestrated experiences. The architecture is modern but not abstract; this is definitely a building, not a sculpture. Familiar features such as arches and colonnades provide scale, as does the hand-hewn sandstone. Safdie has described the art of building as grounded in site, climate, and function, and hence fundamentally different from painting or sculpture. "I think architecture has constraints," he wrote. "They're real. It has to contend with them. Otherwise a building can't fulfill its purpose and the source of its invention—the life that goes on within it." Safdie is critical of the eccentric buildings designed by some starchitects, which he calls conceptual architecture. "It is bound to end up as a caricature of reality, where one aspect of design is exaggerated at the expense of others, where inspiration displaces professionalism; it is the breeding ground for the one-liners, for captivating images that fade in time."

■ ■ ■ ■ ■

Allan Greenberg (b. 1938) is an exact contemporary of Safdie's, and likewise an immigrant. A native of South Africa, he studied architecture at the University of the Witwatersrand in Johannesburg, spent several years in Europe, where he worked for Jørn Utzon on the Sydney Opera House, and came to the United

States for graduate study at Yale, where he later taught. Although Greenberg was first drawn to historicist postmodernism, over time he adopted a more canonic approach to the past. In the early 1980s, a large country house in Connecticut modeled on Mount Vernon, and a new suite of traditionally decorated rooms for the State Department in Washington, D.C., established him as the leading American classicist, and his practice grew to include not only residences but also academic buildings at William and Mary, Rice, Princeton, and the University of Delaware.

In 2016, Rice University turned to Greenberg to design an opera house for its Shepherd School of Music. Two years earlier the school had commissioned an avant-garde firm, but its proposal had been set aside. "The trustees decided they wanted to have a hand in choosing the architect for this opera house," Greenberg told an interviewer. "So they walked around the campus and settled on the two buildings they liked the most and interviewed two architects. I was one of them, and I got the job." The Greenberg-designed building that had caught the eye of the Rice trustees was the Humanities Building, built sixteen years earlier. Its Byzantine-Romanesque style suited the original campus, which had been planned and designed in 1910–16 by Ralph Adams Cram. Cram, who was the university architect of Princeton at the time, favored the Gothic style—which he and Goodhue had used successfully at West Point—for collegiate buildings, but he judged that Houston and the hot Texas plain required something different. Not finding any local historic or stylistic precedents, he imagined an original counterfactual: What if Gothic had emerged in the warm southern Mediterranean instead of cold northern Europe? "I reassembled all the elements I could from southern France and Italy, Dalmatia, the Peloponnesus, Byzantium, Anatolia, Syria, Sicily, Spain, and set myself the task of creating a measurably new style that, while built on a classical basis, should have the Gothic romanticism, pictorial quality, and structural integrity," he wrote in his autobiography. The result was a complex of buildings characterized by shaded arcades, round rather than pointed arches, a mixture of rose-hued brick, pink Texas granite, and multicolored marble tiles, accompanied by attenuated Arab columns and horseshoe arches. Julian Huxley, who was Rice's first professor of biology, described the new campus as an "extraordinary spectacle, as of palaces in fairy stories."

Greenberg admired Cram's architecture, and the new opera house, which terminates the long axis of the campus, incorporates a similar palette of patterned pink brick—basket weave, herringbone, and pinwheel bond—limestone trim, decorative panels, and tall arched windows. Greenberg described the result: "As you approach the building you realize that this is not quite the same as the other buildings at Rice. . . . The building has to serve as an architectural overture

163 Brockman Hall for Opera, Rice University, Houston. Allan Greenberg, 2016–20. The entrance pavilion of the new opera house, which terminates the long axis of the original 1916 campus, displays a palette of patterned pink brick, limestone trim, decorative panels, and arched windows.

to the opera . . . going from one world to another world, from a world of reality to the fantasy world." The centerpiece of the entrance facade is a pavilion that houses a two-story foyer and gala space, a barrel-vaulted, airy room with brightly colored walls and a green and white checkerboard floor. The facade, facing the music school across a small plaza, is unexpectedly low-key—three small, almost whimsical porticos signal the entrance (fig. 163). Because the opera house is also a teaching facility, the wings on either side contain classrooms, rehearsal spaces, opera studios, and practice rooms, as well as a scene shop, costume shop, and dressing rooms. The largely windowless walls are broken up by panels of patterned brickwork, and the south side is dominated by two octagonal turrets and a shaded arcade, recalling the Cram buildings.

The bulky volume of the auditorium projects above the predominantly two-story building. Greenberg modeled the six-hundred-seat horseshoe-shaped hall on the Royal Opera in the palace of Versailles, built in 1765–70 by Louis XV's architect, Ange-Jacques Gabriel (1698–1782). Gabriel, a versatile designer who built the monumental Place Louis XV (today the Place de la Concorde) as well as the jewel-like Petit Trianon at Versailles, created an unusual oval room, and instead of stacking individual opera boxes, which was the practice at that time, he emphasized the curved sweep of the three tiered balconies. The ornately decorated and gilded Baroque decor featured a ceiling with a depiction of Apollo and the Muses. Greenberg's monochrome hall has no ceiling painting, and although it includes chandeliers and ox-eye windows, the design is more muted, as befits a teaching facility—no gilt, no mirrors, no Corinthian columns.

Brockman Hall, as the new opera house is called, incorporates those qualities of "Gothic romanticism, pictorial quality, and structural integrity" that Cram described, but it does so in a self-effacing manner. Greenberg is critical of self-important buildings: "Orchestra halls of the last twenty years are generally erring on the side of sticking out; they impose what you might call a spaceship type of construction and plop it down in human settlements. The problem of these buildings that draw attention to themselves is that nothing ever happens in them to justify that amount of attention," he told an interviewer. "So I think it's better to err on the side of modesty and focus on producing quality activities inside the opera house, rather than creating this strange spaceship and having mediocre performances in it."

The architecture of Brockman Hall is obviously different from that of the Louvre Abu Dhabi and the Khalsa Centre, but all three buildings are a reminder that whatever the architectural vocabulary, the old verities apply. Architecture needs to accommodate practical functions, it must deal with the elements, and it needs to be built to last. In accomplishing these things it also needs to impose a sense of order. This order is often rooted in an expression of structure, but not exclusively so, as Persian and Byzantine architecture demonstrate. Good architecture creates a coherent and self-contained world, but it is always part of a larger setting, natural or manmade. A painting may be moved from one room to another, but a building is always in one place, whether it is the desert coast of the Persian Gulf, the foothills of the Himalayas, or the southeast Texas plain. In addition, a building, especially a public building, represents shared ambitions, an urge to celebrate the present and to pay homage to the past. The way that this is done is experienced viscerally as well as intellectually—that is, being in a good building makes us *feel* good. And good buildings embody another quality. The Doric columns of the Parthenon, the numinous interior of Hagia Sophia, the mosaic muqarnas of Isfahan, and Bernini's giant colonnade at Saint Peter's all testify to their makers' humanity. *We were here. We made this. We cared.*

Afterword

What is generally considered the first successful comparative history of architecture, *A Plan of Civil and Historical Architecture,* was published in 1721 by Johann Bernhard Fischer von Erlach. Fischer was not a historian but an architect, among whose celebrated Baroque works in Vienna are the Schönbrunn Palace and the Karlskirche, but like all serious architects he was interested in history. I was fortunate that history was a key part of the six-year architecture curriculum when I was a student, and that my professor at McGill University, the redoubtable Peter Collins, provided my classmates and me with a comprehensive foundation in that subject. It was thanks to Collins—who was trained as an architect, as he often reminded us—that I gained an appreciation for the role of practice in architectural history. I should also acknowledge E. H. Gombrich, whose magisterial *The Story of Art* served as my beau ideal. Gombrich had the advantage that most of his material was easily accessible in European and American art galleries and museums; my examples are spread farther afield. Of the roughly one hundred buildings that I discuss here, I have visited about half. I've climbed to the Acropolis, although I haven't had the opportunity to go to Isfahan or Kyoto. I've toured the Alhambra and the Forbidden City but not the Great Mosque of Kairouan. I've seen Louis Kahn's work in Ahmedabad, but not his National Assembly in Dhaka. Thus I have been obliged to rely on my experience of other projects by the same architects, as well as on architectural monographs. I should add that the opportunity to travel—if only vicariously, in my memory and imagination—to various parts of the world was a source of support during the prolonged lockdown of the Covid-19 pandemic.

My actual visit to the Acropolis occurred in 1964 during a monthlong car trip with a classmate. We drove a little Renault from Paris to Athens. It was my friend Ralph Bergman who insisted on Athens—I had no great interest in Greek architecture. Or so I thought. Collins had subjected us to a rigorous survey of ancient temples, punctuated by regular slide tests, but nothing had prepared me for the real thing. Even in a ruined state the marble columns had a powerful presence. Like so many architecture students before me I was overwhelmed, and I spent hours on the Acropolis sketching. I also stumbled on an important insight. "The buildings are eminently human, and only make sense if there are people about them," I wrote in my travel diary. "That is why architectural photographs fail to capture their essence. Man is the centre here."

I was twenty-one when I discovered that architecture could move one deeply and emotionally as well as intellectually. That was only three years younger than Le Corbusier when he climbed to the Acropolis and was equally swept away: "The body, the mind, the heart gasp, suddenly overpowered," he wrote. My first encounter with the buildings of Le Corbusier occurred during that same road trip: the Ronchamp chapel, the apartment block in Marseille, several buildings in Paris. I even sought out the apartment building on the rue Nungesser-et-Coli in the 16th arrondissement where Le Corbusier lived, hoping to catch a glimpse of the Great Man. I was too shy to ring the doorbell though I should have; he died the following year. In truth I was a fan—I adopted his spindly style of drawing and the military-style stencil lettering he favored. In the university library I pored over the volumes of the *Oeuvre complète,* and the actual buildings did not disappoint: sculpted walls, crudely roughened concrete, exposed ducts, vibrant colors. It was heady stuff for a neophyte.

Montreal in the mid-1960s had nothing like that. The campus of McGill consisted chiefly of nineteenth-century limestone buildings in a variety of revival styles; the more recent buildings were distinguished by their lack of historical motifs but were otherwise unremarkable. Downtown Montreal boasted two recent modernist skyscrapers, but they were relatively conventional steel-and-glass boxes. Not that the city was without distinctive twentieth-century architecture. The best dated from the 1930s, buildings in the style known as Art Moderne, later called Art Deco. Miami Beach is known for its Art Deco buildings, but Montreal has more—and more varied—examples: office towers and apartment buildings, department stores and movie theaters, public markets and police stations, as well as the dramatic campus of the Université de Montréal, designed by Canada's leading exponent of Art Deco, Ernest Cormier. Cormier's own house was not far from McGill. Whenever I walked by it I gave it a glance. There was nothing crude about its urbane facade, which seduced rather than shocked: smooth ashlar rather than roughened concrete, flower patterns carved into the spandrels below the windows, and a bas-relief of a female form over the front door. I wasn't sure what to make of it. This was definitely not Le Corbusier's type of modernism—but I liked it.

Sometimes the most memorable architecture is not the grandstanding masterpiece or the famous monument, but the building that quietly makes its way into your subconscious. The quirky front door that you pass daily and that gives you a little lift every time; the wonderful museum lobby or railroad station waiting room that makes you pause when you enter, just to savor the moment. Before I embarked on a formal study of architecture, my main boyhood experience of a memorable building was my high school. It occupied a wing of Loyola College, a picture-perfect Jacobean quadrangle in Montreal West built in the 1910s. The brick exterior was decorated with carved stone rosettes and gargoyles, the steep tile roofs were capped by an assortment of towers, turrets, and cupolas. Its Scottish-born architects were undoubtedly influenced by the British Jacobean Revival of the early nineteenth century. The sixteenth-century architecture of the reign of James I was a kind of classicized Gothic, a version of the Italian Renaissance via Flanders and Germany. As a schoolboy I was ignorant of this pedigree, of course. What I remember, other than my cassocked Jesuit teachers, are classrooms with tall ceilings, polished wooden floors, and heavy oak desks, sturdy as carpenters' benches. The five years I spent in these idyllic surroundings provided me with the everyday experience of architectural beauty, an experience that was both unself-conscious and intimate. Did it prompt me to choose a career in architecture? Maybe.

Additional Reading

When I was a student of architecture I owned a copy of Banister Fletcher's encyclopedic *History of Architecture on the Comparative Method.* Originally published in 1896 and regularly updated, the thick tome was full of excellent explanatory drawings. I still own a beat-up paperback of Nikolaus Pevsner's *An Outline of European Architecture,* originally published in 1943. Anyone wishing to consult a more recent comprehensive history could turn to Spiro Kostof's 1985 *History of Architecture: Settings and Rituals.* Readers who would like additional sources on particular periods, buildings, and architects may find the following titles useful.

Part I. The Ancients

More detail on the mastaba of Akhethotep is provided by Norman de Garis Davies, a Scots Egyptologist who, with his wife, Nina, worked on drawing and recording paintings, and who recorded their findings in *The Mastaba of Ptahhetep and Akhethetep at Saqqareh* (Egypt Exploration Fund, 1901). John Romer describes the evolution of the pyramid in *The Great Pyramid: Ancient Egypt Revisited* (Cambridge University Press, 2007). Information on the mortuary temple of Rameses III is provided by Uvo Hölscher, an Egyptologist and architecture professor at the Technical University of Hannover, in *The Mortuary Temple of Rameses III, Part I,* trans. Mrs Keith C. Seele (University of Chicago Press, 1941). In a more general vein is Mary Beard's *The Parthenon* (Harvard University Press, 2003). A comprehensive description of Hagia Sophia is Rowland J. Mainstone's *Hagia Sophia: Architecture, Structure and Liturgy of Justinian's Great Church* (Thames & Hudson, 1988).

Part II. Middle Ages

Richard Krautheimer's *Early Christian and Byzantine Architecture* (Penguin, 1965) discusses San Vitale in Ravenna. Two sources on Islamic architecture are Afif Bahnassi, *The Great Omayyad Mosque of Damascus: The First Masterpieces of Islamic Art,* trans. Batrechia McDonel and Samir Tower (Damascus, Tlass, 1989) and Paul Sebag, *The Great Mosque of Kairouan,* trans. Richard Howard (Macmillan, 1965). Charlemagne's Palatine Chapel and Durham Cathedral are discussed by Kenneth John Conant in *Carolingian and Romanesque Architecture 800 to 1200* (Penguin, 1959). More background on Abbot Suger and Saint-Denis, Notre-Dame, and Sainte-Chapelle can be found in Paul Frankl, *Gothic Architecture* (Penguin, 1962). The visitor to Venice will benefit from James H. S. McGregor's *Venice from the Ground Up* (Belknap Press of Harvard University Press, 2006), which includes a discussion of the Palazzo Ducale and the Ca' d'Oro. John D. Hoag's *Western Islamic Architecture* (George Braziller, 1963) provides background on Islamic Spain and discusses the Great Mosque of Córdoba and the Alhambra. The latter is the subject of Robert Irwin's interesting *The Alhambra* (Harvard University Press, 2004). A detailed review of pre-twentieth-century Chinese architecture is Nancy S. Steinhardt, *Chinese Architecture: A History* (Princeton University Press, 2019).

Part III. A Reimagined World

John Summerson, *The Classical Language of Architecture* (Thames & Hudson, 1963) remains an excellent introduction to the Renaissance, as is James S. Ackerman's essay "Architectural Practice in the Italian Renaissance" in *Distance Points: Essays in Theory and Renaissance Art and Architecture,* ed. Ackerman (MIT Press, 1991). Fifteenth-century Florence is vividly described by Ross King in *Brunelleschi's Dome: The Story of the Great Cathedral in Florence* (Chatto & Windus, 2000). R. A. Scotti, *Basilica: The Splendor and the Scandal. Building St. Peter's* (Viking, 2006) does the same for sixteenth-century Rome. I have written about Palladio in *The Perfect House: A Journey with the Renaissance Master Andrea Palladio* (Scribner, 2002). Absent a visit to Kyoto, *Katsura: Imperial Villa* (Electa Architecture, 2005), ed. Virginia Ponciroli, is a good guide. Howard Hibberd, *Bernini* (Penguin, 1965) and Anthony Blunt, *Borromini* (Harvard University Press, 1979) are excellent sources. Readers interested in Persian architecture could not do better than Arthur Upham Pope, *Introducing Persian Architecture* (Oxford University Press, 1971).

Part IV. The First Moderns

Tim Mowl and Brian Earnshaw's excellent *John Wood: Architect of Obsession* (Millstream, 1988) is the sole biography of this remarkable man. The life of the developer-duke who built the Palais-Royale is described by Tom Ambrose in *Godfather of the Revolution: The Life of Philippe Égalité Duc d'Orléans* (Peter Owen, 2008). There are literally hundreds of books on Karl Friedrich Schinkel and his work. Though most are in German, a notable exception is Barry Bergdoll's *Karl Friedrich Schinkel: An Architecture for Prussia* (Rizzoli, 1994). Still the best description of the building of the Crystal Palace is Christopher Hobhouse's *1851 and the Crystal Palace* (E. P. Dutton, 1937). There are many books on Gustave Eiffel, and David I. Harrie's biography, *Eiffel: The Genius Who Reinvented Himself* (Sutton, 2005), puts the tower in the context of his impressive life's work. George R. Collins, *Antonio Gaudí* (George Braziller, 1960) is an excellent introduction to the subject. The chapter on Gaudí in Robert Hughes's *Barcelona* (Knopf, 1992) rewards close reading. Two books on the Vienna Secession are Kirk Varnedoe, *Vienna 1900: Art, Architecture & Design* (Museum of Modern Art, 1986) and Anthony Alofsin, *When Buildings Speak: Architecture as Language in the Habsburg Empire and Its Aftermath, 1867–1933* (University of Chicago Press, 2006). There are hundreds of books about Frank Lloyd Wright and his work; Paul Hendrickson's *Plagued by Fire: The Dreams and Furies of Frank Lloyd Wright* (Knopf, 2019) is a recent and unusual biography. The story of the Lincoln Memorial is told by Christopher A. Thomas, *The Lincoln Memorial and American Life* (Princeton University Press, 2002).

Part V. New Building

The most comprehensive book on the life and works of J. J. P. Oud is Ed Taverne et al., *J. J. P. Oud: A Poetic Functionalist, 1890–1963/The Complete Works* (Nai Uitgevers, 2001). There are many books and exhibition catalogues about the Bauhaus, whose centenary was celebrated in 2019. Nicholas Fox Webber provides a vivid account in *The Bauhaus Group: Six Masters of Modernism* (Yale University Press, 2011). Duki Dror's 2011 documentary film *Incessant Visions* is an excellent introduction to Erich Mendelsohn. Kathleen James's *Erich Mendelsohn and the Architecture of German Modernism* (Cambridge University Press, 1997) deals with the architect's Berlin years. Bertram Goodhue is neglected today; the sole architectural biography is Richard Oliver's *Bertram Grosvenor Goodhue* (MIT Press, 1983). Paul Cret is likewise largely overlooked, with the notable exception of Elizabeth Greenwell Grossman's *The Civic Architecture of Paul Cret* (Cambridge University Press, 1996). She discusses the Château-Thierry monument in "Architecture for a Public Client: The Monuments and Chapels of the American Battle Monuments Commission," *Journal of the Society of Architectural Historians* 43, no. 2 (May 1984): 119–43. Léon Krier's *Albert Speer: Architecture 1932–1942* (Monacelli, 2013) is a useful source. John Tauranac's *The Empire State Building: The Making of a Landmark* (Scribner, 1995) and Daniel Okrent's *Great Fortune: The Epic of the Rockefeller Center* (Viking, 2003) describe those two landmark projects. The only biography of the great Raymond Hood is Walter H. Kilham, Jr.'s *Raymond Hood, Architect* (Architectural Book Publishing, 1973). The literature on the work of Le Corbusier, Mies van der Rohe, and Alvar Aalto is voluminous. Moshe Safdie describes the story of Habitat in *Beyond Habitat* (MIT Press, 1973). The episode of Wright and the Guggenheim Museum is described by Brendan Gill in *Many Masks: A Life of Frank Lloyd Wright* (G. P. Putnam's Sons, 1987). A good description of the Sydney Opera House affair is Peter Murray's *The Saga of Sydney Opera House: The Dramatic Story of the Design and Construction of the Icon of Modern Australia* (Spon, 2004).

Part VI. After Modernism

There are many books about Louis Kahn's work, and several biographies. An essential text remains David Brownlee and David De Long's *Louis I. Kahn: In the Realm of Architecture* (Rizzoli, 1991). An excellent history of the Pompidou Center is Nathan Silver's *The Making of Beaubourg: A Building Biography of the Centre Pompidou, Paris* (MIT Press, 1994). Peter Rice's *An Engineer Imagines* (Ellipsis, 1994) describes the author's involvement in the Sydney Opera House and the Pompidou Center. I discuss the Sainsbury Centre for Visual Arts at length in *The Biography of a Building: How Robert Sainsbury and Norman Foster Built a Great Museum* (Thames & Hudson, 2011). Ian Volner's *Michael Graves: Designs for Life* (Princeton Architectural Press, 2017) covers the architect's life and work. Mark Girouard's *Big Jim: The Life and Work of James Stirling* (Chatto & Windus, 1998) is a sympathetic and revealing biography. The Sainsbury Wing of the National Gallery, including the controversial competition, is described by Colin Amery in *A Celebration of Art & Architecture* (National Gallery, 1991). Raymond Erith's and Quinlan Terry's careers and work are chronicled in Lucy Archer, *Raymond Erith, Architect* (Cygnet, 1985) and Clive Aslet, *Quinlan Terry: The Revival of Architecture* (Viking, 1986). I have written about the Harold Washington Library Center in "A Good Public Building," *Atlantic Monthly* (August 1992). The buildings discussed in the final two chapters are described in Kurt Forster, *Frank O. Gehry, Bilbao Guggenheim Museoa* (Axel Menges, 1998); *CCTV by OMA* (A+U, 2005); *Zaha Hadid Architects: Heydar Aliyev Centre* (Lars Müller, 2014); *Louvre Abu Dhabi: The Story of an Architectural Project* (Skira, 2018); *Safdie* (Images, 2014); and "A Candid Conversation with Architect Allan Greenberg," on the Future Symphony Institute website.

Acknowledgments

Katherine Boller, my editor, suggested the idea that grew into this book, and I gratefully acknowledge her enthusiastic support and that of the people at Yale University Press, especially Sarah Henry and Heidi Downey, as well as book designer Yve Ludwig. The early observations of Michael J. Lewis were particularly helpful, as were the comments of Demetri Porphyrios, Robert Bruegmann, Stephen Kendall, Lawrence Speck, and Anthony Alofsin. My thanks to colleagues at the University of Pennsylvania for their useful suggestions: David De Long, Nancy S. Steinhardt, Lothar Hasselberger, Liliane Weissberg, Angela Duckworth, and Tingdan Zhang. Moshe Safdie, Allan Greenberg, Karen Nichols at Michael Graves & Associates, and Tom Beeby and Aric Lasher at HBRA helpfully provided illustrations. Thanks also to photographer Paul Hester. My agent Andrew Wylie lent his usual expertise. Finally, I am forever grateful to my late wife, Shirley Hallam, for her help and editorial suggestions, and for accompanying me on many architectural outings during our long and happy life together.

Illustration Credits

Witold Rybczynski: pp. ii, xii, 46, 102, 158, 216, 276; figs. 1, 9, 12, 13, 25, 27, 30, 32, 47, 82, 84, 87, 129, 132, 141, 150, 154
Gerhard Haubold. Licensed under the Creative Commons Attribution-Share Alike 3.0 Unported, 2.5 Generic, 2.0 Generic and 1.0 Generic license: fig. 2
Carole Raddato. Licensed under the Creative Commons Attribution-Share Alike 2.0 Generic license: figs. 4, 16
Dennis Jarvis. Licensed under the Creative Commons Attribution-Share Alike 2.0 Generic license: figs. 5, 28
Willem van de Poll. Dutch National Archives. Made available under the Creative Commons CC0 1.0 Universal Public Domain Dedication: fig. 6
Merlin UK. Licensed under the Creative Commons Attribution-Share Alike 3.0 Unported license: fig. 8
Djehouty. Licensed under the Creative Commons Attribution-Share Alike 4.0 International license: fig. 10
George E. Koronaios. Licensed under the Creative Commons Attribution-Share Alike 4.0 International license: fig. 11
Jebulon. Made available under the Creative Commons CC0 1.0 Universal Public Domain Dedication: figs. 14, 15
Jimmy Walker. Licensed under the Creative Commons Attribution-Share Alike 2.0 Generic license: fig. 17
Courtesy National Gallery of Art, Washington. Made available under Creative Commons Zero (CC0): fig. 19
Nserrano. Licensed under the Creative Commons Attribution-Share Alike 4.0 International license: fig. 22
Mark Ahsman. Licensed under the Creative Commons Attribution-Share Alike 3.0 Unported license: fig. 24
Seier + Seier. Licensed under the Creative Commons Attribution 2.0 Generic license: fig. 26
Marek Szarejko. Licensed under the Creative Commons Attribution-Share Alike 2.0 Generic license: fig. 29
Sailko. Licensed under the Creative Commons Attribution-Share Alike 3.0 Unported license: figs. 31, 55, 56, 59, 71
Sailko. Licensed under the Creative Commons Attribution 3.0 Unported license: fig. 54
CEPhoto, Uwe Aranas. Licensed under the Creative Commons Attribution-Share Alike 3.0 Unported license: fig. 33
Mattbuck. Licensed under the Creative Commons Attribution-Share Alike 2.0 Generic license: fig. 36
Thomas Clouet. Licensed under the Creative Commons Attribution-Share Alike 4.0 International license: fig. 37
Beckstet. Licensed under the Creative Commons Attribution-Share Alike 3.0 Unported license: fig. 38
Peter Haas/Pezi. Licensed under the Creative Commons Attribution-Share Alike 3.0 Unported license: fig. 40
Oldmanisold. Licensed under the Creative Commons Attribution-Share Alike 4.0 International license: fig. 41
Marc Ryckaert. Licensed under the Creative Commons Attribution-Share Alike 4.0 International license: fig. 43
José Luiz. Licensed under the Creative Commons Attribution-Share Alike 4.0 International license: fig. 44
Didier Descouens. Licensed under the Creative Commons Attribution-Share Alike 4.0 International license: fig. 45
Berthold Werner. Licensed under the Creative Commons Attribution-Share Alike 3.0 Unported license: fig. 46
Mervat. Licensed under the Creative Commons Attribution-Share Alike 4.0 International license: fig. 49
G41m8. Licensed under the Creative Commons Attribution-Share Alike 4.0 International license: fig. 50
Daniel Case. Licensed under the Creative Commons Attribution-Share Alike 3.0 Unported license: fig. 51
Siyuwj. Licensed under the Creative Commons Attribution-Share Alike 4.0 International license: fig. 52
Giacomo Augusto. Licensed under the Creative Commons Attribution-Share Alike 3.0 Unported license: fig. 53
Peter1936F. Licensed under the Creative Commons Attribution-Share Alike 4.0 International license: fig. 57
Giovanni Battista Piranesi, c. 1748. Collection of Metropolitan Museum of Art. Made available under the Creative Commons CC0 1.0 Universal Public Domain Dedication: fig. 61
Marcok. Licensed under the Creative Commons Attribution-Share Alike 3.0 Unported license: fig. 62
Quinok. Licensed under the Creative Commons Attribution-Share Alike 4.0 International license: fig. 63
Benjamin Núñez González. Licensed under the Creative Commons Attribution-Share Alike 4.0 International license: fig. 67
Metropolitan Museum of Art. Made available under the Creative Commons CC0 1.0 Universal Public Domain Dedication: fig. 68
Michal Osmenda. Licensed under the Creative Commons Attribution-Share Alike 2.0 Generic license: fig. 69
Afernand74. Licensed under the Creative Commons Attribution-Share Alike 3.0 Unported license: fig. 70
Paolo Monti. Licensed under the Creative Commons Attribution-Share Alike 4.0 International license: fig. 72
Nitot. Licensed under the Creative Commons Attribution-Share Alike 3.0 Unported license: fig. 73
Bernard Gagnon. Licensed under the Creative Commons Attribution-Share Alike 3.0 Unported, 2.5 Generic, 2.0 Generic and 1.0 Generic license: fig. 75
Steve Cadman. Licensed under the Creative Commons Attribution-Share Alike 2.0 Generic license: fig. 76
Self. Licensed under the Creative Commons Attribution-Share Alike 3.0 Unported license: fig. 78
Fowler&fowler. Licensed under the Creative Commons Attribution-Share Alike 3.0 Unported license: fig. 80
Leebrady99. Licensed under the

Creative Commons Attribution-Share Alike 3.0 Unported license: fig. 81
LPLT. Licensed under the Creative Commons Attribution-Share Alike 3.0 Unported license: fig. 85
Ansgar Koreng. Licensed under the Creative Commons Attribution 4.0 International license: fig. 86
Tato Grasso. Licensed under the Creative Commons Attribution-Share Alike 2.5 Generic license: fig. 92
ChristianSchd. Licensed under the Creative Commons Attribution-Share Alike 3.0 Unported license: fig. 93
Till F. Teenck. Licensed under the Creative Commons Attribution-Share Alike 2.5 Generic license: fig. 94
Postcard, 1950. Leo Wehrli. ETH-BNibliothek. Licensed under the Creative Commons Attribution-Share Alike 4.0 International license: fig. 95
Gryffindor. Licensed under the Creative Commons Attribution-Share Alike 3.0 Unported license: fig. 96
Pudelek. Licensed under the Creative Commons Attribution-Share Alike 4.0 International license: fig. 97
Thomas Ledi. Licensed under the Creative Commons Attribution-Share Alike 4.0 International license: fig. 98
Bwag. Licensed under the Creative Commons Attribution-Share Alike 4.0 International license: fig. 99
Jorge Royan. Licensed under the Creative Commons Attribution-Share Alike 3.0 Unported license: fig. 100
Dacoslett. Licensed under the Creative Commons Attribution-Share Alike 3.0 Unported license: fig. 102
Collection of the Buffalo History Museum, Larkin Company photograph collection. Reproduced by permission: fig. 103
Bobistraveling. Licensed under the Creative Commons Attribution 2.0 Generic license: fig. 104
Freiluft. Licensed under the Creative Commons Attribution-Share Alike 3.0 Unported license: fig. 105
Ronakshah1990. Licensed under the Creative Commons Attribution-Share Alike 4.0 International license: fig. 106
Marcela Hernandez Moreira. Licensed under the Creative Commons Attribution-Share Alike 3.0 Unported license: fig. 109
M H.DE. Licensed under the Creative Commons Attribution 3.0 Unported license: fig. 110
Gerhard Dukker. Licensed under the Creative Commons Attribution-Share Alike 4.0 International license: fig. 111
Jean-Pierre Dalbéra. Licensed under the Creative Commons Attribution 2.0 Generic license: figs. 112, 113
Ammordamus. Made available under the Creative Commons CC0 1.0 Universal Public Domain Dedication: fig. 115
Tony Hisgett. Licensed under the Creative Commons Attribution 2.0 Generic license: fig. 116
Jean Ribéry. Licensed under the Creative Commons Attribution-Share Alike 4.0 International license: fig. 117
AndMoKio. Licensed under the Creative Commons Attribution-Share Alike 2.5 Generic license: fig. 120
TomasEE. Licensed under the Creative Commons Attribution 3.0 Unported license: fig. 123
Marc Rochkind. Licensed under the Creative Commons Attribution-Share Alike 4.0 International license: fig. 124
Michiel1972. Licensed under the Creative Commons Attribution-Share Alike 3.0 Unported license: fig. 125
Found in_a_ttic. Licensed under the Creative Commons Attribution 2.0 Generic license: fig. 126
Jules Antonio. Licensed under the Creative Commons Attribution-Share Alike 2.0 Generic license: fig. 127
Leon Liao. Licensed under the Creative Commons Attribution 2.0 Generic license: fig. 128
Tiia Monto. Licensed under the Creative Commons Attribution-Share Alike 4.0 International license: fig. 130
Courtesy Architecture Slide Library, University of Pennsylvania: fig. 131
Jürgen Howaldt. Licensed under the Creative Commons Attribution-Share Alike 2.0 Germany license: fig. 133
Wladislaw. Licensed under the Creative Commons Attribution-Share Alike 3.0 Unported license: fig. 134
PortableNYCTours. Licensed under the Creative Commons Attribution-Share Alike 4.0 International license: fig. 135
Kristoffer Arvidsson, Göteborgs konstmuseum. Licensed under the Creative Commons Attribution-Share Alike 4.0 International license: fig. 136
State Archives and Records Authority of New South Wales. Licensed under the Creative Commons Attribution 2.0 Generic license: fig. 137
Gunnar Klack. Licensed under the Creative Commons Attribution-Share Alike 4.0 International license: fig. 139
Courtesy of Yale University: fig. 140
Nahid Sultan. Licensed under the Creative Commons Attribution-Share Alike 3.0 Unported license: fig. 142
Naquib Hossain. Licensed under the Creative Commons Attribution-Share Alike 2.0 Generic license: fig. 143
Los Angeles. Licensed under the Creative Commons Attribution-Share Alike 3.0 Unported license: fig. 144
Bynyalcin. Licensed under the Creative Commons Attribution 3.0 Unported license: fig. 145
Cristian Bortes. Licensed under the Creative Commons Attribution 2.0 Generic license: fig. 146
Courtesy of Sainsbury Centre for Visual Arts: fig. 147
Ian Beales. Licensed under the Creative Commons Attribution-Share Alike 4.0 International license: fig. 148
Courtesy of Michael Graves & Associates: fig. 149
Fred Romero. Licensed under the Creative Commons Attribution 2.0 Generic license: fig. 151
Richard George. Licensed under the Creative Commons Attribution-Share Alike 3.0 Unported license: fig. 152
The Wub. Licensed under the Creative Commons Attribution-Share Alike 3.0 Unported license: fig. 153
David Iliff. Licensed under the Creative Commons Attribution-Share Alike 3.0 Unported license: fig. 155
Daniel X. O'Neil. Licensed under the Creative Commons Attribution 2.0 Generic license: fig. 156.
Timothy Hursley. Courtesy of HBRA Architects: fig. 157
Ardfern. Licensed under the Creative Commons Attribution-Share Alike 3.0 Unported license: fig. 158
Dayton 12345. Licensed under the Creative Commons Attribution-Share Alike 4.0 International license: fig. 159
Asim Masimov. Licensed under the Creative Commons Attribution-Share Alike 4.0 International license: fig. 160
Francisco Anzola. Licensed under the Creative Commons Attribution 3.0 Unported license: fig. 161
Michal Ronen Safdie. Courtesy of Safdie Architects: fig. 162
Paul Hester. Courtesy Allan Greenberg Architect: fig. 163

Index

Page numbers in *italic* type indicate illustrations.